THE GOSPEL OF DOMITILLA

THE
GOSPEL
OF
DOMITILLA

DID THE EMPEROR'S
NIECE WRITE LUKE?

S.P. LAURIE

Published by Hypostasis Ltd.
71-75 Shelton Street, Covent Garden
London WC2H 9JQ

www.hypostasis.co
Email: info@hypostasis.co

Book cover design by BespokeBookCovers.com
Typeset by Euan Monaghan

ISBN (Print): 978-1-912029-67-9
ISBN (Ebook): 978-1-912029-66-2

Also by S.P. Laurie

THE THOMAS CODE:
Solving the Mystery of the Gospel of Thomas

THE JUDAS WAR:
How an Ancient Betrayal Gave Rise to the Christ Myth

THE ROCK AND THE TOWER:
How Mary Created Christianity

For articles, information and news see:
JesusOrigins.com

For Rose, Isabella and James.

Table of Contents

Introduction

Domitilla

Flavia Domitilla, daughter of a goddess, was perhaps the most fortunate woman in the world at the start of 95 AD. The Roman Empire was nearing its stunning peak, the greatest empire the world had ever known. And Domitilla had been born into what was now the leading family of the empire—the Flavian dynasty. She was the granddaughter of the former emperor Vespasian and the niece of both the former emperor Titus and the current emperor Domitian. Her deceased mother, also called Flavia Domitilla, was deified by Domitian near the start of his reign.

Domitilla had married her cousin, Flavius Clemens, a grandson of Vespasian's brother. The marriage had been a happy one with several children. The offspring were doubly qualified for the imperial throne through both mother and father and were now the sole hope for the survival of the Flavian dynasty. Titus' only daughter Julia was dead, and Domitian's marriage to Domitia had been barren. The emperor could not bring himself to divorce Domitia and had accepted that he was not going to have children. So he had adopted two of Domitilla's sons as his successors, renaming them Vespasian and Domitian.

It looked as if Domitilla would be the matriarch of a line of future emperors. In the Gospel of Luke, when Mary hears from an angel that she is to give birth to a future king, she proclaims: "From now on all generations will call me blessed." Domitilla could have applied these same sentiments to herself. But there was a dark cloud—Domitian was growing increasingly paranoid. And Domitilla had a secret.

In January 95 AD, Clemens was awarded the honor of a consulship with the emperor. A few months later, he was dead, executed by Domitian. As for Domitilla, she was exiled and imprisoned on an island off the coast of Italy. What ultimately happened to her and her children is unknown, for a cloak of silence descended over the family.

We can piece together the couple's supposed transgression from scraps

1

of information. It seems that Domitilla had joined a strange new religious sect from the east; she had become a Christian. Clemens, who was also involved, paid the ultimate penalty, although he was probably just a sympathizer. The emperor was a stickler for traditional Roman religion and would have been outraged at his niece's betrayal. Her offense was particularly grave because of what Domitian would have regarded as her corrupting influence on the boys, one of whom would be the future emperor. He likely only spared her life because she was his beloved sister's daughter, and he had no such compunction about Clemens.

Domitilla's downfall was the first act in the fall of the Flavians and led to Domitian's assassination a year later. The elderly Nerva became emperor, the first of the adoptive emperors who included such figures as Trajan, Hadrian, and the philosopher emperor Marcus Aurelius. As for Domitilla, she would become a Christian saint. She is best remembered today for the early Christian catacombs in Rome that bear her name. But this book makes the case that she left a much greater legacy; she was the author of two books of the New Testament that would have a profound influence on Christianity and Western culture for the next two thousand years.

The Gospel of Luke?

For much of the past, to even question the Bible would have been to invite a charge of heresy. Only in the last few centuries have the individual books that make up the Bible been subject to critical and objective scrutiny. For Christians, the Bible has traditionally been seen as sacred literature inspired by God. Modern scholarship looks at these texts as the work of human authors, the products of a specific time and place. This book is the search for the person who wrote the gospel traditionally called Luke and the Acts of the Apostles (customarily called just "Acts"). We will show that the author of these works was very human; they made mistakes, were carried away by enthusiasms and could, at times, be less than truthful. Self-confident to the point of arrogance, the author had many of the attitudes of the Roman elite. They were also generous, kind-hearted, imaginative and perhaps genuinely inspired.

All the books of the New Testament were written in Koine Greek, the lingua franca of the Roman Empire. The Christian Bible starts with the four gospels Matthew, Mark, Luke, and John, followed by Acts which is the second part, or sequel, to Luke. Next come the letters of the apostle Paul and some miscellaneous letters before ending with the book of Revelation. In our Bibles today, the New Testament is bound together with the so-called Old Testament, the Hebrew Jewish scriptures.

Luke and Acts are the two longest books of the New Testament, accounting for almost 30% of the total. They cover the origins of Christianity from the conception and birth of Jesus, through his mission, crucifixion, and resurrection, and onto the doings of the apostles and the foundation of the church, ending at around 60 AD when the new religion was making inroads across the Roman Empire.

If the author of Luke/Acts were Flavia Domitilla, it would be extraordinary in many ways. Although women played a full part in the early Jesus movement, they were gradually squeezed out from formal roles in the proto-orthodox church which developed an exclusively male priesthood. The signs of struggle between the so-called patriarchal leadership and a female resistance are even visible in the New Testament. The apostle Paul was no feminist, but his letters gave abundant historical evidence for the involvement of women at all levels of the early church. So it was necessary for some unscrupulous individuals to produce fake letters from Paul, and forge interpolations in genuine letters, to make it seem that the great apostle had forbidden women to even speak in church. It was a cruel but very effective hoax: within a few generations, the forgeries were accepted without question by both men and women. The proto-orthodox church won out over the other forms of Christianity that proliferated in the early centuries. It gave rise to the Roman Catholic church in the west and the Orthodox church in the east. So, until very recently, women were excluded without justification from the priesthood. It would be supremely ironic if a substantial portion of the scripture that women were not permitted to preach was actually written by a woman.

We will see the evidence that that some Christian communities as late as the fourth and fifth centuries knew that the third gospel had been written by a female author. This tradition would have been much stronger in the second century. However, proto-orthodox Christians put forward an alternative theory that the gospel was written by a man—Paul's missionary companion, Luke. To be fair, those who promoted the Luke theory would have believed it to be true. And on the face of it, they had a good case.

It is important to understand that Luke is never mentioned in the gospel that bears his name. Both Luke and Acts are anonymous. This is unsurprising; Christianity was a persecuted religion and the identity of the gospel's author had to be kept secret. Luke was certainly a real person. He accompanied Paul on some of his travels and is mentioned in his letters. There is a passing reference in Acts to a Christian from Cyrene in North Africa who bears a very similar name and is probably Luke, but there is not the slightest hint that he was the author.

The theory that Luke had written Luke/Acts was developed in the second century. It came from an analysis of the mysterious passages in

Acts where the narrative suddenly changes from the third-person to the first-person plural—to "we." As these "we" passages all occur in connection with Paul's travels, it was thought that the author must have been a companion of Paul. By comparison with Paul's letters, the potential candidates were narrowed down to just one—Luke. Moreover, Paul appears to call Luke a gentile and a physician. Luke/Acts shows every sign of being written by a well-educated gentile Christian, so it was a perfect fit.

Only the most traditionalist of scholars now believes that Luke really wrote the gospel and Acts. A more rigorous and skeptical comparison of Paul's letters to passages in Acts revealed that the author had no personal knowledge or connection with Paul. Some of Paul's letters are now known to be later forgeries, and inconsistencies with the way Paul describes Luke elsewhere make it doubtful that he was really a gentile. Most likely, the real Luke was a Jewish Christian from North Africa. And Luke/Acts is now typically dated to the 90s AD, much later than the time of Luke, who accompanied Paul in the 50s and early 60s AD.

The Gospel of Domitilla?

It would be remarkable for Domitilla to be the author of Luke in more ways than just her gender. She was intimately close to three emperors who ruled over an empire that extended over much of Europe, the Middle East, and North Africa. Over 30% of the world's population lived under their sway. The emperors were near absolute dictators—providing they could keep the army on their side, which the Flavians, a military family, excelled at. And Domitilla's dearest relations had played a decisive and destructive role in the fate of the Jews in Judea. Her grandfather Vespasian had successfully prosecuted the Jewish War while her uncle Titus had destroyed the temple and much of Jerusalem. For Domitilla to write a work that yearned for the equality of all men and women and the coming of the kingdom of heaven would be truly remarkable.

What is the evidence to support this extraordinary proposition? There are two parts of any case; the circumstantial and the particular. We will cover the circumstantial evidence first by assembling a profile of the author and showing just how well this fits Domitilla. We will start with one vital clue; both Luke and Acts are dedicated to a high-ranking Roman patron called Theophilus. No one with this name has been identified as the likely candidate for the patron. As Theophilus means "God-lover," it is most likely not this man's public name. But even without knowing Theophilus' identity, we can deduce a great deal about the author's situation from the dedication. We will conclude that the author was a high-ranking Roman woman.

There is nothing original about this idea that a woman wrote Luke/Acts. Many others have come to the same conclusion before us. As we will see, there is abundant evidence for female authorship. We will start with the changes that the author of Luke makes to the nativity in Matthew, recasting it from a male-centric to a female-centric narrative. The conclusion is that the nativity was written by a mother who celebrated motherhood. This is backed up by the prominence given to female characters in Luke and Acts. Not only are there far more named women than in the other gospels, but women often occur in positions of higher importance than men. The most telling feature is the way the author often slips into a woman's perspective on events. This is particularly true of the "we" narrative, and provides the clue to the real nature of these passages.

Our profile will go on to show that the author of Luke was a God-fearer before becoming a Christian. The God-fearers were gentiles who were Jewish sympathizers; they read the scriptures and attended some synagogue services but did not become Jews. We know that Judaism attracted many God-fearers, including high-ranking women, but not, it seems, high-ranking men. Many of these God-fearers went on to become Christians and then came into conflict with their former Jewish acquaintances and friends.

The author of Luke/Acts was someone important, a member of the Roman establishment, used to being listened to and obeyed. There are many clues to this, large and small. For example, a parable about servants hiding money is changed in Luke to a parable about a king distributing cites. The author is very well informed but does not show much respect to their sources which they would change markedly. They were particularly fond of miracle stories and would fictionalize a saying or statement to create something very different from the original. Yet they were able to get their imaginative productions accepted as history. Ever since Acts was written, it has preconditioned the way that the development of early Christianity has been seen. Yet scholars, excepting those obliged to adhere to a church view, now see it as largely fiction.

We must add that the author of Luke had many redeeming attributes. They were tone perfect in dealing with emotion, a particularly striking characteristic in contrast with the other gospels. Although of high rank, they were genuinely sympathetic to the poor and those in lowly positions. And they were a brilliant storyteller. If the author were alive today, she would probably be a bestselling novelist.

To show how well this profile fits Domitilla, we need to tell her life history. As all our information about her is fragmentary, this may appear an impossible task. Almost every detail can be disputed, including the identity of her father and whether she was really Christian or Jewish. We will have to approach her primarily through those around her. Only by placing her in the context of her times and her family can we enter her world. The Rome she knew was magnificent and appalling, very different from our own time and yet often strangely similar.

The Flavians retained a significant Jewish connection after the Jewish War, and Domitilla was exposed to Jewish influences throughout her life. The most significant would have been the client king Agrippa II and his remarkable sister, Queen Berenice, who was Titus' mistress. We will find that these individuals whom Domitilla would have known and respected are given an unexpected, and otherwise unexplained, prominence in Luke/Acts.

Another influence on Domitilla was the Jewish general, traitor, and historian Josephus. She would have known Josephus for almost all her life, from when she was a girl no older than ten. They belonged to the same circle of the Flavian court in Rome for over twenty years. We know that she was interested in Jewish matters, and Josephus was the Flavian's pet expert on all things Jewish. She would have learned much about Judaism from him. If Domitilla were the author of Luke, we would certainly expect her works to show his influence.

That Luke/Acts is influenced by Josephus has been obvious for a long time. The very idea of writing Acts was probably suggested by the example of Josephus' Antiquities. At the very least, the author of Luke was familiar with Josephus' works. But we can go further and show that the author of Luke also influenced Josephus. This is the key point. Such mutual influence implies that Josephus and the author of Luke knew each other. It would mean that Luke/Acts was written in Flavian Rome.

Josephus will be our key witness, and in some ways this book is as much about him as it is about Domitilla. We must understand his life history, including the event which brought him and Vespasian together in a collision of cultures—the Jewish War. Intelligent and creative, arrogant and egotistical, Josephus was a conman and a liar who prided himself as a supreme trickster. He took reckless risks with his reputation and even his life to demonstrate his own cleverness. He was also a brilliant individual; it is Josephus who is our primary source of information about Judea and all things Jewish for the period.

With this circumstantial evidence we hope to convince the reader of two things: that the author of Luke was someone just like Domitilla. And that Domitilla was perfectly positioned to be the author of Luke. Neither amount to proof. For that we need to go beyond the circumstantial. In a murder case, it is not enough to show that the suspect could have done it, but that they, and no one else, actually did do it. This requires specific evidence; the fragment of DNA, the spot of blood in the suspect's car, the bullet that could only have come from a particular gun. We do not have a murder, but a literary who-dun-it, and our case has been cold for over 1,900 years. And yet the specific evidence exists.

Our search for this evidence will take us down into the catacombs of Domitilla. There we will find a wall painting, a fresco above a tomb, just a few steps away from the cultic heart of the Christian catacombs. The fresco has been known for over a century, but not understood. Read correctly, it tells us who wrote the Gospel of Luke. The evidence of the fresco will, at first sight, confuse the case. Resolving the confusion will give us one vital piece of information about Domitilla that will help us understand the final evidence.

The Testimonium Flavian

The most controversial passage in Josephus' writings is the Testimonium Flavian, so-called after the Roman name, Josephus Flavius, which he adopted when he became a Flavian client. The Testimonium is the earliest account of Jesus from a non-Christian source. It is found in Josephus' Antiquities of the Jews, which was published 93/4 AD, and is often put forward as the best external evidence for the existence of Jesus. But the Testimonium is odd. It is remarkably positive about Jesus, although everything we know about the Pharisee Josephus leads us to believe that he would have despised Christianity. Scholars have explained this paradox by theorizing that Josephus wrote something skeptical about Jesus which later Christian scribes revised to make it more reverential. Another view, popular among the "mythicists" who believe that Jesus did not exist, is that the entire passage is a forgery. However, later in the Antiquities there is a mention of James "the brother of Jesus called Christ," which supports the idea that Josephus had written about Jesus earlier.

The Testimonium has become central in the war between those who think that Jesus did not exist and those who think he did. In this argument, each side selects the evidence that suits them. Much of the consensus case rests on a reconstruction of what scholars think Josephus initially wrote. Those who base their arguments on this reconstruction tend to forget that it is purely hypothetical and not direct historical evidence. On the other hand, the mythicists have to explain away the embarrassing James reference.

When we consider the evidence in totality, the situation becomes even more confusing and paradoxical. In the 1990s, the discovery was made of a close link between the Testimonium and the conversation on the road to Emmaus in the Gospel of Luke. Both passages have the same detailed structure, a correspondence that extends to nineteen separate points. Not only this, but both passages use an identical odd phrase, a similarity that would be almost impossible to have arisen by chance. None of the existing theories can explain why the Testimonium is so close to this obscure passage in Luke.

After the Testimonium, the next earliest external evidence for Jesus is a passage by Tacitus in his Annals. While dealing with the fire of Rome and Nero's persecution of the Christians in Rome, he gives a brief overview of how the Christians arose from "Christus," who was crucified by Pontius Pilate. The Tacitus passage, written c.120 AD, has been used to support the idea that Jesus existed and that Josephus was likely to have written something about Jesus. But the two passages may be more intimately linked. It was usual for Roman historians to get much of their information from other historians without acknowledging their sources. Tacitus' obvious source for anything relating to Judea would have been Josephus' works. We will see that Tacitus' account of the Christians is based on the Testimonium. As Christians could not have altered Tacitus' copy of the Antiquities, this means that the Testimonium was original to Josephus in something close to its current form.

We are left with an apparent absurdity; that Josephus included a pro-Christian passage in his Antiquities which is very closely related to a passage from the Gospel of Luke. But that is nothing to what comes next. The Testimonium is a very odd thing for Josephus to have written, but the passage that comes immediately afterward is even more peculiar. It is the story of a noblewoman living in Rome who was tricked into an act of prostitution. It is the strangest, most untypical thing in Josephus' extensive writings. And it is followed by another odd story about a second Roman noblewoman who is deceived by an unscrupulous religious conman and his associates.

The two stories are closely related. They are, in fact, two parts of an elaborate satire aimed at the Flavians and Christianity. So we have the remarkable case that the pro-Christian Testimonium is immediately followed by a secret anti-Christian satire. Clearly, any theory about the Testimonium must account for this strange situation. So it is amazing that the two stories are ignored in almost every discussion about the Testimonium.

The satire will give us the final proof we are seeking. We will see how it is not only aimed at Christianity in general but at a specific person. And that this individual, a senior noblewoman living in Rome, must be the same person who wrote the Gospel of Luke. Josephus is not content with just describing her and her husband. The evidence from the fresco will help us see how he even indicates her name.

Domitilla's fate

If one of Domitilla's sons had become emperor, the Roman Empire could have been Christianized two centuries before Constantine the Great's conversion. It is a fascinating "what if" of history. In all likelihood, not much would have changed. The nascent religion was too small and powerless to be widely adopted even with the patronage of the emperor's mother. We do not know if Domitilla's sons were Christians, but there would have been intense pressure for them to conform to traditional Roman religion. Most likely, their mother's religious leanings would have been seen as no more than an oddity. But there would have been a significant impact on Christianity; it would not have been persecuted, and it would have grown faster and achieved respectability sooner.

This brings us to the mystery of what happened to Domitilla and her sons. Why do they just disappear from history? To answer these questions, we need to look at the political circumstances around the assassination of Domitian. The accounts of this key event are strangely silent on certain important matters. Our best source tells us that the assassination was the direct result of Domitian's action against Clemens and that Domitilla's steward was implicated as the chief assassin. Yet Domitilla and her sons were not brought back to continue the Flavian dynasty. Instead, the elderly and ineffectual senator, Nerva, was appointed as the new Emperor. This brings us to further questions. Who was really behind the assassination? Was Domitilla framed in her absence for the killing? And would the new regime allow the real claimants to the imperial purple to live?

1

Britannia

Revolt

Quintus Petillius Cerialis, legionary legate of the Ninth Hispania, led the bedraggled remains of his calvary along the road, urging them to greater haste. It was a bloody and exhausted group of men who trailed along. The injured, who lacked the strength to continue, pleaded for a quick dispatch with the sword. They all knew that any who fell behind would meet a grisly end. A barbarian horde led by a bloodthirsty queen was close on their tails.[1]

The men were all that remained of Cerialis' legionary force. His infantry had been hacked to bits, and the remains of his calvary had been forced to flee. Cerialis was in his mid-thirties and on his first major military command. It looked like it would also be his last—a complete disaster. But no one ever doubted his courage, and his men would follow him to the end.

It was just a few days since the news had come that the Iceni, the chief Roman allies in the east of Britannia, had revolted under their queen, Boudicca. When the Trinovantes joined the Iceni, it looked like the whole province of Britannia was rising up against the Romans. Dio says that Boudicca "possessed a greater intelligence than often belongs to women."[2] She certainly could not have chosen her timing better. The supreme Roman commander in Britannia, Paulinus Suetonius, had taken the main Roman force to the west on a futile military conquest in the rugged hills and mountains of Wales. Tacitus reports that Suetonius was motivated by envy of another famous general, Corbulo. His objective was the Druid's sacred island of Mona (Anglesey), a difficult target separated from the Welsh mainland by the Menai straits about a third of a mile wide.[3]

Suetonius was a military engineer and relished the challenge. His infantry crossed the water in flat-bottom boats while the calvary swam. On the other side, a bewildering sight confronted them. A heavily armed line of native warriors stood ready for battle with wild women leaping among them, brandishing torches. Druid priests with arms raised to heaven uttered magical curses on the Romans. The legionaries were terrified, but their officers commanded them to attack. The battle was short and bloody. The Britons were defeated, and their sacred groves, the site of atrocious rites of human sacrifice (according to Tacitus), cut down.

It was a victory that almost cost the Romans the province of Britannia. The causes of Boudicca's rebellion were complex. Tacitus says that Boudicca's husband Prasutagus had left a will with the emperor as beneficiary alongside his two daughters. A dispute over this will led to the Romans flogging Boudicca and raping her daughters.[4] But how could the Romans have done this while Boudicca was the queen of her tribe and surrounded by her warriors? Perhaps Tacitus has mistakenly confused a reprisal after the revolt for the cause of the war. Cassius Dio, writing later but using early sources, does not mention any flogging or rape. He says that the dispute concerned large sums gifted by the previous emperor Claudius that the provincial procurator, Catus Decianus, was now treating as loans. A Roman noble, Seneca, had also advanced an enormous loan of 40 million sesterces to the Britons, which he was now aggressively calling in.[5]

When Cerialis heard of Boudicca's revolt, he immediately saw the threat to the new Roman colony of Camulodunum (Colchester) in the territory of the Trinovantes and already the largest town in Britannia. So confident were the Romans in the pacification of the island that Camulodunum had no defenses. Fearing the worst, the colonists sent desperate messages for help to the procurator, Catus Decianus, at Londinium (London). In reply, Decianus sent two hundred soldiers. Boudicca's approaching army numbered over a hundred thousand.

Cerialis faced an appalling dilemma. He could march with an inadequate force and attempt the rescue of Camulodunum. Or he could keep his legion deployed defensively and wait for Suetonius to join up with him while abandoning the city to its inevitable fate. The second option was the sensible choice, but Cerialis resolved to go to the relief of Camulodunum. He left either from the headquarters of the Ninth at Lincoln, six days march from Camulodunum, or the fort at Longthorpe, which was three days closer.[6] He had only about half his legion with him, the remainder being deployed widely across the East Midlands.[7]

It was a doomed expedition. Cerialis' force was woefully inadequate against Boudicca's vast army. Tacitus says that the Britons "put his legion to flight and killed all his infantry."[8] The Iceni and Trinovantes took Camulodunum with a vicious orgy of killing by "the gallows, burning and crucifixion."[9] The two hundred soldiers barricaded themselves into the temple to the deified Emperor Claudius, where they held out for two days before they too were slaughtered.

Boudicca's next target was Londinium, a settlement that Tacitus describes as "famed for its large concentration of businessmen and tradable goods."[10]

It is the first mention of London in history and would aptly describe the growing city for the next two thousand years. Confronted with Boudicca's advance, the useless Decianus immediately fled on a boat back to Gaul. The abandoned citizens appealed to Suetonius to save them. Tacitus says that he advanced to Londinium but retreated because of its poor defensive situation. However, it seems impossible that Suetonius could have reached Londinium before Boudicca. In any event, Londinium met the same fate as Camulodunum, as did Verulamium (St Albans). Tacitus puts the number of Roman citizens and allies killed at 70,000. Archaeological investigations have confirmed the massive destruction.

Suetonius' remaining legions were hopelessly outnumbered. Fifty years previously, the Romans had lost three legions in the Teutoburg forest. It looked as if this nightmare in Germania was about to be repeated, and that the province of Britannia would soon be lost.

Cerialis

It is likely that Cerialis had an additional cause of anxiety; the presence of a young wife and perhaps a baby daughter in Britannia. Boudicca's rebellion occurred in 60/61 AD, around the same time that Cerialis had married the daughter of the esteemed general, Flavius Vespasian. His bride, Flavia Domitilla, would have been no more than a teenager. It was customary for senior officers to take their wives and families with them on postings, and we would expect Domitilla to be in Britannia with Cerialis. The couple had one child, a daughter also called Flavia Domitilla, who is the subject of this book.

We cannot be entirely sure of the above picture. There is no direct evidence that Cerialis was married to Domitilla or that our Domitilla was his daughter. But the indirect evidence is strong. Tacitus says that Cerialis was a close relative of Vespasian—the specific word he uses means either brother-in-law or son-in-law.[11] Vespasian's only sister died in childhood, and Domitilla was his only daughter.[12] The inevitable conclusion is that Cerialis was Domitilla's unknown husband. The extraordinary trust that Vespasian would later place in Cerialis supports this conclusion.

Flavia Domitilla's father, Vespasian, had made his reputation in the conquest of Britannia for which he had been granted triumphal honors. Her mother was also called Flavia Domitilla, so we have three women from three generations with the same name. Historians distinguish them by giving them numbers; Domitilla I is Vespasian's wife, Domitilla II his daughter, and Domitilla III his granddaughter. Rather than numbering people, we will use "Domitilla" to mean Domitilla III and indicate the other two as the elder and the younger.

Domitilla the younger was born sometime between Titus (30 December 39) and Domitian (24 October 51). Her year of birth could have been as early as 41 AD. If she had then married and given birth at a young age, Domitilla, her daughter, could have been born as early as 57/8 AD.

We know that our Domitilla had no less than seven children before the death of her husband, an unusually large number for a Roman aristocratic family in the first century. To have so many babies we will assume that Domitilla must have been at least thirty in 95 AD. Even this would involve a much higher birth rate than would be normal for aristocratic Roman women. With these considerations, we get a range of possible birth years for Domitilla of 57-65 AD with the extremes being less likely than the middle.[13]

Cerialis would have been legionary legate of the Ninth Hispania for three or four years, including 60/1 AD. There are two possible windows of opportunity for a marriage. The first is no later than 59 AD before Cerialis left for Britannia. Roman noble girls would marry at fifteen or even as young as twelve. So if Domitilla the younger were born within five or six years of Titus she would have been at the normal age for marriage. If she did marry Cerialis before he left Rome, then she most likely gave birth to Domitilla in the three years or more the couple would have spent in Britannia—say between 60 and 62 AD. This would make Domitilla between 33 and 35 at her downfall. This scenario has the advantage of allowing more time for the birth of Domitilla's seven children.

Alternatively, there may have been a second brief window of opportunity after Cerialis returned from Britannia but before Vespasian departed as proconsul of Africa in 63 AD. If his daughter were still unmarried, Vespasian would have been anxious to arrange a wedding before leaving Rome for three years. Cerialis, however, may still have been in Britannia at this time. If a later wedding did happen it would have been in 62/63 AD with Domitilla being born in Rome in 64 or 65 AD.

There is one other consideration. Any marriage would have been arranged by Domitilla the younger's father and mother. Cerialis would have been an eligible husband before he left for Britannia, but was damaged goods on his return. The Romans abhorred defeat. They would have admired Cerialis' courage but not that he had lost most of his legion. Although not exactly in disgrace, he would have been under a cloud. Would a politically astute man with the reputation and ambition of Vespasian want to marry his only daughter to him? Vespasian would show a lot of trust in Cerialis, which makes more sense if he was already his son-in-law before the Boudicca episode.

Something else that supports a marriage no later than 59 AD is that Domitilla the younger's brother Titus may have been in Britannia under Cerialis.[14] Suetonius reports that the young Titus was a military tribune in both Germania and Britannia.[15] It was usual for a young man to gain his first military experience serving under an older relative. If Titus were present with his brother-in-law Cerialis during the defeat of the Ninth, it would explain an odd story from Cassius Dio. He says that on one occasion when Vespasian was fighting in Britannia, he had been hemmed in by barbarians until rescued by a cavalry detachment led by Titus.[16] As Titus would only have been seven at the time, this would have been quite an exploit! Clearly there is some mistake. The usual explanation is that Titus must have saved Vespasian's life on some unknown occasion in Judea, which has been confused with Vespasian's time in Britannia. However, it would be odd for Dio to place a story relating to the much later Judean campaign under Claudius. A better explanation is that Dio's source recorded an occasion when Titus rescued an older relative in Britannia. This relative was actually Cerialis during the rout of the Ninth, but Dio assumed it must have been Vespasian who had also fought in Britannia.

In conclusion, it is likely that Cerialis married Domitilla the younger before he left for his posting to the Ninth Hispania and that Domitilla was born in Britannia. There is no evidence that Domitilla the younger had any other children, but Cerialis may have.

Some scholars have proposed that Cerialis had one or even two sons by a previous marriage to an unknown woman. So Domitilla may have had a half-brother or brothers, although both candidates are doubtful. The first possibility is Petillius Firmus.[17] A badly damaged stone inscription from Arretium in Italy records that a senator called Firmus who had been acting legate of a Fourth legion, most likely the Fourth Flavia Felix, was given unusual honors under Vespasian. A military tribune called Gaius Petillius Firmus is mentioned in connection with this legion, and it is possible that Firmus took over command after the death of the legate. To explain the unusual honors granted to Petillius Firmus it has been suggested that he was Cerialis' son. However, there is no direct evidence linking Firmus to Cerialis beyond the fact that they both belonged to gens Petillia. And even if they were related, there is no reason for believing that he was a son rather than, say, a nephew. It would be unusual for a son to take neither the father's praenomen (Quintus) nor one of his cognomina.[18] Firmus must have been born no later than c.50 AD and died in his mid to late twenties, for we hear no more about him. If he were Cerialis' son he would have accompanied his father to Britannia as a teenager and been an early presence in Domitilla's life, but the evidence for this scenario is scant.

The other potential half-brother is Quintus Petillius Rufus, who was appointed consul in 83 AD and who would have been at least five years older than Firmus. However, Cerialis himself was likely the consul in question—his full name was Quintus Petillius Cerialis Caesius Rufus—making the supposed son Rufus a phantom.[19]

Domitilla the younger

If Domitilla the younger were with Cerialis in Britannia, she would have lived at Lindum (Lincoln), the base of the Ninth.[20] It may seem odd that a Roman noblewoman would dwell, and even give birth, in a frontier legionary fort. Traditionally the fort has been seen as an exclusively male preserve, with marriage forbidden to soldiers by the ban of Augustus. However, the marriage ban never applied to officers. And it has become clear that there were many women and children within and around Roman forts. Centurions and more senior officers would live with their families inside the fort. The ordinary soldiers would evade the marriage ban by having informal "wives" in the surrounding camp. When they retired after twenty-five years of service with a pension and some land in a colonia, they would formally marry the woman and legitimize their children.[21]

The Romans built all their camps to the same plan so that any soldier would be instantly familiar with the layout. The accommodation for the ordinary legionaries was cramped. They lived in long narrow barrack buildings consisting of ten to fourteen pairs of rooms. Six to eight men would share each pair of rooms which only had a total area of 16 square meters. One room was for sleeping, the other for living in when off duty. At the other extreme, there was a large house near the center of the fort built in a Mediterranean peristyle around an inner courtyard. This was the praetorium, where the legionary legate, his family, and household slaves would live. The praetorium could get quite luxurious, with hypocaust underfloor heating (a necessity in Britannia), wall paintings, sculptures, and private bathing facilities. The Lindum praetorium would have been relatively basic because the fort was newly built. Other senior officers would have occupied similar but smaller houses.[22]

An idea of what life would have been like as a fort commander's wife comes from the inscribed wooden tablets from Vindolanda, a fort near Hadrian's wall in northern England, dating from around 100 AD. The boggy conditions of Vindolanda have preserved perishable materials, including the discarded fort records and correspondence. The forts along Hadrian's wall were occupied by Batavian auxiliaries whose homeland was in the Netherlands. On one famous tablet, the wife of the commander of a nearby fort, Claudia Severa, invites Sulpicia Lepidina, the wife of Flavius Cerialis, the fort commander of Vindolanda, to her birthday party. Flavius Cerialis' nomen tells us that he was granted Roman citizenship under the Flavians. His cognomen would have been given in honor of Petillius Cerialis.

The younger Domitilla came from a much higher social sphere than the two women at Hadrian's wall. Although surrounded by people, it could be a lonely existence. Aside from other officers' wives in the fort, her social circle was limited. The climate would have been miserable for a Roman, the land strange and bleak. She was living at the edge of the known world, the furthest outpost of the Roman Empire.

In the Gospel of Luke, the young pregnant Mary stays for three months with an elder relative, Elizabeth, who is also pregnant. The episode seems odd to the modern reader—why did she not remain with her husband? But it would have made sense in the context of the military world of a Roman frontier province. A pregnant teenager having her first child would have been safer under the watchful eye of a more experienced woman of her own social class. If this were the case for Domitilla the younger, she could have stayed with Suetonius' wife, who lived at the camp city of Viriconium (Wroxeter). Perhaps the baby Domitilla was even born there.

Viriconium, once one of the largest cities in Britannia, was later abandoned; nothing remains today except a few ruins amid empty fields. It lived on in the literary imagination in Houseman's poem: "On Wenlock Edge the wood's in trouble...". A Roman watches a gale move the trees; "the gale of life blew high" through him also before passing, leaving nothing. The gale of life would blow through Cerialis and, in a different way, through his daughter. As for Domitilla the younger, she died as a teenager or in her early twenties, but had the consolation of later becoming a god.

Boudicca and Harry Potter

The army that Suetonius assembled to face Boudicca was woefully inadequate. He had his own Fourteenth legion based at Viriconium and vexillations of the Twentieth along with auxiliary cavalry units. We do not know if Cerialis and the remnant of the Ninth were able to join him.[23] The other legion in Britannia, the Second, was stationed in the southwest under the temporary command of the camp prefect Poenius Postumus. Suetonius had ordered Postumus to march and join forces with him, but, shockingly, Postumus disobeyed the order. Was Postumus' refusal to move out of fear, realistic knowledge of the local conditions, or fatalism in the face of inevitable defeat?[24] It left Suetonius with just 10,000 men facing the opposing force whose numbers are estimated by Roman writers as anything up to an (obviously exaggerated) 230,000.

The Britons were in a holiday mood and had brought their wives and families to witness the fun. Their carts were arranged in a great semi-circle to stop the Romans from running away. They were all ready for the slaughter, and slaughter it was to be.

Boudicca led her forces riding in a chariot along with her two daughters. The Romans adopted a wedge formation, a pointed triangle built up from multiple lines of legionnaires. The Romans' shields protected their formation both at the sides and above their heads. The Britons' javelins bounced harmlessly off, and the Romans began their advance. They thrust their spears between the shields marching remorselessly forward step by step, stabbing down as they walked over their trampled enemies. The Britons' chief advantage, their numbers, were used against them as the wedge cut through the native lines. The panicking warriors attempting to escape the thrust of the spears crashed into those pressing forward from behind. Many were killed in the crush. As the rout developed, Boudicca's fleeing army was hampered by the wagons and the presence of the women. The Romans were indiscriminate in their killing. Tacitus puts the native casualties as high as 80,000 against 400 Romans killed. According to Tacitus, Boudicca ended her life with poison, although Dio says that she sickened and died. Poenius Postumus of the Second Legion committed suicide when he heard of Suetonius' victory.[25]

The most likely site of the final battle is Mancetter in the East Midlands, which matches Tacitus' description and lies on the Roman road between Viriconium and Londinium. Many other less likely theories have been put forward over the years, including that of folklore writer Lewis Spence who argued that the battle was on the outskirts of Londinium in the shallow valley in which King's Cross station now stands. After his pre-war book was published, an urban myth arose that Boudicca was buried beneath the station, between platforms 9 and 10. Harry Potter's Hogwarts train leaves from King's Cross platform 9 3/4, exactly where the queen of the Iceni supposedly lies at rest.[26]

2

Luke and Acts

Luke/Acts in context

Today we encounter the Gospel of Luke and its successor work, the Acts of the Apostles, as sacred literature, as part of the Bible. The books of the Christian New Testament have shaped western civilization for almost two thousand years. At the heart of the Christian Bible are the four gospels; Matthew, Mark, Luke, and John. They tell of the birth, ministry, death, and resurrection of Jesus; there is no part of the world that has not felt their influence.

For most of those two thousand years it has been impossible for Christians to question the truthfulness of the Bible. To do so would invite a charge of blasphemy or, even worse, heresy. Even today, many Christians regard the Bible as inerrant, an attitude that precludes any serious investigation of its origins. At the other end of the spectrum, many would dismiss the Bible as mere superstition, an embarrassing relic of the past. We will approach the New Testament differently, as a collection of texts written by human beings, reflecting their time's historical and cultural context. This is not to rule out the idea that the gospels are inspired and contain spiritual truths. We must never forget that they were essentially religious documents written for a religious purpose. But the authors were real men and perhaps, as this book argues, at least one real woman.

The New Testament as we know it consists of twenty-seven works; the four gospels, Acts, the letters of Paul, Hebrews, miscellaneous letters, and the book of Revelation. It took its current form gradually over several centuries. The myth that Constantine the Great decided which books to include is just that, a myth without any historical basis in fact. The first person to write about a collection of Christian scriptures was the church father Irenaeus in c.180 AD. He developed the concept of the four-fold gospel; the four gospels should be read together as four views of a central truth.[1] The number four was significant: "It is not possible that the Gospels can be either more or fewer in number than they are." There were four winds and four zones of the earth. Irenaeus equated the four gospels to the four creatures in Revelation 4:7; a lion, an ox, a man and an eagle in flight.[2] The lion was John, the calf Luke, the man Matthew and the eagle Mark. This is why the four "evangelists", the gospel authors, are represented as a lion, a calf, a man and an eagle in old images, such as carvings in churches.

Irenaeus lived in a time of many competing types of Christianity. He was a father of the proto-orthodox church and wrote his most famous work, Against Heresies, in opposition to the various gnostic groups he regarded as heretical. The four-fold gospel concept had the advantage of closing the canon against the gospels written and used by these "here-tics." The gospels would be four and no more. Many modern authors and internet posters have drawn attention to the exclusion of the so-called apocryphal writings from the New Testament. It is often said that the four gospels are an arbitrary selection from the forty to fifty gospels in circu-lation. This is simply not true. These other gospels were written after the canonical four, often centuries later. The one disputed exception is whether the Gospel of Thomas is earlier or later than the canonical gospels. (In the Thomas Code and elsewhere, I have argued that the Gospel of Thomas is earlier than any of the four gospels.[3])

Irenaeus' four-fold gospel was one way of solving a problem that has bedeviled Christian commentators from the earliest times—the gospels are all different. While it is true that the overall story is the same, there is a great deal of variation and inconsistency in the details. The four-fold gospel concept implied that all these differences are reconcilable at a higher level. They arise either from our ignorance of actual events or because we are not reading and interpreting the gospel correctly. So, for example, the Gospel of John is inherently a spiritual gospel and should be read as giving the spiritual truth, whereas the other three are more concerned with the literal truth.

As a more questioning and secular approach to biblical scholarship developed, this four-fold gospel concept could no longer be accepted as an adequate explanation. A new popular theory saw each of the gospels as the product of a Christian community in a separate geographical location. If you take several eyewitness accounts of an event, such as an accident, there will always be differences, often striking, between the versions. So if the four gospels were produced by four separate communities, each relying on the testimony of different eyewitnesses, we would expect to find inconsistencies in details. Indeed, it would be suspicious if they were in perfect agreement. So minor discrepancies can be taken as evidence of the essential truthfulness of the overall account.

This new approach accepted that there could be errors and mistakes in the gospels. But it did seem to show an underlying historical reality to Jesus' life, mission, crucifixion—and perhaps even his resurrection.

However, there is one fatal flaw with this theory. It assumes that the gospels were independent productions, but this was not the case. The whole idea of separate Christian communities is suspect; the nascent churches were geographically diverse but not isolated. Communications within the Roman Empire were excellent, and literature spread rapidly between the churches. The successive gospel writers were familiar with the earlier gospels, which they used as sources.

Matthew appears first in the New Testament and was historically supposed to be the first gospel to be written. This theory is called the Augustinian after Saint Augustus who believed that Matthew was written first with Mark, the second gospel, being an abridgment of Matthew.[4] It is now almost universally accepted that it was the other way around. The short and unsatisfactory Gospel of Mark was first to be written. The author of Matthew incorporated nearly the whole of Mark into his new gospel with only a light rewriting, developing it into a more extensive work by adding much new material.

Much of this extra material in Matthew is also found in Luke. The obvious explanation is that the author of Luke used Matthew as a source in addition to Mark. Instead, scholars became fixated on a more convoluted theory called the two-source hypothesis; that the author of Matthew and Luke had independently used Mark together with another source. This hypothetical source was given the mysterious-sounding name of "Q," which stood for Quelle, meaning "source" in German.[5] Q was supposedly a sayings gospel, although it also incorporated some narrative material. Scholars directed much research at reconstructing Q from Luke and Matthew as it was believed to give an insight into the earliest Christianity. But did Q even exist? No manuscript or fragment has ever been found, and none of the church fathers mention such a text.

Scholars believed in Q because of differences in how Matthew and Luke use the Q material. These differences were thought to be best explained if the two authors had independently used a third source. Although many scholars still believe in Q's reality, there is also increasing skepticism. The introduction to Luke strongly suggests that the author was familiar with the Gospel of Matthew. And features that Luke shares with Matthew, such as including a nativity and genealogy, are difficult to explain unless the author of Luke knew Matthew. But if so, then it is unnecessary to invoke the hypothetical Q.

So how do we account for the differences between these two gospels? I have called this the "same but different" pattern.[6] The author of Luke uses Matthew but seems to deliberately change many of the details in an almost perverse fashion. This is explained if the author of Luke was obliged to use Matthew through a lack of alternative sources but wanted their own gospel to be different. It is like a student using another student's essay but changing many details to avoid accusations of plagiarism.

The attitude of the author of Luke to their sources is generally cavalier. Whereas the author of Matthew tends to be very loyal to Mark, the author of Luke is always ready to change Mark's narrative for their own reasons. This tendency to change things makes Luke the least reliable of the gospels regarding fidelity to the source. But the author of Luke is also remarkably well informed with excellent access to both Roman and early Christian material. And they are the best storyteller of all the gospel writers, always sensitive to the emotional side of a situation even though they may be lax on factual detail.

The Gospel of John is the oddball among the gospels. The other three are called the Synoptics, meaning "with one sight." They are closely related, which modern scholars attribute to Matthew and Luke following Mark. The fourth gospel seems to go its own way. It is the most spiritual and esoteric of all the gospels, yet it also shows good awareness of the geography and customs of Judea, suggesting local knowledge. But being different from the other three does not imply independence. The author of John probably knew all the other gospels and is strongly influenced by Luke in particular. But he never copies them word for word. Most likely he has read or listened to them in the past, but is unable or unwilling to consult a manuscript copy as he writes. Such copies would still have been rare.

We can be confident about the relative order of composition; Mark, Matthew, Luke, and John. Assigning precise dates is more challenging. There is virtually nothing in the gospels that can be related to contemporary events. The one exception is the "little apocalypse" in Mark 13, which seems to refer to the coming destruction of the temple by the Romans in 70 AD. Most scholars believe that Mark was written shortly after this event. The following is a typical view for the dates of all the gospels:

Mark	early 70s
Matthew	c. 80
Luke	c. 90
John	c. 100

The crucifixion is typically assigned a date of 30 or 33 AD. So the first gospel, that of Mark, was written around forty years after the supposed date of the crucifixion. We can consider this timing in relation to the Roman emperors:

Vespasian	69-79
Titus	79-81

Domitian	81-96
Nerva	96-98
Trajan	98-117

There is a high probability that Luke was written while Domitian was emperor. We can rule out a date before 81 AD due to Luke's dependence on Matthew, and Acts' likely dependence on Josephus' Antiquities published in the nineties. We can be less definite at ruling out a date after 96 AD.

All the books in the New Testament were written in Koine Greek, the lingua franca of the Roman Empire. A well-educated person anywhere in the empire would be able to write and think in Greek, and the author of Luke was undoubtedly such a person. Greek was in wide everyday use in the east. Although the Romans used Latin as their first language, Greek was the language of learning and philosophy—and of love. Juvenal complains that the women of Rome insist in speaking Greek with their lovers and husbands: "They talk nothing but Greek, though it is a greater shame for our people to be ignorant of Latin."[7] Juvenal exaggerates for satirical effect, but it does show that Roman women of the upper classes were fully conversant with Greek.

All the gospels would have been copied onto papyrus scrolls, and Luke and Acts would have fitted onto one scroll each. They are the two longest works in the New Testament; Luke has 19,400 words, and Acts has 18,400 words.[8]

The Gospel of Luke

The first idiosyncrasy of the Gospel of Luke comes at the very beginning. It starts with something missing from all the other gospels; an introduction and dedication to a man called Theophilus. The opening is followed by the fanciful story of the birth of John the Baptist to two elderly parents Elizabeth and Zechariah. This leads into the pregnancy of the Virgin Mary by the Holy Spirit. Only in Luke do we find the story of Mary and Joseph traveling to Bethlehem for a census where Jesus is born in a stable and placed in a manger. Angels come to shepherds who watch their sheep at night and tell them to go and pay homage to the newborn king.

Jesus' parents take him as a baby and present him at the temple. When Jesus is twelve, he disappears on a journey, and his worried parents find him in the temple questioning the learned scholars. From this point on, Luke stays closer to the narrative of Mark and Matthew. Jesus is baptized by John in the Jordan, and the spirit in the shape of a dove descends onto his head. A voice from heaven says that Jesus is God's son. The baptism is followed by the genealogy of Jesus, "the supposed son of Joseph," which is notoriously different from the genealogy in Matthew. Following his baptism, Jesus goes into the wilderness, where Satan tempts him.

Back in Galilee, Jesus recruits his first fishermen disciples, Simon Peter and a pair of brothers, James and John, the sons of Zebedee. Jesus selects other disciples to make up the group of the twelve. He also has a group of wealthy female followers who give him financial support. Jesus leads this large group around Galilee, performing miracle after miracle and teaching the people about the kingdom of heaven. Jesus, in Luke, is very much a healer. The author of Luke is fascinated by miracles, particularly healing miracles.

Jesus and his followers then leave Galilee to set out for Jerusalem on a journey that takes up the central portion of the gospel. The account of Jesus' last days when they reach Jerusalem mostly follows Mark and Matthew. They arrive at the city for the Passover, and Jesus enters on a colt. The people line the street and greet him as their king, laying branches in front of him. He goes to the temple, where he drives out the sellers and merchants. Having cleansed the temple, Jesus teaches there for the week, but the priests are hatching a plot against him.

Jesus takes the Passover feast, the last supper, with his disciples. He shares the wine, splits the bread, and predicts that one of the twelve will betray him. After the meal, Jesus goes to the Mount of Olives to pray. As he does so, a crowd of armed men approaches led by one of his own disciples, Judas Iscariot. The priests have sent them to arrest Jesus. Judas attempts to kiss Jesus, and one of Jesus' followers strikes the servant of the High Priest with a sword, severing his ear. Luke is the only gospel in which Jesus takes up the ear and places it back on.

In the other gospels, Jesus is tried before the Jewish Sanhedrin and then by Pontius Pilate, the Roman Prefect. But in Luke he also faces a third trial. Pilate sends Jesus to Herod, who concludes he is not guilty of anything and returns him to Pilate. Although the Prefect wants to free Jesus, he gives in to Jewish demands and reluctantly condemns him to death. Jesus is crucified between two robbers at the place named "the Skull" and dies the same day. His body is taken down and buried by Joseph of Arimathea in a newly hewn tomb.

On the third day after his death, a group of his women followers goes early to the tomb to cover Jesus' body with spices, but they find the stone rolled away and the tomb empty. While they wonder what to do, two men in dazzling garments appear and tell them that Jesus has risen. The women report what they have seen to the disciples but are not believed.

Later two of Jesus' followers are traveling along the road to Emmaus, seven miles outside Jerusalem, when they are joined by a stranger. He asks why they are so downcast, and one of the pair, a man called Cleopas, tells him all about Jesus. The stranger tells them not to despair and enlightens them about the meaning of the scriptures. When they come to Emmaus, the two beg the stranger to join them for a meal. They all sit down for a simple supper, and the stranger breaks the bread. At that moment, he is revealed to them as Jesus and vanishes.

Jesus is also said to have appeared to Simon. Finally, he appears to all the eleven remaining disciples showing them his hands and feet with the nail holes and eating a fish to prove he is no ghost. Later Jesus leads them to Bethany. Raising his hands, he blesses them and is carried up to heaven.

Acts of the Apostles

The Acts of the Apostles, like Luke, is dedicated to Theophilus. The joint authorship of the two is widely accepted and rarely questioned. They would originally have circulated together as two parts of one narrative. In the New Testament they are separated by the fourth gospel, John, and Acts serves as the bridge between the gospels and the letters of Paul.

Acts starts where Luke finishes, with the ascension of Jesus to heaven. The former disciples gather together afterward with Mary and the brothers of the Lord in an upper room somewhere in Jerusalem. There are only eleven disciples now because of the suicide of Judas Iscariot. Peter suggests they choose a replacement from two worthy candidates, and Matthias is selected. From now on, the group of twelve will be called the apostles. We might expect that Acts will be about the doings of these twelve, but nine of them are never mentioned again. And the most prominent character will be a man who is not even one of them.

A better title would be the Acts of Peter and Paul. It is a book of two halves. The first half is primarily about the doings of Peter but also introduces Paul. Peter then disappears abruptly from the narrative, and the second half is all about Paul. The prominence of Paul, the self-styled apostle to the gentiles, is one of many clues that the author of Luke was a gentile.

The descent of the Holy Spirit in Acts takes a physical form. When the followers of Jesus are gathered together in Jerusalem at Pentecost, they hear a sound like a violent wind, and tongues of fire appear among them and settle on their heads. They begin speaking in strange tongues so that all the people gathered in Jerusalem from different lands hear them in their own language. The people are amazed, although some say they are drunk with new wine. Peter gives a speech that converts three thousand people on the spot.

Now filled with the Holy Spirit, Peter embarks on his apostolic mission. He heals a cripple and teaches in the temple until he is arrested along with John by the Jewish Sanhedrin. Peter conducts a spirited defense, and the two of them are released. On another occasion, all twelve apostles are arrested and imprisoned. But locks cannot hold them. They walk out of jail and are arrested all over again. The Sanhedrin comes close to condemning them to death, but the Pharisee Gamaliel intervenes, and they are only flogged.

The first martyr in Acts is Stephen. He is accused by the Jews and gives a long speech in his defense but is stoned for blasphemy. Paul, who is called Saul at this stage, watches his execution with approval. He becomes a prosecutor of the church, going house to house and dragging Christians away.

Next comes a strange story about Simon, the magician, who practiced sorcery in Samaria, where he was worshipped as a "great power." When he encounters the apostles, he attempts to buy the spirit from Peter, who angrily rejects him. The church fathers regarded Simon Magnus as the first of the gnostics.

Meanwhile, Saul has continued his war against the church. He has secured letters from the high priest to arrest Christians in Damascus and bring them back to Jerusalem in chains. But as Saul approaches Damascus, he is thrown to the ground by a blinding light from heaven. He hears a voice, "Saul, Saul, why do you persecute me?" He finds he has lost his sight, and the voice instructs him to go to the city and wait. Saul is blind for three days before a man called Ananias comes to him and gives him the spirit, which restores his vision. Saul is then baptized as a Christian. Later, he will take the name Paul.

The narrative switches back to Peter who brings gentiles into the church equal to Jews. First, he has a dream in which he sees a sheet lowered from heaven containing all manner of four-footed animals, reptiles, and birds with the instruction to kill and eat. This removes the prohibition on eating unclean foods. As Peter wakes from this dream, he receives a summons from a Roman centurion called Cornelius, who has been told by an angel to send for him. When Peter travels to Caesarea to meet with the centurion and his household, he announces that God has sent him a message that Jews should no longer keep separate from Gentiles. The Holy Spirit descends upon the gentiles in the room, and they speak in tongues. The Jews who have accompanied Peter are amazed. Peter orders that the gentiles be baptized and stays with them for a few days.

In a new persecution, James, the brother of John and son of Zebedee, is put to death by Herod with the sword. Herod also has Peter jailed, guarded by four groups of four soldiers. His execution seems inevitable, but the night before his trial, an angel comes to release him while sleeping between two soldiers. Peter follows the angel out of prison, thinking it is all a dream until he finds himself in the city and the angel disappears.

Acts now switches to Paul's mission to spread the church to gentiles across the Roman Empire. But first, a pressing issue has to be resolved; should the new gentile converts be circumcised and become Jews? To find out, Paul travels with his missionary companion Barnabas to Jerusalem to meet with the apostles. Paul makes the case that gentiles should not have to be circumcised, and Peter speaks enthusiastically in his support. A shadowy figure called James gives the judgment: the gentiles would not have to be circumcised but must refrain from eating meat sacrificed to idols. The apostles write a letter confirming this to the gentile churches. So everything is neatly resolved. We hear no more of Peter.

Paul's mission takes him to Macedonia and Greece. He preaches to the philosophers in the Areopagus in Athens and causes uproar wherever he goes. He is imprisoned and beaten. Yet he persists. Finally, he embarks on a journey to Jerusalem, echoing the journey that Jesus makes to Jerusalem in Luke. His companions plead with him not to go, but the spirit tells Paul to travel to the city. Once in Jerusalem, the Jews attempt to kill him. He is rescued by the Roman procurator Felix but placed on trial. Felix cannot find that he has done anything wrong but refuses to pronounce judgment, so Paul stays in captivity. When Festus replaces Felix as procurator, Paul is given a hearing in which he exercises his right as a Roman citizen to be tried by the emperor. A second hearing is also attended by King Herod Agrippa II and his sister Berenice. They conclude that they would have released Paul had he not claimed his right to be tried in Rome.

Festus sends Paul by boat to Rome. On the way, he is shipwrecked on Malta but survives along with all the other passengers and crew. No sooner has he reached the safety of land than a viper bites him, but the venom cannot harm him. Eventually, he arrives in Rome, where he is placed under house arrest but allowed to receive visitors and teach, which he does for two years. And that is where Acts ends, with Paul left in limbo. We might also wonder what happened to Peter? According to later tradition, both Paul and Peter were martyred in Rome. Were Luke and Acts conceived as a trilogy with a third part set in Rome? If a third part was intended, it was never produced.

3

Vespasian

Vespasian's rise

Vespasian's family were undistinguished. The Flavians came from the Sabine town of Reate forty miles north of Rome. Vespasian's grandfather had been a centurion in Pompey's army and fled from the battle of Pharsalus where Pompey was defeated by Julius Caesar. He obtained a pardon and settled down in Reate as a debt-collector. His son Flavius Sabinus was that unusual thing—an honest tax collector. He married above himself to Vespasia Polla who came from a long-established distinguished family. Her father, Vespasius Pollio, had been a military tribune three times and prefect of the camp, and her brother was a senator.[1]

Sabinus and Vespasia had three children; two boys called Sabinus and Vespasian and a girl who died young. Vespasian was born on 17 November 9 AD at a little village near Reate called Falacrina. He was brought up largely by his maternal grandmother whose memory he cherished throughout his life. His elder brother Sabinus was the ambitious one and made rapid progress. Vespasian, in contrast, showed no ambition. His mother taunted him with comparisons to his more able brother until he finally took the steps required of a young man to advance in the Roman world.[2]

Vespasian first served as a military tribune in Thrace and then as quaestor in Crete and Cyrene. Back in Rome, he stood for the office of aedile, which he only achieved on his second attempt, and then praetor. As praetor he did not miss any opportunity for flattering the emperor Caligula; on one occasion he gave a speech to the senate thanking the emperor for inviting him to dinner.[3]

Vespasian's family was advancing fast; both brothers had been awarded senatorial rank during the reign of Tiberius thanks to their father's growing wealth and influence.[4] Vespasian, however, made what would have been regarded as a very poor marriage. His wife was Flavia Domitilla, the daughter of a quaestor's clerk and the one-time mistress of a man of equestrian rank, Statilius Capella. She was not even a full Roman citizen, only a Latin citizen until her father, Flavius Liberalis, won a judgment determining their freeborn status. Vespasian had no advantage from this marriage, and it must have been a love match. So it is surprising that he should have a relationship with another woman, Caenis, a former slave and freedwoman of Claudius' mother, Antonia.[5]

By this time, Claudius had succeeded his nephew Caligula as emperor. He suffered from a disability from birth that made him clumsy and an object of ridicule. His speech was also often incoherent, and he was thought to be mentally impaired. In reality, he was an intelligent man who wrote histories. Later Claudius would claim to have acted up his disability in front of Caligula to be regarded as a joke rather than a rival. After Caligula's assassination, Claudius was declared emperor as the only surviving male in the imperial family.

Claudius' government was run by his two chief freedmen, Narcissus and Pallas; Suetonius says that he was too easily ruled by his wives and freedmen.[6] The astute Vespasian managed to win influence with Narcissus, probably through his mistress Caenis.[7] With Narcissus' patronage, he was appointed as legate to the Second Augustus legion in Germania. When Claudius decided to invade Britannia in 43 AD, Vespasian's legion was one of the four selected. In Britannia he served under Aulus Plautius with his brother Sabinus acting as his chief lieutenant. Both Vespasian and Sabinus distinguished themselves in the first major battle of the conquest on the river Medway. After a second battle on the Thames, Aulus Plautius sent for reinforcements that crossed the Channel led by the emperor himself. With this force, Camulodunum (Colchester) was taken and became the Roman capital of the new province of Britannia. Several tribes were subdued, and Claudius was hailed as imperator repeatedly. Vespasian would have served under Claudius personally, although Dio says the emperor was only in Britannia for sixteen days. When he left most of the island was still unconquered, and Vespasian was tasked with advancing into the southwest. Suetonius says that he overcame two powerful tribes, probably the Durotriges and Dumnonii, and established control of twenty "towns," which would have been hill-top forts, as well as the island of Vectis (the Isle of Wight). Modern excavations have revealed a legionary fortress of the Second Augustus at Exeter in Devon and another fort as far west as Bodmin in Cornwall. This shows that Vespasian had penetrated right to the far southwest.[8]

Vespasian was well rewarded for his military accomplishments. Claudius granted him triumphal honors and made him a consul suffectus in 51 AD.[9] Vespasian had made rapid progress but now had a political setback that could have cost him his life. His patron, Narcissus, had a dramatic downfall that started when the emperor's wife secretly married someone else.

Messalina and Agrippina

Claudius' third wife, Messalina, had been having an affair with a young nobleman, a consul-designate, called Gaius Silius.[10] He, however, was beginning to tire of the affair and the risk that it entailed. So she decided to marry him while Claudius, her husband, was away. It was simple madness, a vivid example of the air of unreality that could overcome a member of the imperial family. The two held a marriage ceremony in front of witnesses, took vows, made sacrifices, and signed the marriage documents. They held a bridal feast with their guests and spent the night together openly as man and wife. Her intention seems to have been to shuffle old-man Claudius off to one side while she and Silius ruled the empire as a couple, with her son Britannicus adopted by Silius as the future emperor. But there was no concrete plan to achieve this—it was all wishful thinking.

Narcissus had to take great care in revealing these events to Claudius. He arranged for two prostitutes to break the news to him in his bedroom. Claudius, fearing that he was no longer emperor, set out for Rome. Meanwhile, Messalina was holding an orgy with women dressed as maenads and Silius, handsome in big boots, as Dionysus. When they heard of Claudius' approach, they all scattered to evade the centurions who had been sent to arrest them.

The pretorian camp remained loyal to Claudius, while Messalina was abandoned by everyone. Lacking any other transport, she traveled on a garbage cart to appeal directly to the emperor. Narcissus, seeing her approach, diverted the emperor's attention, for she still had a power of attraction over him. Once in Rome, Claudius condemned Silius to death along with all Messalina's previous lovers, even those who had been forced by her. It was a harder task to get Claudius to condemn Messalina. So Narcissus, fearing that the emperor was beginning to soften, took the risk of ordering her execution without asking Claudius.

Messalina was waiting in a garden with her estranged mother who had returned in her hour of need. Her mother told her that the time had come to kill herself, but Messalina was hesitant. Before she could do the deed, a centurion stabbed her with his sword. Claudius asked no questions and made no remark on her death.

The hunt was on for a new wife for the emperor. Narcissus supported Claudius' previous wife, Aelia Paetina, but was outmaneuvered by the beautiful Agrippina. She had taken full advantage of her rights as a relative of kissing the emperor, and he became besotted with her. The marriage, however, would be incestuous as she was his brother Germanicus' daughter. That obstacle was soon overcome; when Claudius proposed that the Senate change the law to permit an uncle to marry his niece, no one voted against it.[11]

Agrippina turned out to be even worse than Messalina in her scheming but more restrained in her love affairs. She quickly gained control over Claudius and maneuvered for her son Domitius to be engaged to Claudius' young daughter Octavia, even though she was already engaged to Lucius Silanus. The unwanted Silanus was eliminated by a false accusation and pushed to commit suicide. So in 53 AD, Octavia married Domitius who was formally adopted by Claudius as his son and renamed Nero. Agrippina got Nero accepted as Claudius' successor ahead of his own son Britannicus who was not yet of age. She was not powerful enough, though, to arrange the downfall of Narcissus. So Agrippina and Narcissus became locked in a shadow war, each vying for influence with Claudius. The freedman had little hope of surviving the emperor: even if he managed to get Britannicus accepted as successor ahead of Nero, that young man might execute him for the death of his mother, Messalina.[12]

Time was not on Agrippina's side. Britannicus would soon come of age and supplant Nero as the emperor's successor—unless Claudius died first. According to Tacitus, Agrippina took advantage of Narcissus' absence from Rome to poison the emperor on 13 October 54. Many modern scholars are skeptical and attribute Claudius's death to natural causes. Agrippina lost no time getting the sixteen-year-old Nero proclaimed as emperor by the pretorian guards.[13]

Agrippina now had no constraint on her actions, and Narcissus was one of her first victims. She secured his death through a squalid imprisonment. She then went after everyone in his circle, including those, like Vespasian, who had benefited from his patronage. Vespasian managed to survive by adopting a strategy of out of sight, out of mind. He retired into obscurity. We hear nothing about him for a decade after his consulship.[14]

Britannicus died a few months after his father, just days before his fourteenth birthday when he would have assumed the toga virilis, the symbol of manhood. Agrippina was shocked at his death, for she had not arranged it. He had been poisoned by Nero, who had not consulted his mother.[15] Agrippina thought that her son owed everything to her, but Nero was tiring of her interference. In 59 AD, five years after he had become emperor, relations between the two had become so bad that he decided to kill her.[16] With the help of his freedman, former tutor and navel prefect, Anicetus, he came up with one of the most bizarre murder plots in history. The victim would be his own mother, and the murder weapon was a ship designed to collapse and sink.

Nero invited Agrippina to dinner and put her mind at ease by being especially affectionate. He escorted her personally to the magnificent boat he had prepared to take her home up the Tiber. It was a calm starlit night, and most of the crew were completely unaware of the plot. At the prearranged time, a centurion cut a rope holding a heavy lead load that would fall and sink the ship. It was intended to look like an accidental shipwreck. A slave of Agrippina was crushed by the falling load, but the boat did not sink immediately. In a rush to escape, one of Agrippina's attendants claimed to be her and was instantly beaten to death. Now alerted to the murder plot, Agrippina was able to swim to a skiff amid the confusion and then make her way back home.

Agrippina decided that her best approach was to pretend to believe that the sinking was an accident. She sent Nero a message about her escape. But when no one came to congratulate her, she knew that Nero had not been fooled. He was terrified that his mother would have him removed as emperor and got Anicetus to take a contingent of soldiers and complete the deed. They cornered Agrippina in her bedroom, where they battered and stabbed her to death.

Killing your own mother was very bad, even for the Romans. The gods would seek vengeance against a parricide or matricide, and if the murderer were a king or emperor, then misfortune would also fall upon his people. Nero would stay in power for several more years, but perhaps the underlying cause of his eventual downfall can be traced back to the assassination of his mother.

Vespasian and Nero

The removal of Agrippina allowed Vespasian to return to Rome and recommence his career. In 63 AD, he was appointed as governor of the Roman province of Africa. Tacitus says he was "distrusted and disliked," but Suetonius praises his governorship, saying that he was so honest and honorable that he returned to Rome poor. Suetonius adds that Vespasian was pelted with turnips by the inhabitants of Hadrumetum, so the two accounts are not entirely inconsistent.[17]

When Vespasian returned from Africa, he attended Nero's court as the emperor toured around Greece. Suetonius describes Nero's performances at the lyre and the agonies of the audiences who were obliged to watch him. They had to remain seated for hour after hour and cheer and applaud at the correct places. The audience was watched to ensure they showed generous appreciation of the emperor's performance. Anyone who was not sufficiently ecstatic could be beaten by soldiers or, much worse, their names noted for later action. While watching one of these performances, Vespasian fell asleep. He was dragged out and berated by an usher who told him to "go to hell." For this offense, Vespasian suffered exile, which was usually a prelude to the death sentence under Nero. However, Vespasian's friends intervened and saved his life. Perhaps Nero saw that Vespasian was too valuable to lose.[18]

Vespasian returned to grace when Nero looked for a general to deal with the Jewish revolt. He was an unlikely choice in some ways, being almost sixty and not having seen military service for twenty years. But he had enjoyed an excellent reputation under Claudius. Most importantly, the uncouth and unassuming Vespasian was not seen as a threat by Nero because of his lowly family background. So Nero forgave his offense and sent him at the head of an army to Judea in 67 AD.[19]

When Vespasian became emperor, the usher who had assaulted him came to apologize. Another emperor would have had the man put to death. Vespasian just told him to go to hell.[20]

Flavia Domitilla

Vespasian's wife and daughter both died before he became emperor, although we do not know the year of death for either. Domitilla was left without a mother while still a young child.

It is here that we encounter a little mystery. The Romans had three classes of name; a praenomen, a nomen, and a cognomen. The praenomen was chosen from a small selection of names that ran in families. For example, Vespasian's praenomen was Titus, and he passed it on to both his sons. By the first century, the male praenomen was in decline as there were too few names to distinguish adequately between individuals. For women, it was already extinct.

The nomen indicated the gens, which was the family or tribal group. For example, Vespasian's nomen Flavius showed that he belonged to the gens Flavia. Children took their nomen from their father, and a girl would retain her nomen after marriage. Freed slaves would take their nomen from their master and patron, and those granted Roman citizenship would take the nomen of the ruling emperor.

Finally, there was the cognomen or individual name, which was the name Romans typically used for each other. The cognomen was often given in honor of an ancestor or family member. Vespasian's cognomen, for example, alludes to his mother's distinguished gens, the Vespasii.

The cognomen also often ran in families, making things very confusing. Vespasian and his first son shared the same cognomen and praenomen, so their full name was Titus Flavius Vespasianus. To distinguish between them, the son was generally called by his praenomen, Titus, rather than his cognomen, Vespasian.

By the end of the first century, the cognomen had become the most important element of the name. And it was multiplying; it became fashionable for both men and women to take several cognomina, some of which were adopted as an adult. For example, Domitilla's father had three cognomina that we know about; Cerialis, Caesius and Rufus. A cognomen could sometimes refer to an individual characteristic, and such names were often derogatory. The nomen also was also subject to multiplication, particularly where it was a condition of inheritance to take the benefactor's nomen, which was often added to the father's nomen. The trend became even more extreme in the second century; the unfortunate consul of 169 AD whose name is typically abbreviated as Q. Sosius Priscus actually had no less than thirty-eight separate names.[21]

The mystery concerns Domitilla's nomen. As the daughter of Petillius Cerialis, she should have been called Petillia Domitilla even after her marriage. Yet that name is never found—she is always Flavia Domitilla. There are two possibilities; either the younger Domitilla was not married to Cerialis but to an unknown Flavian, or, more likely, Petillia Domitilla had been adopted into Vespasian's family. Such adoptions were common and were treated seriously by the Romans.[22]

Domitilla is called the granddaughter of Vespasian in inscriptions, with no mention of her father. The absence of the father's name is odd no matter who that father was. The best explanation is that she was adopted following her mother's early death. Cerialis would have been a poor nursemaid for a young girl. Vespasian's family had lost their only daughter and sister; it would have been natural to look upon the little Domitilla as her replacement.

An adoption immediately after her mother's death, while Domitilla was still very young, would explain the breaking of the bond with her father. Such an adoption is most likely either before Vespasian went to Africa in 63 AD, when Domitilla would have been little more than a baby, or when he came back at around 66 AD. A later date, after Vespasian became emperor, cannot be ruled out either. Vespasian appointed Cerialis on military assignments that took him away from Rome for years, and it would not have been practical to be accompanied by a girl of less than ten. However, a late adoption would not explain the strange silence about Domitilla's father.

4

Theophilus

The Introduction to Luke

Many have undertaken to arrange an account of the things that have been fulfilled among us, just as they have been delivered to us by those who from the beginning were eyewitnesses and servants of the word. It seemed good to me also, having been carefully acquainted with all things from the first, to write an orderly account for you, most excellent Theophilus, so that you might know the certainty of those things you have been taught. (Luke 1:1-4)

So starts the Gospel of Luke. With this introduction, we are cast into a world apart from the other gospel writers—the world of the educated Roman elite. It is the type of prologue that we might find in a work of philosophy or history. The author of Luke remains anonymous, but the name of their patron is Theophilus.

These few lines give us a great deal of information even though, apart from that one name, it is not specific. Many have already attempted to write arrangements or narrations of events, meaning there are other gospels in existence. These other gospels were based on accounts by "eyewitnesses and servants of the word." But the author has carried out careful investigations to become knowledgeable about all things from "the first." They are now in a position to write an account for Theophilus that he might know the certainty of what he has already been taught.

The introduction aims to establish the credibility of what follows, yet it raises some troublesome questions. The author gives us no evidence about how we can be sure these other gospels are eyewitness accounts. Nor does the author tell us exactly how they have become acquainted with things from the very beginning. What were these existing accounts? One of them would have been the Gospel of Mark, which the Gospel of Luke copies. I would add the Gospel of Thomas, although most scholars would date it to the second century and so after Luke. If you are unhappy with the inclusion of Thomas, you could replace it with the mythical Q. But this still only gives two gospels, not "many." The only other early gospel we know about is Matthew. So the introduction strongly implies that the author was aware of the Gospel of Matthew. This is confirmed by the extensive use of material also found in Matthew.

The author claims their account is superior, offering an "ordered" narrative. Thomas (or "Q") is not a narrative gospel but a collection of sayings. As a literary production, Mark is inadequate. So the real competition is coming from Matthew. We must remember that the author of Luke did not encounter this gospel as sacred literature from the distant past. Matthew was written only a decade or so previously, and the author would have felt no qualms about correcting it. A desire to distinguish the new gospel from Matthew would explain "the same but different" pattern; the author of Luke is greatly influenced by Matthew but changes many of the details.

The Luke introduction is short, which is a characteristic of Roman technical treatises, while histories tend to have longer introductions. Loveday Alexander conducted a survey of Roman prefaces and found the closest resemblance to "scientific" treatises, a group which she defines widely as including writings on mathematics, philosophy and even magic.[1] She suggests that the author must have been a technical person—a perfect fit to the physician Luke.

The argument is unconvincing; Luke is obviously not a scientific text and shows no signs of being written by a technically inclined author.[2] The whole gospel is less than 20,000 words, so a lengthy introduction, more typical of a history, would hardly be appropriate. And even histories did not always have long introductions: Tacitus gave his very substantial work, The Annals, an introduction that amounts to half a page. Besides, the pattern of the gospel genre had been established by Mark and Matthew, neither of which features an introduction. The author of Luke thinks that a Roman work should have an introduction but compromises by keeping it short.

The style of Luke/Acts is something of a paradox. The author of Luke/Acts is the most literary of all the contributors to the New Testament, and yet they show none of the elegant flourishes we would expect from someone trained in rhetoric. Nor does Luke/Acts contain any classical allusions as would naturally flow from the immersive study of Greek literature. The author attempts to follow a high literary style in their preface, and yet the result is undeniably clumsy. Alexander interprets these characteristics as indicating a scholastic scientific personality who lacked the rhetorical and literary education of the elite. But there is another possibility she does not consider—that the author was indeed an aristocrat, but belonged to the 50% who ended their formal schooling in their early teens.

Most excellent Theophilus

Our main lead from the introduction is Theophilus. There is no known person of that name who might be the patron. The name means "lover of God" or "dear to God." This has led many commentators to believe that Theophilus is a pseudonym. Others object, pointing out that Theophilus was a real name. Josephus mentions three individuals called Theophilus; two Jews, including a high priest, and a Greek author.[3] But this does not mean that it was the patron's everyday name in this case. A good pseudonym should be realistic but carry a hidden, or not so hidden, meaning.

Some have gone further and see Theophilus as purely symbolic, the "God-lover" who stands for any potential reader of the gospel. We can rule this out because Theophilus is called by the Greek word *kratiste*, "most excellent," which was a title reserved for a senior Roman. In Acts, two procurators of Judea, Felix and Festus are addressed as *kratiste*.[4] One problem is that we do not know the scope of the title. It has been suggested that *kratiste* was reserved for freedmen who occupied a senior position in the imperial administration. Felix was such a freedman, and Josephus addresses his own patron Epaphroditus, whose name suggests that he might be a freedman, as *kratiste*. But this theory fails in the case of Festus who was not a freedman. The title seems to be applied by the author of Luke to procurators in general.

The problem is that *kratiste* is a Greek expression and can only approximate to Latin titles. Our few examples relate to individuals of equestrian rank, but it may have had a much broader application to senior Romans, particularly those carrying out the imperial administration. Felix was only a freedman, but he was a very special case; the favorite of Claudius, he was married to three princesses in turn. One possibility is that *kratiste* is the Greek equivalent of the Latin *optimus* ("the best"). Pliny the Younger gives this title to an eminent senator and it was even taken by the emperor Trajan.[5]

Whatever the exact scope of *kratiste*, we can be sure that Theophilus was a senior Roman. And this leads on to the most significant question—why would Theophilus allow himself to be the patron of an incriminating, criminal work?

Theophilus' motive

We get the impression from Acts of a softening attitude from the Romans towards the Christians at this time. We should beware of taking this at face value because the author has an agenda of getting Christians accepted by the Romans. So, how accurate is this picture of Roman toleration from Acts? To get an objective view of Roman attitudes towards Christians, we need to turn to authors who are not Christians. We have two such examples, Tacitus and the younger Pliny. Both were contemporaries of the author of Luke and were writing a few decades after Acts. So how do they feel about Christianity?

We start with Tacitus who wrote about the persecution of Christians accused of starting the fire of Rome by Nero. Tacitus expresses some sympathy for the Christians on account of the tortures they endured; they were put to death as a spectacle in Nero's own gardens, burnt alive as human torches or covered with the hides of wild beasts and torn apart by dogs. But overall, his judgment on them is devastating; they were "hated for their shameful offenses." Christianity was a "pernicious superstition" that was "abominable and shameful." The Roman Christians were guilty of "hatred of mankind" and deserving of "exemplary punishment." This is how Theophilus' Roman peers would have regarded him had his Christian associations become known.[6]

Our second example comes from the remarkable correspondence between Pliny the Younger, the governor of Bithynia and Pontus, and the Emperor Trajan dating from 112 AD. Pliny is puzzled as to how he should punish Christians. Should he execute anyone who had ever been a Christian or only those who persisted? His practice was to give those who admitted to being a Christian the opportunity to recant, which they would have to prove by cursing Christ and offering incense and wine to the emperor's image. Whoever refused would be executed unless they were a Roman citizen, in which case they would be sent for trial and likely execution in Rome. To learn more about the Christians, Pliny ordered two female deaconesses who were slaves to be tortured. But he found nothing particularly wrong except "depraved, excessive, superstition."[7]

Trajan approved Pliny's process but told him not to seek out Christians or accept anonymous accusations. This makes it clear that Trajan had not ordered a general persecution. Pliny acted out of his sense that Christianity was an inherently criminal activity that merited the death sentence. His view would have developed in the time he worked in Domitian's administration. Trajan seems to have been more liberal than Domitian on the issue; Christians should be put to death if they become known to the authorities but should not be hunted out.

These examples throw cold water over Acts' attempt to secure Roman toleration. The author of Luke has lost touch with reality and is engaged in wishful thinking. The Roman elite despised Christianity. If Theophilus were identified as a Christian or even a sympathizer, the consequences would have been severe.

A parallel case occurred in the reign of Nero. A woman called Pomponia Graecina, the wife of the same Aulus Plautius under whom Vespasian served in the invasion of Britannia, was accused of "foreign superstition." According to custom, she was tried by her husband in front of a tribunal of relatives. In this case, she was found innocent.[8] Pomponia may or may not have been a Christian, but she must have been the follower of some eastern sect. A man at a level high enough to be called *kratiste* would not have had the luxury of being tried by his spouse and would have faced exile or death.

The gospels were written for wide publication. The Gospel of Luke was a public document that would be copied, distributed, and read out at church gatherings. It could very easily fall into the hands of the authorities, and it would have been essential for the author of Luke to protect the identity of Theophilus. This is why we can be sure he could not be recognized under that name.

That does not mean that Theophilus is a pseudonym. Another possibility is that it was an additional cognomen adopted as an adult. Acts says that the gentile believers in the Jewish God are "fearing God." Theophilus, "God-lover", is one step above these God-fearers. A person would typically be given a cognomen by someone else, such as a family member. We can see Theophilus as a name given by the author of Luke. It would be used among Christians but would be unknown to other Romans, safeguarding his identity.

Even so, this man is taking a tremendous risk. Why would someone of senior rank allow himself to be acknowledged as the patron of two pieces of Christian literature? There are two possibilities:

1. Theophilus is a committed Christian who is prepared to lay down his life if necessary.
2. The bond between the author of Luke and Theophilus is so strong that he is prepared to take the risk on the author's account.

We can rule out the first. Theophilus has been taught certain things but needs to know more, and the author has written the gospel to bring him to "certainty." He is a sympathizer but not yet a full believer and has not been baptized, making his association with Luke and Acts all the stranger. Why should someone who is at most a lukewarm supporter of the movement take the risk? And why would he be the patron of the author of Luke if not already a committed Christian?

We are left with the second possibility; that Theophilus is taking the risk for personal reasons and has an existing strong bond with the author of Luke. Theophilus is the patron, so the author is his client and of lower formal status, which rules out a close male relative. The only remaining possibility is that the author is a woman; Theophilus' mother, sister, or wife.

This is consistent with the repeated pattern that Christianity tended to infiltrate aristocratic families through the female side. A woman is converted first, and she then converts many others in the household, including her slaves and freedmen. She exerts influence on her male relatives, such as her husband, son, or brother, but they do not immediately convert. Even if a man were sympathetic, there were immense practical difficulties. A senior Roman had religious duties; he had to offer sacrifices to the gods and the emperor, which was impossible for a baptized Christian. So a man would tend to postpone conversion until he was facing death.

If the author of Luke were the mother or wife of Theophilus, they would fit perfectly into this pattern. Roman society was built around the client-patron relationship with its mutual obligations and benefits. The head of an elite household would have many clients, such as freedmen who would regularly visit to offer their respects. Formally, a wife was under her husband's authority, so he was her patron. In reality, a wife would exercise tremendous influence over her husband and usually get her own way. A widowed mother might share the same household as her son, in which case she would theoretically be his client. For a sister to live with a brother would be less usual as noble girls would marry young.

We can envisage the author of Luke as a woman who has converted to Christianity and persuaded others in her household to convert also. She has given the name Theophilus to her husband or son, the head of the household and a supporter of the new religion, although not yet a baptized convert. She addresses him in Roman style in Luke and Acts as her patron. Naturally, she calls him *kratiste*, for a woman is always proud of the rank of her husband or son. Although the gospel is formally addressed to Theophilus, it is to be distributed widely among Christians as a rival to the Gospel of Matthew. Theophilus allows himself to go along with all this because he is already heavily implicated as head of a household of Christians. He is into it so deep that he has nothing to lose.

Theophilus is trailing in the slipstream of this woman, the main mover of events. But there is a sense of unreality about her actions. Although Christianity is an illegal sect, she treats it as an acceptable subject for a Roman work of history or philosophy. We get the sense that she is used to being listened to and has the authority to get her works copied and distributed. But she is living in a bubble, unaware of the consequences of the risks she is taking.

But we are getting ahead of ourselves. This conclusion needs collaboration. We must look for more evidence that the author of Luke/Acts was a woman, and will find it in abundance.

5

Five emperors

Nero

Nero woke on his last night to find the palace eerily quiet. The imperial guard had deserted him, and everyone else had fled. The emperor was alone. It had all started when Vindex had revolted in Gaul and declared the elderly Galba, governor of Hispania, as emperor. Initially, Nero had tried to ignore the revolt, although Vindex's insults angered him. Particularly hurtful was the allegation that he was a poor lyre player. This was patently untrue; Nero had repeatedly asked anyone who was a better lyre player than himself to come forth and no one had.

When he heard that Galba and the Spanish legions had joined the revolt, Nero became despondent. Galba's most ardent supporter was a man who had once been Nero's closest friend—Otho, the previous husband of Nero's deceased wife, Poppaea Sabina. They had fallen out over her, and Nero had appointed him as governor of Lusitania (modern Portugal and part of Western Spain) to get him out of the way. Now Otho saw a way of getting his revenge and perhaps eventually becoming emperor himself.

Nero dithered in response to the threat, diverting himself with amusements and coming up with harebrained schemes. An emperor should never lose credibility, but the fear that had held Nero in power was evaporating. He gave a speech to the senate promising death to the criminals, meaning Vindex, but the senators shouted back: "It will be you, Emperor!"

On the day before Nero awoke in the empty palace, he heard that more legions had revolted against him. He tried to put into action his plan to escape to the Parthians, but the soldiers and sailors refused to take him. Everyone was urging him to kill himself. An ordinary soldier had even shouted, "is it really so hard to die?" Nero kept a box of poison by his bed but now, waking in the night, he found his attendants had stolen it. He sent for his friends, but they did not come. All he had left were a few loyal freedmen. One of them, Phaon, suggested they all go to his villa four miles outside Rome. They wrapped Nero in a cloak with a handkerchief covering his face and left on horses. The villa was overgrown with brambles, and they put their cloaks down to escort the emperor to the door.

On the way to the villa, the handkerchief had slipped, and Nero had been recognized. Now the small group around Nero heard rumors that the senate was planning to brutally execute him in public. A tearful Nero ordered his attendants to dig his grave and prepare a funeral pyre. On hearing horsemen approach, he took a dagger and attempted to plunge it through his throat. His loyal freedman and secretary Epaphroditus had to help him guide the dagger home. The centurion who burst in claimed that he had actually come to rescue the emperor. But Nero bled to death anyway. While waiting for the end, he had pronounced his own epitaph: "what an artist dies with me."[1]

Galba and Otho

Nero's rival Galba was in despair in Hispania and contemplating suicide. His position also appeared hopeless. The legions in Germania had remained loyal to Nero and had crushed the revolt in Gaul, killing Vindex. Then came the miraculous news that Nero was dead and the senate had recognized Galba as emperor.[2]

Galba was an unlikely emperor; a severe traditionalist, he was physically unattractive, old, and ill. He depended on a few close advisors who Tacitus calls the vilest and laziest of men.[3] Some rulers have the common touch—Galba had the ability to antagonize just about everyone.

Instead of being magnanimous in victory, Galba had those who had opposed him executed, gaining an immediate reputation as a bloodthirsty ruler. Once in Rome, he began to undo the actions of Nero, whether they had been popular or not. He demoted a unit of marines whom Nero had promoted, turning them back into rowers. When the men angrily protested against this, he decimated the unit—the word means reduced by one-tenth. Decimation was an old punishment that involved the men drawing lots; the one in ten who drew an unlucky lot were executed immediately. The practice had fallen into disuse, and bringing it back against the marines caused anger and dismay throughout the army.[4]

His worst mistake was refusing to pay a donative to his loyal legions. This was a gift of money made to the soldiers to mark the ascension of a new emperor. Those legions that had supported him had been promised a generous donative by their commanders. But Galba rescinded this payment, saying that he was not in the habit of buying soldiers. A conservative like Tacitus might have approved of the principle, but the legionaries on whom Galba depended were outraged.[5]

The legions in Germania had stayed loyal to Nero and had been victorious against Vindex. Instead of being rewarded, they were now being punished for opposing Galba, and they could take it no more. The legions in upper Germania revolted, sending a message to the senate in Rome to appoint anyone but Galba as emperor.[6]

Galba finally realized that he had lost the support of the army. In an attempt to satisfy the German legions, he adopted a successor. The man he chose was Piso Licinianus, whom he formally adopted as his son in the camp of the pretorian guard. The army and the people were not against Licinianus, but they were not for him either. Otho was outraged because he had considered himself as Galba's likely successor. In the days following Piso's adoption, Otho put together a coup.[7]

On 15 January 69, Galba was offering sacrifices at the temple of Apollo. Otho was standing next to the emperor when a messenger told him that the architect and contractors were waiting. This was the prearranged signal that the soldiers were in position to hail him as emperor and escort him to the camp. He made his excuses, pretending to Galba that he was buying a house. When he arrived at the meeting place, he was shocked to find just twenty-three soldiers waiting. He tried to back out, but the soldiers grabbed him, placed him on a litter, and walked through Rome, hailing him as emperor. Others, curious to see what was going on, flocked to his side and then joined in the shouting. By the time he reached the pretorian camp, he was at the head of a large cheering crowd.[8]

When the news reached Galba, he and his advisors took refuge in the palace. They had a heated discussion on how to deal with the threat. The two options were to leave the palace and confront the revolt head-on or take a cautious, defensive position. They were undecided when rumors came that Otho had been killed at the camp. The senators who had been notably absent now thronged to the emperor, regretting that they had not had the chance to kill Otho themselves. The member of the imperial bodyguard who had done the deed, Julius Atticus, came to show the emperor the bloody sword with which he had run through Otho. It is typical of Galba that he did not praise Atticus but reproved him for acting without orders. The newly confident emperor now left the palace in a litter for the forum accompanied by his guard.[9]

Otho, however, was not dead. He had been acclaimed as emperor by the pretorians and was in full command of the camp. Hearing that Galba had left the palace, he dispatched a cavalry contingent to kill him. As the cavalry approached, Galba's guard cast down his insignia, signaling that they had gone over to Otho. The civilians all fled, including the litter bearers who tipped the emperor up in their haste to escape. The seventy-one-year-old emperor lay sprawled on the pavement as the horsemen charged. No one raised a hand to defend him. Galba's head was cut off as a souvenir, and it would be several days before one of his freedmen could retrieve it for burial. A loyal slave hid Licinianus, but he was discovered and his head presented to Otho.[10]

Otho and Vitellius

The first of the four emperors who would rule in 69 AD was dead. Otho was formally elected as emperor by the senate in Rome. The senators and magistrates made haste to pay him homage and declare how they had hated Galba. But a rival emperor, Vitellius, had already been acclaimed by the legions in Germania.

Vitellius had been appointed as governor of lower Germania by Galba. On arriving in the province, he immediately began to undo some of the harm that the emperor's orders had caused, restoring the rank of those demoted for loyalty to Nero. By such actions, he won over the German legions. It was traditional for the legions to redeclare their oaths to the emperor on 1st January. The legions in lower Germania took the oath grudgingly, but those in upper Germania refused. Vitellius' subordinates urged him to declare as emperor, and he had little choice but to agree. By the 3rd January, he was acknowledged as emperor by all the legions in Germania. The legions in Britannia and some of those in Gaul quickly joined them. So when Otho was declared emperor in Rome, there was already an enormous force assembling in the north against him.[11]

The news of Galba's death did not change anything for Vitellius' supporters who were eager to march on Rome. Their plan was for a double-hook attack. Fabius Valens would lead a force through Gaul and into Italy. Caecina was to take a more direct route through the alpine Pennine Pass (now called the Great St Bernard Pass).[12]

In the wider picture, Hispania had first declared for Otho but now switched to Vitellius. Vespasian's force in Judea, the legions in Egypt, and the other legions in the east declared outwardly for Otho but played no part in the conflict. Of crucial importance to Otho were the four legions in Dalmatia and Pannonia, which had declared for him. Using these legions, he assembled a considerable force in northern Italy to oppose Vitellius' advance.[13]

Caecina's army successfully passed through the snowy alps and linked up with other pro-Vitellius units in Italy to control the territory north of the River Po. But Otho's marines secured a victory in Gaul. And when Caecina attempted to attack beyond the Po, he could not take the town of Placentia, even though just a few cohorts defended it. He was forced to retreat across the Po, where his auxiliaries were attacked and slaughtered by Otho's force of gladiators. Even worse was an ambitious attempt by Caecina to ambush Otho's army. The opposing generals got intelligence of Caecina's plan and turned the ambush on the Vitellians. Caecina suffered a humiliating defeat, and his army would have been destroyed except that Otho's chief general, Suetonius Paulinus, the conqueror of Boudicca, called off the attack early out of an abundance of caution.[14]

Things were scarcely any better for Vitellius' other army, which had made slow progress under Valens. At one point, the soldiers mutinied, and Valens had to flee, dressed as a slave. Eventually, the soldiers calmed down, and Valens resumed control. He was finally able to join up with Caecina's army.[15]

Buoyed by these successes, Otho became overconfident. Suetonius Paulinus counselled delay until their considerable reinforcements could arrive. Otho disregarded this advice, perhaps mindful of Suetonius' failure to drive home the victory against Caecina. He instead adopted the plan of his less experienced generals who urged an immediate assault on Vitellius' combined forces. Previously Otho had marched at the head of his troops, disheveled and with a sword in his hand. This had been a huge morale booster for his soldiers, but now it was decided that the emperor should wait out the battle in safety. Spurred on by their leader's impatience, Otho's generals were eager for a quick victory and marched their forces to battle in a line leaving their flank exposed. Valens and Caecina were not going to refuse such an opportunity. They mounted a surprise attack that caught Otho's legions out of formation. The battle was one-sided and the victory complete; those of Otho's soldiers who were not killed surrendered the next day.[16]

When Otho heard the news of his army's defeat, his advisers urged him to regroup. He still had enough legions at his command to fight on. But he had seen how the civil war had ravaged Italy. The battle of Roman against Roman was terrible. He judged, probably correctly, that his chance of winning the war was gone and decided to end it. He made his preparations and sent his friends and subordinates away. He slept that night with a dagger under his pillow and fell upon it in the morning. It was 16th April 69 and Otho's reign as emperor had ended after just three months.[17]

Vespasian and Vitellius

The senate recognized Vitellius as emperor, and he started by ordering the execution of many of his enemies. Otho's former followers simmered with discontent, and the stage was set for another civil war.[18]

When Vespasian had first heard of Nero's death, he had sent Titus to Rome to offer his compliments to Galba. At Greece, Titus heard that Galba had been assassinated and Otho was emperor. Instead of proceeding, Titus turned back to Judea, suggesting that father and son already harbored imperial ambitions. Although Vespasian had his legions take the oath to Otho and then to Vitellius, he was secretly testing support for his own bid. One enthusiastic ally was Licinius Mucianus, governor of Syria, who commanded three legions. Another vital supporter was Tiberius Alexander, who was in charge of the legions in Egypt. Mucianus pressed Vespasian to make his move.[19] But it was the mutiny of the Third legion, recently moved from Syria to Moesia, that triggered a new civil war. They declared for Vespasian and were joined by the two other legions in Moesia who had been enthusiastic supporters of Otho.[20] It became a general theme that Otho's considerable support went over to Vespasian.

On 1 July 69, the Egyptian legions took an oath of allegiance to Vespasian. Two days later, the Judean legions spontaneously hailed Vespasian as emperor. The legions in Syria quickly followed, and enthusiasm for his cause spread widely, with the legions in Pannonia, Dalmatia, and Illyricum all declaring for Vespasian.[21] He was popular with the army, having earned his military reputation as a victorious general in Britannia and Judea. He also had the ideal successor in his son Titus. Everyone loves a hero, and news of Titus' exploits in Judea would have spread widely through the army. Vespasian offered the prospect of a highly experienced, level-headed, and pragmatic Augustus together with a charismatic son and eventual successor as Caesar. It was an attractive double act and a striking contrast with Galba, Otho, and Vitellius, none of whom were military men.

Vespasian's family background was lacking in distinction, but that would not have bothered the ordinary legionnaire. And more important than his birth, the gods had chosen Vespasian. The Jews had an ancient prophecy that the ruler of the world would come from Judea, a prophecy that the Jews applied to themselves. But when Vespasian captured a rebel Jewish general, a man who was also a priest and prophet, the prisoner made a startling revelation. The future ruler of the world was Vespasian himself. The Jew had hailed Vespasian as emperor even though Nero was still alive.

Vespasian was the master of the east, but Vitellius controlled the west. The provinces of Britannia, Hispania, and Gaul had stayed loyal to the emperor, although their support was only lukewarm.[22] Vitellius' real strength lay in Italy and Germania. Vespasian knew that he faced a daunting task in taking Rome from Vitellius' German legions. After discussing strategy with his generals, he decided to establish his base at Alexandria.

Rome depended on the grain shipments from Egypt, which Vespasian now cut off. With Rome starved of gain, Mucianus would lead the military thrust and take the long land route towards Italy—the sea voyage was too hazardous at that time of year. Titus would finish the war in Judea.[23]

In the event, the Flavian generals of the legions closer to Italy decided to move without waiting for Mucianus. They were led by a morally corrupt and hotheaded individual called Antonius Primus. He had been found guilty of forging a will during the reign of Nero, but had been rehabilitated by Galba and given the command of the Seventh legion. He was now an enthusiastic supporter of Vespasian. Tacitus sums him up as a man "abominable in peace but by no means contemptible in war."[24] He persuaded his reluctant colleagues to take advantage of their momentum and advance towards Italy. Soon he was the acknowledged leader of the Flavian legions in Pannonia and Moesia.[25]

Vitellius had become increasingly alarmed as the mutiny of a single legion grew into the revolt of half the empire. Discipline among his soldiers was poor, and the two commanders, Valens and Caecina, were locked into a destructive and bitter rivalry. On the positive side, Vitellius' newly victorious German legions were among the finest in the army. He assembled a large crack force to march to northern Italy to confront the Flavians. Vitellius appointed Caecina to command this army while Valens recovered from an illness. It was his fatal mistake.

Caecina led an enormous force of eight battle-hardened legions. Had he pressed the attack against Antonius he could have destroyed the Flavian forces on the eastern side of the Adriatic and turned the tide of the war. But Caecina was nursing a sense of injustice at his treatment by Vitellius, who had shown favoritism towards Valens. He had been approached indirectly by Flavius Sabinus, Vespasian's brother, and now intended to go over to Vespasian. On the way north, Caecina diverted to Ravenna to meet Lucilius Bassus, the fleet commander. The two of them hatched a plan together.[26]

Caecina began to drag his feet and found excuses for delay instead of pressing the advance. Meanwhile, Lucilius Bassus had persuaded the Ravenna fleet to take the oath for Vespasian, which did not prove difficult because most of the sailors came from Dalmatia and Pannonia, two provinces that had declared for Vespasian. The mutiny of the fleet was the signal for Caecina to stage his revolt. He waited until the camp was quiet with the soldiers out on duty. He then pressed his most trusted centurions to go over to Vespasian. The banners of Vitellius were torn down and replaced by those of Vespasian. But when the legionaries returned to camp, they were outraged. The torn-down banners were replaced, and Caecina dragged away in chains. His revolt had failed—the men were determined to fight for Vitellius.[27]

Vespasian hoped to win a bloodless war by depriving Rome of its grain while assembling a formidable force on Italy's borders, and he forbade his legions to advance into Italy. But Antonius did not want to lose the glory of victory by waiting for Mucianus: he disobeyed the order and marched to Verona. When intelligence of Caecina's failed revolt reached Antonius, he resolved to attack before Valens could arrive from Rome to assume the command.

Antonius first engaged two of Vitellius' legions that had gone on ahead to Cremona. His chief lieutenant, Varus, attacked precipitously, and Antonius' army was almost routed before he regained control through his personal bravery. The tide was turned, and Vitellius' two legions retreated into Cremona.[28]

Antonius was having trouble controlling his soldiers who wanted to attack and sack the city immediately. He was urging them to caution when his scouts brought the shocking news that Vitellius' remaining six legions were fast approaching. They had marched all day to join the battle. The Flavians were exhausted and outnumbered, and it would have been an easy victory for the Vitellians had they only waited until the next day and attacked in good order. But they were without leadership. The soldiers did not wait for the morning but charged in complete disorder. Antonius had managed to arrange his forces in an impromptu line of battle, but the engagement was utterly confused and fought in pitch-black darkness lit only by flaming torches. The Vitellians managed to get their artillery into position on a hill, and the missiles mowed through the Flavian lines. The battle could have gone either way, but the Flavians gained the advantage when the moon rose behind them in the east. It cast strange, confusing shadows which caused the Flavians to loom large in the eyes of the Vitellians. And the Vitellians were now spotlighted by the moonlight, making them easy targets. At dawn, Vespasian's Syrian legion hailed the rising sun, and the rumor spread that Mucianus was approaching with all his legions. The Vitellians broke and the battle became a rout and then a massacre. Vitellius' great army were all cut down or forced to go over to Vespasian.[29]

Antonius now led the Flavians towards Cremona. They had been fighting all day and all night, but Antonius continued to press his advantage. There was another fierce battle before the defenders surrendered and the soldiers were allowed to leave. What followed was the worst atrocity of the civil war. Antonius' soldiers plundered the city, setting the buildings on fire. Anyone attractive, male or female, was repeatedly raped. An attempt by the soldiers to sell the population as slaves failed because no one would buy Italian captives, so they took to killing the civilians unless their relatives paid a ransom. After a few days, Cremona lay in ruins, utterly destroyed. This was no distant province but Italy. Cremona was a severe embarrassment to Vespasian, and he blamed Antonius.[30]

Meanwhile, Valens had been traveling fast to join the legions when the news came of their destruction. He immediately changed direction for Gaul, planning to raise a new army and lead it back into Italy. But he was captured by Paulinus, the energetic pro-Vespasian procurator of Narbonese Gaul, and was later executed. As the news of the battle spread across the empire, other provinces defected: first Hispania and then Gaul declared for Vespasian. The war was entering the end game.[31]

Antonius followed up his victory, aggressively securing control of the whole of Italy east of the Apennines. Nor did he allow the mountains to stop him, although they presented a formidable barrier in winter. Antonius led his troops across through the snow. On the way they met a bedraggled escapee from Rome—Domitilla's father, Cerialis.[32]

Rome

Some of Vespasian's closest family were in Rome which was still under Vitellius' control. Vespasian's older brother, Flavius Sabinus, remained in the city as the praetor urbanus, the chief magistrate. His family would have been with him including his young grandson Clemens, just a boy at the time, who Domitilla would later marry. Vespasian's eighteen-year-old son Domitian was also in Rome, having stayed for his education at a critical age for a young man. Cerialis was part of this family group, and if Domitilla had not yet been adopted by Vespasian, she would have been with her father.

Vitellius' support was drifting away even in Rome. Sabinus' friends assured him that if he led a revolt in the city enough Romans would join him to win, but Sabinus declined to act. Tacitus puts this down to either envy at his brother's success or his "mild temper," but more likely he was obeying Vespasian's instructions to negotiate a deal with Vitellius. The idea was that the former emperor would be allowed to live in peace on an estate in Campania. But Vitellius could never be sure that Vespasian would keep his end of the bargain once he had achieved power.[33]

Cerialis could see the danger that they would all end up as hostages in Vitellius' last stand. He planned a daring escape to reach Vespasian's forces on the other side of the Apennines and urged Sabinus and Domitian to accompany him. Both declined. Sabinus said he was too old and in poor health. Domitian's problem was that he had been detained and was under guard. His guards had promised to help him escape, but he feared this was a trap by Vitellius to give a pretext for his execution. So Cerialis made the attempt alone. If Domitilla were with her father in Rome, she would have been left behind.[34]

Cerialis slipped out of Rome dressed as a peasant. Although the surrounding area was under Vitellius' control, Cerialis managed to slip through the outposts due to his "knowledge of the country." Cerialis met up with Antonius' force in the foothills of the Apennines or while attempting the crossing and was immediately given a senior command.[35]

When the news came that Valens was dead, most Vitellians lost all hope. Whole legions now surrendered to Vespasian. The despairing Vitellius even left the palace to abdicate and become a private citizen, but his soldiers in Rome, who were still up for the fight, made him return. Then as Sabinus passed through the city with an escort, he was attacked. It was only a skirmish, but it started the final phase of the war. Sabinus took refuge in the Capitol, where Domitian and other Flavian supporters joined him.[36]

The Flavians had established their base outside Rome, and for once, Antonius had obeyed Mucianus' instructions not to attack. Tacitus accuses the Flavians of dithering, but Vespasian was keen to avoid a violent assault on the city that could have caused massive destruction. Responding to Sabinus' desperate messages for help, Cerialis attempted to fight his way into Rome by leading a cavalry force of a thousand to enter by the Via Salaria. They were halted on the outskirts outside the gates and fought a pitched battle in narrow streets and market gardens. The Vitellians had the advantage of local knowledge, and Cerialis was obliged to retreat.[37]

Meanwhile, a group of Vitellian soldiers attacked the capitol fortress and threw burning torches in an attempt to fire the doors. The temple of Jupiter Optimus Maximus caught alight, the fire spread and the panicking Flavians were forced out of the burning building. One of Domitian's freedmen disguised him in a linen mantle, the dress of a worshipper of Isis, and smuggled him out among a group of Isis' worshippers. Sabinus was not so lucky. He was captured, dragged before Vitellius, killed and then beheaded.[38]

The Flavians were outraged by the death of Sabinus. There would be no more restraint. Antonius' army advanced to the city walls, ready for the assault. Tacitus says that envoys from Vitellius were met with particular fury by Cerialis' soldiers, reflecting their commander's anger at the execution of Vespasian's brother.[39]

Tacitus compares the final battle to a gladiatorial contest watched by applauding and jeering civilians. The remaining Vitellians fought hard, but their numbers were too small for the outcome to be in doubt. When the city had been taken, Vitellius attempted to hide in the vast empty palace. But he was found, dragged to the Gemonian steps, and killed on the same spot as Sabinus.[40]

Domitian was now hailed as Caesar, a title he held alongside Titus. In theory, he was in command of Rome until his father had made the long journey from Alexandria. In reality, the real power was held by Mucianus whom Vespasian treated as almost a joint emperor.[41] As for Cerialis, he would be put in command of a huge force to put down the Batavian revolt before being sent back to Britannia as governor.

It is ironic that Vespasian's carefully considered strategy had little impact in the end. It was the brutal but courageous Antonius who won the war for Vespasian. He was disappointed at how little reward he received for his services. Vespasian never trusted Antonius. He may have won the war, but he could equally have lost it. Ultimately it came down to chance; Valens falling ill so that the unreliable Caecina was put in charge of the army and the moon rising behind the Flavians on the battlefield.

With Vespasian as emperor, Domitilla's position in society changed utterly. Before, she was the granddaughter of an esteemed general and the daughter of a rather less successful one. Now she was elevated to the imperial family. The young girl had suddenly become the second most desirable match in the empire after her cousin Julia Titi, daughter of Titus. From now on, almost everyone around Domitilla would obey and flatter her. Her importance should have declined over time as Titus and Domitian had children. This did not happen, and she became the last surviving hope of the Flavians, a position of great potential and grave danger.

6

A kick within the womb

The annunciation

The annunciation is one of the most beautiful subjects of renaissance art. The angel Gabriel appears to the Virgin Mary to tell her that she will conceive by the Holy Spirit. The greatest artists loved to paint this scene. Perhaps the most famous version is by Leonardo da Vinci. The angel, kneeling on the left, speaks to a surprised Mary seated on the right. The angel points at her as if to give, and Mary raises her hand to receive. It is a celebration of incipient motherhood. And yet Gabriel only appears to Mary in Luke:

> "Do not fear, Mary, for you have found favor with God. Behold, you will conceive in your womb and give birth to a son, and you shall call his name Jesus. He will be great and will be called the son of the Most High. The Lord God will give him the throne of his father David, and he will reign over the house of Jacob forever, and his kingdom will not end!" (Luke 1:30-33)

Mary asks how this can be since she is a virgin:

> The angel answered and said to her, "The Holy Spirit will come upon you, and the power of the Most High will overshadow you. The holy one to be born will be called the Son of God." (Luke 1:35)

Mary replies that she is the Lord's servant: "may it happen according to your word." (Luke 1:38)

There is no nativity account in Mark or John. The visit of the angel to announce the birth of Jesus is found first in the gospel of Matthew. But in that gospel, the angel does not appear to Mary but Joseph. This is the "same but different" pattern that we find when Luke copies Matthew. The author of Luke takes the idea of the angel's message from Matthew but changes the details, moving the focus from the male to the female. In Matthew, we see events through the eyes of Joseph. In Luke, we see things through Mary and her older relative Elizabeth. This switch in perspective is true not just of the annunciation but of the whole nativity account.

The Matthew nativity

This is how the nativity in Matthew starts:

> Now the birth of Jesus Christ came about like this: his mother Mary was pledged in marriage to Joseph, but before their coming together, she was found to be with child of the Holy Spirit. Because Joseph, her husband, was a righteous man and not willing to expose her publicly, he resolved to send her away secretly.
>
> Having pondered these things, behold, an angel of the Lord appeared to him in a dream and said, "Joseph, son of David, do not fear to receive Mary as your wife, for that conceived within her is from the Holy Spirit. She will give birth to a son, and you are to call his name Jesus because he will save his people from their sins." (Matthew 1:18-21)

Joseph is understandably upset at finding his betrothed is pregnant and naturally thinks she has had sex with another man. As a righteous person, he cannot marry her, but as he is humane and perhaps still loves her, he resolves to avoid public disgrace and secretly put her away. The angel's visit in a dream is necessary to change his mind. He is given the extraordinary news that Mary has not been unfaithful but has conceived from the Holy Spirit. We are not told how Mary felt at being unjustly accused of adultery. Nor are we told anything about her experience in becoming pregnant or whether she had any warning or message. We see everything from Joseph's perspective, and this continues in what follows:

> When Joseph awoke from sleep, he did as the angel of the Lord commanded him and received his wife, but he did not know her until she had given birth to a son. And he called his name Jesus. (Matthew 1:24-5)

Jesus is born in Bethlehem, and his arrival does not go unnoticed. Magi come from the east to ask Herod about the "King of the Jews" who has been born, for they have seen his star. Herod is disturbed but directs them to Bethlehem, where the prophecy predicts the Messiah will be born. The Magi follow the star to Bethlehem:

> And coming to the house, they saw the child with Mary, his mother, and they fell down and worshiped him. And having opened their treasures, they offered him gifts of gold and frankincense and myrrh. (Matthew 2:10-11)

This is the only time in the Matthew nativity that Mary is mentioned without Joseph. Afterward, Joseph has another dream:

> When they had left, behold, an angel of the Lord appeared in a dream to Joseph and said, "Rise, take the child and his mother, and flee to Egypt, and remain there until I tell you, for Herod is about to seek the child to destroy him." And having risen he took the child and his mother by night and departed to Egypt... (Matthew 2:13-14)

An angel warns the wise men to return by another route, but an enraged Herod orders all the baby boys under two in Bethlehem to be killed. When the danger has passed, Joseph is told to return:

> When Herod died, behold, an angel of the Lord appeared in a dream to Joseph in Egypt, saying, "having arisen, take the child and his mother and go to the land of Israel, for those who sought the life of the child have died." And having arisen, he took the child and his mother and went to the land of Israel. (Matthew 2:19-21)

Joseph decides to settle in Nazareth rather than return to Bethlehem, where he would be under the power of Herod's son. In Matthew, the angel appears three times to Joseph but never to Mary. It is always Joseph who takes action, and he never consults his wife. Mary is carried around like a piece of baggage, which is consistent with the male perspective adopted by most ancient literature. The wife's purpose is to give birth to children, and the husband decides everything else. Or so the male perspective would have us believe—real-life relations between the sexes have always been more complex.

The Luke nativity

Turning from Matthew to Luke, we find a very different account of conception and nativity. The Luke version is written entirely from the female perspective and is more appealing to modern tastes—it seems only fitting that the woman should take center stage in a story about giving birth. In fact, the Luke account goes to the other extreme and completely neglects Joseph's point of view. We are not told how Joseph took the news that his future bride was pregnant or how he came to believe that Mary had conceived by the Holy Spirit. The idea that the husband may have had some strong feelings on the subject seems not to have occurred to the author of Luke.

The Gospel of Luke introduces a counterpoint to the main nativity story, with the account of the birth of John the Baptist to his elderly parents, Elizabeth and Zechariah. John features in the other gospels as the prophet who foretells the coming of Jesus and who is present at his baptism. On the face of it, including John's birth is very odd, but it enables the author of Luke to develop a beautiful structure for their nativity account and shows Mary celebrating with another mother-to-be.

In the ancient world, infant and child mortality was high, and the average woman would be pregnant several times in her life. A pregnant woman would be supported by the network of women around her, both family and friends. If she were a girl giving birth for the first time, their help would be vital. Pregnancies would frequently overlap, and pregnant women would want to meet to compare notes. Men would be excluded from such gatherings. In Luke, we are given a privileged view of this feminine world of childbirth.

When she becomes pregnant by the Holy Spirit, Mary goes and stays for three months with her relative Elizabeth, who is pregnant with John. We are not told how Joseph feels about this or why he has not yet married his betrothed. Elizabeth immediately recognizes Mary's special nature: "Blessed are you among women, and blessed is the fruit of your womb!"[1] The two women celebrate their coming motherhood together, and Mary gives a hymn of praise, the Magnificat.

This scene of two women prophesying together with no man present is unique in the New Testament. After Mary returns home, Elizabeth gives birth to John. The story then moves on to the birth of Jesus:

> In those days, a decree went out from Caesar Augustus to register all the world. This registration first took place when Quirinius was governor of Syria. And all went to be registered,

each to his own city. And Joseph also went up from Galilee, from the town of Nazareth to Judea, to the city of David, which is called Bethlehem, because he was of the house and family of David, to be registered with Mary, his betrothed, who was with child. (Luke 2:1-5)

This is completely different from Matthew which does not mention any census. In that gospel, Joseph lives in Bethlehem and only moves to Nazareth after his return from Egypt.

There are three significant errors in the Luke passage above. Most notoriously, the birth of Jesus is supposed to have taken place no later than 4 BC while Herod the Great was king. But the census under Quirinius took place ten years after Herod's death, in 6 AD when Judea became a Roman province. The second problem is that the Romans would never have obliged anyone to travel to their supposed ancestral home. They were a practical people intent on taxation and took the census according to where people lived. Joseph would have been registered in Nazareth, not Bethlehem.[2]

The final problem is that Mary is supposedly only betrothed to Joseph, but the two could not have traveled together unless they were already married. And if Mary were not married at the time of the birth, then Jesus would have been illegitimate. It would seem that the author of Luke has misunderstood the statement in Matthew that they did not have sexual relations until after the birth to mean that the two were not married until this time. In Bethlehem, the baby is born:

While they were there, the days were fulfilled for her to give birth. And she gave birth to her firstborn, a son. She wrapped him in swaddling clothes and laid him in a manger because there was no place for them in the inn. (Luke 2:6-7)

The emphasis here is on Mary; the child is her "firstborn," and she performs all the actions. There is no slaughter of the innocents by Herod in Luke, and shepherds replace the Magi. The author of Luke is well informed about the Herods and would know that Herod the Great had never ordered the murder of infants.

The shepherds are another example of the "same but different" pattern. Luke keeps the structure of a group of men given supernatural directions to come and pay homage to the baby Jesus. In Matthew, a star guides the Magi, whereas angels speak to the shepherds in Luke. When the shepherds visit the stable, they find "Mary and Joseph and the Baby."[3] Note the order of the names. Everyone is amazed at the shepherds' story, and we hear about one person's reaction in particular: "Mary treasured up all these things and pondered them in her heart."[4]

In Jerusalem, both parents bring the child to the temple, and an old man called Simeon gives a prophecy. Both are amazed, but Simeon addresses just one of them, "his mother Mary," telling her that "a sword also will go through your own soul."[5] An elderly woman, Anna, also gives a prophecy about the child at the temple, and afterward, they return to Nazareth.

When Jesus is twelve, the family goes up to Jerusalem again for the Passover. As they return, the parents fail to notice for a day that Jesus is not among the group. They turn around and find him in the temple, talking to the elders and astounding everyone with his questions and answers. Once again, it is Mary we hear from:

> "Child, why have you done this to us?" his mother asked. "Your father and I have been distressed, seeking you." (Luke 2:48)

After they return to Nazareth, we are again given Mary's view on events: "his mother treasured up all these things in her heart."[6] The change in perspective between Mathew and Luke can even be quantified by the number of occurrences of each name:

Matthew—Mary 4, Joseph 7
Luke—Mary 13, Joseph 3

Although many modern novelists are adept at writing from the perspective of the opposite gender, it has required centuries of development to get to this point. Writers in the ancient world were much less able to see things from the other side. This change from a male to a female perspective is evidence that the Gospel of Luke was written by a woman.

The kick of joy

How many times does John the Baptist meet Jesus in the Gospel of Luke? It is something of a trick question.

In the Gospel of Mark, John is a wild man of the desert, dressed in camel skin and living on wild locusts and honey. He is the messenger who comes before Jesus and who baptizes him:

> In those days Jesus came from Nazareth in Galilee and was baptized in the Jordan by John. And immediately coming up out of the water, he saw the heavens tearing open and the spirit

descending on him as a dove. And a voice came out of the heavens: "You are my beloved son; in you I am well pleased." (Mark 1:9-11)

Matthew follows the same storyline but adds a section about John preaching against those "vipers," the Pharisees and Sadducees. Luke copies the same speech, although John now addresses the crowd in general. This is one of the many indications that the author of Luke knew the Gospel of Matthew well. The alternative view is that John's speech was part of Q. But why would a Jesus sayings gospel include a speech by John?

John says he is not the Messiah who is coming and who will baptize with the Holy Spirit rather than water. However, John is imprisoned before Jesus comes on the scene:

> But when he reproved Herod the tetrarch concerning his brother's wife Herodias and all the evils he had done, Herod added to them all: he locked up John in prison. (Luke 3:19-20)

Jesus' baptism follows:

> Now when all the people were baptized, and Jesus being baptized, and praying, heaven was opened, and the Holy Spirit descended on him in bodily form like a dove. And a voice came from heaven: "You are my beloved son; in you I am well pleased." (Luke 3:21-2)

The narrative here is ambiguous. Did John baptize Jesus? Jesus is baptized later than the "people," and John has already been arrested before the Holy Spirit descends upon Jesus. But in the other gospels, the spirit descends on Jesus at his baptism. The implication is that Jesus and John never meet as adults in Luke. But they have already become acquainted with each other while in their mothers' wombs. It is extraordinary that in Luke the meeting between two grown men has been changed into an encounter between their pregnant mothers:

> And when Elizabeth heard Mary's greeting, the baby leaped in her womb, and Elizabeth was filled with the Holy Spirit. (Luke 1:41)

So the unborn John has signaled his recognition of Jesus with a kick in the womb. We see events from the perspective of motherhood. No man would recast a meeting between two adult men as a leap of joy in the womb. A woman wrote that, a mother who had experienced the kick in the womb herself. Including the nativity story of John changes the focus of the account: the new covenant comes through pregnancy and birth, and it is the mothers who are at the center.

Marcion

A little before 140 AD, a man called Marcion arrived in Rome from Pontus on the Black Sea. He was a wealthy shipowner and gave the church in Rome a substantial donation. The son of a bishop, Marcion was acknowledged as a brilliant man, but he and his gift would eventually be rejected.[7] The proto-orthodox church in Rome would come to view him as a heretic. Marcion taught a version of Christianity in which the Hebrew God was the "demiurge," the "half-maker," the wicked creator of a flawed material universe. He revered Paul, but the proto-orthodox Christians claimed he had misinterpreted the apostle. After failing to make progress in Rome, Marcion returned to Pontus and founded a church that was so successful that it became the dominant form of Christianity in the region.[8]

Marcion gathered texts into the first Christian bible, which spurred the proto-orthodox church to produce its own competing version. Marcion's bible was very different from our New Testament. It had only one gospel which he called the "gospel of the Lord." Alongside this, he added Paul's letters but excluded the so-called pastoral epistles, which are now known to be forgeries. What is fascinating is that Marcion's "gospel of the Lord" is a version of what we call the Gospel of Luke. But Marcion's gospel omits the nativity account completely and starts with the descent of the adult Jesus from heaven to Capernaum.[9]

While Marcion claimed that Jewish Christians had distorted the original gospel with additions, the church fathers protested that Marcion had corrupted the Gospel of Luke by taking out those elements that did not support his beliefs.[10] Much of our information about Marcion comes from the hostile Tertullian who was writing seventy years later. He aptly sums up the issue: "I say that my gospel is the true one; Marcion, that his is. I affirm that Marcion's gospel is adulterated; Marcion, that mine is."[11]

It is significant that Marcion did not know that the third gospel was supposed to have been written by Paul's missionary companion, Luke.[12] By 200 AD, the gospel was widely known as the Gospel of Luke, and Tertullian takes it for granted that it was called this in Marcion's day. Tertullian is annoyed and astonished that Marcion does not acknowledge it as coming from Paul's companion. He points out that this would even be to Marcion's advantage, as it could claim the authority of Paul. By this time all the gospels were attributed to an early figure; Matthew and John were preeminent as coming from two of Jesus' disciples. Mark and Luke were secondary accounts from "apostolic men" who did not know Jesus in life but had received the story from the eyewitness accounts of his disciples.[13] Modern scholarship rejects all these attributions as wishful thinking.

Today, most scholars would accept Tertullian's conclusion that Marcion arrived at his gospel by editing out of Luke anything that did not agree with his teachings. Marcion would have excluded the nativity narrative because he believed that Jesus was spiritual in nature and did not have a normal physical body or birth.

Some, however, disagree with this conclusion and maintain that Marcion's gospel was the original. In support of this view, the nativity accounts are stylistically different from the rest of the gospel, showing a strong influence from the Septuagint. Another odd feature of the gospel is the position of the Luke genealogy. In Matthew, the genealogy is at the very beginning, before the nativity. But in Luke, it follows on from Jesus' baptism and is detached from the nativity. So did the original Luke start with the baptism rather than the nativity?

There are problems with this idea that Marcion's gospel was the original. No copy of Luke without the nativity has ever been found. Also, Luke employs Mark as a source and probably also Matthew. Yet two episodes in our Luke, the baptism and the temptation of Christ, that were borrowed from the earlier gospels were omitted by Marcion. Then there is the relationship between Luke and Acts, both written by the same author and dedicated to Theophilus. Acts is not included in Marcion's bible, and his gospel lacks the dedication to Theophilus. All of which shows that Marcion must have edited his gospel to eliminate parts that did not support his views. And if he had eliminated the baptism, temptation and dedication he could have eliminated much else.

Most significantly, if a proto-orthodox Christian had modified Marcion's gospel in the second century, they would not have produced our Gospel of Luke. No proto-orthodox Christian would have made up a new and drastically different nativity and genealogy that conflicted with their favorite gospel, Matthew.

The twin pattern

Marcion's gospel is a red herring. But this does not resolve whether the nativity accounts were originally attached to Luke or why the genealogy comes after the baptism of Jesus. The answers lie in an extraordinary pattern that flows through the nativity account.

Appendix A shows how the nativity account is constructed on a "twin" pattern. Every episode up to the end of the genealogy at Luke 3:38 is twinned with something else. Mostly a John item is twinned with an equivalent Jesus item. So, for example, the appearance of an angel to Zechariah announcing the future conception of John is paired with the appearance of an angel to Mary announcing the future conception of Jesus. The female (Mary) believes, but the male (Zechariah) expresses doubt and is struck dumb until after John's birth.

Essential to the twin pattern is the introduction of Elizabeth and Zechariah as the parents of John to balance Mary and Joseph. The author of Luke attached great importance to the descent of the spirit. Zechariah's angel says that John will be filled with the spirit even in the womb. And through the spirit, the unborn John kicks in recognition of Jesus. The angel likewise tells Mary that she will conceive by the spirit. But nothing is said about Jesus being filled with the spirit because it will not descend upon him until his baptism. So the author of Luke's nativity pattern is not complete until the baptism. The account is chiastic (symmetrical) with linked pairs at the beginning and end:

Ancestors of John's parents, Zechariah and Elizabeth
    Angel appears to Zechariah; John filled with the spirit.
    Angel appears to Mary; she will conceive the Son of God by the spirit.
      John acknowledges Jesus in the womb.
        Seven other twin pairs—see Appendix A.
      John acknowledges Jesus to the crowd.
    Jesus filled with the spirit, acknowledged by God as his Son.
Ancestors of Jesus' supposed father Joseph (the genealogy)

The descent of the spirit onto Jesus at the end is matched at the beginning with two visitations of the angel promising that the spirit will come to John and Mary. The angel promises that Jesus will be the Son of God, and he is acknowledged as this by God at the spiritual baptism.

This structure explains the placing of Jesus' genealogy immediately after this spiritual baptism. The genealogy rounds off the nativity account and links back to the very start of the nativity, where we are told briefly about the family background of Zechariah and Elizabeth. Once again, the author of Luke follows the "same but different" pattern: the author of Matthew starts his nativity with a genealogy, so the author of Luke naturally ends their nativity with a different genealogy.

7

Josephus and the Jewish war

Josephus in Rome

It was dark, and Josephus was up to his neck in water, bobbing up and down in the relentless swell of the Adriatic Sea. He had been swimming all night after his ship broke up in a storm. The other passengers and crew were somewhere around him. Their hope was fading when the first brightening of dawn, at last, glowed in the sky. Daylight revealed the floating bodies of those who had already given up the struggle. But it also showed something else; a distant and indistinct shadowy outline. All around him came cries of "ship," and on the rise of the swell, Josephus could make out a merchant vessel. There would not be room on board for everyone—the ship that had sunk had carried no less than six hundred people—but Josephus certainly had no intention of being left behind. As he recounts in his autobiography: "I and certain others, about eighty in all, outstripped the others and were taken on board." The vessel came from Cyrene and took the survivors to the Italian port of Puteoli.[1]

Josephus, son of Matthias, was born into a priestly family in Jerusalem and traveled to Rome to plead the case of priests who had been sent to judgment before Nero. It was the year 61 AD, and he was twenty-six years old. Not much could have been expected from a youthful Jewish priest who arrived bedraggled in Italy having so narrowly escaped with his life. But Josephus was a remarkable man. By the time he left Rome, he was a favorite of no less a person than the emperor's wife, Poppaea.[2]

He was introduced to Poppaea through an intermediary, a Jewish actor called Aliturus. It was a most un-Jewish thing to be an actor. Not only was acting regarded as an immoral profession, but an actor would have been constantly in the company of gentiles. Most Jewish priests would have crossed the road to avoid being polluted by someone like Aliturus. But Josephus was no ordinary priest. Knowing that Aliturus was an intimate of the would-be-actor Nero, he cultivated his friendship.

Poppaea had a notorious reputation. Before she supplanted Nero's first wife, Octavia, Claudius's daughter, she had long been his mistress. Octavia was childless and a potential focus of rebellion, so when his true love Poppaea became pregnant, Nero decided to get rid of his wife. He divorced and banished Octavia, then ordered her execution on a trumped-up charge. Surrounded by centurions and legionnaires, the young woman's veins were opened. She was so scared that the blood did not flow at first, so she was placed in an over-heated bath to bleed to death. According to Tacitus, her head was chopped off and taken to Poppaea, who viewed it with satisfaction.[3]

Tacitus calls Poppaea a lady "who had to her credit everything but decency." He portrays her as the stereotypical sexually-insatiable female: "She had a modest air but a salacious lifestyle" and "made no distinction between husbands and lovers." Most likely, it is an exaggeration. It is true that she was married to Otho as her second husband while she was Nero's mistress. The three of them formed a love triangle, each having sexual relations with the other two. Eventually, Nero's jealous love for Poppaea grew stronger than his affection for Otho who was sent away.[4]

Josephus would have charmed Poppaea as a young, dashing, and exotic courtier. Her influence enabled him to secure his objective of freeing the Jewish priests. Besides this favor, he received "large gifts" from her before returning to Judea. The episode tells us much about Josephus. He had the capacity and self-confidence to fascinate even the Roman imperial family. That is if we accept his own account.

Josephus is an unreliable narrator and a fluent liar. Was he really a favorite of Poppaea, or is he exaggerating? And did the shipwreck take place as he described it? It sounds suspiciously like an episode that the apostle Paul mentions in his letters.[5] We will see that when Josephus wrote about his visit to Rome, he was keen to portray himself as a second Paul to gain influence with a certain imperial patroness.

Josephus the author

Josephus will be our key eye witness to the identity of the author of Luke. But to understand his evidence we must understand his history and the destructive conflict, the Jewish War, that so entwined his destiny with the Flavians. He is our best source for Jewish history in the era of the Jewish War and the main reason we know more about Judea in the first century than any other part of the Roman Empire. He was a prolific author, and because his writings were of great interest to Christians, they were copied and have survived. His first work was "The Jewish War," published in Aramaic before 75 AD and soon after that date republished in Greek. This was followed much later in 93/94 AD by his magnum opus, "Antiquities of the Jews." His autobiography, "The Life," was written shortly afterward, intended as an appendix to the Antiquities. His final work, now known as "Against Apion," was a defense of Judaism against its many critics.

Much of our knowledge of Josephus himself comes from the first few pages in The Life. This is how we know about his visit to Rome and the shipwreck. It is how we know he married three times and had three surviving sons, Hyrcanus, Justus, and Agrippa, all born while Vespasian was emperor.[6] Josephus' first wife was a gift from Vespasian—a Jewish captive from Caesarea. She would have had no choice in the matter and Josephus says he was obeying Vespasian, implying that he could not refuse either. The two split up when Josephus went to Alexandria with Vespasian.[7] At Alexandria, he married again, and his new wife gave him three children, although only one, Hyrcanus, survived. He writes that he was displeased with her behavior, so he divorced her. His third wife was a Jewish woman from a prominent family in Crete who bore him his two other sons.[8] Josephus never gives us the names of his wives, not even the third whose character he praises as "surpassing many of her sex." To Josephus, their names are unimportant because they were women, an attitude that most men of the time would share. The few women he does name are exceptions that prove the rule; they are all in high positions of power, such as Poppaea or Berenice, sister of King Agrippa.

We must always remember that Josephus was writing for a Roman audience and was regarded as a traitor by the Jews. Josephus presents himself to his gentile readers as a man of distinguished background. One gets the impression from his genealogy that he is descended from the Hasmonean royalty and high priests. But all is not what it seems. His descent from the Hasmoneans is through a distant ancestor on the female side which did not count for the Jews. And none of Josephus' ancestors on the male line was actually a high priest. Josephus does not include the names of any women in his genealogy—we do not know his mother's name, nor the name of the woman through whom he claimed royal descent. And there are suspicious features that indicate that some generations have been omitted.[9]

Josephus wrote his Life to address accusations made by another Jewish historian, Justus of Tiberias. These accusations must have included the charge that he had faked or exaggerated his family background. Josephus claims to have taken his pedigree from "the public registers" to "take leave of the would-be detractors of my family."[10] These public registers were kept in Jerusalem and were burnt twenty-five years previously during the Jewish war. But then Josephus is always careful to ensure that no one can contradict him.

The approach of war

When Josephus returned to Jerusalem, he found a country on the brink of war. The pressure had been growing for years, and Judah was about to explode. Since the 50s AD, a new force of religious nationalism had arrived in Jewish politics. The nationalists were dissident Jews who were not part of the three sects enumerated by Josephus; Sadducees, Pharisees, and Essenes. The Sadducees were the aristocratic and wealthy class from whom the high priests were chosen. The Pharisees were strict religious scholars who studied and applied the Jewish law, the Torah, the first five books of the Hebrew Bible that were supposed to have been written by Moses. Josephus describes the third group, the Essenes, as accepting a sterner religious discipline. Many lived in monastic-like groups of men, refusing to take wives to avoid the promiscuity of women, although other sects did live as families and have children. Many modern scholars think that Josephus effectively created the idea of the Essenes by lumping together many different groups under one label.

Josephus says, surprisingly, that he tried out all three approaches as a young man, eventually choosing the Pharisees.[11] It is difficult to see Josephus as an Essene, and he was probably not rich enough to be accepted as a Sadducee. So his ultimate choice of the Pharisees seems inevitable. The new nationalists did not fit into this neat framework—Josephus calls them "bandits." They first appeared after Felix was appointed procurator in 52 AD when the notorious Sicarii began a reign of terror in Jerusalem. They would hide daggers under their clothes and mingle with the enormous Jerusalem crowds during festivals, approaching their targets unseen. After murdering them, they would melt back into the crowd. As a tactic, it was very successful, with one of their first victims being the high priest Jonathan who had his throat cut.

The Sicarii did not target Roman officials protected by heavily armed soldiers but the Jewish collaborators. There was little that could be done to avoid the attacks, and the establishment Jews in Jerusalem lived in constant fear for their lives.

The Romans ruled their empire in two ways; through client kings appointed by Rome and direct rule through Roman governors. At this time, Judea was ruled directly by a procurator. The Jewish king Herod Agrippa II and his sister Berenice were the local Jewish clients of the Romans. Agrippa's kingdom was to the north of Judea, but he also had an essential role in Jerusalem because he controlled the temple and had the right to appoint the high priests. The Herods were Roman creatures through and through, and Agrippa would never have contemplated rebellion. So the high priesthood was seen by the nationalists as an indirect tool of the Romans.

The rebellion was not just against Rome. All the rebels had the desire to subvert the religious authority of the priests and the Pharisees. Judea was rife with expectation for the coming Messiah, the Christ. Rome was seen as the new Babylon, and God had promised Babylon's final defeat and destruction in the scriptures. Rome might seem supremely powerful, but no human power could stand against God's power. The Jews would defeat Rome.

As well as the "bandits" who were undertaking an armed struggle, there were Messiah aspirants looking more directly for divine intervention. An early example occurred while Fadus was procurator when a man called Theudas emerged claiming to be a prophet. He led an enthusiastic group of his followers to the Jordan where he had promised to part the waters like Joshua. Unfortunately, the waters did not listen to his command, and a detachment of Roman cavalry fell upon his group and massacred them. Theudas lost his head—it was displayed in Jerusalem.[12]

Felix became procurator in 52 AD. Under his relatively long term of six years, the religiously motivated "bandits" became an ever-increasing problem. Josephus attributes this phenomenon to Felix's corruption, but then he uses bribes as a catch-all explanation for almost anything. The real reason was more fundamental: there was a mounting popular discontent with the ruling classes, both Roman and Jewish. This discontent was driven by Messianic expectations.

During Felix's rule, a man called simply "the Egyptian" repeated Theudas' error. He came from the desert with his followers and led a large crowd from Jerusalem onto the Mount of Olives. With the city stretched out before them, the Egyptian raised his hands to heaven and called upon God to cast down the walls so that his followers could take Jerusalem and evict the Romans. When Felix realized what was going on, he sent a detachment of auxiliaries to engage the group. It was another massacre, although the Egyptian managed to escape. In the Jewish War, Josephus says that a total of 30,000 assembled on the Mount of Olives, although this must be a gross exaggeration. He adds that most of the Egyptian's followers were killed, but the local population escaped back to their houses and hid. In the Antiquities, the numbers who died are put at a more modest 400 with another 200 captured.[13]

Felix was followed as procurator by Festus and then Albinus. Festus took vigorous action against the "bandits," whereas Albinus followed a more placatory approach. Both kept the lid on rebellion, but the pressure continued to build. Albinus was succeeded by Gessius Florus, the worst procurator of all. Not only was he venal like Felix, but he was also cruel and incompetent. Under Florus, things finally came to a head. The final explosion was sparked by a piss-pot in an alley.

The outbreak of war

The run-up to the Jewish War was marked by persistent outbreaks of violence between the Jews and their neighbors. There were riots between the Jews and Samaritans and the Jews and the Syrians. A particular flashpoint was the coastal city of Caesarea which had originally been a Syrian town called Strato's Tower. Herod the Great rebuilt it into a beautiful city with a magnificent harbor. He included a most un-Jewish temple dedicated to Caesar Augustus that featured a colossal statue of the emperor in the style of Zeus. The whole city was renamed Caesarea to honor Augustus.[14] By the time of Pilate, it was operating as the Roman capital of the province of Judea.

There was constant hostility between the many Jews who had settled in Caesarea and the non-Jews, who Josephus variously calls the Syrians or Greeks (Hellenists). The Hellenists took every opportunity to bait the Jews. When the Jewish king Agrippa I died, they celebrated his death with wine and feasting. Not content with this, they installed the statutes of princess Berenice and Agrippa's other daughters in the brothels of Caesarea and performed "unspeakable acts" upon them.[15]

Severe rioting and fighting between the two groups broke out while Felix was procurator. The Jews claimed that Caesarea was a Jewish city because Herod had built it. The Hellenists pointed out that Strato's Tower had been a Syrian town and that the pagan temples showed that Herod had not intended it for the Jews. Eventually, Felix sent both sides to Nero, who found in favor of the Hellenists, giving them control of the city.[16]

Such was the background to the incident that started the war. The Jewish synagogue in Caesarea was next to a piece of land owned by one of the Hellenists. The Jews offered an excellent price for this piece of land, but the owner refused to sell it to them. Adding insult to this refusal, he decided to build a factory on the land so that the only access to the synagogue would be through a tiny narrow alleyway. The Jews were outraged, and some of the young men tried to stop the builders at their work. The Jewish leaders adopted a different approach and gave Florus a large bribe of eight silver talents to halt the construction. The Roman procurator accepted the bribe but then simply left the Jews and the Hellenists to fight it out. The next day was the Sabbath, and one of the Caesarean partisans took a chamber pot to the front of the synagogue and sacrificed some birds upon it. This was an extreme provocation to the Jews, and fighting broke out between the two sides. Because the synagogue had been desecrated, the Jews removed the books of the Law and sent a delegation to Florus urging him to intervene and reminding him of the eight talents they had already paid. Florus took this very badly and imprisoned the delegation on the grounds that they had illegally removed the scrolls of the Law.[17]

The people of Jerusalem were infuriated by this injustice. It seems that they withheld some of the tribute due to the Romans, perhaps as putative compensation for the bribe. Florus' response was to send his soldiers to the temple treasury to remove seventeen talents "for Caesar." This action triggered a major riot in the city in which the people shouted insults at Florus—some collected coppers in a basket for him. The procurator was both thin-skinned and hot-headed. The result was a rapid escalation of violence.[18]

Florus entered the city at the head of his grim-faced troops and the next day took his seat on a dais outside the palace. The Jewish leaders appeared before him with a conciliatory attitude to explain the disturbances. Florus simply demanded that they give him the names of those who had insulted him. The priests apologized for the insults and said they had been made by juveniles who were impossible to identify now. Florus was enraged and ordered his troops to take retribution by sacking an area of the city called the Upper Market Place. He ordered his soldiers to kill everyone they found there.[19]

What followed was an atrocity that cast aside the legalistic veneer to reveal the underlying brutality of Roman rule. The soldiers rampaged through the houses of the Upper Market Place, stealing the possessions of the many wealthy inhabitants. The people they found there were flogged and then crucified—men, women, and children without distinction. Josephus puts the total number killed at 3,600. Josephus is particularly enraged that Florus had men of equestrian rank scourged before him and then crucified. Even an ordinary Roman citizen was supposed to be immune from such punishments, with the right of trial before the emperor, yet alone a Roman knight.[20]

King Agrippa was absent from Jerusalem in Alexandria, leaving his sister Berenice in the city undertaking a Nazarite vow which involved shaving her head and abstaining from wine for thirty days. She appeared barefoot before Florus imploring him to stop the slaughter. Not only did he ignore her pleas, but the Roman soldiers tortured Jews in front of her. Josephus says they would have killed the queen had she not been able to get to her palace and the protection of her guards. She spent the night fearing a Roman assault that never came.[21]

The next day the whole city was in a state of grief and anger. The priests were desperately attempting to calm the situation to forestall further reprisals from Florus. He had sent for two more cohorts from Caesarea and demanded that the Jews go out to greet the soldiers to prove their loyalty. The people were very reluctant, but the priests persuaded them. As the crowd walked towards the soldiers, some hotheads began shouting fresh insults at Florus. The Romans attacked, and the people fled back into the city. Many were crushed to death at the gates, and others were hacked down from behind by the Roman cavalry. Inside the city, the Romans were halted in the narrow streets by the press of people trying to escape them. Their cavalry was useless here, and Florus decided to consolidate his forces in the fortress Antonia next to the temple complex. From there, they could control the temple and its treasures. But the Romans' advance was blocked by the people who were now fighting back from the streets and the roofs. Jewish partisans destroyed the colonnade leading from Antonia to the temple, making the fortress useless for its purpose of guarding the temple. So Florus ordered his men to retreat to the camp to avoid getting trapped in the city.[22]

The Romans' situation was becoming impossible, and Florus summoned the high priests to arrange a truce. If they swore to uphold rule in the city, he would withdraw all his troops leaving just one cohort behind. They agreed with the condition that the cohort should be one that had not been responsible for the killing. So Florus withdrew from Jerusalem to Caesarea. The sight of the retreating Romans would have struck joy into the heart of the rebel faction. Perhaps the Romans were not so invincible after all.[23]

Florus immediately sent messages to the governor of Syria, Cestius, reporting that the Jews had revolted from Rome. The magistrates and Berenice sent their own messengers, blaming the disturbance on the brutality of Florus and petitioning for his recall to Rome. Because Judea was only a minor province, its procurator came under the authority of the governor of Syria. A strong governor would have marched to Jerusalem to quell any disturbance and secure the city before holding judgment between Florus and the Jews on the reasons for the trouble. But Cestius just sent a tribune, Neapolitanus, to investigate the situation.[24]

Neapolitanus met up with King Agrippa, who was returning from Alexandria, and the two of them made their way to Jerusalem. Josephus, as ever, is writing with the Romans as his audience. He blames everything on Florus and presents the people as docile and not opposed to Roman rule in general, but only to the tyrannical actions of Florus. According to Josephus, Neapolitanus was convinced in favor of the Jews. But his visit achieved nothing.[25]

King Agrippa attempted to reassert authority over Jerusalem. But when he instructed the people to submit to Florus, he was pelted with stones and had to flee the city. Jerusalem was becoming dangerous even for a king.[26] The establishment was losing control, and everywhere the revolutionary elements were on the rise: a group of rebels successfully took the supposedly invincible fortress of Masada from the Romans. There were even revolutionaries among the priests. The temple captain Eleazar, son of the high priest Ananias, persuaded the priests at the temple to stop the sacrifices offered for Rome and Caesar. This was tantamount to a declaration of independence from Rome. It could no longer be denied that Judea was in revolt.[27]

In one last desperate attempt to retain control, the establishment priests sent messengers to Florus and Agrippa, requesting them to send troops to Jerusalem. Only Agrippa responded, and he sent two thousand cavalry. Using these soldiers, the priests attempted to regain control of the temple from the revolutionaries. There was fighting for seven days between the two factions. Then on a festival day, the Sicarii successfully infiltrated the part of the city controlled by the high priest Ananias' party and gained the upper hand against Agrippa's troops. They burnt down the high priest's house, the palace of Agrippa and Berenice, and the record office. Ananias and the soldiers all fled to the Upper Palace.[28]

A Sicarii rebel called Menahem had achieved control of the insurgency by raiding Herod's huge armory at Masada. Equipped with these weapons, his supporters took Antonia from its Roman garrison, killing all the soldiers. They then laid siege to the Upper Palace. The defenders held out, but their position was hopeless, and they negotiated an agreement allowing the Jews and Agrippa's troops to leave. No such leniency was shown to the Roman soldiers; they decided to fight their way out and occupy three great, impregnable towers that Herod had built into the city walls.[29]

The rebels followed up their victory by killing the high priest Ananias who had been found hiding in a sewer. The revolutionaries were triumphant but divided into factions, and the infighting that was such a feature of the Jewish side throughout the war broke out. Eleazar ambushed and assassinated Menahem and many of his Sicarii followers, with the remainder fleeing back to Masada. Eleazar then negotiated the surrender of the Roman soldiers who had taken refuge in the towers. He promised them safe passage out of the city if they laid down their arms. As soon as they had surrendered their weapons, his men fell upon the soldiers and massacred them all. There could be no forgiveness from the Romans now. The rebels were intent on burning their bridges. If the Jews did not fight together, they would surely die together.[30]

Josephus in Jerusalem

Where was Josephus in all this? In his "Life," written for a Roman audience, he claims he tried to convince his countrymen to submit peacefully
to Roman rule. But the insurgents were too powerful, and he had to
take refuge in the temple for fear of his life. After Menahem was killed,
Josephus came out from the temple and rejoined the establishment party
of the priests and Pharisees. Josephus says they secretly hoped for Cestius
to prevail, which is absurd as the Jews could only look forward to severe
retribution from the Romans.[31]

The rebellion in Jerusalem gave the Hellenists in Caesarea the opportunity to massacre the Jewish population. Josephus says that 20,000 were
killed (doubtless an exaggeration), with the remainder enslaved by the
Romans. In the towns and villages all around Palestine, Jews and Syrians
were at each other's throats. Josephus gives a long list of Syrian towns
and villages destroyed by the Jews; it starts in the Decapolis, goes around
Galilee and down the coast to Caesarea. The populations of these places
were killed; Josephus talks about an immense number of Syrian dead.
Whole communities were slaughtered by their neighbors, with their land
and possessions taken by the victors. The propensity of ethnic groups
in the ancient world to slay each other like this is a terrible reminder of
human nature.[32]

The trouble spread further. There was a habitual conflict between Jews
and gentiles in Alexandria, and the rebellion set off rioting between the
two groups. This ended with the Romans brutally putting down the
disturbance amongst the Jews.[33] Later, the people of Damascus in Syria
massacred their own colony of Jews who numbered over 10,000 according
to Josephus.[34] But these were the exceptions. The diaspora of millions of
Jews had already spread across the Roman world, and outside the immediate area around Judea, there was little trouble. The Jews in other places
did not support the rebellion, nor were they punished for it.

The Syrian governor Cestius finally took action. He put together a large
force consisting of the Twelfth legion, cohorts from the other legions, and
auxiliary forces supplied by the local kings Agrippa, Antiochus, and
Soaemus. Cestius marched his army down to Caesarea, subduing the
towns and villages in the countryside, his soldiers killing and burning,
pillaging and looting. From Caesarea, he marched to camp at Gibeon, six
miles from Jerusalem, to prepare for the assault on the city.[35] But he was
surprised by a ferocious attack by the Jewish partisans who were disor-
ganized and untrained but full of religious fervor. The Roman line barely
held.[36]

Seeing the strength of the opposition, King Agrippa attempted to negotiate a peace deal. His ambassadors, however, were attacked by a partisan faction. This action in defiance of the protocols of war led to internal disagreement and fighting amongst the Jewish side. Cestius saw his opportunity; he attacked, routed the partisans, and advanced right up to the city walls. He waited three days for the Jews to surrender before entering Jerusalem. The battle inside the city raged for six days until the legionnaires, marching slowly in tortoise formation, reached the temple wall and gates, which they began to undermine and fire.[37]

Josephus represents this as the critical moment. He says that the rebels were starting to flee, and the Jews inside the temple were ready to surrender. But just as the Romans were on the brink of victory, Cestius gave the order to withdraw. Josephus claims, absurdly, that some of Cestius' officers were bribed by Florus to provide him with bad advice. More likely, the Romans realized they were seriously outnumbered and that even if they took the temple, they would be trapped, surrounded by hundreds of thousands of Jews ready to fight in the narrow streets of Jerusalem.[38]

Their retreat, though, was undoubtedly a disaster. The insurgents gained heart from the sight of the Romans' withdrawal and constantly harassed Cestius' army: it took a whole night and a day to cover the short distance back to Gibeon. There Cestius rested his men for a couple of days, but the delay meant that a vast number of Jewish fighters had time to join the rebels surrounding the camp. Cestius had no option but to withdraw further. Abandoning most of their baggage, the Romans marched out in good order but were ambushed in a narrow ravine. Only the coming of night saved them from complete annihilation and enabled the remnant of the Roman army to take refuge in the town of Beth-horon.[39]

The town was put under siege by the Jews, and Cestius had to resort to a clever trick to extract his men. He moved his army out silently at night, leaving behind guards to shout the passcodes, to fool the Jews into thinking the camp was fully occupied. The trick worked, but the guards paid with their lives when the first light of day revealed the empty camp. By then, the Romans had a three and a half mile lead which was enough to reach safety.[40]

Cestius had suffered substantial losses, with nearly 6,000 of his men killed, according to Josephus.[41] The Romans did not easily forgive defeat. Even after the Twelfth participated in the final Roman victory, they were still in a state of disgrace.

It was now clear to the Jews that the prophecies were coming true. A citizen army of brave Jewish fighters had defeated a fully prepared and equipped Roman army and forced them to flee for their lives. The Jewish God was stronger than the Romans. Writing much later, and with the benefit of hindsight, Josephus says that the victory was disastrous for the Jewish nation because it emboldened the rebels.[42] But we may wonder if he also was carried away with nationalistic enthusiasm. He places himself among those Jews who opposed the revolt. Indeed, from his account, he would appear not to have had any military experience whatsoever nor played any part in the rebellion. So it is all the more surprising that he would emerge as the leading general on the Jewish side.

8

A female gospel

Women of the Way

Luke and Acts explicitly include many women among the people of the Way, and the individual women we come across are almost always named. How many female prophets are there in the New Testament? If we take the five narrative works (the gospels and Acts), we can find five separate episodes of female prophecy:

1. Elizabeth in Luke 1:41-45. She is filled with the Holy Spirit and makes a prophecy about Mary's child.

2. Mary in Luke 1:46-55. Her hymn, the Magnificat, is a prophecy about the Christ child.

3. Anna in Luke 2:36-38. She recognizes the baby Jesus when he is brought into the temple and gives a prophecy about him.

4. The slave girl in Acts 16:16-18. She has a spirit of divination and recognizes that Paul and his companions are servants of the Most High God with a message of salvation.

5. The four daughters of Philip in Acts 21:8-9. We are told that they were unmarried and prophesied.

These five episodes concern eight female prophets, and they all come from either Luke or Acts, with not a single female prophet in the other three gospels. Indeed, only Luke/Acts makes it clear that women can be prophets:

This is what was spoken by the prophet Joel: "And in the last days, God says, I will pour out my spirit upon all flesh. Your sons and daughters will prophesy, your young men will see visions,

your old men will dream dreams. And even upon my male servants and my female servants will I pour out my spirit in those
days, and they will prophesy." (Acts 2:16-18)

Acts follows this up by showing how women and girls were among
the very first Christians. The group baptized by Philip in Samaria, who
would later receive the Holy Spirit from Peter, consisted of "both men
and women." And when Saul/Paul persecuted the church, he "bound
both men and women with chains."[1] In Luke/Acts, women play a full part
in the early church; they get baptized, receive the Holy Spirit, prophesy,
and suffer persecution. The other gospels tend not to be explicit about
female involvement; we have to guess whether women are supposed to
be included with the "brothers"—they probably are, but only Luke/Acts
makes this clear.

This is just one example of how Luke/Acts pays more attention to
women than the other gospels. It is not that the other gospels are anti-
woman but that they fade into the background to the point of invisibility.
Females tend to come into ancient narratives when they impinge upon
the male as wives, lovers, or mothers. Yet women keep popping up in
unexpected places in Luke and Acts.

Take, as an example, the story of a married couple, Ananias and
Sapphira.[2] They were Christians who sold a field but kept some of the
proceeds back rather than donate the whole to the common fund as they
had promised. When confronted separately by Peter, each of them drops
dead. It is a rather silly story, but it treats the couple as complete equals.
The wife, Sapphira, is named as well as the husband and is a party to
the deception. Indeed, the story reaches its climax when Peter confronts
Sapphira, who lies to him about the price of the field, not knowing that her
husband is already dead. Emphasizing the woman of a couple is unusual,
evidence that we are looking at things from a female perspective.

Then there is the servant girl in the story of Peter's rescue from prison by
an angel.[3] Peter comes to the house of Mary, the mother of John and James,
and knocks on the door. There is a little comic interlude as the servant girl
is so surprised that she runs to tell the others without opening the door.
The people in the house dispute with her whether it is Peter or his angel
before they think to let him in. We learn that the girl's name is Rhoda, a
detail that would be too incidental to merit a mention in the other gospels.

There is a whole group of Christian women, the widows, whose existence at this time would be unknown if not for Acts.[4] We learn about
them when the "Hellenist" Christians in Jerusalem complain about their
widows being overlooked in the daily distribution of food. The resolution
is the appointment of seven men to oversee the food arrangements. We

may doubt that the author of Luke has any actual knowledge of the situation in Judea in the 30s AD, but the existence of groups of poor widows dependent upon their fellow Christians for support would have been familiar from their personal experience.

The widows also come into the story about the resurrection of Tabitha called Dorcas in Greek.[5] Tabitha was a good woman occupied in charitable works who died unexpectedly. The widows arranged her body in an upper chamber and called Peter. They showed Peter the clothes that Tabitha had made, giving us another little insight into the feminine world. Women of all classes would be involved in weaving and making clothes—Tabitha's charity was a very practical affair of clothing the naked. Peter sends everyone out of the room and utters the words, "Tabitha arise!". The dead woman's eyes open, and she sits up.

All is not as it seems in this story. When put in Aramaic, Peter's words differ in only one letter from Jesus' invocation, "little girl, arise!", which he uses to resurrect Jairus' daughter in the Gospel of Mark (we are not told her name!)[6] It seems that the author of Luke is aware of the mystic formula but has confused Talitha, "little girl," for Tabitha, meaning Gazelle, which is Dorcas in Greek. As for Tabitha's garments, they probably relate to the spiritual garment of the resurrection, which frequently appears in early Christian sources. The author of Luke has misunderstood a saying that was about the spiritual resurrection and turned it into this story about a dead dressmaker.

At the other end of the social spectrum from the widows are the two sisters of Herod Agrippa II—Drusilla and Berenice. Drusilla is mentioned in passing in the account of the trial of Paul before her husband, Felix. More significant is Berenice's involvement in Paul's second trial. The procurator Festus has decided to hold a hearing in front of Agrippa and Berenice.[7] Queen Berenice is described as being seated in pomp alongside the king and Festus. She is among those who discuss the case and conclude that Paul is innocent.[8] Although Berenice would have had no formal role in the proceedings, she is shown as a person of influence who would make decisions and be listened to. We will look further at Agrippa II and his sisters later.

Not all women in Luke and Acts are dependent upon the male. When Paul visits Philippi, he converts a businesswoman called Lydia, a dealer in purple fabrics. It seems that Lydia is the mistress of her own household—there is no mention of any man. She is baptized along with her whole household and insists that the apostles come and stay at her house.

As well as being prophets and leaders of house churches, women could be teachers educating men in matters of doctrine. In Acts, the married Christian couple, Aquila and Priscilla, meet Paul in Corinth and then travel with him to Ephesus. Paul continues further while another Christian preacher, an Alexandrian Jew named Apollos, comes to Ephesus. He is eloquent, "well versed in the scriptures," and teaches accurately about Jesus. He only knows, however, the baptism of John and not that of Jesus:

> When Priscilla and Aquila heard him, they took him in and explained to him the way of God more accurately. (Acts 18:26)

The episode is a travesty of the situation from Paul's letters. Aquila and Priscilla are mentioned by Paul but not in connection with Apollos, who came to Corinth after Paul and taught a different and more spiritual Christianity. Paul wrote 1 Corinthians to address the situation that Apollos' visit had caused. Many of the Corinthians had begun to doubt Paul's teachings and even his credentials as an apostle. The author of Luke concocts the story that Apollos only knew the baptism of John until instructed by the couple to try and explain this embarrassing situation. I have suggested that Apollos was actually teaching from the Gospel of Thomas, which, according to the scholarly consensus, is not supposed to exist at this time. The significant point here is that the author places the woman, Priscilla, ahead of her husband. The implication is that Priscilla takes the lead in enlightening Apollos, an example of a woman instructing a male Christian teacher.

There is even a passing reference in Acts to a female philosopher. When Paul lectures to the philosophers of Athens, he creates an uproar and gains a few new followers, "including Dionysius the Areopagite and a woman named Damaris."[9] We hear nothing more about Damaris and it is uncertain whether a woman could have been a philosopher in first-century Athens. We do know, however, that many of the elite Roman ladies took an interest in philosophy and engaged in philosophical discussions alongside men.

Women who minister

In the Gospel of Luke, a group of women bankrolls Jesus' ministry:

> And it came to pass that he (Jesus) was traveling through city and village, preaching and proclaiming the good news of the kingdom of God. The Twelve were with him, and certain women who had been cured of evil spirits and infirmities: Mary called Magdalene, from whom seven demons had gone out, Joanna, the

wife of Herod's steward Chuza, Susanna, and many others. They were ministering to them out of their own means. (Luke 8:1-3)

This fascinating passage has been much discussed. Not only are women included among Jesus' followers, traveling around with him and the twelve disciples, but they also "minister" to them out of their "own means." So they are rich enough to provide sustenance for the whole group. Only Luke mentions these women at this point. In the other gospels, a group of women, including Mary the Magdalene, appear at the crucifixion and resurrection. The ultimate source is the description of the women at the crucifixion in Mark:

And there were also women looking on from afar. Among them were Mary the Magdalene, Mary the mother of James the least and Joses, and Salome. They had followed Jesus and been ministering to him while he was in Galilee, and there were many other (women) who had come with him to Jerusalem. (Mark 15:40-1)

We can see how the author of Luke has developed this passage. The idea of women "ministering" to Jesus is moved from the crucifixion to near the start of Jesus' ministry, which makes good narrative sense. The author of Luke has also made some significant changes. Most obviously, the women's names are different, with only Mary the Magdalene in common between the two lists. The change could be justified because the Mark passage talks about "many others" who have followed Jesus to Jerusalem.

The most significant difference, though, is the nature of the assistance that the women give to Jesus. The word in Mark is *diakoneo,* which has given us the title of "deacon" for a Christian minister. The early Jesus movement employed this term, "to minister," in a mystical and spiritual sense; it meant to feed the followers of Jesus with spiritual food and drink. But the author of Mark interprets it literally. The everyday meaning of *diakoneo* was to serve food and drink. So the Mark passage implies that the women were lodging and feeding Jesus and his followers in their houses as he moved from place to place. We know this is the type of support that settled Christians gave to itinerant teachers and apostles in the early Jesus movement.

At a more exalted level, *diakoneo* could mean the hospitality of a wealthy hostess. She would cater to all the needs of her guests but would certainly not prepare their food with her own fair hands. It is illuminating that the author of Luke interprets the word in this second sense—the women minister "out of their own means." They are not humble village housewives, cooking and offering a spare bed, but rich patronesses who provide for all the needs of Jesus and his followers out of their purses. Most significantly, they now travel with Jesus from place to place.

It is one of the many little clues that show that the author of Luke looks at the world through a rich person's eyes. In reality, it would have been impossible for wealthy women to have followed Jesus around in this way in first-century Judea. A woman traveling with a group of men would be regarded as a prostitute—unless perhaps her husband were one of the men, and maybe even then. It might be argued that Mary the Magdalene did have a reputation as a prostitute. Another woman, Susanna, is only mentioned in the gospels in this one place, and she appears to have no husband. It is possible that both Mary and Susanna accepted a reputation as prostitutes to follow Jesus. But the third woman, Joanna, proves beyond doubt that the story is fiction.

Joanna, like Susanna, appears only in the Gospel of Luke, and she is described as the wife of Chuza, the steward of Herod. Such a steward would typically be a freed slave, but this should not blind us to the seniority of the position. This was an age in which there was no national administration separate from a ruler's household. A steward would not only manage the king's estates but his whole kingdom. A modern equivalent might be the office of prime minister, although, unlike a democratically elected prime minister, the steward would remain very much a servant of the king.

Joanna is married to the most senior official in Herod's kingdom. The ancient world was an honor-shame culture. A woman who acted as Joanna was supposed to have in Luke would have brought extreme shame on her husband. And the shame of Herod's senior official would have rebounded on Herod himself. Quite simply, it is not going to happen. A wife had no power to defy her husband. Joanna is going to be brought back, and the men she was with are going to be punished and probably executed.

A woman like Joanna can only follow Jesus in fiction. The author of Luke would have been all too aware of the restrictions on a senior woman's behavior, but the story is set in the distant land of Judea. Besides, Jesus is the son of God, and the normal rules are suspended. The author is free to fantasize; she imagines a woman of exalted position wandering the roads of Judea with Jesus, providing for him and his disciples from her considerable wealth. It is a fantasy that tells us much about the author.

Women of a better class

Let us take another look at Mary who lives in Jerusalem with her household, including her servant, Rhoda. When Peter has escaped from prison, he knocks on the door of her outer gate. This means that Mary's house had its own inner courtyard and was substantial, even palatial, like the high priest's house. It is certainly large enough to act as the house church and meeting place for the Christians in Jerusalem. Mary, then, is portrayed as a wealthy lady with an establishment. The episode is fascinating, and I have analyzed it in more depth in the Rock and the Tower.[10] Just to point out here that the real Mary would have been poor—the "saints" in Jerusalem had no money. The author of Luke grossly exaggerates her social standing and elevates her to the elite. This is consistent with her treatment of Mary the Magdalene, who is turned into a rich benefactress.

There is a pattern here. The author of Luke sees the world through elite eyes. They have spent their life living in splendid houses, and they automatically think anyone important must have done the same. We see this bias towards high-ranking women in some revealing passages in Acts.

When Paul travels to Pisidian Antioch in Phrygia, he speaks at the synagogue, and many of the "Jews and devout converts" are persuaded by him. He comes again on the following Sabbath and finds almost the whole city assembled to hear him. The episode is fanciful; Pisidian Antioch was a gentile city in a gentile province, and the Jews would have been a small minority. There is no way the whole town is going to turn out to listen to Paul. And if they had, the synagogue would be far too small for such a crowd. But then, to be fair, exaggerated numbers are typical of ancient sources. Up to now, the Jews have been acting generously towards Paul. But this changes when they see the influence he has achieved:

> The Jews incited the worshipping women of prominence and the principals of the city, and they stirred up a persecution against Paul and Barnabas and expelled them from the district. (Acts 13:50)

The "worshipping women" must be gentile God-fearers who worship in the synagogue. We have a picture of high-status women attracted to Judaism who use their influence with the "principals," the men who run the city, to get the Christian preachers expelled. Judaism attracted many God-fearers from the freedmen class. But Acts shows how there were also God-fearers, mainly women, among the nobles. These aristocratic women influence the leading men, their husbands, fathers, and sons, who would have been sympathetic to Judaism but not God-fearers themselves. There are many indications in Luke/Acts that the author had been just such a God-fearing noble before converting to Christianity.

When Paul comes to Thessalonica, he meets more opposition at the synagogue but also finds supporters:

> Some of the Jews were persuaded and joined Paul and Silas,
> along with a large number of God-fearing Greeks and quite a
> few leading women. (Acts 17:4).

The leading women here are listed separately from the Greeks. They
are likely Romans, the wives and daughters of senior administrators and
army officers. Like the Jews and the "God-fearing Greeks," they worship
in the synagogue—they are God-fearers. Note how there is no mention
of leading men. It seems that the male nobles did not become God-fearers,
but their wives could and did.

Paul received a warmer welcome from the Jews of Berea who scruti-
nized the scriptures to see if he was speaking the truth:

> As a result, many of them believed, along with quite a few prom-
> inent Greek women and men also. (Acts 17:12)

In this sentence, it is the women who are Greek and prominent, with
"men also" added as an afterthought. This reverses the usual pattern
among ancient writers in which the men come first, with the women added
at the end, if at all. Once again, the high-status women are singled out. It is
these women who would establish house churches and become the most
prominent Christians in their cities.

Mary the Magdalene

The author of Luke is regarded as a misogynist by many Christian feminists. This may come as quite a surprise given the prominence of women
in Luke and Acts and the obvious pro-female viewpoint of the author. The
reason is entirely due to Luke's treatment of Mary the Magdalene.

For the modern Christian feminist, the Magdalene is an icon. She is a
strong woman, one of the closest followers of Jesus, and an apostle and
teacher in her own right. Some go further and believe that she was married to Jesus. The Gospel of Luke, however, appears to minimize her role.

Although Mary the Magdalene is an early follower of Jesus, she is joined
by Joanna, Suzanna and "many others," reducing her importance. Most
significantly, her special role at the resurrection as "apostle to the apostles"
seems to be denied by Luke. In Matthew and John, the Magdalene is the
first person to see the risen Christ, and she gives the news to the disciples/
apostles. The same is true of Mark if we include the so-called long ending
to that gospel. But in Luke, she is just one of a party of women who go to
Jesus' tomb with spices. They find the tomb empty and see two angels who

tell them that Jesus has risen. The women do not see Christ for themselves, and when they return in a group to give the message to the disciples, they are not believed.[11]

Not content with reducing the Magdalene's importance, it is further alleged that the author of Luke blackens her name. Mary the Magdalene has been traditionally known as a reformed prostitute. As a repentant sinner, she was extremely popular in the medieval church. In the renaissance, she became a favorite subject of western art, painted in lascivious poses, often completely naked. Most modern scholars have rejected the idea that the Magdalene was a prostitute. Some feminists go much further and see a conspiracy in which a female role model was turned into a sexual object by the "patriarchal" church. So where did this tradition about Mary the Magdalene as a prostitute come from? The finger of blame is pointed towards the Gospel of Luke.

These feminists see the author of Luke as a man threatened by the Magdalene as an early female leader of the church. So he sabotages her by taking away her special role as first witness of the resurrection. He then goes further by implying she was a prostitute. His purpose was surely to elevate the competing early church leader, Peter, at her expense. The case against the author as a misogynist appears dark indeed. But it is always suspicious when an argument fits the modern zeitgeist so perfectly.

When we look at the evidence in detail, it melts away to nothing. Take the charge that Luke demotes Mary the Magdalene as the first witness to Jesus' resurrection. The resurrection account in Luke is actually ambiguous, and it is unclear who saw the resurrected Jesus first, although there is a suggestion it could be Simon Peter. The author of Luke, like all the gospel writers, is struggling with conflicting sources for the resurrection. Our earliest account is not a gospel, but Paul's letter to the Corinthians written twenty years before Mark. Paul says that Christ appeared first to Cephas (Peter) and then the twelve. He does not even mention Mary the Magdalene or any other woman.[12] The author of Luke must have regarded Paul's statement as authoritative because the order of resurrection appearances in Luke and Acts follows that set out by Paul.

Turning to the gospels, we find that Mark says that the resurrected Jesus appeared first to Mary the Magdalene, but only in the disputed long ending. The consensus among scholars is that the long ending is a much later addition, and if we ignore it, then Mark indicates that Jesus appeared first to Peter and the disciples. Mary the Magdalene would have heard the angel's message, as she does in Luke, but would not have witnessed the resurrection. So Luke would be following two out of the three earlier sources in not having Jesus appear to the Magdalene.

Things, however, are more complex than this. Appendix B deals with the long ending in more detail and shows that it must have been attached to the Gospel of Mark very early, before either Matthew or Luke was written. And we will later see strong evidence that the long ending influenced Acts. So the author of Luke was aware that Mark gave priority to the Magdalene but chose to accept the account of Paul over both Mark and Matthew. This position is understandable given the esteem with which the author regarded Paul. Later, we will see that the author had an additional personal reason for preferring Peter, one which had nothing to do with the Magdalene.

The accusation that the author of Luke implies that Mary the Magdalene was a prostitute is easily dealt with, because the gospel of Luke says nothing of the sort. The author has moved two episodes concerning women from the crucifixion account in Mark and Matthew and positioned them much earlier in their gospel. One of these episodes concerns the rich benefactresses of Jesus. The other is about an unnamed woman who comes to anoint Jesus' head with expensive ointment shortly before his crucifixion. In Luke, this woman becomes a "sinner from the town," meaning a prostitute. She comes to Jesus as he is taking a meal with the Pharisee Simon and other guests, lets down her hair and anoints Jesus' feet.

Reading all four gospels together gives the impression that the sinful woman was Mary the Magdalene. In Luke, the episode is immediately followed by the passage introducing the Magdalene as someone from whom Jesus has cured of an infirmity by casting out seven demons. I believe that the author of Mark is drawing upon traditions that do indeed go back to the Magdalene. But as this woman is unnamed in Mark and Matthew, the author of Luke does not know this. The Magdalene comes immediately after the sinful woman in Luke because both passages have been moved from the crucifix account in Mark. And Mary the Magdalene actually appears in the passage along with several other women; Joanna, Susanna, and "many others." Are they all prostitutes?

Most significantly, the Magdalene cannot be the same as the sinful woman because she is described quite differently. Jesus forgives the prostitute her sins, but he casts out seven demons from the Magdalene. Forgiving sin and casting out demons are not the same thing in the gospels. Possession by demons is what we would call mental illness; a demon will provoke a person to self-harm or make them sick. Sin, however, is a matter of a person's own volition. Jesus casts out demons to make a person well. He never casts out demons to stop a person from sinning—he forgives them and tells them not to sin again.

The author of Luke never intended the woman from the town to be the same as the Magdalene. Far from being a misogynist, the author of Luke gives us another remarkable female portrait with the sinful woman. This is the only time a prostitute appears in the gospels, and she is described sympathetically. She approaches Jesus in tears, with her love and devotion overflowing from her heart. Her gratitude for being forgiven her sins contrasts with the judgmental attitude of Simon and the other men who would expel the woman from their company. And this surely is the point, the real reason why the woman is called a sinner in Luke. The story compares Jesus' forgiveness of sinners to the Pharisees' self-righteous condemnation.

And yet the actions of the woman are undeniably erotic. She lets down her long hair, an act of sexual provocation, and pours expensive ointment upon it. Then she kneels submissively, rubbing and cleaning Jesus' feet with the richly perfumed wet hair. It is the sexiest moment in the New Testament (not a phrase one would expect to read!) We may wonder if the imaginative author of Luke is indulging in her own secret fantasy.

Mary and Martha

We have left the most sensitive female portrait in Luke to last. The two sisters, Mary and Martha, are followers of Jesus who only appear in Luke and the latter Gospel of John. In one famous story, Jesus visits Martha's house:

> She had a sister named Mary, who sat at the Lord's feet listening to his words. But Martha was distracted by much service. She went up to them and said, "Lord, do you not care that my sister has left me alone to serve? Speak to her, that she might help me."
>
> "Martha, Martha," the Lord replied, "you are anxious and troubled about many things. But only one thing is necessary, and Mary has chosen the good portion that will not be taken away from her." (Luke 10:39-42)

The story is brief but perfect. Note the significant elements:

1. The two women apparently live alone together, with no mention of a man. As this is very unusual, it is unsurprising that the Gospel of John gives them a brother, Lazarus.
2. Mary is shown as a pupil-disciple of Jesus, listening and absorbing his teachings. This is the only time a woman is portrayed like this in the gospels.
3. The subject is women's work.
4. The story revolves around the relationship of the two sisters.

There was a strong separation between male and female work in the ancient world. The two sexes lived different lives in this respect with little cross-over. Male authors of the time show no interest in women's work which is scarcely ever mentioned. Yet the toil and trouble of cooking for a sizeable group are central to this story. A man would be interested in the quantity and quality of a feast but not in the effort required to prepare it. We see things here from a female perspective. Note the relationship between the two sisters. We can smell the sexual jealousy behind Martha's complaint; Mary gets to sit at the "Lord's feet" while she, Martha, is left preparing the food.

This is not something that a man in the ancient world would write. Had it really happened, the episode would have been too slight to have left any record. Yet it is very relevant to a woman; it shows a hostess abandoning her traditional responsibilities to attend to the teachings of Jesus. It would have had particular resonance for a woman who had perhaps neglected her own family and household to find time to research and write a gospel.

9

Josephus and Vespasian

Josephus the general

Josephus gave an account of how he became the general in charge of the rebellion in Galilee in his Jewish War. He says that following the defeat of Cestius, almost everyone was persuaded to the cause of the rebellion. The few exceptions were some of the leading citizens who escaped "like swimmers from a sinking ship" and went over to the Roman side. A mass meeting of the victorious rebels was held in the temple to appoint generals in charge of the various regions, and Josephus was given the important area of Galilee.[1]

Galilee is in the far north and was separated from Judea by Samaria on the west side of the Jordan and the trans-Jordan on the east side. At the center of Galilee was Lake Gennesaret, also called Lake Tiberius or the Sea of Galilee. The lake was famed for the quality of its fish, and the surrounding land was productive and fertile. The main towns were Tiberius and Tarichaeae, both granted to King Agrippa, and the Hellenized city of Sepphoris. Tarichaeae was always for the revolt, Sepphoris stayed loyal to the Romans, and Tiberius would waver between the rebels and Agrippa.

Josephus always refers to himself in the third person in the Jewish War. He describes how "Josephus," having arrived in Galilee, immediately implemented an efficient system of civil administration appointing a council of seventy elders with seven magistrates in each town to hear more minor cases. Then, preparing for war, he oversaw the fortification of numerous towns and cities. At the same time, he raised an army of 100,000 men equipped with whatever weapons were available. Josephus organized this force on Roman lines, complete with decurions, centurions, and tribunes. He trained his army on Roman principles, insisting on obedience and discipline. And, following the Roman practice, the men were drilled relentlessly in the arts and maneuvers of war. But Josephus despaired at achieving Roman levels of competence in the short time available.[2]

These well-laid plans were disrupted by the arrival on the scene of a despicable schemer called John of Gischala. This John had started as a bandit but rapidly built up his own mini-army based in his hometown. His real interest was to control the olive oil trade, in which he achieved a monopoly and made a fortune. When Josephus attempted to limit John's activities, John plotted to kill him.[3]

It is all nonsense. This is clear from Josephus' later conflicting account in his Life which was written in response to accusations by Justus of Tiberias and is almost entirely concerned with Josephus' time as a general in Galilee. The Life contains its own set of deceptions, but by comparing these with the deceptions in the Jewish War we can begin to make out the truth. For example, the seventy elders supposedly appointed by Josephus were, in reality, hostages he took to ensure the compliance of the towns and villages in the area.[4]

The army of 100,000 men, organized and trained on Roman principles, is pure fantasy. Josephus actually commanded a rag-tag force of mercenaries and former bandits, along with villagers and townspeople. There is no mention of any training or military discipline in the Life, and the numbers involved in the fighting are pitifully small. John used a force of 1,000 against Josephus at Tiberias, and a rebel called "Jesus the brigand" had an army of 800 men, which was believed to be sufficient to defeat the supposed commander of 100,000.[5] In Josephus' first real military engagement, one of King Agrippa's men called Aebutius came against him with a trained force of only 100 cavalry and 200 infantry. Aebutius was forced to retreat but suffered a mere three casualties. Josephus says he followed up this victory by leading 2,000 men on a raid, but many of these would have been farmers and peasants.[6]

These skirmishes would not have impressed a Roman general, which was Josephus' aim when writing the Jewish War. His imperial patrons were the former generals Vespasian and Titus. Roman generals were formally appointed by the emperor and commanded large, highly-disciplined, well-organized, and well-trained forces. Josephus presented himself as the Jewish equivalent of such a general.

In the Jewish War, Josephus says the assembly in Jerusalem appointed him as military commander in Galilee. But it strains belief that the rebels would have chosen a man without prior military experience or revolutionary credentials to lead their forces in such a vital region. In the Life, we get a very different account. Josephus was sent to Galilee by the Jewish establishment as part of a three-man commission. Josephus says their mission was to persuade the Galileans to surrender their arms, but this is not credible. The commission seem to have been appointed primarily as tax collectors so that the establishment Jews, who had lost control of the temple and its treasury, could use the taxes to buy arms in Jerusalem. Certainly, the other two members returned to Jerusalem with the tax collection. Josephus claims that they had collected the money to enrich themselves, but this makes no sense and is typical of his accusations against others.[7]

With the departure of his two colleagues, Josephus, the opportunist, was free from constraint. As de-facto administrator of Galilee, he began to assemble a force of mercenaries under his command: in the Life, he claims that he recruited these men to stop them from fighting the Romans![8] At some point, his military command must have been confirmed by the assembly in Jerusalem as an acknowledgment of the facts on the ground.

As for John of Gischala, he is a very different man in the Life from the upstart bandit war-lord of the Jewish War. We learn that John was already well established as a leader in Galilee before Josephus even arrived on the scene. He had heroically retaken and then rebuilt his hometown of Gischala, which had been destroyed in ethnic violence at the beginning of the war.[9] And Josephus lets drop the surprising information that John was an intimate friend of the revered Simon, son of the famous Pharisee Gamaliel.[10] So John was no small-town bandit but a well-educated individual with connections at the very highest levels of the Jerusalem establishment.

When John of Gischala appealed to Jerusalem to have Josephus recalled, he was successful. A committee was sent to Galilee at the head of an armed force to take Josephus back under guard to Jerusalem. If he resisted, he was to be killed.[11] The same establishment priests who had sent Josephus to Galilee were now very unhappy with him. Josephus represents this attempted recall as being due to envy at his success, the scheming of John, and the corruption of the priests who were ever ready to take bribes. But in reality, it seems that Josephus was accused of being a corrupt individual who had enriched himself at the expense of the rebellion.

Josephus the thief

The casual reader of Josephus' works will find the accusation that Josephus was a thief surprising. For he continually tells us that he is not corrupt. In the Life, he gives an eloquent eulogy on his upright character. But then it is characteristic of dishonest people that they tend to protest their integrity too much. Honest people do not brag about their honesty. Deceitful people also project their own dishonesty onto those around them—particularly their rivals and enemies. And this is something that Josephus does all the time. If we take Josephus at face value, he was a shining moral example in a sea of corruption.

Josephus talks a lot about money in his account of his time in Galilee. He starts with two scams by his arch-enemy, John of Gischala. Josephus accuses John of appropriating money intended for rebuilding the wall of Gischala and making large profits by cornering the olive oil trade with the Jews in Caesarea Philippi (not to be confused with the Caesarea on the coast). But if we compare his two accounts carefully, we can see that Josephus was involved in both of these scams.[12]

The money for the wall came from selling grain stolen from the Romans, something that Josephus keeps very quiet about in the Jewish War. Who gave John permission for this sale? In the Jewish War, Josephus says he gave John this permission. In the Life, he says he perceived John's intention of misusing the funds and refused his permission, but his two colleagues, Joazar and Judas overruled him because they had taken bribes from John. This is unbelievable as elsewhere Josephus describes the two as "men of excellent character."[13]

As for the olive oil, John could buy it in Galilee and sell it for ten times the price in Caesarea Philippi because he had been granted a monopoly on the trade. Who gave him this monopoly? —Josephus. Once again, his excuses are unbelievable. He claims in the Life that he only agreed to this under duress while staying with John in Gischala: "My permission I gave reluctantly from fear of being stoned by the mob."[14] If so, then why did he not rescind the monopoly as soon as he left Gischala? In reality, John and Josephus seem to have been in cohorts together at this early stage. Josephus admits that he was initially delighted by John's "energy."[15] Presumably, they fell out when Josephus did not get his full cut of the proceeds.

Two other situations were more profitable for Josephus. When the commission of the three priests arrived in Galilee, they commanded that Agrippa's palace at Tiberias be burnt down. Josephus claims the Jerusalem authorities ordered this for religious reasons. The townspeople objected, and the order was not immediately carried out. In the event, Josephus and his colleagues were preempted by Jesus, son of Sapphias. Josephus is as dismissive of Jesus as he is of John, describing him as a rabble-rouser and the leader of sailors and the poorer citizens. In reality, Jesus was the chief civil authority in the town—Josephus calls him elsewhere the "chief magistrate."[16] While Josephus was absent, Jesus ordered Agrippa's palace to be burnt and took the opportunity to massacre all the non-Jewish residents of the town.[17]

Josephus claims that Jesus was motivated by greed at the sight of the gold roof. But this is surely not the case: he comes over as a religious fanatic who was utterly committed to the revolution. He would twice accuse Josephus of financial crimes; on both occasions Josephus would come within a hair's breadth of execution. For his part, Josephus was outraged by the loss of life in Tiberius and even more so at the loss of furniture: "I...devoted my energies to recovering from the plunderers as much as I could of the palace furniture, namely some candelabra of Corinthian make, royal tables, and a large sum of uncoined silver."[18]

The fate of this stash of expensive goods and silver was to form one of the accusations against Josephus. He would claim that he put it aside for King Agrippa by appointing some principal citizens to safeguard the treasure "with injunctions to deliver it to none but myself."[19] It is wildly implausible that Josephus ever intended to return the treasure to the king.

Even more profitable than the palace's treasures was the booty from a daring guerrilla raid carried out by young partisans from the village of Dabaritta. They had ambushed the wife of Ptolemy, the steward of Agrippa (we are not told her name). She was traveling in "great state" with an escort of cavalry from Agrippa's territory to Roman-controlled territory. The fighters attacked the cavalcade, and the woman and her guard were obliged to flee, leaving behind the baggage mules. The baggage was brought to Josephus and found to contain rich apparel and a substantial amount of money; a large pile of silver and five to six hundred pieces of gold. Josephus took control of this treasure which would soon have the whole of Galilee in an uproar.[20]

Josephus gives two conflicting accounts of what happened to the money. In the Jewish War, he says that he reproved the fighters of Dabaritta for violence against Agrippa's servants and put the money into the care of Annaeus, a citizen of Tarichaeae, for eventual restoration to its owners. In the Life, he says that he told the fighters that he was keeping the money back to repair the walls of Jerusalem, which he admits was a lie. Instead, he gave the money to two friends of Agrippa, Dassion and Jannaeus[21], with instructions to send it immediately to the king. He swore them to silence and even threatened them with death if they told anyone. Doubtless, this was intended to explain why no one had heard this story before. Agrippa could not contradict Josephus by pointing out that he had never received the money because he was dead by this time.[22]

The idea that Josephus would have contemplated returning treasure and money to the enemy is absurd. He had incited the cities that belonged to Agrippa in Galilee to revolt against the king and the Romans. He ordered Agrippa's palace to be burnt down. And he fought Agrippa's soldiers on the field of battle. When the city of Tiberias attempted to go back to the king, Josephus played a clever trick to prevent them. Josephus would never have given the enemy the financial resources to wage war against himself.

Josephus claims that the Jewish law would not allow him to keep another's property even if it belonged to an enemy: "If you encounter your enemy's ox or his donkey going astray, you shall bring it back to him."[23] But no other Jew interpreted this law as applying in war. And Josephus seems to have forgotten his scruples when he boasts of how he led a raid to steal a large quantity of grain belonging to Queen Berenice.[24]

The people of Galilee were outraged at Josephus' attempt to appropriate the money. He says that a crowd of 100,000 (an obvious exaggeration) gathered in the hippodrome at Tarichaeae in anger. The chief prosecutor was Jesus, son of Sapphias. Holding a copy of the Torah in his hand, he accused Josephus of violating the law, which can only be a reference to the commandment "you shall not steal."[25]

The assembly appointed Jesus to take armed men to Josephus' house and kill him. Josephus was asleep until woken by his guard, who urged him to commit suicide before the crowd could get hold of him. But suicide was not Josephus' way. He sneaked out of the house and went by a back route to the hippodrome. To the crowd's surprise, he entered dressed in black with his sword hanging from his neck and flung himself on the ground as a remorseful sinner. The tears streamed down his face, and the crowd was moved to allow Josephus to speak. That was always a fatal mistake.[26]

He started by admitting his guilt but said he only wanted the money out of love and care for the people of Tarichaeae so he could rebuild their fortifications. This pleased one-half of the audience, but to win over the others, he had to extend his promise to cover the walls of Tiberias. Josephus boasts of how he turned the foolish people in his favor with these lies.[27]

Not everyone was convinced, and a group of 600 men later came to his house to set it on fire. Josephus told them he would give back the money if they sent in a delegation. The people waited outside while they thought a negotiation was in progress, but Josephus was actually having the men severely flogged so that the flesh fell away from their backs in strips. One man had his hand cut off and hung around his neck. They were sent back to the shocked crowd, who fearfully melted away.[28]

Josephus won on this occasion, but John of Gischala did not give up. He sent a delegation to Jerusalem led by his brother Simon to get Josephus replaced. Through Simon, son of Gamaliel, an approach was made to the high-priests Ananus and Jesus, son of Gamalas, "to clip my sprouting wings and not allow me to mount to the pinnacle of fame," as Josephus puts it. Ananus was persuaded to order his recall. As ever, Josephus attributes this to corruption—his opponents bribed Ananus. Yet in the Jewish War, Josephus said that Ananus was "of the highest integrity" and "always put the public welfare above his own interest."[29]

The priests sent four envoys to Galilee under the leadership of a Pharisee called Jonathan, accompanied by 1,000 soldiers. Their instructions were to send Josephus back to Jerusalem, and if he offered any resistance, they were to execute him. When Josephus heard about the approaching delegation, he decided at first to go with them peacefully despite the appeals of the Galilean people who "were overcome with grief and besought me with tears not to abandon them." But he had a dream telling him to stay and gave in to the popular demands out of "compassion" for the people.[30]

In the Life, Josephus gives a very long account of the cat and mouse game that he played to evade the delegation. There are some hints of the accusations against him; he was not a good general and lived in luxury while the burden of the war fell on the common people.[31] Despite Josephus's clever plans, he did eventually fall into the hands of Jonathan's delegation.

At this point of crisis, Jesus, son of Sapphias, interrogated Josephus with the army of John of Gischala fast approaching. Intriguingly, the questions asked by Jesus are all about the misappropriation of funds. What happened to the furniture and silver from the palace? And what happened to twenty pieces of gold from the sale of bullion? Jonathan, presiding, came to a hurried judgment, found Josephus guilty, and condemned him to death. Josephus says that the charge was being a "despot" and making "deceitful speeches", but the real accusation was surely corruption. In this dire extremity, Josephus' supporters came to his aid and helped him escape by boat across the lake with just minutes to spare before John's army arrived.[32]

Ultimately, Josephus outmaneuvered his opponents. He had sent his own embassy to Jerusalem, and they aroused enough popular indignation to get the order for his recall rescinded. Frustrated by this result, two of the delegation, Jonathan and Ananias, set out for Jerusalem to freshly accuse Josephus of maladministration and get the decision reversed. But they were both captured by Josephus' forces. He was also able to trick the other two delegates into his hands. He then packed all four of them off to Jerusalem for good.[33]

Josephus the trickster

Josephus was a supremely confident trickster. Like Odysseus, he was a "resourceful" man of many schemes and stratagems. Take an example. The citizens of Tiberius were unenthusiastic revolutionaries. At one point, they sent to Agrippa for help, and thinking that the Roman forces were nearby, declared for the king and closed their gates against the rebels. Josephus was just along the lake at Tarichaeae but without an army. He improvised by sending out an armada of empty boats onto the lake with one steersman in each. He instructed these boats to stay well out from the city, packing his own boat with the few soldiers he could muster and approaching close to Tiberius to negotiate. The Tiberians were fooled into thinking that Josephus had an enormous force on the lake. He accepted their surrender and took hostages of their leading men in batches until the entire council was in captivity. In this way, Josephus won the victory with just a handful of soldiers.[34]

Josephus could trick a man into cutting off his own hand. He did just this in the aftermath of his Tiberius stratagem. It was necessary to punish the ringleader who had persuaded the town to go back to Agrippa, a young man called Cleitus. With no more than his few soldiers, Josephus confronted the much larger crowd of Tiberians. He ordered one of his soldiers to go into the crowd and sever Cleitus' hand, but the man was too fearful to carry out the order. So Josephus called out to Cleitus and told him he would have both his hands cut off. Cleitus begged for mercy, and Josephus pretended to be moved by his distraught pleas. He said that if Cleitus severed one of his hands, he would spare the other. Cleitus drew his sword and hacked off his left hand.[35]

This may seem brutal, but any other general would have executed Cleitus along with many others. Josephus was an egotistical and deceitful conman, but he had one redeeming virtue; he was remarkably reluctant to kill people. The Romans would never have allowed a city like Tiberius to escape without reprisals. Their approach was to sack conquered cities and massacre most of the population, often using crucifixion. As for the Jews, many thousands were slaughtered in their factional conflicts. Yet, as far as we know, Josephus never ordered the death of a single person outside the heat of battle.

Vespasian comes to Galilee

Josephus had little contact with the Romans until Vespasian came to Judea. He spent most of his time in petty squabbles against other rebels in Galilee with the occasional action against the troops of King Agrippa. Everything would now change. Vespasian was given his commission by Nero in Greece. He immediately sent Titus to Alexandria to fetch the Fifteenth legion while he headed to Antioch to join forces with King Agrippa.[36]

Even without Vespasian, there were ominous signs for the Jews that their victory would be short-lived. After the defeat of Cestius, their next target was the fortified town of Ascalon and its Roman garrison, about sixty miles from Jerusalem. The Jews greatly outnumbered the defenders, and elated by the prospect of victory, they attacked with the same reckless courage they had shown earlier. But this time the outcome was very different. The Romans were fighting on their ideal ground on the plain in front of the city. The legionnaires kept their discipline and inflicted two massive defeats on the Jews, who lost 18,000 killed according to Josephus.[37]

While at Antioch, Vespasian had dispatched a garrison to the friendly city of Sepphoris. Josephus did not want this Roman force in his midst and immediately attacked the town. But his men proved no match for Roman soldiers, and he was forced to withdraw. The inhabitants of the country around Sepphoris paid the price as the garrison conducted a brutal campaign of reprisals.[38]

Meanwhile, Vespasian had met up with Titus at Ptolemais. He had three whole legions under his command, the fifth, tenth and fifteenth, along with additional cohorts and auxiliary cavalry, bowmen, and foot-soldiers from the three client kings, Antiochus, Agrippa, and Soaemus. Josephus gives the total size of Vespasian's army at 60,000. Vespasian now marched this army into Galilee. At their approach, Josephus' army ran away.[39]

Josephus himself fled to Tiberius and wrote to Jerusalem, begging them to make peace. He knew the Jews had no chance against such a well-organized and trained force. The Jews of Jerusalem, too busy with their internal fighting, paid no attention.[40]

Vespasian's first target was the town of Gabara which was almost undefended. It was easily taken, and the whole male population was slaughtered except for small children. Vespasian would have seen the deaths as regrettable but tactically necessary. The example of Gabara caused panic throughout Galilee. Most other places would now surrender without a fight.[41]

Jotapata: the siege

Vespasian next moved on to Jotapata, a well-fortified town in the mountains where many of the rebels had taken refuge. The chief obstacle was the town's natural defenses, surrounded as it was on three sides by deep ravines. It was only approachable on the fourth side, which abutted the mountain slope, and Josephus had made this side more defendable by extending the town fortifications.[42]

The existing road to Jotapata was an unsuitable rough mountain track which the Romans rebuilt to their high standards in just four days. On the fifth day, Josephus slipped into Jotapata. He claims in the Jewish War that when the Romans heard the news, they were delighted and immediately sealed off the town. With his usual lack of modesty and talent for exaggeration, he adds: "if Josephus could be secured, then all Judea would be captured." The sight of the great Roman force taking up positions around the town, with Vespasian conspicuously camped on the slope high above, filled the townspeople with dread. As Romans closed in to surround them, the Jews sortied out of the gates and attacked. It should have been an unequal match, but the Jews were fighting for their lives, their families, and their God. They battled the Romans before the walls for five days until their manpower and energy were sapped, and they had to withdraw back into the city.[43]

All that stood between the Romans and victory now were the walls. They began tackling this problem by building a platform of earth and wood to reach the top of the wall on the side of the slope. A framework of hurdles supported by wooden uprights protected the soldiers at work on the platform. They also battered the city with missiles from 160 siege engines that hurled javelins, stones, and great rocks. The Roman archers kept up a continual onslaught of arrows over the walls. The Jews did what they could to interrupt the work; they threw rocks down from above and mounted frequent sorties to attack the workers and tear down their structures. The platform, however, got ever higher and was soon nearing the top of the wall.[44]

The town would fall if the platform reached its objective, but Josephus came up with an audacious plan—they would build the wall higher. He protected his workmen with a framework of stretched animal skins. This framework stopped the arrows and smaller missiles completely. When a large rock hit it, it would collapse, but the structure would absorb most of the projectile's kinetic energy. Now shielded, the men were able to build the wall, complete with towers, another 20 cubits higher. Encouraged by this feat, the Jewish defenders increased their guerrilla attacks on the Roman platform, burning and destroying as fast as the Romans could build.[45]

Vespasian was patient and did not want to waste too many of his soldiers on the siege of one town. He hoped that the blockade would have its effect in starving the people to surrender. The city had plenty of grain but lacked a good water supply.[46]

For all his bravado, it was now clear to Josephus that the town would fall. So he planned his escape. But when he disclosed his intention to sneak through the Roman lines, the chief citizens were outraged. They had a strange idea that the commander should stay with the sinking ship and not leap overboard: "It would be unforgivable for him to run away from his enemies and abandon his friends." Josephus "concealed his anxiety for his own safety" and told them he was leaving for their sakes. If he was free, he could organize a relief force. This did not fool the people as Josephus could not possibly assemble a force large enough to tackle Vespasian's army. They insisted that he stay, and Josephus had to pretend to agree, or "he would be watched."[47]

With his escape foiled, Josephus turned his considerable talents and energies to the last-ditch defense of the town. Vespasian had brought another siege engine into play; a great tree trunk suspended from beams with the iron head of a ram attached to one end. This "battering ram" was aimed against the city wall. At the first strike, the whole wall shook as if by an earthquake, and the people cried out, thinking the end was upon them. The hastily constructed walls would not hold for long. The battering ram had to be stopped. Josephus came up with a plan to lower straw sacks on ropes to blunt the force of the impact, but the Romans countered with blades on long poles to cut the ropes.[48]

At this extremity, the Jews made a heroic attack on the ram with fire. They charged out of the gates and set everything in reach ablaze. Much of the equipment was constructed of wood and bitumen and burnt fiercely. One hero even captured the ram's head: he was shot through with arrows but died in a moment of glory. The Romans had to look on as their work went up in flames, but this was nothing but a minor setback. Another ram's head was brought forward, and the siege engine rebuilt. Soon it was pounding the weak walls again.[49]

By nightfall, the fires lit by the Jewish attack were still raging. Their light dazzled the defenders on the wall who could see nothing of the Romans beyond. They would hear but not see the approaching missiles as they whizzed through the air. A man's head would suddenly be carried off by a rock. In the town, the people would hear the repeated thud of bodies falling from the wall. The night air was full of the wailing of women and the groans of dying men. A great heap of corpses was piled at the foot of the battlements.[50]

In the hours before daybreak, part of the wall gave way and collapsed into a large pile of rubble. Vespasian allowed his men a brief rest before starting the assault at dawn. A heavy barrage of arrows was intended to kill the defenders in the area of the breach. Ladders would be raised to the intact walls to create a distraction. Then gangplanks and ramps would be lowered onto the rubble pile to enable the heavy infantry to begin the real assault followed by the cavalry.[51]

Josephus had anticipated these plans. He positioned his best fighters around the breach, shielding them against the barrage. The old and infirm he sent to defend the walls. The Romans fired their arrows, and the ramps were put in place under their cover. The Roman legionnaires began to march up the ramps in "tortoise" formation. Heavily armored, their inter-locked shields protected them front, sides, and overhead. Taking step after step forward, they stabbed between their shields with spears and swords.[52]

It was an invincible remorseless advance—or so the Romans believed. But Josephus had devised a tactic against the tortoise. He arranged for boiling oil to be poured down on the Romans from the walls above. The oil flowed over and between the shields, running over the men, getting down their necks and backs, and burning their flesh. Fatty oil retained its heat much more than water and continued to burn as it flowed beneath their armor. The tortoise fell apart as the screaming men grappled with their armor, trying to get it off, and fled in agony. It was the first use in recorded history of pouring boiling oil on attackers from walls, a tactic that would become popular in medieval times.[53]

When the Jews ran out of oil, they tried another ruse. They poured a liquid made from a herb called fenugreek over the ramps. It was super-slippery, and the Roman infantry lost their footing as they marched up the ramps. The heavily armored men slid and slithered off onto the rubble, where the agile partisans would charge down to dispatch them. The Romans' well-planned assault had descended into chaos. They could make no headway up the ramps. The calvary watched helplessly, unable to get over the rubble. Vespasian abandoned the attack at nightfall.[54]

The Romans now concentrated on building the platforms higher and encasing them in iron, making them fire-proof. They used towers on the platforms to redouble the barrage of the city. Eventually, the tower reached the height of the wall. But that very night, a Jewish deserter had given Vespasian some vital intelligence. The Jews were so short of manpower, and their remaining men so tired, that the sentries would fall asleep in the hours before dawn.[55]

It might be a trick, but it was worth an attempt. Titus personally led a small force of Romans to quietly climb the rubble in the early morning hours. They saw that the guards were indeed asleep and dispatched them silently. Others followed over the breach, and before the Jews knew what was happening, the town was taken, and the massacre began. The Jewish fighters could not mount a defense, and the Romans spared no one. They killed everyone in the open and then hunted out the hiding places. Josephus writes that so one-sided was the final victory that the Romans only suffered a single casualty.[56]

Jotapata: the cave

Two days later, the town of Jotapata was a smoking, stinking holocaust. The Romans had pulled down the walls and buildings and set fire to whatever would burn. Everywhere lay the bodies of the inhabitants. The air was full of the stench of decomposition, the ruins alive with flies. The surviving Jews had taken refuge in the sewers, caves, and cisterns under the city. The Romans hunted them out one by one. Some of the women and infants had been allowed to live. Josephus says that 1,200 were taken as slaves. The other 40,000 Jews in the town had been slaughtered.[57]

Where was Josephus? He had taken refuge in a large cave under the city. Josephus says that he had jumped into a pit and found the cave by accident. This is frankly unbelievable. The cavern was well prepared and provisioned for many days. The entrance was carefully disguised so that it was invisible from above. Josephus says he found "forty people of importance" already in the cave. It was a hiding place for the elite. Somewhere they could sit out the destruction and wait for the Romans to leave.[58]

Josephus must have known about the cave and fled to it straight away. The others would not have been keen to see him. The Romans were looking for Josephus, dead or alive, and would continue looking until they found him. Escape from the cave was impossible: each night, they looked out, but the Roman sentries remained in place. On the third day, a woman left the cave and attempted to slip out of the town, but she was captured and gave the secret away. Vespasian sent two tribunes to offer Josephus safe conduct and persuade him to come out. But Josephus feared that it was a trick to capture him alive and torture him. Vespasian then sent another tribune, Nicanor, an old friend of Josephus. We do not know how Josephus became friendly with a tribune in Vespasian's army—possibly they met in Rome, or perhaps Nicanor was on the staff of Agrippa in Jerusalem. Nicanor "enlarged on the habitual kindness of the Romans to the vanquished." Given the evidence of slaughter all around, this may seem darkly ironic. However, a code of gallantry applied between the elite, although not to the lower orders or the foreign. Evidently, the Roman officers already saw Josephus as "one of them." This view was not shared by the ordinary soldiers who wanted to build a fire at the cave entrance and kill everyone inside. Nicanor managed to hold them off.[59]

Josephus began to waver. He attributed this not to cowardice but to God. The meaning of certain dreams and prophecies suddenly became clear to him. God wanted him to live, and Josephus had to bow to the divine will. He started to climb out of the cave, but the others pulled him back.[60]

His fellow Jews behaved very unreasonably, drawing their swords and crowding around him. They pushed and shoved him, reminding him how many people had given up their lives due to his persuasion and his orders. They called him a fool for ever believing the Romans' false promises. Then they held out a sword for him—he had a choice. Use it on himself and die bravely as their commander, or they would use it on him, and he would die as a traitor.[61]

What happened at this moment of crisis? According to the Jewish War, Josephus gave a long, elegant philosophical speech on how it would be impious to commit suicide and reject life if God chose to offer it to them. Such unrealistic speeches were a literary convention in histories of the time. Josephus' speech rather misses the point because only he had been offered the chance to live. He passes over the fate of the others in silence.

But, in any case, the speech did no good. His compatriots surrounded him, their weapons drawn and pressed against his throat.[62]

Josephus says that "in this predicament, his resourcefulness did not forsake him." He concocted a plan. While appearing to accept the inevitability of mass suicide, he took control of the situation and set the rules. They would each draw lots. Whoever drew the first lot would be the first victim, and the man pulling the second lot would kill him quickly with the sword. The person drawing the third lot would then kill the second and so on. The last man alive would kill himself.[63]

Josephus said he had placed his trust in divine protection. If so, then divine protection came good. One by one, the men were killed, but not Josephus. He was left with just one other man, "whether through divine providence or just luck." The odds were now even, one to one. He suggested they both surrender and live, and the other man agreed.[64]

Readers down the ages have concluded that Josephus somehow fixed the lots. The episode is so disreputable that it is amazing Josephus did not keep quiet about it. The ancient world admired courage, and for the Romans suicide in defeat was a noble death. But Josephus never could resist boasting of his tricks: he had got a whole cave of people intent on his death to kill each other, leaving him alive.

Josephus before Vespasian

Josephus was taken from the cave to Vespasian. The Romans crowded around and pressed forward to get a glimpse of the enemy who had caused them so much trouble. Josephus says that while many called out for his execution, others felt their anger melt away at the sight of him. Titus, in particular, was impressed by his "courageous bearing" and felt "pity for his youth." They were actually a similar age, Josephus around thirty and Titus twenty-seven.[65] Josephus had begun already to exert a fascination over Titus, which would only grow. Josephus claims that Titus influenced his father to spare his life, but Vespasian intended to send him to Nero for judgment.[66] This would have been the real motivation for taking Josephus alive. The capture of the Jewish general would show the emperor that Vespasian was making good progress with the war. And it would allow Nero to execute a prominent rebel in public, visible proof that the Jewish rebellion was being brought under control.

Josephus must have been expecting something like this. Once he was sent to Nero, his fate would be sealed. He must prevent that at all costs. So he put into action the plan that had come to him in the cave. Josephus requested a private audience with Vespasian and Titus to impart important information. Vespasian asked everyone to withdraw except for Titus and two others. They must have been expecting some piece of intelligence about the rebellion, but Josephus gave them a message from God. He told Vespasian not to send him to Nero, for he would not be emperor for much longer. God had chosen Vespasian to rule the earth. Such was the implication of the Jewish prophecies and Josephus' own dreams. He had chosen life rather than an honorable death to be the messenger who told Vespasian that he was the true Caesar and emperor.

It was a brilliant, reckless move. Vespasian could not possibly send Josephus to Nero now. If Josephus repeated his prophecy in front of the emperor, the outcome was inevitable. A fast boat would be sent from Rome with orders for Vespasian and Titus to turn their swords on themselves. The centurions sent with the boat would do the deed for them if they refused. What Josephus had just said was high treason, the private meeting evidence of complicity. Vespasian's safest option would have been to have Josephus killed immediately and swear everyone else to silence.

Josephus was gambling that he had read Vespasian's political situation correctly. He judged that the general would secretly harbor imperial ambitions, if only as a protection against a mentally unstable emperor. It was a desperate throw of the dice—life or death—but Josephus won again. Whether or not Vespasian believed in prophecies, the people did. An ancient Jewish prophecy interpreted by a Jewish priest would carry credibility. Particularly as that priest was an enemy general who had fought Vespasian. The prediction would provide the legitimacy otherwise lacking in Vespasian's modest family background. Josephus had made himself into a high-ranking card. But it was a dangerous card, a trump to be played if the game went the right way or discarded if not. Vespasian told the others that Josephus had spoken nonsense to save his own life. But actions speak louder than words. He kept Josephus close by him, guarded carefully but treated well. Josephus would be allowed to live—for now.[67]

10

Luke and the "we" passages

The "we" passages

The "we" passages are one of the enduring mysteries of Acts. Although Acts is written generally in the third person, it switches to the first-person plural—to "we"—every now and then. The only obvious pattern is that the "we" passages concern the travels of Paul and often involve a sea journey. Many theories have evolved to explain the "we" passages. The most significant of these are:

1. The "we" passages demonstrate that the author of Luke and Acts was a companion of Paul. They indicate where the author was directly involved in events.

2. The "we" passages show where Acts draws upon a traveler's log of sea journeys written by a companion of Paul.

3. The "we" passages are a sophisticated forgery by the author of Luke who wrote much later than the time of Paul. They were intended to create a false impression that the author was an eyewitness of events.

To see which, if any, of these theories fits the evidence, we will start with an overview of the "we" passages. They commence when Paul has a vision of a man in Macedonia:

> Now when he had seen the vision, we immediately sought to leave for Macedonia, concluding that God had called us to preach the gospel to them. Having sailed from Troas, we made straight to Samothrace and the following day to Neapolis. From there to Philippi, the leading colonia city of that district of Macedonia. We stayed in the city some days. (Acts 16:10-12)

Here we have two typical features of the passages; (i) the "we" is introduced abruptly without explanation; and (ii) there is an almost day-by-day itinerary of a sea journey. At Philippi, Paul and his companions meet Lydia and Paul drives the demon out of the slave girl. At this point, the "we" ends, and the narrative continues in the third person. The casting out of the demon has caused a loss of revenue for the slave girl's owners, and Paul and Silas find themselves in prison and beaten with rods.

The "we" only reappears four chapters later. Much happens in the meantime. Paul travels around Greece and gives a lecture to the philosophers of Athens. He lives in Corinth for a year and a half before leaving with Aquila and Priscilla for Syria. After traveling to Antioch via Ephesus, he tours Galatia and Phrygia. Returning to Ephesus, Paul teaches for two years and three months before making another journey:

> Now after these things were fulfilled, Paul resolved in the Spirit
> to pass through Macedonia and Achaia and go to Jerusalem,
> having said: "After I have been there, I must see Rome as well."
> (Acts 19:21)

Paul's proposed journey is illogical; Macedonia and Achaia (Greece) are in the opposite direction to Jerusalem. It would be much shorter to visit Jerusalem first and then go to Rome via Macedonia and Achaia. The real reason for this strange route is revealed in Paul's letters: he is arranging a collection for the Christians in Jerusalem. In 1 Corinthians 16:1-8, Paul, writing from Ephesus, tells the Corinthians he will visit Macedonia and Corinth to arrange this collection. Messengers will take the money to Jerusalem, and Paul hopes to accompany them. By the time he writes his letter to the Romans, he is ready to leave Corinth with the money:

> Now, however, I am on my way to Jerusalem ministering to the
> saints. For Macedonia and Achaia were pleased to make a cer-
> tain contribution for the poor among the saints in Jerusalem.
> (Romans 15:25-26)

After he has completed this service, he intends to visit Rome on his way to Spain. The situation then is much as described in Acts. The visit to Spain is omitted, which is understandable as Paul never got there. What seems less explicable is that Acts never mentions the collection, which was the sole purpose of Paul's long journey. In Acts, Paul does not actually leave from Corinth but goes to Macedonia because of a plot against him by "the Jews."[1] And here, after Acts gives a list of Paul's traveling companions, the "we" passages start again:

> But these, having gone ahead, waited for us in Troas. We then sailed away after the days of the unleavened bread from Philippi, and within five days, we came to them at Troas, where we stayed seven days. (Acts 20:5-6)

Is it just coincidence that the "we" passages recommence in the exact place, Philippi, that they left off? Something like seven years has elapsed between them stopping and starting again. The fact that they start again at Philippi is the clue that the "we" passages were originally a continuous narrative that has been incorporated into Acts with the addition of new material, including these seven years.

At Troas, Paul raises a boy from the dead. The story starts as a "we" passage:

> In the first day of the week, having come together to break bread, Paul, who was ready to depart the next day, talked to them and continued speaking until midnight. Now there were many lamps in the upper room where we were assembled. (Acts 20:7-8)

But Acts then shifts to the third person with the account of the miracle:

> A certain young man named Eutychus sitting by the window was overpowered by deep sleep as Paul talked on longer. And having been overpowered by sleep, he fell down from the third story and was picked up dead. Paul, however, descended, threw himself on the young man, and embraced him. "Do not be alarmed!" he said. "For there is life in him!" Then having gone back upstairs, he broke bread, and having eaten and talked until daybreak, he departed. And they brought the boy away alive and were greatly comforted. (Acts 20:9-12)

There is much that is strange here. After Eutychus falls out the window, Paul rushes down and announces that the boy is alive. They all then go back to the room and happily continue their meeting until daybreak, eating and talking while Eutychus lies as if dead on the ground below. He only revives after Paul has left. The last line of the "we" passage states that there were many lamps in the room. What came next in the original "we" source would have been replaced by the miraculous resurrection of Eutychus, which mirrors Peter's resurrection of Dorcas.

The "we" narration resumes with a travelogue: they go by ship to Assos to pick up Paul, who has taken the land route. Their boat then visits Mytilene, Chios, Samos, and Miletus but bypasses Ephesus:

Paul had decided to sail by Ephesus so as not to spend time in
the province of Asia because he hastened to be in Jerusalem, if
possible, by the day of Pentecost. (Acts 20:16)

Here is a little detail that tells us volumes about the author's perspective. They assume that Paul could decide whether or not the ship calls at
Ephesus, even though he is just a passenger. Someone like Domitilla would
have the power to direct a ship's movements, but not an ordinary traveler.

The "we" is absent from Paul's speech to the elders of Ephesus which
does not sound like the other "we" passages. The "we" appears again as
they leave the elders, and there is a detailed list of waypoints; the isle of
Cos, the city of Rhodes, and on to Patara, where they change to a ship
bound for Phoenicia. Passing by Cyprus, they come to Tyre, where the boat
unloads. The disciples at Tyre are filled with the spirit and warn Paul not
to go to Jerusalem, but they continue the journey. From Tyre, they go by
ship to Ptolemais, and then on to Caesarea, where they stay at the home
of Philip, one of the seven.[2]

While at Caesarea, a prophet named Agabus comes down from Judea to
warn Paul not to go to Jerusalem, as he will be bound and handed over to
gentiles. But Paul simply replies, "the Lord's will be done."[3]. So they travel
on to Jerusalem and meet with the leadership of the church:

On the following day, Paul went in with us to see James, and all
the elders were present. (Acts 21:18)

At this point, the "we" passages end again for several chapters. Paul is
seized by a Jewish crowd at the temple and almost killed. He is taken into
Roman custody but freed to face a trial before the Sanhedrin, who are so
divided about his case that a riot ensues. The Romans take him back into
custody and transfer him with a massive armed guard to Caesarea. He
spends years in prison with hearings before Felix, Festus, King Agrippa,
and Berenice. They finally agree that Paul could have been freed had he
not appealed as a Roman citizen to the emperor. But now, he must be sent
for judgment to Rome.

The "we" passages recommence with the journey to Rome, culminating
in an exciting shipwreck. We are granted a privileged viewpoint, for it just
so happens that the narrator is one of two Christians who accompany Paul
on the ship, the other being Aristarchus who is mentioned in Philemon.[4]
Such privileged viewpoints are typical of fiction—think of Dr. Watson
narrating the Sherlock Holmes adventures.

A centurion of the cohort of Augustus named Julius takes custody of
Paul for the journey to Rome. Domitilla would have been familiar with

the Augustan cohorts which belonged to the emperor. They board an Adramyttium ship traveling north along the coast of the Roman province of Asia. There is a daily account of waypoints until they have passed Cyprus and come to Myra in Lycia, where they change to an Alexandrian ship bound for Rome, one of the many grain ships that plied the Mediterranean from Alexandria to Rome and back again. The Alexandrian ship had traveled due north to the coast of modern-day Turkey and would now turn west. But the season was dangerously advanced: all navigating ceased by November, for the seas were too hazardous for ancient vessels in the winter months.[5]

Progress was slow, for they were facing a contrary wind. Eventually, they reached the isle of Crete and came to a harbor called Fair Havens near the town of Lasea. Paul offered his advice that they should overwinter there, but strangely the pilot and the shipowner do not listen to the prisoner. The centurion agrees with the pilot to press on to the larger Cretan port and harbor of Phoenix. Initially, the wind is a gentle southerly, but it turns suddenly into a Northeaster cyclone which blows the ship out to sea.[6] They are driven helplessly before this wind. The account contains some fascinating detail:

> Running to the lee of a small island called Cauda, we were able, with difficulty, to secure the lifeboat. After hoisting it aboard, they used cables to undergird the ship. And fearing that they would run aground on the sandbars of Syrtis, they lowered the gear and were driven along. (Acts 27:16-17)

In the wind shadow of the island they have a brief respite and haul their small skiff onboard. They also tie rope cables around the ship—ancient vessels would be equipped with such cables to strengthen the hull in a storm. Because they fear that the storm would drive them onto the distant sandbanks of north Africa, they lower their "gear," meaning a sea anchor, to slow their progress. These precautions are not enough, and the next day they jettison some of their precious cargo and even the ship's "apparatus," meaning everything movable and non-essential.

Paul gives a speech to the company, reassuring them that an angel had visited him and told him not to be afraid: "You must stand before Caesar." God has also granted Paul the lives of all those who sail with him, but he predicts they will go aground on an island.[7]

On the fourteenth night, the ship is still being driven by the storm when the sailors sense they are approaching land: the depth soundings give twenty fathoms deep and then fifteen. They set anchors, and some of the sailors attempt to escape on the lifeboat, but the soldiers cut it adrift at

Paul's urging. At dawn, they see that they are close to a sandy beach and aim the ship to run onto it. First, they lighten the vessel further by casting the remaining grain into the sea. Then they cut the anchors and set the sail for the beach, but the ship runs aground on a sandbank and begins to break up. The soldiers are going to kill all the prisoners to stop them from escaping, but the centurion, wishing to save Paul's life, prevents them. Those who can swim take to the water, and the others cross the sandbank on planks and wreckage. By this means, all 276 onboard are saved.[8]

The island is Malta, and the natives show them great kindness. Just as everyone is safe, something happens to Paul that seems to show he is cursed by God. While adding wood to the fire, a viper jumps out and fastens to his hand. They all expect him to swell up and die, but he comes to no harm. The islanders now say Paul is a god.

This is the first of two miracles that Paul performs on the island, the other being the cure of the father of Publius, the chief official. They overwinter on the island for three months and then catch another Alexandrian ship with the Dioscuri, the Gemini twins, as the figurehead. The voyage is uneventful. They stop for a few days at the great city of Syracuse in Sicily before crossing to the coast of Italy and reaching their destination, the port of Puteoli in the bay of Naples, where the passengers disembark. Paul stays with Christian brethren for a week, although he is supposed to be a prisoner. They then have a long journey up the Appian Way to Rome. Christians come out from Rome to meet Paul at two waypoints; the Forum of Appius (forty-three miles from Rome) and the Three Taverns (thirty-three miles). Once in Rome, Paul is placed under house arrest with a soldier to guard him.

The "we" passages come to an end here, but it is not quite the end of Acts. Paul continues to teach and preach in Rome under house arrest, where the local Jewish leaders visit him. A few are converted, but most eventually reject him. Paul predicts that God's salvation has come through the gentiles who will listen. Acts ends with Paul staying in his rented house for two years, receiving anyone who visits and proclaiming the kingdom of God.

Did Luke write Luke?

In the second century, Christians took the view that the "we" passages demonstrated that the author of Luke had traveled with Paul. This raised a fascinating possibility that the author might be identified by comparing parallel passages in Acts and Paul's letters. The conclusion was that the gospel and Acts were written by the Luke who Paul mentions three times in his letters:

Colossians: Paul includes Luke (Loukas) among his non-Jewish companions, calling him "the beloved physician."[9] This description seems to fit the author of Luke perfectly. As a doctor, Luke would be an educated man able to write in Greek. And like the author of the gospel, Luke was a gentile Christian.

Philemon: Paul, writing from prison, includes Luke among those who are with him, but not prisoners: "Epaphras, my fellow prisoner in Christ Jesus, sends you greetings, as do Mark, Aristarchus, Demas, and Loukas, my fellow workers."[10] This reflects the position at the end of Acts, where both Luke and Aristarchus have accompanied Paul to Rome.

2 Timothy: Paul, a prisoner apparently in Rome, tells Timothy that "only Loukas is with me."[11] Again this is consistent with Acts, where the author stays with Paul in Rome.

But there was one obvious problem. Luke was with Paul in Rome, so why does he not include Paul's trial and martyrdom in Acts? It seemed to show that Acts must have been written in Rome before the trial, dating it to the early 60s. The Gospel of Luke would have to be even earlier.

From the late second century until the nineteenth century, it was widely accepted that Luke was the author. But under critical scrutiny, the case began to fall apart. The first problem was that 2 Timothy was increasingly regarded as not being written by Paul. Those who wished to defend the letter attributed it to a "pupil" of Paul—the more critical called it a forgery. Disregarding 2 Timothy, the case fell largely on Colossians. But that letter was also coming under suspicion. Most traditionally minded scholars still believe Paul wrote it, but there are multiple indications of forgery. And we should note that there is another potential reference to Luke in Paul's letters that contradicts Colossians:

> Timothy, my fellow worker, greets you; so do Loukios and Jason and Sosipater, my kinsmen. (Roman 16:21)

It would be quite a coincidence for Paul to have two supporters called Loukas and Loukios; most likely, these are two variant spellings of the same name. If so, then Luke was a kinsman of Paul, which does not mean that he was a relative but that he was Jewish. This is a blatant contradiction with the information in Colossians that Luke was a gentile. And if we discredit Colossians, there is no evidence that Luke was a physician. Loukios is also mentioned in Acts:

> Now there were in the church at Antioch prophets and teach-
> ers, Barnabas, Simeon who was called Niger, Loukios of Cyrene,
> Manaen who was brought up with Herod the tetrarch, and Saul
> [Paul]. (Acts 13:1)

Would Luke include himself in a list of people like this without any comment or hint that he is the author? The Acts passage is consistent with Loukas/Loukios being a Jewish companion of Paul from the city of Cyrene in North Africa. So the real Luke does not sound like the gentile author of the third gospel and Acts.

As belief in Luke as the author began to fade, so did conviction in that early date. The author of Luke obviously used Mark, and that gospel was being dated to the early 70s AD, so Acts could not have been written in the 60s AD. Even worse were the connections between Luke/Acts and the works of Josephus. We will see that Acts draws upon the Antiquities of the Jews, which was not published until 93/4 AD, some thirty years after Paul's imprisonment in Rome. Indeed, the Antiquities has been identified as a major influence for the concept of Acts: Antiquities was a history of the Jews, and Acts a history of the Christians. It became apparent that Luke/Acts should be re-dated to the 90s AD, if not even later.

That effectively destroyed the idea that the author of Luke was a companion of Paul. But then, it had already become clear that the author of Acts could not have known Paul. There were too many differences between the Paul of the letters and the Paul of Acts. We have already come across one example: if the author were Luke, he would have been one of the messengers charged with delivering the collection to Jerusalem, so why is this collection never mentioned? Acts ignores the prosaic reality of the collection in favor of the idea that Paul went to Jerusalem by divine command so that he would testify about Jesus as a prisoner in Rome.

This shows a characteristic of Luke/Acts that everything is exaggerated and made more miraculous. For example, Joseph's dream of the angel in Matthew turns into the visitation of a real angel to Mary in Luke: the angel is physically present, and the two converse.

For Paul, "talking in tongues" was to talk apparent gibberish that had a spiritual meaning. He advises the Corinthians not to speak in tongues when they have visitors present, or the guests would think that the Christians are all mad or drunk.[12] That was not good enough for the author of Luke. When the apostles talk in tongues at Pentecost in Acts, all the foreigners gathered can hear them speak in their own language. The author turns a disturbing spiritual practice into a spectacular miracle with thousands of witnesses. The person who wrote the Acts account of Pentecost had certainly not attended a speaking-in-tongues session with Paul.

The same desire to make miracles more spectacular and to include witnesses is present in Acts' story of Paul's conversion. In his letters, Paul talks of a private, spiritual experience of Christ, saying that God chose "to reveal his son in me." Paul told no one about this experience: "I did not consult with flesh and blood," nor did he visit the apostles in Jerusalem. Instead, he went straight to Arabia, where he must have lived for a significant period before he "returned to Damascus." Only after three years did he go to Jerusalem to confer with Cephas.[13]

Acts' famous story of the conversion of Paul on the road to Damascus deviates markedly from Paul's own description. Paul, called Saul at this time, has been sent by the priests to Damascus to bring Christians back in chains to Jerusalem. This is completely unrealistic as the Jewish priests had no religious jurisdiction in Damascus in the province of Syria. As Saul is traveling on the road approaching Damascus, he is struck blind by an unbearable light from heaven and hears the voice of Jesus. The men accompanying him also hear the voice but do not see the light. They take the blind and helpless Saul to Damascus, where he remains in this state for three days. On the third day, he receives a visit from Ananias, a Christian who has come in response to a vision. Ananias places his hands on Saul's head and gives him the Holy Spirit. Saul's sight is restored, and he is baptized. He then spends several days with the brethren in Damascus. He begins preaching about Jesus in the synagogues, but the Jews conspire to kill him. Some of the disciples help him escape by lowering him down the city walls in a basket from a window at night. Saul then goes from Damascus to Jerusalem.[14]

There are blatant inconsistencies with Paul's account that have long worried commentators. Paul says he did not go to Jerusalem until three years had passed, but in Acts, the time is measured in days; the "three days" for which he is blind, "several days" with the brethren, and "many days" in which he preaches in Damascus.

The most significant difference is that Paul stresses that he had no contact with the church after his experience, nor spoke to anyone about it. Instead, he went to Arabia for a period of solitude and contemplation. The Acts account is completely different: he is baptized by Ananias, spends time with the other brethren in Damascus, and does not even go to Arabia.

Why make such drastic changes? The problem was that Paul's own account sounds dangerously like the gnostics who claimed direct spiritual experience of Christ without the intermediation of the proto-orthodox church. So, in Acts, Paul is shown as receiving both baptism and the Holy Spirit from the church. For the author of Luke, the spirit was passed down through a chain of the faithful going back to the disciples and apostles who had known Jesus. This is one of several areas in which the author makes Paul's experience conform to what she thought should have happened at the cost of contradicting his own words.

The long ending and the "we" passages

We have eliminated the first theory, that the author of Luke and Acts was a companion of Paul. But this does not remove the possibility that the "we" passages were an eyewitness account. The author could have written Acts in the 90s but incorporated an earlier travel account into the narrative.

There is also a theory, advanced by Bart Ehrman, that the "we" passages are a sophisticated forgery to present Acts as an eyewitness account. This seems unlikely as there is plentiful evidence that the author of Luke was quite a naive writer. We will show that this forgery theory is wrong because the "we" passages existed as a text before Acts was written. However, they were not an eyewitness account but a literary creation.

The evidence comes from comparing the miracles in the "we" passages with those in the long ending of Mark. This shows that the "we" source was a fictional narrative composed by someone familiar with the long ending. Scholars had missed this connection because the long ending was not supposed to exist when Acts was written, at least not according to the scholarly consensus. The reader is again referred to Appendix B for why the consensus is wrong.

Paul performs three definite miracles in the "we" passages:

1. He casts a demon out of the slave girl in Philippi.
2. He is bitten by a snake on Malta but does not die.
3. He cures the father of Publius on Malta.

The case of the resurrection of Eutychus is less certain. The first-person plural is used before and after the miracle, but there is no "we" within the miracle story itself. If we look at the list above, we find a close correspondence with the predictions made by the resurrected Jesus in the long ending:

> "And these signs will accompany those who believe; in my name they will cast out demons; they will speak in new tongues; they will pick up snakes with their hands, and if they drink anything deadly it will not harm them; they will lay their hands on the sick, and they will be well." (Mark 16:17-18)

Compare these miracles with those in the "we" passages.

Casting out demons
Long ending: "in my name they will cast out demons"
Acts 16:18: "Having been distressed, Paul turned and said to the spirit, 'In the name of Jesus Christ I command you to come out of her!' And it came out of her at that very moment.

Speaking in new tongues
Not present in the "we" passages.

Picking up snakes/drinking poison
Long ending: "they will pick up snakes with their hands, and if they drink anything deadly it will not harm them."
Acts 28:3;5: "Paul gathered a quantity of sticks, and having laid them on the fire, a viper, driven out by the heat, fastened itself to his hand.[...] But having shaken off the creature into the fire, he suffered no ill effects."

Curing the sick
Long ending: "they will lay their hands on the sick, and they will be well."
Acts 28:8-9: "The father of Publius was sick in bed from fever and dysentery. Paul, having entered and prayed, laid his hands on him and healed him. After this had happened, the rest of the sick on the island came and were healed."

The miracles appear in the same order and are described in the same language. There is no drinking of poison, but this is basically the same miracle as being unaffected by the venom of snakes. The miracle of speaking in tongues does not occur in the "we" passages as they exist in Acts, but it may have been in the original. The missing miracle would fit in anywhere after Philippi and before the shipwreck. As the author of Luke interpreted speaking in tongues as speaking in foreign languages, the best place for the miracle would be Jerusalem, where Jews speaking many different languages gathered for feasts. In Acts, the apostles speak in tongues after the descent of the spirit at Pentecost. And there is a clue that this miracle was originally in the "we" source:

> Paul had decided to sail by Ephesus so as not to spend time in the province of Asia, because he hastened to be in Jerusalem, if possible, by the day of Pentecost. (Acts 20:16)

Paul hastens to get to Jerusalem by Pentecost, suggesting that something should happen there on that feast day. But nothing does! Pentecost is not mentioned again. The "we" source may have had Paul and his companions speaking in tongues at Pentecost in Jerusalem. When Acts was written, the miracle was moved near the beginning to be performed by Peter.[15]

The equivalence between the miracles is strong evidence that the long ending was a literary source for the "we" passages. The precise correspondence only emerges when we extract the "we" passages from the rest of Acts, demonstrating that they existed as a stand-alone source. They are not a forgery, but neither are they an eyewitness account.

A woman's perspective

The narrator of the "we" passages accompanies Paul on his journey to Rome. This is odd. Would the Romans really allow men, particularly young men, to accompany prisoners on board a ship? It would greatly increase the risk of escape. A woman would be more acceptable. Prisoners had to be fed and cared for out of their own resources. So a female slave or wife accompanying a male prisoner would have been a familiar sight on Roman ships.

This is one instance of the "we" passages adopting a female viewpoint. In the Roman world, the experiences of the sexes were very different, and this difference inevitably comes out unconsciously when writing. The idea of accompanying a prisoner is more likely to occur to a female author. And the author of the "we" passages looks at the world through a woman's eyes. The first example comes when the travelers arrive at Philippi:

> On the Sabbath day, we went outside the city gate by a river where there was a customary place of prayer. After sitting down, we spoke to the women who had gathered there. (Acts 16:13)

This seems to be a place where Jewish women and their gentile supporters, the God-fearers, gathered for prayer. For some reason, they did not have a synagogue which only required ten Jewish men (women did not count).[16] It would be natural for a God-fearing or Christian woman to meet up with the local women worshipping the Jewish God. But men would seek out the local men and not approach women. The sexes were very much divided in the ancient world, just as in traditional societies today. Women had protective and potentially jealous husbands, brothers, and fathers. Men entering a strange new city would have to be particularly careful to avoid incurring the wrath of the local male population.

While speaking to the women, Paul and his companions meet a local business person:

> And a certain woman named Lydia, a seller of purple from the
> city of Thyatira, a worshiper of God, was listening. The Lord
> opened her heart to attend to the things spoken by Paul. And
> when she and her household had been baptized, she urged us,
> "If you have judged me faithful to the Lord, come and stay at my
> house." And she persuaded us. (Acts 16:14-15)

We have already come across Lydia, the dealer in purple cloth. She controls her household and takes her own decisions without consulting any man. She seizes the initiative to persuade Paul and the others to stay with her. It would be expected for Roman women to importune other women to stay with them, particularly when abroad. (One may think of Claudia Severa urging Sulpicia Lepidina to come to her birthday party.) But would a woman really invite men like this?

While staying with Lydia, the group revisit the place of prayer. Note how much time they are spending with the women! On the way, they come across a female at the opposite end of the social spectrum to Lydia:

> One day as we were going to the place of prayer, we were met
> by a certain slave-girl having a spirit of Python, who brought
> her masters much gain by fortune-telling. This girl followed
> Paul and the rest of us, shouting, "These men are servants of
> the Most High God, who proclaim to you the way of salvation!"
> (Acts 16:16-17)

The girl has a spirit of Python, the prophetic serpent slain by Apollo. It means that she has a spirit of divination from Apollo, similar to the oracle at Delphi. Although possessed by a pagan spirit, the girl's prophecy is valid, and she recognizes the real nature of Paul. Surprisingly, Paul is annoyed at her following him and continually shouting her proclamation, so he casts her spirit out. Here, we get a glimpse of the mythical world of the gentile author who has converted to Christianity but not entirely left paganism behind.

The "we" passages end for four chapters. They continue when Paul and a group of male companions start their sea voyage from Philippi with their ultimate destination of Jerusalem. They stay seven days at Tyre where the Christian disciples plead with Paul not to go to Jerusalem, but as he must obey God's command they leave:

> But when we completed the days, we set out on our journey.
> All accompanied us with wives and children, as far as outside
> the city, and knelt down on the beach to pray. And having said

farewell to one and other, we went onto the ship, and they returned home. (Acts 21:5-6)

There is an explicit mention of wives and children, two groups usually passed over in silence. The emotion seems overwrought for a stay of just a week. However, such farewells were a regular part of life for the Roman ruling classes as senior appointments lasted around three to four years. The wife of a senior official would be in company for that time with the wives of local officials and junior officers, such as centurions, who would be permanently based in the province. The deep friendships forged by women and children would be severed when the tour of duty came to an end. One can imagine the tearful farewells when it was time to embark on the ships, and the prayers for a safe voyage, for sea travel was always hazardous.

Their final landfall is Caesarea, where they stay with Philip. But this also turns out to be quite a female household:

Leaving the next day, we went on to Caesarea and entered into the house of Philip the evangelist, who was one of the Seven and stayed with him. He had four virgin daughters who prophesied. (Acts 21:9)

The "we" passages temporarily end when Paul arrives in Jerusalem, and they start again with Paul's final voyage to Rome. There is no explicit mention of women on the sea journey.

All these female-related episodes occur on land, and most of the "we" passages are set at sea. There is an extraordinary concentration of female interest in the first part of the "we" narrative leading up to Jerusalem. The "we" passages amount to less than 100 lines in total, of which 60 lines are the account of the shipwreck voyage. The first part consists of just 38 lines, and in this short section, we have five different female interest episodes. This is even more remarkable as much of the remainder is a list of places passed or visited at sea. We encounter five of the eight female prophets who appear in the narrative works of the New Testament in these 38 lines.

The author of the "we" passages

We can summarize our deductions about the "we" passages:

1. They formed a continuous narrative that has been split up in Acts.
2. The narrative was written as an adventure story with an emphasis on the sea voyages and a climax of the shipwreck.

3. The narrative was exclusively focused on Paul and loosely inspired by Paul's letters and 2 Corinthians in particular.

4. The story used the long ending of Mark as a source. The three (most likely originally four) miracles performed by Paul match the miracles that the followers of Jesus will perform after his resurrection.

5. The author was interested in prophecy and miracles but not theology.

6. The story was written by a woman who continually lapses into a female perspective on events.

The concerns of the "we" passages are very much the concerns of the rest of Acts and Luke. So the evidence points to the "we" passages having been written by the author of Luke/Acts. There are certainly some stylistic differences, most strikingly the almost obsessive listing of a day-by-day account of the places visited on the sea voyages. But this would be explained if the "we" passages were an early, immature work.

The specifics of the sea voyages are very accurate. The author had an excellent knowledge of sea travel in the first century. Most likely, the "we" passages are partly based on a log of actual sea voyages. Such knowledge would have been commonplace in the Roman world. Many ships were plying the Mediterranean carrying a vast number of passengers (Josephus says that his own ship carried several hundred). Most members of the Roman ruling classes would have made multiple sea journeys. And even someone who had no personal acquaintance with sea voyages in the eastern Mediterranean could draw on the experiences and records of those around them. Access to a sailor, merchant, official, or soldier who had served time in the east would be ideal.

And so we come to the mundane explanation of the "we" passages:

1. They started life as a short early work by the author of Luke/Acts. This text dealt with the travels of Paul to Macedonia and then to Jerusalem, the subsequent arrest of Paul, and his voyage to Rome for trial. It was a simplistic account involving miracles, prophecy, and a shipwreck.

2. After writing the Gospel of Luke, the author decided to expand this short work into something much grander—the Acts of the Apostles.

3. The first half of Acts, including the Peter section and the conversion of Paul, were wholly new and bridged back to the ending of Luke.

4. With further study of Paul's epistles, the author realized that her former account of his travels was inadequate. So she added the extensive

seven-year interpolation in which Paul travels from Philippi and back to Philippi.[17]

5. The section dealing with Paul's arrest and trials in Jerusalem was greatly expanded, replacing the original "we" narrative. Most likely, Paul's visit to Jerusalem had included a Pentecost "speaking in tongues" miracle, but this was moved to the start of Acts.

6. A short account of Paul's time in Rome was added at the end of Acts.

It is clumsy that the "we" passages were incorporated into Acts without changing them to the third person. This accusation of clumsiness is unavoidable regardless of what theory we adopt to explain these passages. If they were an eyewitness account, this should be signaled more clearly. If they were a sophisticated forgery, then the author should have made it obvious to the reader who was supposed to be narrating. Just switching to "we" at odd times is careless. For all the pretensions of Luke/Acts as history, the author is an amateur compared to, say, Tacitus or Josephus.

The author as an amateur follows on from the author being a woman. Literacy is a complex topic in the Roman world. High-ranking women, as well as men, would rely heavily on trained scribes, slaves or freedmen, for writing and perhaps even reading. This does not mean that they could not read and write for themselves. We have at least one example of a Roman woman's handwriting: Claudia Severa, at Vindolanda, added a postscript to her birthday invitation in her own, untidy hand.

More generally, Roman girls did not receive anything like the same education as boys. Upper-class girls would marry young and immediately start their careers of childbirth. This was not to say that women were uneducated. The great teacher of rhetoric, Quintilian, believed that mothers should be as well educated as fathers for the sake of a child's upbringing.

Social life centered around the main meal, which was eaten reclining on couches, often with guests present. Women would take a full part in the conversation, which might revolve around literary, political, and philosophical subjects. In the second century, philosophy became something of a craze among the elite, with many women laying claim to philosophical knowledge. They would have read and studied philosophy and literature to participate equally with men in the discussion.

But for all that, a girl would not receive the formal training in rhetoric and other intellectual subjects that a boy would. So even a woman in Domitilla's exalted position can be seen, in one sense, as self-taught. She had an abundance of resources to call upon but little formal training.

Can we acquit the author of Luke from a charge of forgery if the "we" passages started as a stand-alone production? After all, the "we" passages were written as if by an eyewitness. But a better analogy might be with fan fiction. The author of Luke would have placed herself in the role of the narrator, accompanying Paul on his travels. There is nothing in the "we" passages, or Acts as a whole, that are as duplicitous as the detailed greetings in the fake Paul letters. It is better to see the "we" passages as the outpourings of a vivid imagination rather than a cold-blooded device to deceive the reader.

11

Alexandria and Jerusalem

Galilee

At first the people of Jerusalem lamented Josephus' presumed death at the fall of Jotapata. But when they heard that he had gone over to the Romans, they were incensed at his cowardice. Josephus was starting his new life as a traitor and turncoat.[1]

Vespasian wintered his legions in Caesarea and Scythopolis, taking the opportunity to eliminate the pirate base that had grown up at Joppa. He spent the time enjoying the entertainment and lavish hospitality of King Agrippa. He decided to repay the favor by subjugating the remainder of Galilee and restoring the king's territory. The lakeside towns had few defenses against the advancing Roman force. At Tiberius, the citizens accepted the inevitable and negotiated a surrender. There was a hitch when Jesus, son of Sapphias, stole the Roman ambassadors' horses. But Vespasian overlooked this provocation, and the city avoided bloodshed.[2]

Tarichaeae was not so lucky. The rebels, including Jesus, son of Sapphias, made a stand at the city. Vespasian sent his best cavalry under Titus, and they charged the rebels' line in front of the city and forced them to retreat behind the walls. Most generals would have waited for reinforcements and siege engines. But Titus could hear disputes and panic from the other side of the walls. He immediately led his horsemen into the lake to swim around the defenses and into the city. Caught by surprise, the Jews were defeated in a bloody slaughter. The fleeing rebels had to leap into the boats to escape.[3]

Titus had taken the city, but many rebels remained in the boats on the lake. The Romans set out with rapidly made rafts manned with legionnaires. A strange naval battle followed, with hand to hand fighting in small vessels until the lake was red with the blood of the Jews.[4]

Vespasian decided to spare the surviving townspeople of Tarichaeae. He tricked the rebels by saying they could leave without their arms. Their freedom was illusionary. They were shepherded along the road to Tiberius and herded into the amphitheater. Vespasian selected 6,000 of the fittest to send to Nero. The old and infirm had no commercial value, and over a thousand were killed. The remainder were sold as slaves. Some of them were citizens of Agrippa's territory, and Vespasian courteously offered the king the choice of what to do with them. Agrippa opted to take the profits from their sale.[5]

After Tarichaeae, most Jewish towns and villages in Galilee surrendered to the Romans. But one town, Gamala, across the lake in Agrippa's realm, continued to support the rebels. The citizens were relying on their town's strong defensive position, built as it was on a mountain ridge. The houses seemed to tumble down the steep slope with a pinnacle, the citadel, standing proud in the center. But nothing was impregnable to the Romans. They broke through the walls with battering rams and surged into the town. The streets were too narrow to give room to fight, so the Romans climbed onto the roofs to get more space. But the buildings began to collapse beneath their weight, trapping many in the ruins. It was perhaps the most dangerous moment in the whole campaign for Vespasian. He had advanced far into the town and was now isolated with just a small guard. Titus was away in Syria and could not come to his rescue. Vespasian and his men had to fight their way back as the town collapsed in rubble around them.[6]

The townspeople had won an unexpected victory. The Romans had been forced to retreat and had suffered many casualties. But it was nothing more than a temporary setback. Vespasian's men undermined and collapsed a tower in the walls. When Titus returned, he led a cavalry detachment secretly into the city and took it by stealth. Many townspeople fled to the central peak, where they hurled themselves and their families over the cliff.[7]

The town of Gischala still held out under Josephus' rival John. Vespasian sent Titus to take the town with 1,000 cavalry. The citizens had no stomach for a fight. So John told Titus that they were ready to agree a peace deal but could not negotiate on the Sabbath. Titus accepted the delay of a day and held back from the attack. But John and his supporters quietly slipped away in the night. The Romans started after them at dawn, catching and killing the hindmost. But John of Gischala was able to reach Jerusalem to become the leader of a major faction of rebels. Vespasian's army had subdued the whole of Galilee, but the daunting task of taking Judea and Jerusalem was still ahead of them.[8]

Civil war

Another fighting season was over, and Vespasian overwintered his army at Caesarea. His next task was to subdue the countryside in preparation for the assault on Jerusalem. In early spring, Vespasian led his army out of Caesarea and progressed through Antipatris, Thamma, Lydda, and Jamnia, devastating areas of resistance and making a base at Emmaus where he stationed the Fifth. Emmaus is identified with Nicopolis, about twenty miles from Jerusalem. It is probably the same Emmaus that is famous for the story of Jesus' resurrection in the Gospel of Luke.[9]

Vespasian continued with the conquest of Idumea, which lay to the south of Judea. He returned through Emmaus, up to Neopolis in the north, and down to Jericho, east of Jerusalem. The Romans found the city of Jericho deserted; the inhabitants had all fled. Supposedly, people could not sink in the dense salty waters of the Dead Sea. Vespasian decided to conduct a Roman-style experiment to see if this was true. Two captives who could not swim were bound and thrown into the sea. The experiment was a success as the men floated and did not drown.[10]

The Romans now had complete control of the area around Jerusalem. The city was rife with internal divisions and had become a battleground between three competing factions. Any sensible person could see that there was only one possible outcome. The inhabitants could only pray that God might intervene before the Romans conquered the city. And, remarkably, it looked as if their prayers had been answered.

Just as the Romans were closing in to finish the war, Vespasian was stopped in his tracks. In the summer of 68 AD, news reached the army that Nero had committed suicide in Rome. A Roman general's commission was personal to the emperor, and Vespasian's mandate had expired with Nero's death. He dared not start the siege of Jerusalem without fresh instructions from the new emperor, Galba. So he waited until winter for orders that did not come. Eventually, he sent Titus, accompanied by King Agrippa, to give his compliments to Galba. They had a hazardous winter voyage in a warship hugging the coast as far as Greece, where they heard that Galba had been assassinated and replaced by Otho. Agrippa continued on to Rome, but Titus decided to return to his father.[11]

With Titus back, Vespasian recommenced military operations but held back from an attack on Jerusalem. He would have spent this time seeking support for a bid for power. When the news came that Otho was also dead, defeated by Vitellius, Mucianus publicly implored Vespasian to declare as emperor, which Vespasian did on 1 July 69. On the same day, Tiberius

Alexander, the prefect of Alexandria, instructed the legions in Egypt to take an oath of loyalty to Vespasian.[12]

It was now time to play the Josephus card and make the story of his prophecy public. He was brought forward and formally released from his imprisonment. At the urging of Titus, he was not only freed but had the chain of his fetters struck through, removing the stain of any offense. Josephus' gamble had paid off spectacularly.[13]

The story of the prophecy spread around the Roman world and was valuable propaganda for Vespasian. Suetonius, writing around 120 AD, gives the Roman perspective:

> According to an old and established belief widespread through-
> out the East, it was fated that at that time men coming from
> Judea would take control of the world. This prediction, which
> events later revealed to concern the Roman emperor, the Jews
> took to refer to themselves and rebelled, killing the legionary
> commander, and besides this, routing the governor of Syria
> who was bringing reinforcements, and seizing one of his eagles.
> (Suetonius, Vespasian 4)

Suetonius also mentions Josephus: "And one of the captives, of noble birth, Josephus, when he was thrown in chains, insisted that the same man would shortly set him free but that he would then be emperor."[14] It was absurd to view Vespasian as the Jewish Messiah, but Josephus knew his Romans. He had counted on their overwhelming ignorance of Jewish matters and he was not disappointed.

Alexandria

Vespasian traveled to Antioch in Syria, from which he sent Mucianus with a large force to Rome. He then moved his own base to Alexandria to control the grain supply. If Vespasian had adopted Domitilla on her mother's death, as seems likely, we would expect her to have accompanied Vespasian to the east. The family would have been located well out of the war zone, probably in Antioch and then Caesarea, both places prominent in Acts. Vespasian would have taken his family with him to Alexandria to keep them by his side while events were uncertain.

Domitilla would only have been around eight, but she may have met Josephus. He was treated with honor by Vespasian and Titus after his release and would have been a frequent guest at gatherings. He was now a client of the Flavians and part of their family circle. A brilliant courtier like Josephus is likely to have taken notice of the beloved granddaughter of the emperor, knowing that this child would grow into a person of power and influence.

Josephus never calls Vespasian the Messiah, the Christ. The word appears only twice in his works, and both are disputed references to Jesus. It was wise to keep the Romans in ignorance of the true nature of the Messiah prophecies. But did he believe any of it himself? Perhaps. In the Jewish War, Josephus describes Vespasian's advance into Galilee with a team of road makers going before him "to straighten out bends in the road, level rough surfaces and cut down obstructive woods."[15] His description matches a prophecy of the Messiah in Isaiah: "make straight in the desert a highway for our God. Every valley shall be lifted up, and every mountain and hill made low; the uneven ground shall become level, and the rough places a plain."[16]

The gospels show Christ performing many healing miracles. Vespasian was said to have accomplished some surprisingly similar miracles. In Alexandria, there were two men, one blind and one with a withered hand. The Egyptian god Serapis appeared to both men telling them to go to Vespasian. The men went and appealed to the emperor to cure them. He was skeptical and reluctant to agree for fear of ridicule, but his advisors urged him to attempt the cure. He took some of his spittle and rubbed it into the eyes of the blind man who had his sight restored. He then imprinted his heel on the other man's withered hand and it was made whole. There were many witnesses, and Tacitus reports that those present attested to the miracles "to this day." There was no motivation for them to lie, for, by that time, the Flavian dynasty was extinct.[17]

Jesus uses his spittle for two miracles in the gospels. He cures a deaf and dumb man in Mark by rubbing spittle onto his tongue. And he mixes spittle with clay to rub it into the eyes of a blind man in John.[18] It may be significant that the Mark miracle story is the only one that the author of Matthew did not use. Perhaps it was uncomfortably close to Vespasian's miracle.

Vespasian's healing power supposedly came from Serapis rather than the Jewish God. While the outcome of the conflict in Rome was still uncertain, Vespasian went alone to the temple of Serapis to take the auspices and forbade anyone else to enter. After making his offerings to the god, he turned around and saw that the freedman Basilides had brought him sacred branches, garlands, and cakes. He found out later that Basilides was actually ill in bed many miles away and unable to walk. When Vespasian came out of the temple he heard that Vitellius' army had been defeated at Cremona and that his rival was dead.[19] This was taken as further proof that Vespasian was specially favored by Serapis.

As soon as the winds were favorable, Vespasian left Alexandria for Rome. Family members, such as Domitilla, may have accompanied the emperor in his victorious procession or they may have traveled more directly to Rome. If Domitilla went directly by sea, she would have followed the same route as Paul did in his Alexandrian ship in the "we" passages. The journey would have made a great impression on a young girl, and she may have kept a day-by-day log to record her adventure. But this is just speculation as we cannot even be sure that she had been adopted by Vespasian at this time.

Titus had been in Alexandria to collect reinforcements, and he and Josephus left early to continue the Jewish war. If she were in Alexandria, Domitilla would have remembered the departure of her glamorous uncle. And here we find a coincidence. Josephus gives a short but very particular account of their journey back to Judea.[20] For example: "his second day march brought him to Heracleopohs, the third to Pelusium. Having halted here two days to refresh his army, on the third he crossed the Pelusiac river-mouths, and, advancing a day's march through the desert, encamped near the temple of the Casian Zeus, and on the next day at Ostracine."[21] It is virtually a day-by-day account, and there is nothing like it anywhere else in the Jewish War. It reads, in fact, just like the "we" passages in Acts. Did Josephus and Domitilla agree to keep a log of their respective journeys? And did these logs find their way into their literary works? It is a nice thought, but once again, pure speculation.

Jerusalem

Jerusalem had descended into civil war. More than just a rebellion against the Romans, the conflict was also a religiously-motivated revolution against the Jewish establishment. The young tended to support the revolution while their elders were more cautious and reluctant to abandon the status quo.[22]

In Jerusalem, the moderates and the remnant of the establishment gathered under the leadership of two former high priests; Joshua, son of Gamaliel, and Ananus, son of Ananus. The opposing party, the Zealots, was much smaller but attracted fit young fighters and held the temple. Moved by a democratic instinct typical of young revolutionary movements, the Zealots decided to choose the next high priest by a lottery. Josephus was shocked to the core by this idea; what use was a noble birth as proved by genealogies and distinguished ancestors if just anybody could be high priest? That, of course, was the point. All Jews were equal before God, so why have nobles? Give power to the people.[23]

It was a nice theory, but as others have found through the ages, the practice proved rather different. The lot fell to a farmer, Phanni, son of Samuel, who had to be dragged from his smallholding. He had no idea what to do as high priest and was nothing more than a puppet dressed up for ceremonies.[24] The real leaders were Eleazar, son of Simon, and Zachariah, son of Amphicalleus.[25]

Ananus knew that if the city were to survive, he would have to expel the Zealots. So he assembled a force to attack the outer court of the temple. The battle was vicious, and the Zealots, motivated by religious extremism, fought back hard. But Ananus could draw upon the townspeople who were becoming sick of the war and fearful of the outcome. They captured the outer court, confining the Zealots to the inner court and the main temple building. Had he pressed forward, he would have defeated the Zealots, opening the way for a peace deal with the Romans. Jerusalem could have been saved.[26]

Josephus blames his old enemy, John of Gischala, for what happened next. He claims that John appeared to be on Ananus' side but was really working as a spy for the Zealots. It is more likely that John was a committed revolutionary who had initially favored Ananus' faction. The accusation he made against Ananus, that he intended to negotiate a surrender with Vespasian, was probably true. This would be unacceptable for John, who had fought and outwitted the Romans in Galilee. So he joined up with the Zealots and persuaded their leaders Eleazar and Zachariah to seek outside help. They appealed to the Idumaeans, a people who lived to the immediate south of Judea and who had converted to Judaism over the centuries; they sent an army of 20,000. On the approach of this army, Ananus closed the city gates against them. There was now a double siege: the Idumaeans were besieging the city, and the city was besieging the Zealots in the inner temple.[27]

It looked like a stalemate. But one night, Ananus failed to make his regular checks on the guards surrounding the temple. The guards fell asleep, and the Zealots began to saw quietly through the metal of the temple gate. Once through, they crept through the city to the main gates, which they opened to the Idumaeans. Their combined force assembled at the temple and set about massacring the large guard which Ananus had placed around the compound. Then they pillaged the whole city.[28]

Both Joshua and Ananus were killed. The two former high priests were denied burial with their naked bodies thrown out for the dogs. The Zealots then commenced a reign of terror, murdering and torturing thousands of young nobles who refused to join their side. They held show trials of their enemies, with the execution of the accused as the inevitable conclusion. Events were following a revolutionary trajectory repeated again and again throughout history.[29]

Once the plundering was over, the Idumaeans began to lose enthusiasm for their Zealot allies. Most, although not all, went home. John of Gischala was now the accepted leader of the revolutionary faction and the master of Jerusalem. But his total grip on power would not last long.[30]

A new rebel leader, Simon, son of Gioras, had emerged in the countryside outside Jerusalem. Simon had been allied with the Sicarii at Masada, but left that desert fortress to further his wider ambitions. Leading a group of guerrilla fighters, he secured control over the hill country. Simon does not seem to have been particularly interested in religion. He proclaimed a revolution of the proletariat, freedom for slaves, and rewards for the free. As more and more rebels joined him, he expanded his operations to the towns on the plain. Josephus hated Simon, saying he attracted all the "scum" to his cause. But he admitted that Simon's popularity went beyond the lower classes, and he appealed to many middle-class citizens from the towns. The Zealots in Jerusalem came out to attack Simon, but his army won the battle and drove them back into the city.[31]

Now with an army of 20,000 men, Simon invaded Idumaea. An initial battle was inconclusive, but eventually, he gained control of the kingdom; through treachery, according to Josephus, who represents Simon as a brutal despot. There may have been an element of jealousy here; Simon comes over as the best military commander on the rebel side, with a much more impressive record than Josephus. He took advantage of the Roman period of inactivity to carve a significant territory out of nothing. Simon would next seek the biggest prize of all—Jerusalem.[32]

Josephus paints the city under John of Gischala as being hopelessly depraved. He claims that John allowed everyone to do as they wished, including murdering rich men and stealing their possessions. One of the surprising new freedoms was cross-dressing! A disgusted Josephus reports how many of the men were "plaiting their hair and attiring themselves in women's apparel, drenching themselves with perfumes and painting their eyelids to enhance their beauty. And not only did they imitate the dress, but also the passions of women..." It reveals a very different side to the Jews from the stereotypes; the difference between them and other peoples in the Hellenistic Roman Empire was less stark than it sometimes appears. But such behavior would have shocked religiously observant Jews, including John's allies, the fundamentalist Zealots. More generally, the ordinary people were becoming weary of the revolutionary chaos.[33]

John's rule over the whole city ended when the remaining Idumaeans deserted him and joined the remnants of the establishment side under a former high priest, Matthias. They attracted many of the townspeople to their cause and together were able to push back John and the Zealots to the temple area. Then Matthias made a fatal mistake. Thinking that the enemy of my enemy is my friend, he opened the gates to Simon, son of Gioras. He was expecting Simon to assist in expelling the Zealots from the city. But Simon was ruthless in his pursuit of power and would eventually have Matthias and his sons executed. Matthias pleaded to be the first to die, but the sadistic Simon made him watch as his sons were killed before he himself was executed.[34]

Simon quickly consolidated his rule over the city. He assembled his army for an assault on John and his Zealots, but, for once, he was unsuccessful. With its high colonnades, the temple was an excellent defensive position, and the Zealots inflicted heavy damage on the attackers below without suffering much in return. Simon had to retreat, leaving John in command of the temple and its environs. But John faced another revolt when a Zealot faction under Eleazar, son of Simon, broke away and took over the inner temple. So, there were now three rebel factions in the city, all fighting each other. Simon, son of Gioras, controlled the lower city, John controlled the upper city including the outer temple, and the Zealots controlled the inner temple. In this manner, the Jews prepared for the return of Titus and the Romans.[35]

The siege

Titus had four legions under his command; the Fifth, the Tenth, the Fifteenth, and the disgraced Twelfth, eager to make amends for its defeat under Cestius. Vespasian had depleted the legions to make up the army he sent to Rome, and now they were made up to full strength with Titus' reinforcements from Alexandria. They were joined by a large force of auxiliaries provided by the client kings.[36]

As the army approached Jerusalem, Titus went ahead with a few hundred cavalry to reconnoiter the city's defenses. Seeing that all was quiet with the Jews shut up within the walls, he approached closer. A gate suddenly opened, and the citizens piled out armed with swords and spears to attack. Titus was cut-off with a few companions and had to flee, dodging missiles to get back to the main group. This would be typical of Titus' recklessness throughout the campaign.[37]

The Romans spread out around the city and began building their camps. The sight of the formidable force on the hills around the city would have shocked the Jews. But their courage did not fail them even now. As the Tenth began constructing their camp on the Mount of Olives, they were surprised by a sudden assault. The Jews surged over the brook Kidron and up the hill. The Romans were unprepared and fell back in panic.

Titus came to the rescue with reinforcements and pushed the attackers back down to the brook. But when he ordered the soldiers back to their work, the Jews thought the Romans were fleeing and charged again. Titus was once more in danger until the legionaries of the Tenth came to his assistance.[38]

While the Romans were making their preparations, the factions inside the city were beginning to consolidate. At Passover the Zealots in the temple under Eleazar allowed other Jews through the half-open gates to worship. John smuggled some of his men into the temple and was able to bring the Zealots back under control. Now there were two sides, John and Simon. As the Romans began their assault, the two entered into an uneasy truce and joined against the common enemy.[39]

Titus repeatedly used Josephus to try and persuade the Jews to surrender the city. Josephus would shout his speeches below the walls, while the people atop hurled abuse and missiles down at him. On one occasion, his companion, Nicanor, was struck in the shoulder by an arrow. On another, Josephus was hit on the head by a stone and was carried away unconscious. Jerusalem rejoiced at his death. Josephus' mother and father were in prison in Jerusalem, and when his mother was told her son was dead, she replied that she might as well have had no son. But Josephus was just concussed and revived.[40]

Jerusalem was protected by three walls with the strongest around the temple area. The Romans started to attack the weakest wall, which had been built around a newer part of the city by Agrippa I. The foundations were massive, and had the walls been as strong, the city would have been impregnable. But Agrippa, fearful that the emperor would think he was planning rebellion, had deliberately made them weak. Titus ordered the battering rams to begin their work on this section of the wall. They had little effect, so a massive ram nicknamed Victor was brought into play. It soon made a breach, and the Romans threw down the wall on either side and moved into the northern suburbs.[41]

This was little loss for the Jews who had retreated into the better-defended sections of the city. The Romans started on the second wall, and Victor took only four days to batter through. Titus impatiently pressed through with some of his men without waiting to widen the breach. The Jews attacked, and Titus was trapped once again: the gap was only wide enough for one person to pass through at a time. Titus showed considerable bravery in holding the position to enable his men to get out. Once they were all back on the Roman side, he took care to demolish a large section of wall before advancing again.[42]

All that remained now was the fortified area around the City of David. The walls here were too old, thick, and strong for the battering ram, so the

Romans began laboriously constructing siege towers to surmount them. Their other weapon was hunger. Titus ordered a wall to be built around the city to prevent supplies from getting in or people getting out. Josephus claims it was completed in just three days. The city was ill-prepared for a lengthy siege. Large areas, including grain stores, had been destroyed by the factional fighting. The rebel fighters searched door to door to requisition any food while the non-combatants died of starvation. Josephus tells the story of one woman, Mary, daughter of Eliezer, who cooked and ate her own baby. Whether such tales were true or not, they served as useful propaganda for the Romans.[43]

Anyone caught slipping out to find food was tortured and crucified in sight of the walls. The area was filled with crosses, as many as 500 a day. The Romans did allow those who wished to leave the city free passage, but these deserters ran other risks. First, they had to get past the Jewish partisans who would kill anyone attempting to flee. They then had to face the Roman soldiers who did not always obey their instructions to allow the refugees to live. One citizen was seen extracting gold coins from his excrement: he had swallowed the coins to smuggle them out of the city. So soldiers began slitting open the bellies of fleeing citizens in the hope of finding gold.[44]

The Romans' chief difficulty was getting enough timber to build their siege platforms which the Jews kept burning. The area around Jerusalem was a scene of desolation. The Romans had felled every tree within ten miles of the city and now had to transport timber from afar. As well as working on the platforms, the Romans began attacking a section of wall by the fortress Antonia with battering rams. Although the Jews were confident that the wall would not fall to the rams, John ordered a tunnel to be dug underneath it to sink the Roman platforms. He had unknowingly undermined his own wall. A group of legionaries worked all day under an onslaught from above to pry out a few stones. It was not much, but enough; that night, the wall collapsed.[45]

Things were still not easy for the Romans. Another wall had been constructed to block their way, and there was fierce fighting as they struggled to get their troops into the temple area. Titus had the fortress Antonia demolished and a broad ramp made to eliminate the bottleneck. The next obstacles were the wall and gates protecting the temple's outer court. The battering rams made no impression on the finely crafted and fitted stone blocks in the temple walls. The high colonnades were attacked using ladders, but the defenders pushed these over. So Titus ordered a fire to be built around the gates that were made from wood gilded with gold and silver. The heat melted the metal, the wood caught fire, and the gates collapsed.[46]

Josephus' account of what happened next is not believable. He claims that Titus held a council of war and decided that the temple building must be preserved. Fate, or God, intervened. A soldier acting on his own initiative threw a burning faggot into the temple. Others followed his example, throwing more brands into the fire. Titus urgently shouted orders to stop, but they did not hear him. The temple caught fire and burnt down.[47]

In reality, it seems that Titus ordered the destruction of the temple. He entered the temple building before it burnt down to view the treasures and may have gone into the holy of holies.[48] And the Romans had plenty of time to loot the contents, such as the magnificent gold candelabra. This is shown being carried off on the arch of Titus in Rome.

Josephus the historian was writing imperial propaganda. And Josephus the priest had his own reasons for denying that Titus had ordered the destruction. Jewish religion was centered on the temple. Yet, now he was working for the desolators under their commander in chief, Titus, who was his friend and patron. All traitors must eventually face the implications of their betrayal. Josephus handled this dissonance by arguing that it was the will of God to destroy the temple. Titus was not guilty, and the Romans were only doing God's work. It is an argument that Josephus puts forward at several points in The Jewish War. The rebels had brought the destruction upon themselves. They were the guilty ones. He, Josephus, was working for the good guys.

The legionaries celebrated their triumph over the Jewish God by sacrificing to the legion's eagle in the temple court in front of the burning sanctuary.[49] It is believed that they offered a pig, the ultimate insult to the Jews. Josephus says that the temple was destroyed on the "10th of Loos", the same day of the year that the Babylonians destroyed the first temple.[50]

The aftermath

Even now, the siege was not quite over. There was a mopping-up operation to capture the upper city district. Then the whole city was sacked and set on fire. Josephus reports that 1.1 million died in Jerusalem, and although this is undoubtedly an exaggeration, it does show the scale of the tragedy. Those not killed were taken as slaves. As no one would purchase the elderly, they were all slain. The prime fighters would die as gladiators in the arena. The most attractive young citizens were selected for the victory parade through Rome.[51]

Josephus reports that so much gold was pillaged from the city that the price went down all over the east.[52] The same must have happened to the cost of slaves with such an abundant new supply. Those who now faced a life of slavery were the lucky ones. Many of the captured would have been crucified, the only limitation being the lack of timber for the crosses.

The two rebel leaders, John and Simon, hid separately in the sewers under the town. John eventually surrendered, forced out by hunger. Surprisingly, he was allowed to live although imprisoned for life. Simon tried a trick, emerging dressed in gaudy silks like an apparition in full sight of the Romans. Unlike Josephus, he did not receive any mercy from Titus who ordered him to be taken back to Rome for execution in the triumph.[53]

Titus told Josephus to take whatever he wanted from the wreckage of Jerusalem. But Josephus chose only the freedom of some of his acquaintances, numbering about two hundred and fifty. Titus also made him a present of some sacred books. On one occasion, Josephus was riding with a large cavalry contingent outside the city when they came across a group of crucified Jews, including three of Josephus' acquaintances. He went in tears to Titus, who ordered the three to be taken down and given medical attention. Only one of them survived.[54]

Josephus' land in Jerusalem was on the site of a new Roman garrison, so Titus gave him a better estate in exchange. But Josephus knew that staying in Jerusalem was not an option. The few hundred people he had helped did not alter the hatred directed towards him. Thousands of ex-partisans would have relished the chance to slip a knife between the traitor's ribs. So Josephus accepted an offer from Titus to accompany him to Rome. He would not see his homeland again.[55]

12

A Roman apologist

Blame the Jews, not the Romans

Luke and Acts show the Romans in a remarkably favorable light. The author of Luke goes out of her way to avoid blaming them. Where some culpability is inevitable, such as for the crucifixion, the author minimizes Roman guilt. This strategy requires a scapegoat, a burden that falls upon "the Jews." In Acts, they become matinee villains, forever stirring up trouble.

We might conclude that the author of Luke felt racial hatred towards the Jews, but it would be closer to the truth to say that the author of Luke loved the Jews. She is well informed about Jewish matters and has read the scriptures extensively. The author sees Christianity as supplanting Judaism but is still fascinated by Jewish culture. And many individual Jews are shown in a positive light.

A good narrative, however, needs villains. Following the lead of Mark and Matthew, "the Jews" become the perennial enemies of the Christians. But it is nothing personal; the anti-Jewish attitude of Luke/Acts is really a pro-Roman bias. The author cannot blame the Romans because she is a Roman, and a high-ranking Roman at that. We will look at the evidence that supports this conclusion.

Good centurions

When John the Baptist harangues the crowd in Luke, it is surprising that soldiers are among his audience. John gives them the type of advice that any member of the Roman upper-classes might agree with: "Do not exhort or falsely accuse; be content with your wages."[1] The idea that Roman soldiers could be followers of John would never occur to a Jewish Christian, and it demonstrates the Roman-centric worldview of the author of Luke.

Roman centurions feature in a surprisingly positive way in the New Testament, particularly in Luke/Acts. The Gospel of Luke has two stories involving centurions. In the first, Jesus cures a sick slave of a centurion at

Capernaum, a miracle also found in Matthew. It is illuminating to compare the two versions. In Matthew, the centurion represents a despised class, on the same level as a tax collector or prostitute. He comes to Jesus to ask him to heal his servant. Jesus offers to go with him, but the centurion tells him he is unworthy to even have Jesus in his house:

> But only speak the word, and my servant will be healed. I also am a man under authority, with soldiers under me; and I say to one "go," and he goes; and to another "come," and he comes, and to my slave, "do this," and he does it. (Matthew 8:8-9)

Jesus is amazed at the centurion's faith and heals the servant from a distance. A Jew would be made unclean by just entering the centurion's house, but faith can save even a Roman. The author of Luke does not like the suggestion that a Roman would be automatically despised by the Jews and changes the story:

> When the centurion heard about Jesus, he sent some Jewish elders begging him to come and save his servant. They came to Jesus and pleaded with him earnestly, saying: "He is worthy for you to grant this, for he loves our nation and has built the synagogue for us." (Luke 7:3-4)

The centurion is now highly respected by the Jews who act as his intermediaries; he is a God-fearer. In Matthew we see things from the perspective of the occupied, in Luke from the perspective of the occupiers. The centurion is a model of how the author of Luke would like us to see the "good" Romans; they are the friends and patrons of the Jews.

In the Gospel of Mark, a centurion witnessing the death of Jesus says: "Truly this man was the Son of God!"[2] Jesus has just suffered an ignominious death on the cross, and the only sign in Mark, the tearing of the temple veil, would not be discernable to the centurion. Why then does the centurion make this surprising statement? The authors of Matthew and Luke both address this problem. In Matthew, the death is marked by a spectacular earthquake, and the dead rise and walk into Jerusalem. In contrast, Luke tones down the centurion's statement: "Surely this was a righteous man!"[3]

We find more centurion stories in Acts. One concerns the gift of the Holy Spirit to gentiles involving a centurion called Cornelius. He is based in Caesarea and is from the Italian cohort, which is the sort of fascinating Roman detail that we only get from Luke/Acts. He and his household are "devout and God-fearing." So Cornelius is another God-fearer who gives to the poor and prays to God regularly. One day he is rewarded by a vision telling him to summon a man called Simon Peter who is staying in Joppa. Meanwhile, Peter is on a roof, having his own vision of a sheet lowered from heaven and hearing a voice telling him that all foods are permitted. As he pondered the meaning of the vision, three messengers from Cornelius arrived.

The next day, Peter accompanies them to Caesarea. Cornelius falls to his knees, but Peter makes him rise. He tells Cornelius that he now understands that God does not show favoritism and that no man is unclean. They all get together in Cornelius' house, and the Holy Spirit descends onto the gentiles, and Peter baptizes them.[4]

This episode shows gentiles brought into the church equally with the Jews and the removal of the requirements of the Jewish law. Significantly, the author of Luke chooses a Roman military household to illustrate this crucial development.

Domitilla came from a military family and would have been very familiar with centurions. The Roman army was organized on class lines, and the senior officers came from the nobility. The system was based on hereditary privilege, but it worked well because of the centurions. Nominally in charge of one hundred men, the centurions were highly experienced soldiers recruited from the ranks purely on merit. Any legionnaire could aspire to be a centurion, and they were rewarded with privileges well above those of the ordinary soldiers. Unlike the higher officers, centurions remained with the same legion, which developed loyalty and competition between legions.

Centurions were some of the most competent people around and were highly valued. Officers would give their orders to the soldiers via the centurions. And they were used by the senior levels up to and including the emperor for all sorts of missions and errands. So there was a great deal of daily contact between nobles and centurions.

Paul is sent to Rome for trial under the charge of Julius, the centurion of the cohort of Augustus. The centurion is responsible for other prisoners besides Paul and exercises authority on the grain ship they travel on, making decisions in conjunction with the pilot. Julius is shown favorably. He treats Paul with considerable respect allowing him to visit friends and listens to his advice. Most significantly, when their boat is shipwrecked and the soldiers intend to kill the prisoners, he intervenes to save Paul's life.[5] Domitilla would have been very familiar with centurions like Julius. When she traveled by ship, as senior Roman women often did, a centurion would have led her escort.

We also encounter centurions in Acts in contexts where they do not form a major focus of the action. When Paul's speech provokes the Jews to riot, the cohort commander Lysias leads a force of "soldiers and centurions" to arrest him.[6] Later he orders Paul to be flogged, but the apostle is saved when the centurion hears that he is a Roman citizen.[7] When Paul's sister's son comes to warn him of a plot against him, Paul asks a centurion to take the young man to Lysias.[8] The cohort commander responds to the plot by ordering two centurions to assemble an escort to convey Paul to Felix.[9] And Felix assigns a centurion to keep Paul under guard.[10]

We see the senior Romans, both the cohort commander and the procurator, operating through centurions. This is the type of realistic detail that only an insider will get right. It shows that the author of Luke was familiar with the operation of the Roman army at a senior level.

Paul, the Roman citizen

Acts gives us two pieces of vital information about Paul; he came from the city of Tarsus in modern-day Turkey and was a Roman citizen. Both points are doubtful. Paul never mentions Tarsus in his letters nor says he was a Roman citizen. From the evidence of the letters, he likely came from Judea: he had trained as a pharisee, which suggests Jerusalem, and he persecuted the early church in Judea. From Acts we learn that Paul's "sister's son" lives near Jerusalem, indicating that Paul's family was based there.[11]

In Galatians, Paul says that immediately after his conversion, he went into Arabia. From there, he returned to Damascus before going down to visit Jerusalem and then going into the "regions of Syria and Cilicia".[12] As Tarsus was the chief city in Cilicia, this does provide evidence for an association of the apostle with that place. However, there is no hint that he came from this area. It could be that Christians from Tarsus claimed Paul as one of their own because of traditions about his very early missionary activities.

Was Paul really a Roman citizen? Unfortunately, Acts does not explain how his family came to have citizenship. If Paul were really a Roman citizen, it would have been a reward granted to his father or grandfather. However, the letters provide positive evidence to the contrary. Paul says that he was beaten by rods three times, a punishment that he differentiates from receiving the thirty-nine lashes five times from the Jews.[13] The rod beating was administrated by the Roman lictors and was not a punishment that could be meted out to a Roman citizen. The author of Luke understands the problem, for Acts includes a story where Paul and his companion Silas are mistakenly beaten with rods. When the magistrates realize that Paul is a Roman citizen, they apologize.[14]

The second time Paul is about to be flogged by the Romans in Acts, he tells the centurion he is a citizen. The commander is amazed when he hears this:

> "I paid a high price for my citizenship," said the commander. "But I was born a citizen," Paul replied. (Acts 22:28)

You could not buy citizenship except by bribing an official. So Paul is presented as a more legitimate citizen than the cohort commander.

Acts' explanation for Paul's beatings does not really work. It does not explain why he did not claim his rights as a Roman citizen before the first beating, nor why he was beaten with rods three times. Was the rule against beating a Roman citizen applied as zealously and conscientiously as the author of Luke assumes? Most citizens would stay in the same place, and local records would affirm their status. But Paul was a wandering vagabond. There would be no way of checking whether he was a citizen and no come-back for a magistrate who ordered him flogged. It is odd that Paul never claims to be a citizen in his letters. So, on the balance of probabilities, he was probably not one.

Why then does the author of Luke make Paul a citizen? In part, this is to claim him for Rome—as a Roman citizen from the cosmopolitan city of Tarsus, Paul would be respectable for a Roman audience. He would be "one of us." It also fits in with the narrative line of Acts, that Paul was sent to Rome because he claimed his right of citizenship. If Domitilla were the author of Luke, she would have known whether or not Paul had been sent to Rome for trial. But you did not have to be a citizen to be sent to the emperor for judgment. An example is the case that first brought Josephus to Rome: "At the time when Felix was procurator of Judea, certain priests of my acquaintance, very excellent men, were on a slight and trifling charge sent by him in bonds to Rome to render an account to Caesar."[15] These priests would not have been Roman citizens. Felix would have sent them to the emperor because the case was too contentious to resolve himself. A Judean procurator may have concluded that it was more appropriate for Paul to be tried in Rome because he was notorious for his actions in many provinces. The author of Luke, however, wanted to avoid any suggestion that Paul had been condemned by the Romans.

Guilty of Paul's martyrdom?

We can discern the broad outline of Paul's fate in Rome. He was held in prison for a while and then put to death, probably as part of Nero's actions against the Christians following the fire of Rome. Tacitus writes about the fate of these Christians: "Covered with hides of wild beasts, they perished by being torn to pieces by dogs; or they would be fastened to crosses and, when daylight had gone, burned to provide lighting at night."[16]

Most likely, this is how Paul died. So it is astonishing that the author of Luke turns the story around so that the honorable Romans save Paul from "the Jews." We will look at the account of Paul's arrest and multiple trials in Jerusalem when we come to the links between the author of Luke and the circle of Herod Agrippa II. Just to point out here how the Romans are consistently shown as doing the right thing. They save Paul's life from a Jewish conspiracy and grant him a large escort to get him to safety. They treat him with considerable respect in captivity and are minded to release him while giving him every opportunity to continue teaching and preaching. Felix orders Paul to be well treated. The centurion Julius allows him to visit Christians on the way to Rome, and Paul is even permitted to stay with Christians for seven days at Puteoli in Italy.[17] In Rome, he is placed under a very light house-arrest with a single soldier guarding him. Apart from remaining in the house, no constraint is placed on his activities:

> Paul stayed there two full years in his own rented house, and welcomed all who came to him. He proclaimed the kingdom of God and taught about the Lord Jesus Christ with unhindered freedom of speech. (Acts 28:30-31)

So Acts ends with Paul enjoying considerable freedom under the benign Romans. We may even consider it a happy ending, which is surely the real reason why the ultimate fate of Paul is not covered in Acts. To include his trial and execution would be disturbing and spoil the pro-Roman story.

Throughout Acts, the Romans and the Roman appointed authorities refuse to take action against Paul and his associates. The one exception is the beating with rods, and even that merits an apology. In Thessalonica, the Jews are enraged by Paul's preaching and make a serious accusation to the city authorities that the Christian brothers deny Caesar's decrees and say that there is another emperor, Jesus. The city authorities are concerned but release the brothers on a surety of good behavior by Jason, a prominent citizen.[18]

In Corinth, Paul is so disgusted by his reception by the Jews that he brushes the synagogue dust off his cloak and utters a curse that echos the condemnations of the Gospel of Matthew: "Your blood is on your own heads." From now on, Paul says, he will go to the gentiles. He moves his base next door to the house of a God-fearing gentile called Titius Justus. The name shows that Justus is a Roman who must have been rich for his house to be large enough to accommodate the church. But it is not in the author's nature to give a blanket condemnation of the Jews as a people; the synagogue leader, Crispus, also converts along with his household.[19]

A more serious legal attack on Paul came when the Jews brought him before the tribunal of Gallio, the Roman proconsul of Achaia, in modern-day Greece. The Jews accused Paul of inciting people to worship contrary to the law, but Gallio dismissed the charge. Gallio was the brother of the younger Seneca and was proconsul of Achaia around 51/52 AD. He was caught up in his family's downfall and fell victim to Nero in 65 AD.[20] Once again, we see the author of Luke getting the Roman details correct.

At Ephesus, Paul's supporters suffered a different kind of adversary. Demetrius, a silversmith who made shrines and images for Artemis, found his business in decline because Paul was persuading people that idols were not real gods. He led a riot under the slogan "Great is Artemis of the Ephesians." The city clerk quelled the disturbance, reaffirming the status of Ephesus as the place where the image of Artemis had fallen from the sky. But he gives a favorable verdict on the Christians: "they are guilty neither of sacrilege nor of blasphemy against our goddess."[21] He suggests that Demetrius should make his charges in court—but going through official channels is never the way of the demagog.[22]

The author of Luke raises all the charges that a Roman might bring against Christians:

(i) they see Jesus as a greater ruler than Caesar;
(ii) they persuade people to abandon traditional religion;
(iii) they encourage sacrilege against pagan gods such as Artemis.

In Acts, these charges are considered one by one by the Roman appointed authorities. In each case, they find Paul and the Christians innocent. In this way, the author of Luke attempts to persuade the skeptical Roman reader that Christianity is blameless and should be allowed to flourish without persecution. It is ironic that each of these charges was actually true, as would become brutally evident to pagans when Christianity finally did take over the empire.

A client king

One of the strangest parables in Luke is based on Matthew's parable of the talents.[23] In Matthew, a master is about to embark on a long journey. He gives his three servants his money to look after. To one servant, he gives five talents, to another two talents, and to a third one talent. (A talent was a large weight measure of silver; it amounted to about 3,000 shekels.)

When he returns, he finds that the servant who has received five talents has invested them to make another five. Likewise, the servant with two talents has made another two. He rewards them both with additional responsibilities. However, the servant with one talent is afraid because his master is a hard man: "reaping where you have not sown and gathering where you have not scattered seed."[24] So he has buried his one talent to safeguard it for his master's return. The master reproves him for his laziness and gives it to the servant with ten talents. The punchline is that one who has will be given more, and one who has not, the little they have will be taken away from them. Behind this Matthew parable is a spiritual saying of the Jesus movement. A person with spiritual riches will put their gifts to work and become richer. A person without spiritual gifts will not even use the little they have, so losing even that. The author of Matthew, however, is not content with that conclusion. They add a punishment: "and throw that worthless servant into the outer darkness, where there will be weeping and gnashing of teeth."[25]

The author of Luke takes this Matthew parable and changes it according to the "same but different" tendency.[26] Instead of three servants, there are now ten who are each given one mina (about 50 shekels). However, the author then reverts to the Matthew pattern of three. The first servant makes ten more minas, the second five more, and the third retains his initial one. This luckless servant has his mina taken away from him and given to the servant with ten.

The most unexpected change is that the master is now a man "of noble birth" who is going into a distant country to claim his kingship. His servants hate him and send a delegation in an attempt to prevent him from becoming king. This makes it clear that the model for the parable is a Roman client kingship, such as the Herods. The delegation is unsuccessful, and the nobleman returns as king. He rewards the servant who has made ten minas with the governance of ten cities and the one who has made five minas with five cities. The servant with one mina is not punished, but the king orders the execution of those who opposed his rule.

The parables are everyday stories that illustrate some feature of the kingdom of heaven. For the author of Luke, the everyday seems to include kings awarding the oversight of cities. There are some parallels to Herod the Great's son, Archelaus, who journeyed to Rome to get his kingship acknowledged by Augustus and faced a delegation from his citizens. On his return, he treated his subjects brutally and eventually lost his kingdom and was exiled. Josephus recounts the story in both the Jewish War and the Antiquities. However, the king in the parable represents Jesus and not Archelaus. The subjects who are killed are the wicked who reject Jesus' rule and who will be brought to judgement and punished in hell.

As a parable, it is a failure. But it gives us insight into the author of Luke's perspective on life.

Guilty of the crucifixion?

Even the author of Luke struggled to make the Romans innocent of Jesus' crucifixion, but that did not stop her from trying. In the other gospels, Jesus is arrested, tried, and condemned by the Sanhedrin. He is taken to Pilate, who finds him innocent and offers to release either Jesus or Barabbas. The crowd choose Barabbas and call upon Pilate to crucify Jesus. Pilate reluctantly agrees and has Jesus scourged. This was a vicious flogging with a whip containing fragments of sharp bone or metal that would inflict serious damage. After the scourging, Jesus is led into the praetorium, where the soldiers give him mock homage. They dress him in a robe of purple and place a crown of thorns on his head and hail him as King of the Jews. They then strike him on the head with a staff and spit upon him before leading him away to crucifixion.

The episode shows the Romans as sadists not content with simply putting someone to death, not even by crucifixion. Unsurprisingly, the author of Luke is unhappy with this portrayal of Roman brutality. So the Gospel of Luke eliminates some of the Romans' worse actions. This is achieved by changing the story to follow what should have been the correct legal procedure. Jesus is supposedly from Galilee and should come under the jurisdiction of Herod Antipas, the tetrarch of Galilee. The Roman governor should have sent Jesus to his king for judgment. We find examples of this practice in Josephus: Vespasian had condemned Justus of Tiberius to death but sent him to Agrippa II because he was a subject of that king.[27]

So, in Luke, Pilate sends Jesus to Herod Antipas. This introduces a blatant contradiction to the other gospel accounts where Jesus is taken from the priests to Pilate and then straight to crucifixion. It also gives problems with the timescale, which is already ridiculously short. The Gospel of Mark allows only three hours for the Jews to condemn Jesus, for him to be taken and tried by Pilate, for the mock homage and preparations for crucifixion, and the journey to the cross. An additional trial in front of Herod, after which Jesus is sent back again to Pilate for judgment, makes the timescale even more absurd. In reality, a hearing before Herod would have taken several hours or even days. The king must be available, and his advisors would have to investigate and brief the king. Then there is the time for the hearing itself, for Herod "questioned him for some length."[28]

The real purpose of including the trial before Herod is to shift blame from the Romans. In Luke, it is Herod's soldiers and not the Romans who give Jesus mock homage:

> Herod with his soldiers ridiculed and mocked him. Dressing him in a splendid robe, they sent him back to Pilate. (Luke 23:11)

The mocking no longer takes place in the praetorium and has been considerably toned down. There is no crown of thorns, no contemptuous acclamation of Jesus as "King of the Jews," and certainly no spitting or striking on the head. And any blame rests on the Jewish soldiers of Herod, not the Romans.

The brutal, vicious scourging is completely omitted. Instead, Pilate suggests a whipping for Jesus in an attempt to save his life: "Therefore I will punish him and release him."[29] The word here for "punish" is that used for the chastisement of a child, and nothing like the scourging that could maim or even kill.

Guilty of the destruction of Jerusalem?

Domitilla's family was guilty of the destruction of Jerusalem and the temple. She would have found it very difficult to blame her uncle and her grandfather for these events, so we should expect to find apologetics in Luke/Acts shifting the blame. Josephus, the client of Vespasian and Titus, faces the same problem. He blames the rebel Jews for causing the destruction through their rebellion, their immoral behavior, their takeover of the temple, and their actions against the priestly establishment. Josephus sees the Romans as the instruments of God's wrath cleansing Jerusalem: "They entered your gates to purge with fire the filthiness within you: you were no longer the place of God."[30]

The author of Luke follows a similar strategy but assigns blame differently. It is now due to the Jews' failure to understand Jesus and what he was offering them:

> As he drew near and saw the city, he wept over it and said, "If only you had known on this day the things of peace! But now they are hidden from your eyes. For the days will come upon you when your enemies will barricade you and surround you and hem you in on every side. They will level you to the ground and your children within you. They will not leave one stone upon another, because you did not know the time of your visitation." (Luke 19:41-44)

Jerusalem will be destroyed because the people did not recognize Jesus as Lord and God. Although the passage does not explicitly mention the Romans, there is a clear reference to Titus' siege of the city: "your enemies will barricade you and surround you" and "they will level you to the ground." If only the Jews had eyes to see "the things of peace" that Jesus brought, they would have avoided this fate.

In Mark and Matthew, Jesus warns about the destruction of Jerusalem when he leaves the temple: the Jews will see "the abomination of desolation standing where it should not" and must flee to the mountains.[31] Although the warning is obscure, the "abomination of desolation" must have something to do with the Romans. The author of Luke does not like Jesus calling the Romans an "abomination" and changes the passage:

> But when you see Jerusalem surrounded by armies, you will know that her desolation is near. Then let those who are in Judea flee to the mountains, let those in her depart, and let those in the country not go into her. For these are the days of vengeance, to fulfil all things that are written. (Luke 21:20-22)

There is no longer an "abomination of desolation," only a "desolation", *eremosis*, that applies to the city, not the Romans. The phrase "days of vengeance" justifies the Roman destruction as divine punishment on the Jews. So the Gospel of Luke subtly shifts the blame for the destruction onto the Jews while making the Romans the tools by which the prophecy comes true: "...and Jerusalem shall be trampled by the nations, till the times of nations be fulfilled."[32]

13

Rome

The journey to Rome

Titus' triumphant progression began at Caesarea Philippi. There he celebrated his victory by watching his defeated enemies die in the arena; they were thrown to wild beasts or made to fight and kill one another. He went next to Caesarea on the coast, where he celebrated Domitian's birthday with games in which 2,500 Jews died. The gladiators slew each other in staged battles while some fought wild beasts, and others were simply burnt alive. The fun continued as Titus made his festive way through Syria. The spectacle would have delighted the Syrians who were locked in a mutual hatred with the Jews.

Did Josephus attend any of these entertainments? Did he sit near Titus Caesar, watching his compatriots die as he ate and relaxed? Did he cheer as a Jewish gladiator was speared through by another Jew? Or did he demur to attend on religious grounds? To do so would have been dangerous. Josephus claimed that Vespasian was the Messiah whom God had appointed to lead the world. So how could he excuse himself from celebrating the victory in Roman style? And whether he attended or not, how did Josephus feel at the endless killing?

At Antioch, the capital of Syria, the citizens came out to greet Titus Caesar. They joyfully requested the expulsion of the Jews from the city or, failing that, the rescinding of the Jew's rights and privileges. But Titus flatly refused. For both Titus and Vespasian, there was a stark difference between how they treated affairs of war and civil society. The Jews in the arena were paying the price of fighting Rome. The Jews of Antioch had not revolted, and Titus refused to see an injustice done to them.[1]

One provision that did apply to Jews everywhere concerned the temple tax. It had been a religious obligation recognized by Roman law for Jews throughout the empire to pay a tax of half a shekel or two drachmas to the temple in Jerusalem. This was the source of the immense riches of the temple. Now that the temple was no more, the tax was not relevant, but the Romans were not going to forego revenue. In the future, the Jews would pay the money to the temple of Jupiter Optimus Maximus in Rome. This action changed a religious contribution into a civil tax on the Jews as a people.[2]

Titus progressed from Antioch back to Jerusalem and then Alexandria, where he took Josephus with him on a ship bound for Rome. Unlike Josephus' last sea journey to Rome, the voyage was uneventful. The senate had declared separate triumphs for Vespasian and Titus, but they decided modestly to share a single triumph. The two generals slept the night before the triumph at the Temple of Isis. They took breakfast at the Portico of Octavia, where they were met by cheering crowds and soldiers, and then entered the city.[3]

The triumph astonished the spectators. Rich and abundant treasures were carried in possession. The highlights were the temple furniture including a gold table weighing several hundredweight and the magnificent seven-branched gold lampstand. Even the captives were finely dressed—Josephus adds that their garments hid any disfigurements they had suffered. The greatest spectacle of all were the traveling stages representing the battle scenes of the war. They were three to four stories high, and people feared that they might topple over. The war was depicted in grisly detail, with the general of each captured town displayed as part of the scene. The possession paused at the temple of Jupiter, where they waited for the execution of Simon, son of Gioras, in the Forum. Then all of Rome celebrated with sumptuous banquets.[4]

Did Josephus play his part in the display? He was, after all, the defeated general of Jotapata, one of Vespasian's most challenging conquests. Did he have the humiliation of standing in the rags he wore when captured as the crowds gawked and jeered? Josephus must have been an eyewitness to the display but is silent about his own role. We will see how he later took a literary revenge on Vespasian for this triumph.

Vespasian would set up a temple to Peace to house art and artifacts from around the known world. He deposited most of the Jerusalem temple treasures in this museum. The book of the law and the curtain to the inner temple were taken to the palace. This is the same temple curtain which, according to Mark and Matthew, split into two upon the death of Jesus. The author of Luke loved miracles but, for some reason, omitted this particular one: perhaps she was too familiar with the intact curtain.[5]

Josephus

By 71 AD, both Josephus and Domitilla were in Rome. The two would belong to the same circle in the same city for the next twenty-four years. Josephus took the name Josephus Flavius reflecting his new status as a Flavian client. Vespasian set him up in his own former house in Rome. Domitilla would have been very familiar with this house as it was likely her childhood home. Even if Vespasian did not adopt her until later, she would still have spent much time there.

Now that he had patronage, leisure, and comfort, Josephus reinvented himself as a historian. He always had an eye for how he could be useful to the powerful. The Jewish war had been the principal military accomplishment for both Vespasian and Titus. By becoming the chronicler of their war, he intended to set himself up for life. A historian had to be a former man of affairs in the ancient world. Only someone who had experienced command could adequately understand the forces that shaped military engagements and the destiny of peoples. But it was unusual for the historian to have been on the opposite side to Rome, which is why Josephus was very keen to portray himself as a Roman-style general rather than some exotic barbarian chief.

It may seem odd that he first wrote the Jewish War in Aramaic, which his Roman audience would have been unable to read. At this stage, Josephus was unpracticed as an author and not confident reading or writing in Greek. He says that the intended readership for the Aramaic version was the Parthians, the Babylonians, the people of Arabia and Adiabene, and, more broadly, the Jewish diaspora living beyond the Euphrates.[6] This very odd audience would have been difficult to reach from Rome. Josephus is likely covering up for the rough quality of his draft. He could show it to friendly Jews for their comments and opinions, and the fact that his Roman patrons could not read it would be an advantage. The supposed Jewish audience beyond the Roman Empire in the east was conveniently distant—he could boast, without fear of contradiction, that his book was read avidly by the Parthians. No copy of this Aramaic version has survived, and we cannot judge its quality. But the real audience for the Jewish War was the Flavian court, and Josephus soon began work on the Greek version.

Writing in the 90s AD, he admits that assistants helped with the Greek—they would have been slave or freedman scribes—and does not mention any prior Aramaic version.[7] The high literary quality of the Greek Jewish War is due to these unacknowledged collaborators who turned Josephus' stumbling translations into polished prose. The work has been completely rewritten leaving no sign of an Aramaic original. Most likely these assistants were highly-trained imperial slaves provided by Vespasian. Even twenty years later, Josephus struggled with Greek:

> "I have also labored strenuously to partake of the realm of Greek prose and poetry after having acquired practice in writing, although the habitual use of my native tongue has prevented my attaining precision in the pronunciation." (Antiquities 20:263)

He denigrates the skill of writing with "smoothness of diction" as something practiced even by freedmen and slaves. Josephus was above such things, being one of only two or three individuals who had mastered the full depth of Jewish learning.[8] It seems that Josephus always had to rely on scribes for his Greek composition.

The Greek version of the Jewish War was published sometime between 75 and 79 AD and was acclaimed by the Flavians.[9] Both Vespasian and Titus gave it official approval, with Titus even signing the volumes to vouch for their accuracy and ordering their publication. King Agrippa purchased a copy and wrote sixty-two letters promoting the work. Another member of the Herodian dynasty also bought a copy, as did other prominent Jews in the Roman world. The Jewish War became the official version of the truth, and if you wanted to be anyone in Flavian Rome, it was wise to be familiar with it or, even better, own a copy.[10] It looked like Josephus had it made. But fate has the habit of interrupting even the best-laid plans.

Domitilla and Julia

Flavia Domitilla must have been adopted by Vespasian no later than the beginning of his reign, if not earlier. Cerialis was almost constantly engaged in military operations for several years, first putting down the Batavian revolt and then as governor of Britannia. He was awarded the consulship both in 70 and on his return from Britannia in 74.

Domitilla spent her teen years growing up in Rome in the 70s as a Flavian while her grandfather Vespasian was Emperor. She would have been a highly desirable match for any ambitious aristocrat. But she was not alone. Her cousin Julia Titi (also known as Julia Flavia), was the child of Titus and either his first wife, Arrecina Tertulla, or his divorced second wife Marcia Furnilla. She would have been around the same age as Domitilla or perhaps a year or two younger.[11]

As Julia was the only surviving child of Titus, the likely future emperor, the man who married her could have a claim to be emperor himself. The Flavians were well aware of this danger, and Titus offered her as bride to her uncle Domitian. He, however, was infatuated by Domitia Longina, daughter of the esteemed general Corbulo, a victim of Nero. She had to divorce her husband, Aelius Lamia, to marry him.

This did not stop the Flavians from keeping their heiresses safely in the family. The two girls were married to two brothers, the grandsons of Vespasian's deceased brother, Flavius Sabinus. Julia's husband was also called Flavius Sabinus and was the son of yet another Flavius Sabinus who had been consul suffectus in 69 AD and 72 AD.[12] Domitilla was married to the younger brother, Flavius Clemens.

We do not know the precise dates of the marriages, but both must have occurred by around 80 AD. Titus intended to continue the Flavian dynasty through Julia, and when Domitian refused the match, he turned to the next most eligible Flavian male, Sabinus. This implied that Julia's and Sabinus' hoped-for-sons would be Titus' intended successors rather than Domitian. Titus may even have inclined towards Sabinus as a more immediate potential successor rather than the unsatisfactory Domitian. It would have been natural for Titus to eventually make Sabinus a Caesar alongside Domitian. And Titus gave Julia the title of Augusta, customarily reserved for the emperor's wife. She was thus singled out as the highest-ranking woman in the empire.

That left Domitilla and Clemens as the spare couple. All we know about Clemens' character is the remark by Suetonius that he was a man of "most contemptible idleness."[13] Commentators have long speculated what Suetonius meant by this. Christian apologists have interpreted it as implying that Clemens was reluctant to undertake pagan religious duties. But it seems more likely that he was an unambitious stay-at-home who refused military service or posts abroad. No one ever saw Clemens as emperor material, which would explain why he out-survived his brother for so long under Domitian. In fact, Domitilla and Clemens fade almost unnoticed into the background until thrust into the limelight by the fertility of their marriage. Julia's beautiful face is known from her coins and statue busts, but we have no known contemporary image of Domitilla.

Were Julia and Domitilla close? We might expect so from the similarity of their age and relationship, being both cousins and sisters-in-law. However, that does not always follow, and we simply do not know. Both their lives would end in tragedy. But Julia, unlike Domitilla, left no enduring legacy.

Berenice, Agrippa and Drusilla

Josephus was not the only Jewish influence in Domitilla's life. While in Judea, Titus had fallen hopelessly in love with Queen Berenice. She was already the subject of considerable scandal, for she was rumored to be in an incestuous relationship with her brother Agrippa. We find this rumor reported by Josephus in his Antiquities, published 93/94 AD.[14] Both Agrippa and Berenice must have been dead by that time, or Josephus would not have mentioned the incest gossip. Juvenal, who was writing in the late first or early second century, repeated it as fact:

> A diamond of great renown, made precious by the finger of
> Berenice. It was given as a present long ago by the barbarian
> Agrippa to his incestuous sister, in that country where kings
> celebrate festal sabbaths with bare feet, and where a long-estab-
> lished clemency suffers pigs to attain old age. (Juvenal 6:156-60)[15]

Agrippa and Berenice were certainly very close, cohabiting for long
periods. But perhaps this arrangement just suited them both. Agrippa
never married and was not interested in women beyond the company of
his sister. He accepted Berenice as his equal, which enabled her to rule her
kingdom without the interference of a husband.

Berenice was born in 28 AD and was sixteen when her father, Agrippa
I, died. She was already on her second marriage. Her first husband,
Marcius Julius Alexander, had died, leaving her a very young teenage
widow. She was immediately remarried to her uncle, Herod of Chalcis.
The marriage produced two sons, but he also died in 48 AD. So, aged
around twenty, she started to live with her brother. The rumors of incest
grew so strong that several years later, she requested to be married again.
A suitable match, King Polemo II of Pontus, was found. Agrippa insisted
that he convert to Judaism and be circumcised. The king agreed, motivated more by Berenice's wealth than desire for her person. The union
did not last long—Berenice soon deserted him and moved back to her
brother.[16]

In the year of the four emperors, Berenice put her influence and her
money firmly behind Vespasian. While Titus had turned back in Greece,
Agrippa had continued to Rome to pay homage to the new emperor, whoever he might be. He now received a secret summons, doubtless from
Berenice, to return. Tacitus makes an ironic comment on her support for
the Flavians:

> "His sister Berenice showed equal enthusiasm for the cause.
> She was then in the flower of her youth and beauty, and her
> munificent gifts to Vespasian quite won the old man's heart too."
> (Tacitus, The Histories 2:81)

The implication is that while Titus was won by her beauty, Vespasian,
whom Tacitus accuses of meanness, was won by her money. In reality,
Berenice was making a daring and risky gamble that paid off handsomely.
Reading the strategic situation correctly, she pulled all the strings of her
considerable connections to ensure Vespasian had full support in the east.
She would have been motivated in part by her relationship with Titus.
Although eleven years his senior, she exercised a fascination over him.

According to Suetonius, Titus had a "great passion for Queen Berenice to whom he is said to have promised marriage."[17]

It is extraordinary that Agrippa and Berenice did not come to Rome until 75 AD. It seems that there was political opposition against Titus' relationship with Berenice. Some point to Mucianus as the culprit. He exercised a huge influence in Flavian Rome and died in the mid 70s.[18] But it is not clear why Mucianus should object to a liaison which weakened his rival. It is more probable that the opposition came from Titus' father. Vespasian may have liked the queen, but that does not mean he would have been happy to see his son marry her. She was foreign, eastern and Jewish, all of which made her unpopular with the people of Rome. She was also too old to have children and Titus had no sons. But the lovers ultimately won out, and Berenice and her brother were permitted to reside in Rome. Agrippa was made a praetor while Berenice lived openly in the palace with Titus as if they were married.

We can imagine how glamorous her uncle's Jewish mistress must have appeared to Domitilla. Berenice had ruled in her own right and lived life on her own terms. She was courageous and moved events. Now nearing fifty, it looked like she would be empress alongside Titus who would have to look to his daughter, Julia, to provide his heirs.

Whatever the basis of Berenice's attraction, it was not just looks. She was not even the beauty of the family, that distinction belonging to her sister Drusilla. Born in 38 AD, Drusilla was ten years younger than Berenice. She was just six when her father Agrippa I died but already betrothed to Epiphanes, son of the king of Commagene. The marriage never took place because Epiphanes refused to be circumcised. Instead, her brother married her as a young teenager to Azizus, king of Emesa, who did get circumcised.[19]

The marriage did not last long. As Josephus puts it: "While Felix was procurator of Judea, he saw this Drusilla, and fell in love with her; for she did indeed exceed all other women in beauty." Josephus gives a strange story of Felix employing a Jewish magician called either Simon or Atomos (the manuscripts differ) to persuade her to divorce Azizus and marry him.[20] But from Josephus' description, it seems that she had already separated from Azizus and was living with Agrippa and Berenice:

> Accordingly she acted ill, and because she was desirous to avoid her sister Berenice's envy, for she was very ill-treated by her on account of her beauty, was prevailed upon to transgress the laws of her forefathers, and to marry Felix; and when he had had a son by her, he named him Agrippa. (Josephus Antiquities 20:143)

Antonius Felix, or Claudius Felix (depending on whether we believe Tacitus or Josephus), was a remarkable example of upward social mobility in the Roman world, for he started life as a slave. His brother Pallas was the most favored slave of the future emperor Claudius' mother Antonia and was freed by her. When Antonia died, Pallas served her son Claudius and was one of the two freedmen, alongside Narcissus, who effectively ran Claudius' administration. The modern equivalent to Pallas would be the finance minister, and he became very rich on his own account. Suetonius jokes that Claudius often complained of being short of funds, but he would have had plenty if he had become the partner of his two prominent freedmen.[21]

Pallas' younger brother Felix would have been freed by either Antonia or Claudius, hence the confusion over his name. Felix became a favorite of Claudius, who put him in charge of "cohorts and cavalry divisions." In 52 AD, he was appointed governor of Judea, an office he held until his recall under Nero in 60 AD. Suetonius says that Claudius married him off to three queens. Tacitus gives the additional information that he married Drusilla, a granddaughter of Antony and Cleopatra, making him Antony's grandson-in-law, whereas Claudius was Antony's grandson.[22] This woman may be the daughter of Juba II of Mauretania in North Africa and Cleopatra Selene II, or perhaps the next generation of this line. What about her name Drusilla? She cannot be the Jewish Drusilla who was not related to Cleopatra. Tacitus has either confused two wives of Felix, or there is a coincidence of names.[23] We know nothing about the identity of the third queen.

The Jewish Drusilla would have been Felix's final wife, and he married her at the very end of Claudius' reign. After Felix's recall, the couple would have lived in Rome. We hear nothing more about Felix and only one uncertain mention of Drusilla. Were they still alive in the mid-70s? Felix would have been quite old for the time, around sixty, but Drusilla was much younger and still in her thirties.

Josephus is surprisingly neutral about Felix in the Jewish War but changes his tone in the Antiquities. Most strikingly, the Antiquities includes the accusation that Felix arranged for the Sicarii to kill Jonathon, the high priest, and so was responsible for starting the terrorist violence. This improbable story is not believed by scholars. The Antiquities also includes the account of the seduction of Drusilla and says that Felix would have been punished for corruption on his recall to Rome except for the intercession of Pallas. Although Josephus was careful not to upset Felix and Drusilla when he was writing the Jewish War around 75, they must have both died by the 90s when he wrote the Antiquities.[24]

We can expect Drusilla, with or without Felix, to have been a familiar part of her brother's and sister's circle in Rome. Drusilla and her son Agrippa may have been occasional visitors rather than permanent residents: both mother and son were in the Bay of Naples area towards the end of the 70s.

Agrippa and his sister would have brought with them a wider Jewish entourage. The Herods would have continued to practice their religion surrounded by other Jews; freedmen, slaves, minor family, and hangers-on. Domitilla would have been exposed to this considerable Jewish influence, and she would have had the example of Titus' intimate relationship with Berenice. The family grouping of Agrippa and his sisters in Rome did not last beyond a few years. Popular opinion was firmly against Berenice, who was seen as a second Cleopatra. To ensure his succession as emperor, Titus reluctantly agreed that Berenice would have to leave Rome for a time.[25]

The Jewish influence on Domitilla would account for the author of Luke/ Acts' considerable knowledge of Jewish practices. Domitilla would have regarded Berenice and Agrippa as her social equals. Josephus, however, was not on the same level. She would have admired his talent and erudition, but socially he was just a Flavian client. We will see the evidence for a mutual influence between the author of Luke and Josephus later. But first, we will show how Luke and Acts reflect the Herodian connection centered on King Agrippa and his sisters.

14

Agrippa II and his circle in Luke/Acts

Agrippa II's kingdom in Luke

The mission of John the Baptist in Luke is dated by a comprehensive statement:

> Now in the fifteenth year of the reign of Tiberius Caesar, Pontius Pilate being governor of Judaea, and Herod being tetrarch of Galilee, and his brother Philip, tetrarch of Ituraea and of the region of Trachonitis, and Lysanias, the tetrarch of Abilene, during the high priesthood of Annas and Caiaphas, the word of God came to John, son of Zechariah, in the wilderness. (Luke 3:1-2)

This sets the scene for Jesus' mission and is quite unlike anything in the other gospels. It gives a list of Roman or Roman appointed rulers starting with the highest authority of the emperor and working down in importance. It shows how the author is writing from a Roman perspective and copying the conventions of historical writing. Two of the rulers, Pilate and Herod, will interact with Jesus, but the others are not mentioned again.

The statement starts with a date, the fifteenth year of the reign of Tiberius. Unfortunately, we cannot be sure if we should count Tiberius' reign as starting when he succeeded Augustus as emperor or two years earlier when appointed as joint ruler. So the fifteenth year is either 26/27 or 28/29 AD. Next in importance after the emperor is the Roman governor of Judea, Pontius Pilate, and then Herod Antipas, the tetrarch of Galilee. After Herod, the list becomes increasingly strange. Why mention Philip at all? His kingdom was across the Jordan, and the two places named are distant from Judea; Ituraea far to the north of Galilee and Trachonitis, a rocky region further to the east.

The most puzzling and obscure of all is "Lysanias, the tetrarch of Abilene." The tetrarch Lysanias who ruled Abila, also called Abilene, as part of a much larger territory, lived sixty years previously and was put to death by Mark Antony in 33 BC due to Cleopatra's machinations. Apologists contend that there must have been a later ruler of the same name who governed part of the former Lysanias' territory. But Josephus, who has a comprehensive knowledge of the minor kings in the region, never mentions such a person. Nor are there any coins in his name. Josephus says that Zenodorus (probably Lysanias' son) later leased the "house/estate of Lysanias" and also talks about the "kingdom called that of Lysanias." which shows that Lysanias' name continued to be attached to the kingdom long after he died. So the idea that Lysanias lived at the time of John the Baptist seems to be a mistake made by the author of Luke.

The real mystery, though, is not Lysanias himself but why the author of Luke should mention such an unimportant, distant place as Abila/Abilene. The ancient town of Abila Lysaniae lay in Syria, twelve miles northwest of Damascus. It had no connection with Judea and is never mentioned again in the gospel.

A further mystery concerns Ituraea. The Ituraeans are an obscure people perhaps of Arab origin and known mainly from a few passing remarks made by ancient historians. They had a bad reputation among their neighbors as robbers and raiders. The Romans, however, made use of their military prowess and esteemed them highly as archers. There were cohorts of Ituraean archers in the Roman army as late as the third century, although by this time they would have largely ceased to exist as a separate ethnic group having been absorbed into the Syrians.

In the first century BC, there was an identifiable Ituraean kingdom. Both Lysanias and Zenodorus were Ituraean minor kings, as was Lysanias' father, Ptolemy, son of Mennaeus. Their capital was Chalcis and all three issued coins on which they styled themselves "tetrarch and high priest." The Ituraean heartland was the Lebanon and Anti-Lebanon mountain ranges and the Biqa valley which lies between.[1] This area is far to the north of the lands ruled by Philip and immediately west of Abila Lysaniae.[2]

So why does Luke call Philip tetrarch of Ituraea when Josephus never mentions Ituraea in connection with his tetrarchy.[3] There is some evidence of Ituraeans in Gaulanitis, the modern-day Golan Heights, which lies to the north of Galilee and which Josephus does assign to Philip.[4] But Philip never ruled the Ituraean homeland in Lebanon.[5] Calling him the tetrarch of Ituraea would seem to be a misunderstanding by the author of Luke, albeit one we can sympathize with given the ethnic and political complexities of the area.

How can we make sense of this odd list in Luke? None of the places listed after Galilee were Jewish and there is no reason why John or Jesus should be involved with remote Syrian areas such as Ituraea or Abilene. There is, however, one common factor for the places on the list; all of them after Judea belonged to Agrippa II's kingdom. His father, Agrippa I, had been an intimate friend of Caligula before he became emperor. Tiberius imprisoned Agrippa for expressing a wish for his death so that Caligula could succeed him. When Tiberius did die, Agrippa was released by Caligula and granted the former tetrarchy of Philip, along with "the tetrarchy of Lysanias."[6] Agrippa was in Rome when Caligula was assassinated, and he helped smooth the way for Claudius' ascension. The new emperor rewarded him handsomely by adding Judea and Samaria to his kingdom, as well as other outer districts ruled by his grandfather, Herod the Great.[7]

When Agrippa I died in 44 AD, Claudius decided that the seventeen-year-old Agrippa II was too young to inherit his father's kingdom, so he made Fadus procurator of Judea. Four years later, the king of Chalcis died, and Agrippa II was given his small tetrarchy, the former heartland of the old kingdom of Ituraea.[8] Later, Claudius would exchange Chalcis for some of the other territories his father had ruled:[9]

> When he completed the twelfth year of his reign he granted to Agrippa the tetrarchy of Philip together with Batanea, adding thereto Trachonitis and Lysanias' former tetrarchy of Abila. (Jewish Antiquities 20:138) [10]

There are several common points with the Luke passage; the tetrarchy of Philip, Trachonitis, the tetrarchy of Lysanias, and Abila (Abilene). The parallel passage in the Jewish War adds "old tetrarchy of Varus" after the kingdom of Lysanias.[11] Most likely this "tetrarchy of Varus" refers to a mountainous area of Lebanon that was part of Ituraea but which lay outside the tetrarchy of Chalcis.[12] Nero added to Agrippa II's kingdom the city of Julias and the two Galilean towns, Tiberius and Tarichaeae.[13]

We can summarize the relationship of Agrippa II to all the districts that Luke lists:

Galilee: although Agrippa II did not control all of Galilee, he had a strong interest in this area, possessing two of the three major cities, Tiberius and Tarichaeae, and their hinterland.

The tetrarchy of Philip, including Trachonitis: all of Philip's tetrarchy was subsequently ruled by Agrippa II. Philip did not rule Ituraea although his tetrarchy included Gaulanitis which probably had an Ituraean population in the Golan Heights.

Ituraea: Agrippa II first ruled the former Ituraean capital Chalcis and its hinterland. He lost this city when he was given additional territory which included the tetrarchy of Varus, most likely the mountainous area of Lebanon which had been a part of the Ituraean heartland.

Lysanias' former tetrarchy of Abila: another part of Lysanias' former kingdom granted to Agrippa II and previously ruled by his father.

The author of Luke seems to have started with a list of Agrippa II's territories, including Abilene and Ituraea in Syria. These were then allocated to the kings who ruled them in the late 20s AD. Josephus was one of the author's sources for this exercise, but not the only one. The author made two mistakes; thinking Lysanias was still alive in the 20s AD and allocating Ituraea to the tetrarchy of Philip. It all shows the importance placed on the lands ruled by Agrippa II and is the first clue of a special link between the author and the king.

Felix and Drusilla

If the territory of King Agrippa II features near the start of Luke/Acts, the king himself will appear near the end. When Paul is arrested in Jerusalem, he is held in Antonia by the Romans for his own safety. However, more than forty Jews make an oath to ambush and kill him. Paul's sister's son hears about the plot and informs the tribune, Claudius Lysias, who sends Paul to the Roman headquarters in Caesarea. He assembles a large force to defend him; two hundred legionaries, seventy cavalry, and two hundred auxiliaries—a total of almost five hundred men.[14] This must have been a sizeable proportion of the total Roman garrison at Antonia. The author of Luke seems to think nothing of such a contingent, and perhaps, for them, it was a perfectly reasonable guard. In reality, no Roman commander would have committed so many men to defend a vagabond preacher simply because he claimed to be a Roman citizen. A handful of soldiers would have been assigned to guard such a person. The Jews knew that anyone who dared attack the guard would end up crucified.

Paul has been sent to Caesarea for trial before the procurator Felix, the husband of Agrippa II's sister, Drusilla. Lysias writes to him saying that there is no charge "worthy of death or imprisonment" and that the case concerns the Jewish law. From the Jewish side, the high priest Ananias and the orator Tertullus travel to Caesarea to accuse Paul as "the ringleader of the sect of the Nazarenes."[15] Paul gives his defense, and Felix adjourns the case until he can consult with Lysias, which should take no more than a few days. But the case stays adjourned for years.

Felix is addressed by the same title, *kratiste*, as Theophilus. He is said to be "well informed" or "had exact knowledge" (*akribos*) "about the Way."[16] The "Way" is the author of Luke's expression for the Jesus movement. In the introduction to Luke, the author uses the same word *akribos* to describe how they had become "well informed" to instruct Theophilus. So how has Felix has become well instructed about Christian beliefs? Most likely through Drusilla.

Felix orders Paul to be treated well, keeps him under arrest, but allows him some contact with others. And, surprisingly, he seeks to learn from Paul:

> After several days, Felix with his wife Drusilla, who was a Jewess, sent for Paul, and heard him concerning the faith in Christ Jesus. As Paul talked about righteousness, self-control, and the coming judgment, Felix became frightened and answered: "Go for now. When I have the opportunity, I will call for you." (Acts 24:24-5)

Although scared by the moral requirements placed on Christians and the implications of the coming judgment, Felix continues to listen to Paul:

> At the same time he hoped that riches [chremata] would be given him by Paul. So he sent for him often and talked with him. (Acts 24:26)

Almost invariably, this is translated as meaning that Felix wanted a bribe from Paul, but what Felix wants cannot be literal money. A poor itinerant Christian apostle like Paul had nothing of worldly value to offer to a wealthy Roman governor. And if Felix were open to a bribe to settle the case, the Jewish establishment could pay more handsomely than Paul.

The word *chremata* can mean riches, money, or more generally, something that one uses or needs. Felix is shown as someone knowledgeable about Christian doctrine and keen to listen to Paul talk about the Christian faith. It makes sense for that which he hopes for to relate in some way to Christianity. In the Gospel of Thomas, "riches" is used in two opposed senses; worldly riches, which are condemned, and the riches of the spiritual kingdom of heaven that are esteemed. It must be this second type of riches that Felix wants from Paul. He desires the spirit but is not willing to pay the moral price it entails. Felix defers judgment for two years to keep listening to Paul. But when he is recalled to Rome, he leaves Paul in prison to avoid upsetting the Jews.

The key to understanding this extraordinary episode is that Felix stands for Theophilus. They are both called by the same title *kratiste*, and they are both well-informed about the Way, but neither are full Christians. Felix has come under the influence of his Jewish wife Drusilla to learn something about Judaism and Christianity. Likewise, Theophilus has been instructed by the author of Luke who is his wife or mother. Felix feels the call of Paul but is not prepared to make the sacrifice the apostle demands. He wants to be "made rich" with the spirit but is unwilling to pay the price.

Ultimately Felix fails the test and will come to the judgment he fears. The author of Luke is holding up Agrippa II's brother-in-law as a warning to Theophilus. Will you be like Felix or take the step he would not?

Festus, Agrippa and Berenice

Felix was replaced as procurator by Festus. On arriving in the province, he traveled to Jerusalem, where, according to Acts, the priests tried to get him to send Paul to the city for trial so that they could ambush him on the way. The Jewish priestly establishment would have never taken such a risk in reality. Festus is suspicious and insists that the hearing be held in Caesarea. The Jews make their accusations at the hearing, and Paul gives his defense. Although Festus is inclined to send him to Jerusalem for trial, Paul claims his right as a Roman citizen to be tried before the emperor in Rome. So Festus rules that Paul will be sent to Rome.[17]

This second trial sets up Acts for the climactic conclusion of a third trial in Rome before the emperor. But it never happens. Instead, an unnecessary third trial takes place in Caesarea. Festus decides to hold another hearing in front of his guests, King Agrippa and Queen Berenice. Supposedly, this is to inform Festus of what to write to the emperor as the Jews have not given him specific charges. Strangely, the Jewish accusers have not been invited, and only Paul speaks.[18]

Paul starts by praising Agrippa as "acquainted with all Jewish customs and controversies." He recounts his own history of how he persecuted the church until his experience at Damascus. He affirms the resurrection of Christ and claims he has said nothing that Moses and the Jewish scriptures do not predict. At this point, Festus interjects: "You are mad Paul! Your great learning makes you mad!" Paul responds calmly, addressing Festus by the title *kratiste*, most excellent. He appeals to Agrippa: "I am persuaded that none of this has escaped his notice, because it was not done in a corner." Paul then plays a salesman's trick of asking the king a leading question he cannot deny: "Do you believe the prophets?" The king bats the question back, giving him an ambiguous reply: "Within so little time would you persuade me to be a Christian?"[19]

Some see this as a dismissive sarcastic remark by Agrippa. Others regard it as a genuine appreciation of Paul's argument, meaning; "even saying so little you have almost persuaded me." Paul replies to Agrippa:

I would wish to God, both in a little and in much, not only you but also all those hearing me this day to become such as I am, except for these chains." (Acts 26:29)

This wish that Agrippa and Berenice would become Christians, along with the Romans, comes from the author's heart. Agrippa, Festus, and Berenice go apart to discuss the case, saying: "This man has done nothing to deserve death or imprisonment." Agrippa gives the verdict: "This man could have been released had he had not appealed to Caesar."[20]

It is the first of the two climaxes in Acts, the other being the shipwreck, and it is clumsy. We would expect a full trial before the emperor, not this extempore hearing before Agrippa and Berenice. But it was not possible, emotionally or politically, for the author to show the trial and execution of Paul in Rome.

Domitilla as author

If Flavia Domitilla were the author of Luke, this would explain the unusual prominence given to King Agrippa II and his circle in Luke/Acts. It is not just that the king, his two sisters, and his brother-in-law appear in Acts. There is a chiastic structure in Luke/Acts that stresses the importance of the Herods:

A. After the nativity, Luke starts with a statement of the territories (i) ruled by the procurator of Judea and (ii) which would later form the kingdom of Agrippa II.

B. Acts' first climax, before Paul's journey to Rome, is the hearing in front of the procurator of Judea, King Agrippa, and Queen Berenice. Those at the hearing were the current rulers of all the territories listed in A, and they find Paul innocent.

Christianity is on trial along with Paul. The author of Luke would like Rome to conclude that a Christian has "done nothing to deserve death or imprisonment." But, alas, it is fantasy.

Domitilla would have grown up thinking of Agrippa and Berenice as almost another uncle and aunt, given the queen's relationship with Titus. As for Drusilla and her husband, Felix, they were the black sheep of the family. So it would be fitting for Domitilla to cast Felix as a warning for her own undecided husband, Clemens/Theophilus.

Ironically, Agrippa was almost certainly a persecutor of the Jesus movement, although Domitilla would not have known that. He was a conservative stickler for Jewish religious traditions, insisting that his sisters' gentile husbands be circumcised. Of course, these religious scruples were put aside for the Roman imperial family. There was every reason why Agrippa should seek to destroy the Jesus movement who were religious rebels undermining the priesthood and the Jewish establishment. Agrippa was the embodiment of that establishment.

We will see later how Agrippa can be linked to the death of James. It would be consistent for him to have arranged for Paul to be sent to Nero in Rome for trial and execution, and this is perhaps the truth behind the Acts account.

If Domitilla were the author, the most likely source for her information would have been Agrippa himself. After the death of Titus, his political situation was precarious. The relationship between his sister and Titus would have become a handicap under Domitian. Agrippa would have needed whatever influence he could muster. As the niece of the emperor and the mother of the likely future emperor, Domitilla would have been a key patron. So he could not let her know the truth about his past as a persecutor of the Jesus movement. For her own part, Domitilla would have been unwilling to contemplate the idea that an old and dear family friend had put her Christian heroes to death.

So we have the apologetic version of the trials in Acts; Agrippa and Berenice would have freed Paul had they been able to. But the fact that they were involved in the hearing suggests that they were pushing a reluctant Festus to deal with Paul. Whatever it was that Festus wrote, it would get Paul executed.

We hear no more about Berenice after the death of Titus. Josephus would not have talked about Agrippa and Berenice in the way he did in the Antiquities had either still been alive. And in the Life, intended as an appendix to the Antiquities, Josephus implies that Agrippa was already dead.[21] Agrippa is now thought to have died c.92 AD which would be before Acts was written.

15

Vespasian to Domitian

Cerialis

Cerialis was in bed with a woman called Claudia Sacrata when he was roused in the night by shouts and cries. It was 70 AD, and he was in command of the legions fighting the Batavian rebels. His fleet was returning down the Rhine from Novaesium and Bonn. The escort, marching along the shore, had fallen behind. Instead of staying on his flagship, Cerialis had slipped out to spend the night with his mistress. Now, virtually naked, he looked out to see the astonishing sight of his flagship being sailed away by the Batavians. His assignation with Sacrata may have saved him. The sentries had fallen asleep, and the Batavians thought they had captured the Roman commander.[1]

Losing your flagship was like losing an eagle—a very real humiliation. Tacitus recounts the episode gleefully and criticizes Cerialis for slack discipline in his army. But Cerialis always had a way of turning a setback around.

The Batavians' homeland was a marshy river "island" between the Rhine and the Meuse in Germania Inferior (the Netherlands). They were the Romans' most prized auxiliaries. As the elite special forces of the Roman army, they were particularly adept at fighting in water. Highly accomplished horsemen, they could swim their hoses through fast-flowing rivers while wearing full armor, a tactic that would take an enemy by surprise. The population of Batavia was quite modest, but the revolt of such spirited fighters was serious.[2]

The Batavian's leader was a chief called Civilis, a long-standing veteran who had fought for the Romans in the conquest of Britannia. He rose up after being mistreated by Nero and Vitellius. In the chaos of the year of the four emperors, he persuaded neighboring tribes to join the rebellion. Vespasian initially looked to Civilis as an ally because he tied down some of Vitellius' legions in the Rhine area. But as emperor, he had to confront a rebellion that had got out of hand. Civilis' forces had destroyed two legions, and two others had reluctantly joined his side.[3]

Vespasian appointed Cerialis to put down the rebellion and assigned him an enormous force; it included the Eighth, Eleventh and Thirteenth legions, which had been loyal to Vespasian, the Twenty-first, which had fought for Vitellius and the newly-enrolled Second. These legions were supplemented by the Fourteenth, summoned from Britannia, and the First and Sixth from Hispania.[4] This was a greater force than either Vespasian or Titus had commanded in Judea. A Roman general could march on Rome with such an army. That Vespasian put such trust in Cerialis is further testimony to their close relationship, with Domitilla the living link between the two.

Cerialis' loyalty was tested twice. First, Civilis offered to make him emperor of all Gaul if he changed sides, but Cerialis brushed aside his proposal.[5] The second occasion was a strange approach from Domitian. He asked whether Cerialis would transfer his army to his own command if he were to come to him. Tacitus presents this as an attempt at rebellion by Vespasian's son, but we must remember that Domitian was demonized after his death. It is most likely that the boy Caesar just wanted to get involved in the action and match his brother's victory against the Jews by defeating the Batavians. Cerialis made a diplomatic but noncommittal response to Domitian's suggestion which went nowhere.[6]

Cerialis made rapid progress against the Batavians. He quickly won back the legions that had deserted and reintegrated them into the Roman army without reprisals. At Rigodulum (Riol), he achieved a significant victory against a rebel general, Valentinus, who was captured. This enabled him to enter the rebel town of Trier. His army wanted to sack the city, but Cerialis refused to allow this.[7]

At Trier, Cerialis suffered a similar incident to the later seizure of his flagship. The rebel generals had argued over whether to attack Tier quickly or wait. Civilis, who wanted to wait, had to yield to the other rebel commanders, Classicus and Tutor, and order an immediate attack. The Batavian's dawn raid took the Romans completely by surprise. Cerialis was staying in the town when he was awoken from his bed by the sounds of battle. The Batavians had forced their way into the legionary camp and taken the bridge over the Moselle. It was a rout with the Romans fleeing for their lives.[8]

Caught without his armor, Cerialis ran and grabbed some of his fleeing soldiers. He forcibly turned them around and led them to the bridge. Under his leadership, the group managed to retake the crossing. Once he secured the bridge, he attempted to assemble his legions to mount a fightback. The breakthrough came when the Twenty-first was given enough time and space by the enemy to regroup. They held off an attack by the Batavians and then went on the offensive. The tide of battle turned, and it was the German tribes' turn to flee. Cerialis gained a stunning victory. In a typically double-edged comment, Tacitus said that Cerialis' carelessness had almost caused a disaster, but his bravery had saved the day.[9]

By the time of the flagship episode, Cerialis was well in control of the war. His reply to the loss of his flagship was a push deep into Batavian territory. The last major action of the war came when Civilis assembled a fleet including the captured vessels and paraded them in the delta of the Rhine and Maas (Meuse) rivers. Cerialis attempted to attack with his own boats, but the tides and winds allowed Civilis' fleet to escape.[10]

The Batavians, however, could see the writing on the wall. With a Roman army in their midst, they pushed Civilis to negotiate a surrender.[11] Tacitus expresses grudging admiration for Cerialis' campaign:

> He was a man of sudden resolves and brilliant successes. Even when his strategy had failed, good luck always came to his rescue. Thus neither he nor his army cared much for discipline. (Tacitus Histories 5:21)

Cerialis was an intuitive general, more in the mold of Titus than Vespasian. He had won a rapid victory. The lost legions had been successfully recovered and reintegrated into the Roman army.[12] The casualties of the conflict, although substantial, were much lower than would have been expected. Remarkably, the war ended with the Batavians forgiven and happily fighting for Rome again. Claudia Severa and Sulpicia Lepidina, the two wives who wrote to each other at Vindolanda thirty years later, were Batavians. Lepidina's husband, Flavius Cerialis, had been given his cognomen in honor of Cerialis.

It was to Britannia that Cerialis was sent next. Vespasian appointed him as governor of the province in 71 with a mission to subdue the Brigantes of northern Britannia. One of his senior officers was Julius Agricola, legate of the Twentieth and future father-in-law of Tacitus. Agricola gained his military experience under Cerialis fighting in Britannia. A few years later, he would become the provincial governor and briefly take the Roman Empire to its furthest extent by invading Caledonia (Scotland). But it was Cerialis who had established the groundwork that enabled Agricola's advance. Tacitus wrote his first work, Agricola, about his father-in-law's achievements. Tacitus always believed that Cerialis had overshadowed Agricola due to his connection to the imperial family. Modern military historians think that this led Tacitus to underrate Cerialis' abilities as a general.[13]

Cerialis returned to Rome in 74 and became consul suffectus in that year for the second time. He is not mentioned again in the surviving written histories (we lack Tacitus' account of Domitian's reign.) But he seems to have been appreciated by Domitian. Most likely, he is the Q. Petillius Rufus who is recorded as full consul in 83 along with Domitian.

Vespasian

Vespasian was a popular ruler. The elite were relieved of their constant fear under Nero and accepted, in return, Vespasian's rustic and unpolished manner. He was never ashamed of his modest background and relished being a man of the people. When some flattering courtiers attempted to trace back the Flavians' origins to semi-mythical ancestors, he just laughed. When he undertook the repair and rebuilding of Rome after the devastation of the civil war, he started by symbolically helping the workmen clear rubble with his own hands, carrying it on his back.[14]

Each day he would get up before dawn to read letters and reports from his officials. He would receive friends and associates while he dressed and then go through the day's business. He was very approachable and would personally hear all petitioners, including the common people. After working, he would go for a walk and lie with one of his mistresses before taking a bath and having dinner. (Following the death of his wife, his long-term attachment was to his concubine Caenis. But when she also died, he took several mistresses.) He was renowned for his witty remarks and was particularly jovial at dinner.[15]

Vespasian was remarkably tolerant as emperor, even with people who went out of their way to be rude to him. He tried to avoid executing anyone and disliked watching gladiators kill each other in the arena, preferring wild beast hunts. Philosophers he detested and had them all expelled from Rome. When he heard that Demetrius the Cynic continued to insult him in exile, he sent him a message: "You are doing everything to force me to kill you, but I do not slay a barking dog."[16]

In the eyes of his contemporaries, his one vice was meanness. But even this seems more like astute management of the imperial finances than a personal love of money. He insisted on the payment of taxes and clamped down on what we would call tax avoidance. When he discovered someone was paying bribes for access to him, he ordered the bribe to be paid into the imperial treasury instead. When some citizens made a subscription to build a statue to honor him, he held out his hand as the "base"—meaning he would take the money rather than the statue. But he could also be generous: when an inventor came to him with an ingenious device for moving large columns to the Capital "with almost no cost," he rewarded him unstintingly. However, he declined to use the invention because it would put poor people out of work. (We would love to know what the device was!) Vespasian would lighten his supposed meanness with jokes. When Titus complained to his father that he had even put a tax on urine (used in industrial processes), Vespasian held up a gold piece raised from the tax and asked, "Does it smell?"[17]

For Domitilla, this would have been a blessed time. She was secure and in a happy marriage, and she likely had her first children by the end of the 70s. Surrounded by every comfort she could desire, she would have been much sought after. Domitilla was used to being listened to, used to being obeyed.

Vespasian was the perfect emperor in every respect except that of age. In the early summer of 79 AD, he came down with what seemed like a minor ailment but which developed into a more serious digestive problem. He took to his bed from where he continued to work and hear cases. As he felt death approach, he made his most famous remark: "Alas! I think I am becoming a god." He asked to be raised up as an emperor should die on his feet and died in his attendants' arms. He was a few months short of his seventieth birthday and had been emperor for almost ten years.[18]

Titus

It was widely feared that Titus would be a second Nero. He had a reputation of living a dissolute life in Rome with his exotic eastern queen and mistress, Berenice. His father's reign would have been a frustrating time for Titus. The commander of armies was much honored and given some extraordinary powers, including that of praetorian prefect, normally held by an equestrian. He fretted, however, that he could not rule on his own account but only act for his father. Like others in this position, he became a playboy.[19]

Titus' drunken lifestyle was not the only problem. He was also suspected of some dark, Neronian intrigues. In 79 AD he invited Aulus Caecina, a former consul, to dinner. As Caecina left, Titus had him run through with a sword. Titus claimed to have discovered a written speech in Caecina's handwriting promoting a conspiracy. He used this supposed evidence to secure the death of Eprius Marcellus, an influential senator who had been an informer for Nero.[20] It was widely believed that the speech was a forgery and that Titus had invented the supposed conspiracy to eliminate two members of an opposing faction. Marcellus was the principal target, but Caecina was also a potential rival because he was Vespasian's close friend. The emperor would have been deeply upset by his son's actions and the removal of Berenice from Rome may have been Titus' punishment.[21]

Everything changed when Titus assumed the purple. He was a

vigorous man in the prime of life, and he had the bit between his teeth again. Contemporary historians are astonishingly favorable about Titus as emperor. The army respected Vespasian but loved Titus. He was young, heroic, and an able commander. He benefited from his father's work in bringing the finances of Rome back into order. Titus, by nature, was generous, and his largess compared favorably with Vespasian's supposed meanness.

As well as inheriting a solvent financial position, Titus gained from another legacy of his father. The building of the Flavian Amphitheatre was initiated by Vespasian but completed under Titus. We know it as the Colosseum, and it is the most impressive surviving monument from ancient Rome. People at the time would have been amazed by its size and grandeur. Titus loved the games and his favorite Thracian gladiators. He liked to engage in friendly banter with opposing supporters in the crowd.

Titus brought Berenice back after his father's death, but she remained unpopular and he was forced to bow to widespread opposition: "He sent Berenice away from Rome at once, although neither of them wished it."[22] Titus, the ruler, bore no grudges. Forgiving and good-natured, he went even beyond his father in refusing to take action against anyone who insulted or lampooned him.

Titus' failure to get Berenice accepted would have taught him a painful but valuable political lesson—the importance of carrying public opinion on your side. Titus might have been an emperor rather than a president, but he had all the skills of a modern democratic politician. Naturally charismatic, he knew how to empathize with the people in times of crisis. He needed all his political talent to deal with what looked like the end of the world.

Vesuvius

The region in Campania around the Bay of Naples was a favorite resort for the Romans. Wealthy Romans flocked to the coast around Mount Vesuvius and the affluent towns of Pompeii and Herculaneum. The scenery was spectacular, the climate favorable and much healthier than pestilent Rome. The only disadvantage was the earth tremors. In 62 AD, a major earthquake destroyed large parts of Pompeii and the surrounding areas.[23] Two years later, Nero was making his public singing debut in the theatre in Neapolis (Naples) when an earthquake shook the building. After the performance, when everyone had left, the building collapsed.[24]

Vesuvius had been dormant throughout the Roman period, but that ended when the volcano erupted in November 79 AD—the long-accepted

date of 24/25 August 79 AD is contradicted by archaeological evidence
unearthed in recent years. We have a remarkable eyewitness account from
Pliny the Younger, who witnessed the eruption from Misenum on the Bay
of Naples and wrote two letters about it to his friend Tacitus.[25] It started
when his mother noticed a strange cloud far away on the other side of
the bay. They were staying with his uncle, Pliny the Elder, who was in
command of the Roman fleet. Pliny's mother pointed out the cloud to her
brother, who, after taking a bath, gave it a closer examination. It appeared
like an umbrella pine, with a tall, straight trunk and branches spread out
in a circle. But it was too far away to tell how it originated. Pliny the Elder
was a famous naturalist and wanted to investigate this phenomenon closer,
so he ordered a ship to be prepared. He invited the younger Pliny to go
with him, but the young man preferred to stay at home and read a book.
It was a wise decision.

As Pliny was leaving, he received a messenger who had traveled around
the Bay of Naples by the coast road. He had come from an acquaintance
of Pliny, a woman called Rectina who implored Pliny to rescue her. She
was trapped on the coast in her villa at the foot of Vesuvius, which was
showering the area in ash and burning stones. For the first time, Pliny
realized the seriousness of the situation. He ordered the fleet to set sail to
rescue Rectina and anyone else who was trapped.

The winds were in the right direction, and the voyage across the bay
took only a few hours. As the fleet got closer, the sky grew black, and hot
ash and pumice fell constantly on the ships. It proved impossible to get
close to Rectina's villa: the water level had dropped, creating dangerous
shoals, and accumulations of ash blocked the beach. Instead, they pro-
ceeded further along the coast to Stabiae near Pompeii. There Pliny met
up with his friend, Pomponianus, who had already prepared boats for
escape. But the winds were contrary, and the rescuers found themselves
trapped. They decided to wait to see if the winds changed, and Pliny made
use of the time by having a bath and a good meal at Pomponianus' house.
During that night, they could see fires high above on the mountain. Pliny
said they were farmer's fires, but in reality, it was a sign that the eruption
had entered a new and deadlier stage. As the situation got ever worse, the
group faced a dilemma. Should they flee with pillows tied to their heads to
protect against falling stones? Or should they wait it out in the buildings?

Everyone in the area had faced the same dilemma. Herculaneum was
upwind of the volcano and suffered only a minor ashfall on the first day.
The roads were easily passable, and almost all the inhabitants escaped to
safety. The situation in Pompeii downwind of Vesuvius was very different.
The ash and pumice falls made travel difficult and eventually impossible
as acclamations reached several feet. Many people decided to stay within

buildings and not risk death on the roads. But most of those who left early enough escaped. The real killers were the deadly pyroclastic surges of superheated gases and material that came on the eruption's second day. They rolled down the sides of Vesuvius to Herculaneum, Pompeii, and other towns on the coast, killing everyone in their path. Temperatures reached 300 centigrade, which was not survivable either inside or out. Both Herculaneum and Pompeii were buried under tephra deposits which also changed the coastline.

The body of Pliny the Elder was found on the third day. He most likely died from a heart attack or asthma attack as his body was found unharmed with his clothing intact. His companions had survived by fleeing overland. It is believed that Pliny's action in organizing the evacuation saved many lives.

The eruption reached as far as Misenum, where the younger Pliny and his mother had a terrifying ordeal. After waiting a day for news of the elder Pliny, they finally decided to leave the town. It was daytime but as black as night with ash falling thick around them. A great crowd of people joined them on the road as Pliny helped his mother stumble along. In the distance, Vesuvius was lit by strange fires brighter than lightning. His mother pleaded with him to leave her and save himself, but Pliny refused. As a dark day gave way to a pitch-black night, they sat down a little way from the road and waited for death. The crying of women and children was all around them. They had to periodically sweep the ash off themselves to keep from being buried. But eventually, the day came, and the ash-sky began to thin a little. A blood-red sun penetrated the clouds. They would live.

Another mother and son were not so lucky. Drusilla and her son Agrippa died in the eruption. That is the most likely meaning of Josephus' ambiguous phrase that the "young man (Agrippa) with the woman (Drusilla)" died in the Vesuvius eruption.[26] The alternative translation that the "young man (Agrippa) with his wife" died is less likely because the passage is about Drusilla. Josephus rarely mentions wives or women unless they are the center of the action. He promised to relate how the two died in due place but unfortunately never did.

The volcanic cloud reached as far as Egypt. It darkened the skies above Rome, where the people thought the world was ending. Titus was exemplary and generous in dealing with the consequences for the people of Campania. While he was in Campania supporting the people, another disaster befell Rome. A great fire destroyed much of the Capitol area. Once again, Titus gave every support to the victims, including selling some of his property to fund the restoration.[27]

Was a connection made between these events and Titus' destruction of the Jerusalem temple? The Vesuvius eruption happened very early in his reign. And the fire destroyed many Roman temples, including the Temple of Jupiter to which the Jews were obliged to pay the temple tax. After the volcano had settled down, some survivors dug through the tephra in an attempt to retrieve statues and belongings. In Pompeii, one such survivor, either a Jew or a Christian, scrawled a message on a wall to give their verdict—"Sodom and Gomorrah."

Domitian

It looked as if Titus would be one of the most successful emperors. But after just two years, he was stricken with an illness while traveling to his Sabine estate. As his condition deteriorated, he said he regretted nothing in his life apart from a single deed. Historians, ancient and modern, have come up with many theories for what he meant. Suetonius repeats a rumor that it was an affair with his brother's wife Domitia, but this was strongly denied by her and seems unlikely. Dio thinks it was not putting Domitian to death and so allowing his brother to kill him. Against this theory, there is no evidence that his brother had any hand in Titus' death. Or perhaps Titus was thinking of his failure to marry Berenice.[28]

There is another explanation that makes more sense than any of these. It must have occurred to Titus that three misfortunes had struck within the few brief years he had been emperor; the eruption of Vesuvius, the fire that destroyed the temples of Rome, and now his illness. Had he brought divine wrath upon himself and Rome by destroying the Jerusalem temple? Did he now repent, hoping for forgiveness from the Jewish God? If so, then forgiveness did not come.

Titus died on the same estate as his father on 13 September 81 AD, aged 41. Domitian lost no time in getting himself accepted as Emperor by the pretorian guard. By some accounts, this was before Titus had died. One legend has Domitian keeping his brother alive in ice until he had been declared emperor.[29] Vespasian had to wait six months after his death before "becoming a god," but Domitian deified Titus immediately. Does this prove that Domitian loved his brother? Cassius Dio says that Domitian would pretend in public the opposite of his real feelings.[30]

It would be closer to the truth to say that Domitian's reign was shaped by hatred of his dead brother. He claimed that he should have been joint emperor with Titus, and that Titus had cheated him by forging their father's will. Whether or not this is true, the gallant, battle-tested leader of men was always going to be accepted by the army and the people over the untried and relatively youthful Domitian. His father had never allowed

Domitian to prove himself, perhaps because he doubted his character. Domitian deeply resented the comparison people made between him and Titus. He even claimed to have bestowed the empire upon his father and brother, for he had been in Rome while they were in the east.[31]

Domitilla had enjoyed security under both Vespasian and Titus. But she and Clemens would have been shocked by something that happened a few months after Domitian became emperor. The consuls appointed at the start of 82 were Domitian and Flavius Sabinus, the brother of Clemens. Shortly after his appointment, Sabinus was executed. This habit of honoring someone and then ordering their death would be a recurring and particularly unpleasant aspect of Domitian's reign. According to Suetonius, on the day of the consular election, the herald announced Sabinus as future emperor rather than as consul. So Domitian had Sabinus killed.[32]

No herald would ever have made such a mistake. The real reason behind the execution was the elimination of a rival. Sabinus was married to Titus' daughter and was expected to be the father of the next emperor. Titus may have planned to appoint Sabinus as a second Caesar alongside Domitian. It would be typical of Domitian to exact an ironic revenge on Titus by having the herald formerly announce Sabinus as Caesar, and then use that announcement as a pretext for his execution.

That left Julia as a childless widow. Suetonius says that Domitian had seduced her while Titus was still emperor and loved her openly after she had lost her husband and father. Dio repeats this rumor and adds that the two lived together as husband and wife while Domitia was temporarily separated from Domitian. Suetonius goes on to say that Julia became pregnant by the emperor and that he ordered her to have an abortion which resulted in her death.[33] We should be careful about taking these rumors at face value: they circulated after Domitian's reign when the incoming regime wanted to blacken his name.

Domitian is known to have been a stickler for sexual morality. He established provisions against women who had been found guilty of adultery and punished one man for taking back an adulterous wife. And he condemned senators and men of equestrian rank who had played the passive role in sexual acts with other men. More positively, he forbade the practice of castrating slaves to make them eunuchs. All of this was part of a campaign to improve public morals.[34]

His most notorious action was against those Vestal Virgins who had broken their vows of virginity. The Vestals were aristocratic women selected as young girls to remain virgins for thirty years in service to the goddess Vesta. However, the application of the absolute requirement for virginity had become lax. Domitian decided these laws needed to be fully enforced. Three of the Virgins were found guilty of sleeping with men and allowed to choose their own means of death while the men concerned were exiled. But when the senior Vestal, Cornelia, was also convicted, she was sentenced to the traditional penalty of being buried alive. Her supposed lovers were beaten to death with rods. The conviction of Cornelia was secured by confessions made under torture. Pliny the Younger thought she was innocent and reported how she had gone bravely, and with dignity, into the tomb that had been prepared for her.[35]

Against this background, we can see why those wanting to discredit Domitian would accuse him of having an incestuous affair with his niece. But the stories about the two do not add up. Why should Domitian order the abortion of his own child when he had been trying for years to have an heir? In truth, Domitian was in love with Domitia. He sent her away after their baby son died, probably because of her lack of fertility. But he soon relented and took her back again.

A better explanation for Domitian's treatment of Julia is his hatred of Titus. He wanted to ensure that no grandchild of his brother would ever become emperor. So after killing Julia's husband, he forbade her to marry again. These actions were misinterpreted as evidence of jealous love for Julia. But although Domitian could refuse her permission to marry, he could not stop her from having an affair. She became pregnant by an unknown lover, and Domitian ordered her to have an abortion. This would be consistent with his actions against other women accused of sexual immorality. Julia died c.90, supposedly from complications arising from the abortion. She was just twenty-five years old. The dead Julia was no longer a threat, so Domitian deified her.

Domitian's real feelings towards Julia are illustrated by his actions while she was alive. Julia had been made Augusta by her father, a title which Domitian could not remove. But he immediately gave the same title to Domitia, giving rise to the strange and unique position of having two living women who were both Augusta. The relative standing of the two can be gauged by their number of provincial coin issues. Domitia Augusta appears on 117 such issues during Domitian's reign and Julia Augusta on just 3.[36] The provincial issuers would have been keen to curry favor with the emperor. They understood that Domitia was "in" and Julia very firmly "out."

The death of her husband's brother and the treatment of her cousin Julia could not fail to have affected Domitilla. Ironically, in one sense, she benefited from Sabinus' demise. Domitilla, like Julia, was Domitian's niece, but unlike Julia, she was not the daughter of the hated Titus. Domitian had her mother, the younger Domitilla, deified early in his reign with the title of Augusta. We find coins issued to honor "Divi Domitilla" that can be dated somewhere between 82 and the start of 85, with 82-83 being the most likely date for the earliest of these coins. To give such honors to a long-dead sister was so unusual that some scholars have suggested that the elder Domitilla, Domitian's mother, was the one deified.[37] The evidence against this is a verse from the poet Statius written for the dedication of an enormous statue of Domitian erected in 91 AD:

> Son and brother, father and sister will come to your embrace;
> one neck will make room for all the stars" (Statius Silvae 1:1:97-8)

These "stars" who come down from the heavens are Domitian's divine relations. His infant son, brother, and father were all deified, so the verse implies that his sister was also. The counterargument is that Statius was writing hurriedly. Perhaps he used "sister" as a loose term for niece, meaning Julia, who had recently been deified. However, to interpret "sister" as "niece" is quite a stretch. And the idea that Statius was careless does not allow for Domitian's nasty habit of executing people. A contemporary poet would have taken great care to get the details of the emperor's family correct.

The decisive point is that Statius does not list Domitian's mother among the "stars." Such an omission would be inexplicable if she had really been deified. We can conclude that it was his sister and not his mother who he made into a god.

Supporting evidence comes from a gold Aureus dated 82-83 AD with Vespasian on one side and the deified Domitilla on the reverse. On most coins, the portraits of the Flavian women are generic and so stylized that it is impossible to distinguish individuals. But on this coin, there is a striking similarity between the divine Domitilla and Vespasian; she has a softened version of his very distinctive and rather odd features. Whether or not the engraver had a good likeness to work from, he depicts the woman as Vespasian's daughter rather than his wife.[38]

So why did Domitian deify Domitilla the younger? Perhaps he had a close relationship with his older sister, who would have been a constant presence in his childhood until her marriage. We do not know exactly when she died, but she most likely returned with Cerialis from Britannia, allowing brother and sister to bond again. Domitian would have been no more than about fourteen at the time of her death, and it must have had a devastating impact upon him. There are also some indications that Domitian was close to Cerialis. His suggestion that he come and take command of Cerialis' army for the Batavian war is more explicable if the two had a strong relationship, as is Domitian's forgiveness of Cerialis' diplomatic refusal. In the absence of Vespasian in the east, he may have looked upon Cerialis as a father figure.

Domitian's sibling war with Titus is likely to have also played a part.

He was laying claim to his dead sister and using her to counterbalance Titus and Julia. Like Titus, she was deified and like Julia, given the title of Augusta. Domitilla would have been drawn in as the alternative niece from Julia.

At around the time that Domitian was deifying his sister, he likely made Cerialis consul for the third time. There is some dispute whether the "Q. Petillius Rufus", who was joint consul ordinary with the emperor in 83 AD, was Cerialis himself or an otherwise unknown son by a previous marriage.[39] The only evidence supporting the son hypothesis is an inscription from Smyrna recording that Rufus was on his second consulship, *Cos II*, whereas Cerialis should have been *Cos III*. But this could be a mistake by the provincial stone mason.[40] There are two reasons why the consul in 83 is probably Cerialis. The first is that it is unlikely that Cerialis, who was first made a consul in 70 AD, could have a son old enough to be made consul for a second time as early as 83 AD. Indeed, there is no evidence for a first consulship for this hypothetical son.[41]

The second and more significant reason is the importance of the appointment. To be made full consul jointly with the emperor was a considerable honor; the ordinary consul of 83 was only the second of Domitian's reign after the unfortunate Sabinus. Domitian would have used this position to signal the foremost man in his regime, someone who was perhaps even his intended successor. Domitilla's husband, Clemens, would be far too young and, besides, Domitian had just executed his brother! Domitian's closest male relative of an appropriate age and distinction was Cerialis who was his brother-in-law and the father of his niece, Domitilla. The appointment of Cerialis as ordinary consul is to be expected, but the appointment of his son by a previous marriage would be extraordinary. Such a son would not be closely connected to the emperor, being neither a Flavian nor a blood-relation. And given the prominence of this appointment, it would be strange that we hear nothing about this son from any of our historical sources. We can conclude that the consul Q. Petillius Rufus was almost certainly Q. Petillius Cerialis Caesius Rufus.

Cerialis' third consulship is further evidence that he was the father of Domitilla and the husband of the deified Domitilla the younger. The joint honor to Domitilla's parents suggests that Domitian was considering her children as his potential successors as early as 83 AD. His plan A would have been to have his own offspring succeed him as Emperor. But when he and Domitia had no surviving children, he would turn to plan B and adopt Domitilla's sons. Domitilla would be firmly in the limelight. In Domitian's Rome, this was a dangerous place to be.

16

Josephus and Luke/Acts

The influence of Josephus

It would be odd for any gospel writer to use the works of Josephus as a source. A Pharisee and senior member of the Jerusalem establishment, Josephus was at the opposite end of the social spectrum to the apostles of the Jesus movement. After defecting to the Romans and being present at the destruction of the temple, most Jews would have seen him as a traitor. Among the Romans, interest in Josephus' writings would have declined after the deaths of Vespasian and Titus. As a Jew who had fought on the rebel side, he did not fit Roman expectations for a history writer. So it is surprising that Luke/Acts shows a strong influence from Josephus.

By the 90s AD, Josephus' audience would have been drawn from the small minority of Romans interested in Jewish politics and history. These would have included the God-fearers and those Jews throughout the empire participating in the Roman administration. To have access to Josephus' books implied that you were one of the elite. Producing any book before the invention of the printing press was expensive. So how many copies of the Jewish War would have existed in the first century? Probably hundreds because Vespasian and Titus had personally endorsed it. We know that Agrippa wrote sixty-two letters promoting the work, which gives us some idea of the likely market size.[1] Copies signed by Titus would have sat in the villa libraries of wealthy Romans and Jews. Possession of a copy would have been the preserve of the rich, but others would have been able to read those copies; members of the family, their guests and clients, scribes working for the owner, and the tame philosophers and scholars who were often attached to large households. The most excellent Theophilus can be expected to have owned a copy of the Jewish War, and the author of Luke, being either a family member or client, would have had access to that copy.

So in one respect, the use of the Jewish War as a source by the author of Luke is nothing remarkable if we accept that the author was attached to the Roman ruling class. But to have knowledge of the Antiquities of the Jews would be a very different matter. For a start, it would seem to push back the date of Luke/Acts to the mid-90s at the very earliest because

Josephus did not publish the Antiquities until 93/94. By this time, Josephus had lost his imperial patrons. King Agrippa II was dead, bringing the Herodian dynasty to an end, and Domitian, seeking a return to traditional Roman religion, was hostile towards the Jews and their Roman sympathizers. Antiquities was also a very long work, and copies would have taken a highly trained scribe over a year to produce. It was an expensive book with limited appeal, and the distribution would have been correspondingly small.

Even more radical is the idea that Luke/Acts also shows knowledge of Josephus' Life that was not written until 94/95. The Flavian dynasty came to an end in 96 AD, and the distribution of the Life must have been minimal. Only a person close to Josephus was likely to have access to a copy.

The influence of Josephus on the author of Luke is pervasive and accepted by most scholars. At the highest level, we can sense the flavor of Josephus in Acts. The concept of Acts, a history of the Christians, seems to have been inspired by the example of the Antiquities, a history of the Jews. There are also specific passages in both Luke and Acts which echo passages in Josephus.

Whether Acts did use Antiquities as a source has been hotly debated. Some traditional Christian apologists reject the idea because of the implications for the dating of Luke/Acts. The more general influences depend on a sensitive reading and are easily dismissed by the skeptic. But we will start with a specific case that is difficult to explain away.

Theudas and Judas the Galilean

When the Pharisee Gamaliel addresses the Sanhedrin in Acts, he uses the example of two former rebels:

> And he said to them, "Men of Israel, consider carefully what you are about to do with these men. Some time ago, Theudas rose up, claiming to be somebody. A number of men, about four hundred, joined him, but he was put to death, and all who were persuaded by him were dispersed, and it came to nothing. After this man, Judas the Galilean rose up in the days of the census and drew away people after him. And he perished, and his followers were scattered." (Acts 5:35-37)

So Acts says that Theudas came before Judas the Galilean who rose up in the "days of the census." This is the same census under Quirinius in 6 AD that the nativity account in Luke wrongly places before 4 BC. So

Theudas' rebellion must have occurred in 6 AD—or if we believe Luke, 4 BC. But Theudas, a would-be prophet who led a revolt, was actually killed by the procurator Fadus in 45/46 AD. The author of Luke has placed him at least forty years too early. Why would they have made such a mistake?

If we turn to Antiquities 20:97-103, we find the answer. Josephus first gives the story of Theudas and Fadus. He then moves on to the next procurator Tiberius Alexander who ordered the crucifixion of James and Simon, the two sons of Judas the Galilean. Josephus then reminds his readers how Judas the Galilean had led a revolt while Quirinius was taking the census. So the passage covers both Theudas and Judas in that order, even though Judas lived long before.

The author of Luke has imperfectly remembered the passage and made the mistake of thinking that Judas came after Theudas. Christian apologists who believed the Bible to be inerrant cannot accept this. They claim that there must have been an earlier rebel called Theudas. But Josephus mentions no such person, and the name is rare.[2] More pertinent is the apologist's argument that not all the details in the Acts passage come from Josephus. The number of Theudas' followers is explicitly given as four hundred in Acts, although Josephus does not mention the number. However, the number four hundred does appear in the Antiquities in connection with another rebel, the man called "the Egyptian." Josephus reports how a force commanded by the procurator Felix fell upon the Egyptian and his followers, killing four hundred and capturing two hundred.[3] The two episodes of Theudas and the Egyptian are so close that it is easy to see how the author of Luke could have recalled the number four hundred and applied it to the wrong rebel. The Egyptian also makes a brief cameo appearance in Acts when the legionary tribune asks Paul whether he is the Egyptian. Here, it is said that the Egyptian had four thousand followers.

Since the author of Luke has made a mistake about Theudas and Judas that depends upon the order in which Josephus deals with them, we must conclude that she is aware of the Antiquities. And yet her use of the Antiquities is muddled, indicating that she is working from memory or incomplete notes. Had she consulted a copy of the Antiquities, she would not have made these mistakes.

Confirmation of the author's awareness of the Antiquities passage comes from other links. We can compare the eight lines of the Antiquities from 20:97 to 20:104 to Acts:[4]

Both have the revolt of Theudas (as above).
Both have the revolt of Judas the Galilean at the time of the census (as above).

Both have a famine in the reign of Claudius (Ant. 20;101; Acts 11:28-29).

In both cases, the famine in Judea is relieved by help from outside. In Antiquities, this help comes from the Jewish convert Queen Helena, and in Acts, it comes from the Christian community of Antioch.

In both cases, the famine is followed shortly afterward by an account of the death of "Herod"; he is the brother of king Agrippa I in Ant. 20:104, and Agrippa I himself in Acts 12:20-3.

There are too many points of similarity to be a coincidence. The author of Luke knew of Antiquities 20:97-104, most likely through attending a reading. We also get a sense of competition between the two authors. While Josephus uses the famine to show the generosity of Helena, Acts goes one better by having the prophet Agabus predict the famine so that the Christians can alleviate it in advance.

It is also suspicious that both Josephus and Acts fix on the same three rebels. Josephus tells us that there were many rebels and false prophets arising in Judea at this time. He illustrates the "many" by giving just three examples; Judas the Galilean, Theudas, and the Egyptian. But these are also the only three Jewish rebels mentioned in Acts. Josephus does not give the name of "the Egyptian," and the author of Luke does not know it either. It would be an amazing coincidence if Josephus and the author of Luke just happened to choose the same three examples. We can conclude that the author of Luke took their knowledge of these rebels from the Antiquities.[5]

The death of Agrippa I

In both the Antiquities and Acts, there is a story about the death of Agrippa I, and they are similar enough to indicate dependence. Our most reliable version comes from Josephus. Agrippa was in Caesarea celebrating the games in honor of Caesar for which he wore a gown woven entirely of silver thread. It dazzled the crowd as it shone in the sun, and the people were so amazed they hailed the king as a god. Agrippa did not rebuke them and was immediately struck with intense pain in the stomach. It lasted for five days until he died.[6]

In Acts, Agrippa had been in dispute with Tyre and Sidon, but the people of these cities wanted peace because Agrippa controlled their food supply.[7] So they arranged an audience with the king through the services of an official:

> On the appointed day, Herod put on his royal robes, sat on his throne, and addressed them. And the people were crying out,

"This is the voice of a god and not of a man!" Immediately an angel of the Lord struck him, because Herod did not give glory to God, and he was eaten by worms and died. (Acts 12: 23)

Comparing the Acts story with Antiquities, there are several similarities:

In Antiquities, the death of Agrippa takes place at Caesarea. Although the Acts story does not explicitly mention Caesarea, the audience would have taken place there as Tyre and Sidon are a short distance along the coast.

The death is preceded by a dispute between Agrippa and the Roman governor of Syria (Josephus) or Syrian cities (Acts).[8]

In both cases, there is a reference to Agrippa's robe.

In both cases, Agrippa is acclaimed by the people as a god.

Agrippa is "eaten by worms" in Acts. In Antiquities, he has severe abdominal pain.

The Acts version, however, does not make sense. Agrippa had no power to restrict the food supply to a Roman province. And Josephus says that the people of Tyre were the bitterest enemies of the Jews, so they are not going to call Agrippa a god.[9] Acts does not explain why Agrippa is acclaimed as a god by the people, and the king's robe does not play any part in the rest of the story. We need to turn to Antiquities to see how the robe is the real reason for the acclamation and how the occasion was actually the games held for the people of Caesarea.

The Acts story is a distorted version of the Antiquities account. The author of Luke was apt to change sources significantly for their narrative. But even so, it seems unlikely that they have access to a written copy of Antiquities as they write. The Acts version must be based on a faulty memory of the Antiquities story or a verbal account from Josephus.

Schools of philosophy

Josephus and the author of Luke are both grappling with a similar problem; how to make their respective religions acceptable to the Roman elite. Josephus' strategy is to present the various Jewish religious groups as if they were schools of philosophy. In one famous section of the Jewish War, he sets them out as the Sadducees, Pharisees, and Essenes, which he calls three "schools."[10] Scholars have noted that Josephus' description of the Essenes seems to owe much to the Greek Stoics: his idealized Essenes are very different from the assorted dissident religious groups revealed by the Dead Sea scrolls.

The author of Luke employs a similar strategy for the Christians. In Acts, Paul even lectures the philosophers of Athens and engages them in debate. After the spirit descends upon the Christians, they form an ideal community holding all property in common:

> The multitude of believers was one in heart and soul. No one claimed that anything he possessed was his own, but all things were held in common. (Acts 4:32)

We know from Paul's letters that this is not an accurate depiction of early Christian communities. Paul is continually lecturing his churches about money. He is frustrated with some of the Corinthians for maintaining social distinctions to the extent of not even sharing a meal with the poorer brethren in church meetings. He urges his readers to give generously to his collection for the poor saints in Jerusalem. The recipients of these letters have obviously not donated all their money and possessions to a common fund. Even Acts seems to cool on the idea because holding property in common is not mentioned again. Wealthy Christians, like Lydia, continue to maintain their own households after conversion.

The sharing of possessions fits in with a theme in Luke that the poor will be rewarded and the complacent rich punished. Mary proclaims that the Lord has "brought down rulers from their thrones and exalted the humble."[11] When Jesus preaches, he promises good news for the poor, but not for the rich: "But woe to you who are rich, for you are receiving your reward."[12]

So was the author of Luke some kind of primitive socialist or communist? Many have thought so and concluded that the author opposed the ruling classes. But this is belied by the prominence given in Luke/Acts to the wealthy and the ruling elite. It is a fact of human nature that no one includes themselves in such rhetorical denunciations. And to view the author as a rebel of the proletariat is to misunderstand Roman culture.

It was customary for the Roman elite to denigrate "the rich" and praise poverty. Consider, for example, the sentiments of Seneca:

> We talk much about despising money, and we give advice on this subject in the lengthiest of speeches, that mankind may believe true riches to exist in the mind and not in one's bank account, and that the man who adapts himself to his slender means and makes himself wealthy on a little sum, is the truly rich man. (Seneca Epistles 108.11)[13]

Seneca claims to despise wealth in favor of the riches of the mind. Yet this is the same Seneca who made that enormous loan of 40 million sesterces to the Britons. His actions in calling in the repayment of this loan were one of the triggers for Boudicca's revolt, which resulted in over a hundred thousand deaths.

The idea of holding all property in common draws upon one of the most pervasive and powerful myths of Roman culture—that of the golden age. Before the ages of iron and bronze had come the age of gold when that metal was plentiful and the earth bountiful. There was no private property because there was no need. Everyone shared and was wealthy alike. In Acts, the gift of the Holy Spirit puts the first Christians back into this golden age.[14]

Josephus similarly presents the Essenes as sharing all property:

> Riches they despise for they are communists to perfection. None of them are better off than the rest: their law is that novices admitted to the sect must surrender their property to the order, so that neither humiliating poverty nor excessive wealth is ever seen among them, but each man's possessions go into the pool and, like brothers, their entire property belongs to all. (Jewish War 2:122)

As Steve Mason has pointed out, the author of Luke does not mention the Essenes but substitutes the Christians as the "third way" after the Pharisees and Sadducees. It seems that the author of Luke has modeled the idea that Christians hold all property in common on Josephus' Essenes. The notion put forward by Josephus that a novice must surrender all their property makes sense of the episode of Ananias and Sapphira; they are struck dead for keeping back some proceeds from the sale of their field.

Josephus alone among Jewish writers describes the Jewish religious movements as "schools" as if they were pagan philosophers. But we find the same terminology in Acts, where the Pharisees and Sadducees are described as hairesis or philosophical schools.[15] In Acts 26:5, Paul calls the Pharisees the "most exact school," the exact same phrase used by Josephus. Because this way of talking was unique to Josephus, we can be confident that Acts is borrowing from him.[16]

Steve Mason goes further than this and argues that the author of Luke presents Christianity as a philosophical school in imitation of Josephus' treatment of the Essenes. We need not stretch Josephus' influence quite this far. An upper-class Roman would have absorbed philosophical thinking with their mother's milk. And to the author of Luke, the Christians are not just another "school" as their Jewish opponents call them, but the Way—something that supersedes all that has gone before.

Influences in Josephus' "The Life"

Was the author of Luke also influenced by Josephus' "The Life"? One possibility is Josephus' shipwreck account which could be the inspiration for the story of Paul's shipwreck in Acts. There are some close similarities; both Paul and Josephus are on their way to Rome when shipwrecked, they are both shipwrecked in the sea of Adria, they both continue their journey in a different ship which lands at the identical port, Puteoli, in Italy.[17] The similarities are suspicious although none of these coincidences is particularly unlikely. Shipwrecks were common in the ancient world; Paul says he was shipwrecked three times. The sea of Adria continued much further south than what we call the Adriatic Sea, so a shipwreck on a voyage from the east to Rome might well take place in this area. The journey would have to be continued on another boat and Puteoli was the usual passenger port for Rome. There are also marked differences between the two stories; in Acts, the ship is beached near an island with passengers able to cross to shore on timbers, whereas Josephus swam all night in the open sea.

However, the obvious source for the Acts shipwreck is Paul's letters. And this brings us to the idea that the author of Luke has influenced Josephus. His shipwreck description is suspiciously close to Paul's words: "Three times I was shipwrecked, I passed a night and a day in the deep."[18] Paul spent a day and night on the open water, and Josephus had to swim all night before being rescued after daybreak. If Domitilla had discussed Christianity with Josephus, she would most likely have quoted from Paul's letters. Josephus' shipwreck story seems a mixture of Paul's own account and the Acts' shipwreck. So Josephus could be attempting to impress Domitilla by presenting his own experiences as matching or exceeding those of Paul.

Another coincidence supports this idea. Josephus' only story about his boyhood is very similar to the only story about Jesus' boyhood in the gospels. In the Gospel of Luke, the twelve-year-old Jesus accompanies his parents to Jerusalem for the Passover. On the return journey, his parents find that Jesus is missing and go back to search for him:

> And after three days they found him in the temple, sitting among the teachers, listening to them and asking them questions. All those who heard him were amazed at his understanding and his answers. (Luke 2:47)

Compare this with Josephus:

> While still a mere boy, about fourteen years old, I won universal
> applause for my love of letters; insomuch that the chief priests
> and the leading men of the city used constantly to come to me
> for precise information on some particular in our ordinances.
> (Josephus, The Life 8-9)

In both cases, the subject is called a "child," and their age is given; for
Jesus, it is twelve, but Josephus, with his superior knowledge of Jewish
custom, makes it a more realistic fourteen. Both Jesus and Josephus
amaze their listeners with their answers to learned questions. However,
while Jesus seeks out the wise men to ask them questions, the wise men
approach Josephus to ask him. The Josephus story is more impressive,
but also absurd. No high priest is going to lose face by consulting a boy
on questions of the law, no matter how clever that child was. Josephus is
writing at around age sixty in Rome, safe in the knowledge that no one can
contradict him. We can see the Josephus story as a fiction suggested by the
Gospel of Luke. The alternative view is that the author of Luke has copied
Josephus. But there is no reason why they should pick on an episode from
Josephus' Life and apply it to Jesus.

In Luke the story of the boy Jesus visiting the temple is immediately
followed by the account of John the Baptist in the wilderness.[19] In The
Life, Josephus follows the story of the priests consulting him on matter of
the law with an account of how, at age sixteen, he became the disciple of
a holy man in the wilderness:

> ...on hearing of one Bannus, who dwelt in the wilderness, wear-
> ing only such clothing as trees provided, feeding on such things
> as grew of themselves, and using frequent ablutions of cold
> water, by day and night, for purity's sake, I became his devoted
> disciple. (Josephus, The Life 11)

The comparison to John who practiced baptisms of water for purity is
obvious. The idea of anyone wearing clothing that the trees provided is
odd. The description of John in Mark and Matthew is different and memorable; he was clothed in camel's hair with a leather belt and ate locusts
and wild honey.[20] The Gospel of Luke, however, omits these particulars.
In Luke, John does tell the people to "bear fruits" and warns that "every
tree that does not bear good fruit is cut down."[21] A hazy memory of this
passage could have given Josephus the idea that John used the products
of the tree. Whether or not this is so, the coincidence between Luke and
Josephus' Life is striking; in both cases the elders consult the boy Jesus/
Josephus who then, when he attains manhood, follows a baptizer in the

desert. We know that the Gospel of Luke is not copying Josephus here, because Luke is dependent on Mark and Matthew for John the Baptist. So Josephus must be copying Luke.

There is one more example. When the Jerusalem priests send a delegation to arrest Josephus and bring him back to Jerusalem, he says he was inclined to go with them. But something happens to change his mind:

> That night I beheld a marvelous vision in my dreams. I had retired to my couch, grieved and distraught by the tidings in the letter, when I thought that there stood by me one who said: "Cease man from thy sorrow of heart, let go all fear. That which grieves thee now will promote thee to greatness and felicity in all things. [...] Remember that thou must even battle with the Romans." (Josephus, The Life 208-9)

In Acts, Paul has a remarkably similar experience:

> But the following night the Lord stood by him and said, "Take courage! As you have testified about me in Jerusalem, so also you must testify in Rome." (Acts 23:11)

Paul and Josephus are both distressed when they receive a divine visitor at night. In both cases, the visitor stands by them to give them courage. The visitor predicts that each will have an encounter with the Romans; Josephus will battle them, and Paul will "testify," meaning to be tried, in Rome.

Josephus' account is egocentric, talking about his "greatness and felicity." It refers to his prediction of Vespasian becoming emperor and the good fortune that it brought him. Twenty years earlier, he described quite differently how he came to have this prophecy in the cave of Jotapata. He talked about vague dreams concerning the fate of the Jews and the Roman emperors, the meaning of which came to him in a flash of inspiration in the cave.[22] The story of the celestial visitation has been made up for the Life. It is not like Josephus' normal matter-of-fact style but closely resembles the miraculous visions that occur so often in Luke/Acts. Josephus was no mystic, and this is the only time he describes himself as having an explicit supernatural experience.

Mason points out that this dream comes in the very center of the Life, which he believes has a chiastic structure.[23] The story then serves a literary purpose as the centerpiece of the history of Josephus' time in Galilee and a prediction of his future good fortune. It must be based on Paul's vision in Acts.

So on four separate occasions, Josephus uses Christian sources for something in the Life. And three of the four, the shipwreck, the boy genius and the holy teacher in the desert, come successively within eight verses out of a total of over four hundred in The Life. Why should Josephus use Christian texts in this way when they would have been entirely obscure for most of his Roman readers? The influences are from three different works; Luke, Acts, and the letters of Paul. We can expect him to have listened to Domitilla recite from all three. We should note that the three consecutive episodes are then followed by a story about the emperor's wife granting special favors for Josephus. We can deduce that Josephus is trying to impress the Christian imperial lady, Domitilla, by making himself the equivalent of Paul and even Jesus.

There is a story in Antiquities book twenty, written a short while before the Life, that supports this idea.[24] It starts with King Agrippa II deciding to build a new dining room onto his palace to take advantage of a superb view over Jerusalem. Agrippa could now recline at meals looking down on everything that went on in the temple. The priests were outraged; the king and his guests could spy on their sacrifices and sacred rituals. So they built a new high wall to hide the sightline to the inner temple. Agrippa was furious that his view had been spoilt, and the Roman governor Festus even more so because the wall hid the inner temple from the colonnade. Roman soldiers were forbidden as gentiles to enter the inner courts of the temple and would use this high colonnade to monitor activities in these courts. So Festus ordered the priests to tear down the new wall, but they objected, pleading that no part of the temple could be demolished.

The case ended up with Nero in Rome. According to Josephus, it was decided in the Jewish priests' favor due to the intercession of Poppaea. Josephus says something very unexpected about her—that she was a "worshipper of God." This is hard to believe given her notorious conduct. Josephus is once more trying to influence his audience. He gives Poppaea as a role model, a God-fearing imperial wife who was favorable towards the Jews and generous towards Josephus personally. His target here may be Domitilla or Domitia or possibly both. It shows how Josephus, the salesman, was always willing to bend the truth to achieve his desired result.

17

The fall

Mother of seven

Domitilla was the mother of no less than seven children. We know this from a cemetery inscription now in the church of Saints Nereus and Achilles:

Tatia Baucylis, nurse of seven great grandchildren of the deified Vespasian, and children of Flavius Clemens and his wife, Flavia Domitilla, granddaughter of the deified Vespasian, whose beneficence established this burial place for the benefit of her freedmen and freedwoman and their posterity. (CIL 6:8942)

Domitilla is described as the wife of Clemens and the granddaughter of Vespasian with no mention of her father. The inscription was set up by the freed nurse of Domitilla's children, Tatia Baucylis, or by her family and records that Domitilla had established the burial place for her male and female freedmen and their descendants.

Domitian adopted two of Clemens' and Domitilla's sons as his heirs and had them renamed Vespasian and Domitian. The adoption must have taken place a few years before 95 AD as Suetonius says it happened "only recently."[1] Quintilian was appointed tutor for these two boys, and he writes about them in the preface to book 4 of his great work on rhetoric, the Institutio Oratoria:

But now Domitian Augustus has entrusted me with the education of his sister's grandsons, and I should be undeserving of the honor conferred upon me by such divine appreciation if I were not to regard this distinction as the standard by which the greatness of my undertaking must be judged. For it is clearly in my duty to spare no pains in molding the character of my august pupils, that they may earn the deserved approval of the most righteous of censors. The same applies to their intellectual training, for I would not be found to have disappointed the expectations of a prince pre-eminent in eloquence as in all other virtues. (Quintilian, Oratoria 4 Preface 2-3)[2]

Quintilian was an excellent choice of educator for the boys. He was the leading teacher of oratorical skills in Rome who believed that education was about creating the whole person. He wrote that the influence of the people around a young child was of crucial importance. The nurse should speak with good diction; the pedagogue (the slave charged with the early education) must be well trained; and both the child's parents should be well educated. He believed it was important for pupils to love their learning. For very young children lessons should be made amusing and fun so that they do not come to hate them when they are older. Quintilian's education theory was founded on his central idea that no one could be a master of rhetoric, able to sway the populace with eloquence, without first being a "good man." Unfortunately, this is an opinion that history has debunked.

We may think that Quintilian's praise for Domitian is excessive, but one statement rings true, although perhaps not in the way intended; Domitian was "the most righteous of censors." One thread that runs through all his actions is a return to traditional Roman ways and morality.

After concluding that he and Domitia were not going to have any children, Domitian adopted the grandsons of his beloved sister, the younger Domitilla. He intended for the boys to be brought up according to his own principles, to make them worthy of their new names. A good influence from the parents was vital for his plans.

After this adoption in the early 90s, Domitilla would have been at the height of her influence. As the mother of the future emperor, everyone would have aimed to please her, and no one would have been able to say no to her.

We can attribute the writing of Luke and Acts to this time. To be surrounded by flatterers and people ready to obey your every wish detaches a person from reality. It would have been essential for Domitilla to hide her Christianity and keep it secret, yet she appears to have been reckless. We can deduce that Clemens, as Theophilus, was not a baptized Christian but that Domitilla worked hard on his complete conversion. She must have been broadcasting her new literary creations and perhaps holding private readings for them. Like her father, she could not avoid playing with fire.

Downfall

In 95 AD, Clemens was given the honor of being appointed full consul alongside the emperor. A few months later, he was executed on the orders of Domitian: "He put Clemens to death all of a sudden, on the slightest of grounds and when he had barely come to the end of his consulship."[3] We can expect the consulship to have lasted to April, so this would place the execution of Clemens around May 95. Domitian was becoming increasingly paranoid, but it still seems extraordinary that he should have torn up his carefully crafted succession plan for "the slightest of grounds." In the same passage, Suetonius calls Clemens "a man of most contemptible idleness," which hardly suggests that he was conducting a rebellion or that anyone saw him as an emperor aspirant.

We get a sense that something is missing from Suetonius' account. He does not mention Domitilla directly, but says that Clemens' execution led to the death of Domitian. He then describes how Domitilla's steward was the main assassin. It points to the motivation for the assassination being revenge for Domitilla. Whatever Clemens had done, she was implicated and suffered the consequences.

Suetonius is writing biography rather than history, which explains why he is often a frustrating source and selective in the information he gives us. To get the full story of Clemens' and Domitilla's downfall, we would like to turn to Tacitus. The account of Domitian's reign and assassination was the culmination of the Histories and would have been our best possible early source had it survived. But the extant manuscripts include only the first third of the Histories and end long before Domitian became emperor. We have to make do with Cassius Dio, who wrote his Roman History c. 200 AD. Not only is this later than we would wish, but the relevant book is only available as an epitome, a précised selection. Still, Dio had access to much earlier sources and is generally reliable. His information helps us understand what is missing from Suetonius while giving rise to even more questions:

> And the same year Domitian slew, along with many others, Flavius Clemens the consul, although he was a cousin and had to wife Flavia Domitilla, who was also a relative of the emperor. The charge brought against them both was that of atheism, a charge on which many others who drifted into Jewish ways were condemned. Some of these were put to death, and the rest were at least deprived of their property. Domitilla was merely banished to Pandateria. (Dio, Roman History Epitome 67:14:1-3)[4]

Here we see that both Clemens and Domitilla were charged with "atheism" along with many others who had "drifted into Jewish ways." This could indicate Christianity as well as Judaism because most Romans did not distinguish between the two. It was not rebellion but religious belief that caused the couple's downfall. Domitian would have been particularly sensitive to this aspect because they were the parents of his chosen successors.

The charge of "atheism" meant not giving sacrifice to the Roman gods, including the cult of the emperor. Most of those charged with atheism were Christians because their religion forbade them to worship other gods. Although the Jews were "atheists" for the same reason, they had been granted a special dispensation, and they did not have to participate in pagan worship as long as they paid the Jewish tax. Domitian was very insistent on the collection of this tax:

> Besides other taxes, that on the Jews was levied with the utmost rigor, and those were prosecuted who without publicly acknowledging their faith yet lived as Jews, as well as those who concealed their origin and did not pay the tribute levied upon their people. I recall being present in my youth when the person of a man ninety years old was examined before the procurator and a very crowded court, to see whether he was circumcised. (Suetonius, Domitian 12)[5]

It used to be accepted almost without question that Dio's words meant that Domitilla and Clemens were Christians. The couple fitted perfectly into the Victorians' and Edwardians' belief in clean family-orientated Christian living and their equal fascination with the debauched and immoral ancient Roman culture. Domitilla became a shining and pure example of Christian womanhood against the intriguing, darkly-erotic background of Roman decadence. Over-enthusiasm resulted in an inevitable reaction in the twentieth century. Revisionist historians began to attack what they saw as the Domitilla myth. They argued that she and Clemens had not even been Christians—they were Jewish God-fearers.

The weak underbelly of the Domitilla story was the issue of the catacombs. The Victorians indulged in absurd historical fantasies around these catacombs, which they regarded as a refuge and romantic trysting place for the persecuted ancient Christians of Rome. The catacombs of Domitilla were a particular focus, and there was a strong desire to establish a connection with Domitilla and the Flavians. This was encouraged by archeological finds that appeared to link Domitilla to the catacombs, and it was hoped to find her tomb.

More careful archeological work shattered this cozy picture. The cata-combs had never been meeting places out of sight of the Roman authorities. And they were not as early as had been supposed. The catacombs of Domitilla were constructed a century after her time, and the oldest parts were pagan and not Christian. It seemed that Domitilla had been nothing more than the owner of the land on which the catacombs had later been built. We will see whether this was actually true later, but it was all impe-tus to the revisionist cause.

The revisionists also critiqued the conclusion that Dio's words implied Christianity. Rather than explicitly saying that Clemens and Domitilla were Christians, as he could have done, Dio says that they (or their asso-ciates) fell into "Jewish ways." No one disputes that this could include Christianity, but it is a matter of probability. That expression "drifting into Jewish ways" seems more likely to mean they were God-fearers than Christians. This would be quite understandable given the Jewish influence on the Flavians and Titus' relationship with Berenice.

There are two other pieces of evidence linking Domitilla to Christianity that the revisionists had to tackle. One was a passage from Eusebius, the other an early tradition that Domitilla was a Christian martyr and saint. We will deal with these shortly. Just to say here that the revisionist approach is to explain these away by assuming that the Christians appro-priated Domitilla from the Jews.

Revisionist historians are not always correct. There is often a suspicion that they are too intent on debunking what has come before and have put on their own blinkers. In this case, we have several independent strands of evidence that point to Domitilla being a Christian. We will examine the evidence piece by piece.

Let us start again with Dio's account. The problem with the idea that Domitilla and Clemens were God-fearers is that the charge was atheism, and God-fearers were not atheists. The Romans had absolutely no problem with anyone worshipping the Jewish God. In fact, they identified him with Jupiter/Zeus or Saturn. A problem only arose when a person refused to worship gods other than Yahweh. But God-fearers were not prohibited from worshipping other gods because they were not Jews. This is a point that seems to be missed in discussions of Dio's statement.

To be a Jew was a binary condition—a male could only be a Jew if he were circumcised. The position for females was less clear, but at a practical level, whether a woman was a Jewess or not would have been determined by her family. Domitilla would not have been regarded as a Jewess unless her husband, Clemens, had been circumcised. The God-fearers were uncir-cumcised Jewish sympathizers and were classed as well-meaning gentiles.

This is a vital distinction because the Jews had different laws for gentiles and Jews. The law of Noah applied to gentiles, and it was very basic, little more than do not commit murder. The law of Moses applied to Jews and was far more onerous and complex. Most famously, it involved the ten commandments, including the requirement not to worship idols or other gods.[6] The Christian church dropped circumcision, and the commandments were taken as applying to all Christians even though they were, theoretically, free from the law. For the Jews, circumcision was fundamental. An un-circumcised God-fearer remained a gentile and was not under the Law of Moses. As there was nothing in the Law of Noah about idols or other gods, there was no reason why a God-fearer could not go through the motions of pagan worship. They might not believe in the gods in their hearts, but Roman religion was not concerned with conscience but doing the right thing in public.

If Domitilla and Clemens were God-fearers, they would have been able to demonstrate that they were not atheists by offering sacrifice to the gods and the emperor. To be guilty of atheism implies that they could not do this, which means one of two things:

1. Clemens had been circumcised so that both he and his wife, Domitilla, were Jews under the law of Moses.
Or
2. Domitilla and Clemens were Christians.

Although conversion to Judaism was permitted in general, Domitian would never have allowed a Roman noble, yet alone a member of his own family, to do such a thing. So either of these would account for Domitian's action.

We know from a range of sources, including Galatians, that there was great reluctance for adult males to be circumcised. Nor is there any evidence that many gentiles did become circumcised; the Jews essentially remained an ethnic group. In many ways, a God-fearer had the best of both worlds. They earned Yahweh's favor by assisting the Jews and participating in Jewish worship and there was little incentive to go on and become circumcised. This was particularly true for Roman nobles, for whom the consequences of becoming a Jew would have been severe. Christianity was more popular because it offered the would-be convert a better deal; it did not require circumcision and had a more definite version of eternal life. Unsurprisingly, Christianity expanded among gentiles much faster than Judaism and gained many more converts. On the balance of probabilities alone, it is much more likely that the couple were Christians than that Clemens was a circumcised Jew.

Dio says that many others were involved, that some were executed, and others had their property confiscated. But he only gives one other name, Glabrio, a consul alongside the future emperor Trajan in 91 AD.[7] Bizarrely, Dio adds that Glabrio's main crime was his prowess in fighting as a gladiator in the arena with wild beasts. Domitian was jealous at the way that Glabrio, while consul, had fought and dispatched a lion while Domitian was holding a festival at his Alban estate. Perhaps Glabrio converted to Christianity or Judaism shortly afterward, but it is more likely that two unrelated episodes have been conjoined in the epitome. The others would have included members of Domitilla's house church if she were a Christian. Jews and God-fearers associated with the couple may also have been caught up in the emperor's rage, and these could well have included Josephus, for we hear no more about him after this time.

There is also a passing mention to the couple's downfall in Philostratus' Life of Apollonius, although it does not inspire confidence; Domitilla is called the sister of Domitian, and there is no mention of her exile.[8] Domitian orders her death three or four days after Clemens' execution and is assassinated at that time by her freedman, Stephanus, in an attempt to save her life.[9] In reality, the assassination took place a year after Clemens' death.

Two Domitillas?

Our other major source is the church historian Eusebius who was writing c. 315-325:

> The teaching of our faith shone so brilliantly in those days that even historians foreign to our beliefs did not hesitate to record in their pages both the persecution and the martyrdoms to which it led. They also indicated the accurate time, noting that in the fifteenth year of Domitian, Flavia Domitilla, daughter of the sister of Flavius Clemens, a consul at Rome that year, was with many others, because of testimony to Christ, taken to the island of Pontia as a punishment. (Eusebius, Ecclesiastical History 3:18)

There are close similarities with Dio's passage and some striking differences. It is clearly the same event, but Domitilla is called the niece rather than the wife of Clemens and is exiled to the island of Pontia and not Pandateria. Eusebius says his source gave the precise date as the fifteenth year of Domitian and the same year in which Clemens was consul. As Domitian's reign started on 14 September 81, this would imply that the persecution was not earlier than mid-September 95. Based on Suetonius alone, we would date Clemens execution to May 95, but September/October is not inconsistent with his vague statement that Clemens was barely out of his consulship.

In the parallel passage in his Chronicles, Eusebius identifies his main source as the Roman historian Bruttius who was writing in the second or third century. So Eusebius' testimony gives us independent confirmation about the downfall of Clemens and Domitilla from a source contemporary to Dio.[10] Eusebius unambiguously identifies Domitilla as a Christian. He further boasts that the testimony to the Christian faith given by the martyrs shines through even in the writings of those who disagreed with it. He would not have put things this way unless he had found definite information about Domitilla's Christian belief and persecution in Bruttius—not some vague statement about "Jewish ways."

This leaves the question of whether Eusebius' Domitilla is the same as Dio's. Are the wife and niece the same person or two separate individuals? Eusebius' account has tended to dominate the later Christian perception of Domitilla. She becomes a virgin saint very different from the mother of seven, reflecting a growing preoccupation with virginity and chastity among Christians in the early centuries. The archetype of the female saint was a beautiful and youthful virgin barely into womanhood who dedicated herself as the bride of Christ, rejecting all human suitors. It became harder for Christians to relate to a saint who was a mature and experienced woman.

If there were two different women, we would have some remarkable coincidences:

1. The two women are both named Flavia Domitilla.
2. They were both exiled at the same time for Christian or Jewish religion.
3. They were exiled to two different islands in the same group.
4. They are both identified in relation to the same man, Flavius Clemens.

There is not a shred of contemporary evidence for a Domitilla who was the daughter of a sister of Clemens. As names ran in families, a niece could have been called Flavia Domitilla, although there are a couple of points against this idea. First, the unknown sister would have had to marry another Flavian for her daughter to be a Flavia as the nomen came from the father. Second, "Domitilla" was a family name on Domitilla's side and came ultimately from Vespasian's wife. It was not a family name for Clemens or his sister (if he even had one). More significant than either of these objections is the last point that both sources identify Domitilla by her relationship with Clemens. It would be very unusual for a woman to be identified in relation to her uncle rather than her husband or father. More likely, there is one woman behind both accounts— Domitilla, the wife of Clemens.

It would be easy for the two islands to be confused as Pontia (Ponza) and Pandateria (Ventotene) are both in the Pontine group, separated by 25 miles. Both were suitable residences for a disgraced imperial lady. This type of discrepancy invariably arises in independent historical accounts of the same event. Domitilla may even have started her exile on one and been moved to the other.

There is also an excellent explanation for Domitilla being thought to be Clemens' niece. That mistake could have arisen through a grammatical ambiguity. The phrase "his sister's daughter" can be ambiguous, with doubt about who is meant by "his." Eusebius mentions three people in his passage; Flavia Domitilla, Domitian, and Clemens. Domitilla is said to be Clemens' sister's daughter, but she was actually Domitian's sister's daughter. This would be quite a coincidence and indicates that the source has been misread.[11] Suppose that source said something like this:

In the fifteenth year of Domitian, in which Flavius Clemens was consul, Flavia Domitilla, his sister's daughter, was exiled to Pontia for being a Christian along with many others.

In this sentence, is Domitilla Domitian's sister's daughter or Clemens' sister's daughter? She could be either. This ambiguity can exist in Latin or Greek, similar to English. Eusebius would have misunderstood his source as meaning that Domitilla was Clemens' sister's daughter when she was actually Domitian's. This is the simplest explanation for the two Domitillas.

Saint Domitilla

In Eusebius' statement, it is Domitilla who is Christian and not Clemens. He does not even tell us that Clemens was executed by Domitian. Nor is there evidence that Clemens was venerated by Christians in the early centuries. If he had died as a Christian, his death would have been a very significant martyrdom.

It was Domitilla who became a saint, even though she was only exiled and not killed. Her saint day was 12 May which she shared with two other saints, Nereus and Achilleus, with whom she is closely associated, along with the unrelated Saint Pancras. The Greek Orthodox church accepts her as the wife of Clemens, but in the Catholic church, she is his niece. She was removed from the Catholic calendar in 1969, but retains her status as a saint.

Domitilla was only added to the calendar quite late. The justification was an apocryphal text known as the Acts of Nereus and Achilleus, which could more accurately be called the Acts of Domitilla. In the twentieth century, this imaginative work was unsurprisingly deemed to be historically unreliable. Although the Acts of Nereus and Achilleus cannot be accepted at face value, it does record traditions extant among Christians in Rome when it was written in the fifth or sixth centuries. The explanations for these traditions might be fictional, but the Acts cannot be totally disregarded.

In the Acts, Nereus and Achilleus are two attendants on Domitilla who are also Christians and share in her exile on the island of Pontia. Many other saints are brought into the saga, each demonstrating some link to Domitilla. A digression brings in the story of Peter's daughter, called Petronella, who becomes a martyr. This introduces the shadowy Saint Petronella who will become central to our quest. The foursome of Domitilla, Petronella, Nereus, and Achilleus will be repeatedly encountered together.

The Acts are not our earliest evidence for a cult of Domitilla. That is a letter written by Jerome after the death of Saint Paula, who traveled to the Holy Land:

> The vessel touched at the island of Pontia ennobled long since as the place of exile of the illustrious lady Flavia Domitilla who under the Emperor Domitian was banished because she confessed herself a Christian; and Paula, when she saw the cells in which this lady passed the period of her long martyrdom, taking to herself the wings of faith, more than ever desired to see Jerusalem and the holy places. (Jerome, Letters 108:7)

Paula made this journey to Jerusalem at around 385. So by the end of the fourth century, the cult of Domitilla the martyr was already long-established on Pontia. Whether the "cells" in which she was supposed to have spent her exile had any relation to the historical Domitilla is a different matter. But Jerome's evidence does show that Christians already esteemed Domitilla as a martyr and saint.

18

The Domitilla Catacombs

Discovery

In 1593 an eighteen-year-old youth called Antonio Bosio arrived in Rome, having traveled from his home on the island of Malta.[1] He had abandoned his law studies to embark upon a most unusual quest—he was searching for catacombs. His imagination had been inflamed by news of the discovery in 1578 of a catacomb on the Via Salaria. This gave the first glimpse, for the modern age, into the underground burial grounds of ancient Rome. Bosio knew that many more catacombs had existed, and he was determined to find them.

He began exploring the countryside outside the city walls of Rome, following clues in ancient Christian writings. He had beginner's luck and discovered an access route down into a hypogeum, an old burial chamber. Following corridors that led from this chamber, he was soon hopelessly lost in a dark labyrinth of underground passageways and staircases. He walked mile after mile of tunnels between bones piled in the cavities to each side. Unable to find an exit, the young Bosio feared for his life. It looked as if he were fated to join the dead who had lain undisturbed for so long. To show some sign he had been there, he wrote a graffito recording his name and the date—10th December 1593.[2] It was only after several hours of wandering that he found the entrance again and was able to climb back into the light of day. Bosio did not know it at the time, but he had discovered the catacombs of Domitilla.

The catacombs were the practical solution to a pressing problem caused by the explosive growth of the population of Rome—what to do with the dead. It was illegal to bury a person within the walls, so the cemeteries had to go outside. Families would want to visit their deceased loved ones, so these cemeteries had to be within easy walking distance of the city. There was a severe shortage of suitable land. The problem was particularly acute for Christians as they favored burial over cremation, and burials took up more space. The solution was to dig downwards. The soft tufa rock in the area of Rome was eminently suitable for the construction of tunnels. So the cemeteries developed into catacombs, enormous underground multi-level structures. These would mainly consist of corridors on different stories, each with several levels of "shelves" hollowed out on their sides.

Typically, the newly dead would be left on a shelf wrapped in a grave cloth. The bones would be moved to a permanent resting place when the body had decayed. When everyone had forgotten the deceased, the bones would likely end up piled up in communal shelves along with hundreds of others. It was a very efficient use of space.

Those who were wealthy or more eminent would have individual tombs which were sometimes richly decorated with frescos. Other frescos would adorn arches and public spaces, including the rooms in which feasts would be held in memory of the dead. From such images and tomb inscriptions, we can learn a great deal about the early Christians of Rome. But the catacombs were not just Christian: most catacomb burials in the early centuries were pagan, and the large Jewish community also buried their dead in catacombs.

With the fall of the western Empire, the population of Rome decreased to a fraction of its former size. The catacombs were no longer used for the internment of the dead from the fifth century onwards but found a new role as the center of the pilgrimage tourist trade. The pilgrim came to Rome to visit the tombs of the many early martyrs. Guidebooks called "itineraries" dating from the seventh and eighth centuries attest to the importance of the catacombs and the trail of the martyrs. In the ninth century, the popes began moving the relics of the saints out of the catacombs and into specially constructed churches. Rome was reinventing itself, changing from an imperial capital into the capital of Christianity. Denuded of the bones of the martyrs, the catacombs no longer served a purpose for the living and were left for the dead. The entrances collapsed or were buried, and they faded from memory for seven hundred years.

Bosio undertook the first systematic exploration of the catacombs, and it took his whole life. His method was to comb through the surviving Christian literature from antiquity for any clues. Once he had a rough position for a catacomb, he would start the long, laborious search for any sign on the ground. If he were lucky, he would find the remains of a filled-in staircase or an old lighting shaft. He would then excavate and go down and explore, taking care not to get lost again. By his death in 1629, he had discovered no less than thirty sites.

The posthumous publication of his book, Roma Sotterranea, marked the commencement of the modern exploration of the catacombs. It also made the location of the catacombs known to treasure hunters. There was much looting and many of the frescos were removed, often destroyed by a heavy-handed extraction. In the nineteenth century, the church exerted more control, and the archaeologist De Rossi was appointed to undertake a thorough scientific excavation.

It was De Rossi who first properly identified the catacombs of Domitilla, which included the so-called Flavian Hypogeum, the underground burial chamber found by the young Bosio. This was mistakenly believed to have been built by the Flavians in the first century but actually dates from the second half of the second century. The Domitilla catacombs developed as several smaller sites which were joined together to make a complex with 13 km of tunnels. De Rossi was able to link the catacombs to Domitilla with evidence that seemed cast iron certain until the twentieth century revisionists got to work.

The link was supported by three stone epigraphs.[3] The first records a grant of land by Flavia Domitilla to one P. Calvisius Philotas for a burial place for the use of both himself and his descendants.[4] This was found on the Tor Marancia estate where the Domitilla catacombs are located. It would seem to unambiguously link Domitilla to the burial site, so the revisionists were forced to argue that this was another, later Flavia Domitilla. There is no evidence for the existence of this other Domitilla although it is always possible that an unknown descendant may have taken the same name.

A second inscription found at the church of Saint Clement relates to Domitilla as the granddaughter of Vespasian.[5] It has clearly been taken to that church from somewhere else—it was widely believed that Saint Clement was the same person as Domitilla's husband, Clemens. The third and most interesting inscription is that by Tatia Baucylis, the nurse of Domitilla's children, which explicitly records that our Domitilla made a grant of land for the burial of her freedmen.[6] It seems to have been associated with the Domitilla catacombs, although the revisionists deny that it was necessarily found there.

The revisionists adopt a "divide and conquer" approach to the evidence, and each individual point can indeed be disputed.[7] And yet the cumulative case for a link with Domitilla is impressive. As well as the inscriptions we have the sixth century Acts of Nereus and Achilleus that record that the burial place of these two saints was on land that was owned by Domitilla. The Acts demonstrate a strong tradition c.500 that Domitilla had established the place as a burial ground. It is difficult to explain how such a tradition could have developed unless Domitilla were really connected with the site. And then there is the inscription recording a grant of land in the immediate area by "Flavia Domitilla." Even if this were a later Domitilla, it would still establish a family link to the earlier cemetery. And we know that Domitilla did dedicate land for the burial of her freedmen—if this was not at the catacombs of Domitilla then where else? There is no evidence connecting any other burial site with her.

The Basilica

Within the Domitilla catacomb is a church that De Rossi excavated. He found that it was dedicated to Saints Nereus and Achilleus, which was a surprise as there was a church containing the relics of these saints located near the baths of Caracalla. That second church was built c.800 and the saints' remains were probably relocated from the Domitilla catacombs at that time. They are supposedly interred alongside the remains of Saint Domitilla, although these bones are unlikely to have any genuine connection to her.

Pope Damascus (366-384) probably built the original basilica at the Domitilla catacombs. The church was certainly in existence during his pontificate, for he left an inscription the text of which was recorded in the Pilgrim Itinerary of Einsiedeln:

> Nereus and Achilleus, martyrs, had put their names down as soldiers and fulfilled a cruel duty, together giving regard to the orders of the tyrant and ready to serve through fear. Wonderful to believe, they put aside their fury and being converted, they fled the impious ranks of the tyrant, and threw away the shields, their trophies and bloody javelins. Confessing, they rejoiced in winning the victories of Christ. Believe, by means of Damascus, what the glory of Christ is capable of.

So, Nereus and Achilleus were soldiers who, upon conversion, refused to obey the orders of the "tyrant" and laid down their arms. The implication is that they were martyred for refusing to fight. It is all quite vague, without context or timeframe. Scholars have come to the conclusion that Pope Damascus actually knew almost nothing about the saints he was commemorating.[8] The remains of two fallen pillars were uncovered in the church; one had Achilleus' name and a depiction of his martyrdom in military dress by beheading. The other, which was incomplete, would have recorded the same about Nereus.

The church was built half above ground and half below. The reason for this odd floor level is that the focal point of the building was an earlier sanctuary. This had been constructed c.320 by excavating the surface to just above the level of the catacomb tombs. Some of the walls of this earlier building were incorporated into the new church. So there were at least three successive stages;

(i) the catacomb tombs of Nereus and Achilleus dating to no later than the third century;

(ii) an earlier small sanctuary built c.320;

(iii) the enlarged church built by Pope Damascus c.380.

There may have been an earlier stage; the catacomb tombs may not have been the first graves of the two martyrs as remains were often moved. This basilica formed the sacred heart of the catacombs; Christians wanted to be buried close to the martyrs. But there are two puzzles about the dedication to Nereus and Achilleus. The first is why there was no dedication to Saint Domitilla. The catacombs of Domitilla are only identified as such in the itineraries quite late. Yet the author of the Acts of Nereus and Achilleus knew that the saints had been buried on land belonging to Flavia Domitilla. And this is supported by the inscriptional evidence. So awareness of Domitilla's association with the catacombs must have been passed down for hundreds of years from the late first century. Why then was she not included among the saints honored at the site?

The second mystery concerns Saint Petronella. By the sixth century, the church would be dedicated to her, but she is not mentioned in the inscription by Damascus. However, in the Acts of Nereus and Achilleus, the two male martyrs are buried close to Petronella's monument or tomb. The issue is confused by the later identification of Petronella as Saint Peter's daughter. One possible explanation is that the cult of Petronella only developed comparatively late because of this false identification. But we know that this is not the case.

In the catacombs below the church, there is a mosaic decorating the tomb of a woman called Veneranda, which shows another young woman escorting the deceased to paradise. The name of this second woman is "Petronella mart (martyr)". We will analyze this painting in the next chapter. Just to say here that the fresco is dated to c.356 and the artist shows Petronella in the fashions of the early centuries. The tomb of Veneranda is positioned immediately behind the church's apse and very close to the tombs of the two male martyrs. So there is evidence for a long-established cult of Petronella associated with Nereus and Achilleus.

Why was the church not dedicated to Petronella alongside the other two? It was Pope Damascus who was instrumental in developing the cult of the martyrs by remodeling catacomb sites as places of worship. He favored pairs of male saints, such as Nereus and Achilleus, and was notorious for diminishing or eliminating female saints.[9] There seems to have been a power struggle between female teachers and preachers and those, like Damascus, who wanted a more masculine Christianity. Damascus wrote some sixty elegies for the martyrs to be inscribed at their sanctuaries, including the one he wrote for Nereus and Achilleus. Only one of these elegies is for a female martyr.

Damascus was also concerned to fight what he saw as heresy. In the fourth century there were competing versions of Christianity and the development of the martyrs' cults was often a matter of private initiative and not under the control of the church. Damascus aimed to propagate the official story of the martyrs and suppress what he saw as heretical beliefs.[10] We will see that Petronella was the centre of what, to Damascus, would have looked like an appalling heresy.

Another question is whether the remains of Petronella were really at the site. Although her tomb was reputed to be close to the other two martyrs, it has never been found. It is true that the supposed sarcophagus containing her remains was transferred to Saint Peter's in the eighth century. But, as we shall see, the only real connection between this sarcophagus and the early martyr is the name "Petronilla (sic.)." There was a tremendous economic advantage in possessing the relics of the saints, and they were often misidentified. A sarcophagus, unlike a tomb, is movable by nature; it could have been found elsewhere and brought to the church.

De Rossi thought that the sarcophagus had belonged to Petronella and that he had identified the niche in which it had once lain under the circular wall encompassing the apse.[11] His confidence in this theory disguised the fact that he never offered a single piece of hard evidence linking the niche with Petronella. And this niche occupies a curious half-in half-out position. Why would the church be built with Petronella's tomb under the wall rather than under the floor of the apse like the tombs of Nereus and Achilleus? De Rossi's answer was that Petronella had not been a martyr like the other two and so was relegated to this secondary position on the fringe. However, this is contradicted by the contemporary evidence of the fresco which De Rossi himself discovered. We could not have more eloquent evidence that Petronella was regarded as a martyr at the time the church was built.

De Rossi never considers alternative explanations for this niche. Christians wanted to be buried as close as possible to the saints and the niche occupies the ultimate high-status position on the very edge of the apse without intruding into the martyrs' sacred space. It is likely that it belonged to a rich patron, perhaps the person who had funded the building of the church.

It is also significant that the Acts of Nereus and Achilleus details the burials for all the martyrs except for Petronella. She is mentioned a little later in the account of the burial of Nereus and Achilleus:

Speciosus, a follower of theirs and a domestic slave of the holy virgin Domitilla, stole their bodies at night, carried them by boat to Rome, and buried them in the sandy crypt at Domitilla's suburban villa. The burial place is about one and a half Roman miles from the city walls, quite close to the monument [or tomb] of Peter's daughter Petronilla. We learned this from Speciosus' account. He wrapped the bodies of the saints in their burial shrouds. (Acts of Nereus and Achilleus, 18:11-14)[12]

So when the Acts was written c.500, there was a monument/tomb to Petronella near the two martyrs' graves, although this could be a reference to the Veneranda fresco. If the author were familiar with her sarcophagus, supposedly carved by Saint Peter, we would expect this to be mentioned.

The idea that the two were buried in a sandy crypt of Domitilla's villa is plainly false, although it is an understandable conclusion if the author thought that the two, as contemporaries of Domitilla, had been buried on a site belonging to her. The author of the Acts would not have known that the catacombs were only built a hundred years after her time. If the two had really lived in the first century, then their bones must have been moved from their original resting place into the new stone tombs carved out in the catacombs. Such translations of saints' bones from another nearby location were common. We must remember that the martyrs would have been regarded as criminals at the time of their deaths and Christians would have buried them quickly and inconspicuously in whatever poor grave was available. The tombs would have taken time and labor to prepare so we can be confident that they are not the original graves. The bones must have been moved into new tombs worthy of the martyrs from somewhere else.

A Christian catacomb

We know that a major Christian catacomb developed on land which Domitilla had donated as a burial ground for her male and female freedmen. Initially, this was seen as supporting the idea that Domitilla was a Christian. But archaeologists failed to find evidence for early Christian burials and concluded that the Christian catacomb only began developing in the third century. Some scholars think that this implies that Domitilla had no connection with the catacombs—she had simply once owned the land on which they were later built.

The conclusion does not follow. It would be surprising if we were to find early Christian burials at the site because there is virtually no evidence for such burials anywhere in Rome. Christians had yet to develop their own burial practices in the first two centuries and Christian burials are indistinguishable from pagan burials.[13] Besides, the original cemetery that Domitilla established has long since disappeared.

The evidence of the catacombs is completely consistent with a Christian Domitilla. We know that she granted the cemetery for her freedmen. If she were Christian, the early burials would have been a mixture of Christian and pagan freedmen: her imperial household would have been large and Christians would have been a small minority. We also know that Domitian's persecution claimed more victims than just Clemens, and we would expect these victims to include freedmen members of Domitilla's house church. These martyrs would have been buried in the cemetery alongside their pagan colleagues, which would explain why the site later developed into a significant Christian catacomb and cultic center.

If Domitilla were Jewish, there would have been no early Christian connection. So the development of the Christian site on land that she granted would have to be pure coincidence. We would also expect a Jewish Domitilla to have established a Jewish cemetery. But there is no evidence for Jewish burials on the site.

Was Domitilla Jewish?

The case for Domitilla being a Jewish sympathizer rather than a Christian uses a "divide and conquer" approach to the evidence. Each point is considered in turn, and arguments produced for why the evidence does not necessarily mean that Domitilla was a Christian. The flaw with this method is that it makes no allowance for the fact that several independent lines of evidence all point in the same direction. We evaluate each of these lines below to show the extent to which it is consistent with Domitilla's religion being either Christianity or Judaism:

1. Cassius Dio's statement that Domitilla and Clemens fell into "Jewish ways" might suggest Judaism. However, the charge of atheism implies Christianity unless Clemens was actually circumcised, which is very unlikely.

2. Eusebius' evidence is entirely consistent with Christianity and not consistent with Judaism unless Eusebius was lying or making a mistake. His source, Bruttius, is independent of Dio and is backed up by Jerome's evidence of an early cult of Domitilla on Pontia

3. The evidence of the catacombs of Domitilla is entirely consistent with Christianity. We know that Domitilla established the cemetery for her freedmen, and if she were a Christian, we would expect a mix of Christian and pagan burials. The presence of early Christian graves, some of early martyrs, would explain why the catacombs later developed into a major Christian catacomb and cultic center.

If Domitilla were Jewish, then the fact that her burial ground emerged as a significant Christian burial ground would have to be assigned to coincidence. There is also some contrary evidence; we would expect a Jewish Domitilla to have given rise to a Jewish catacomb, but there is no evidence of Jewish burials.

4. The emergence of Domitilla as a saint in both the Greek Orthodox and Catholic churches is, of course, consistent with Christianity. Those who think that Domitilla was Jewish must assume that Christians went around appropriating anything Jewish. But there is no other example of a Jewish figure contemporary to the Christian church being appropriated in this way. Christians honored their own saints and martyrs and did not have a favorable view of Jewish converts. So if Domitilla were Jewish, she would be a unique case of appropriation.

All the evidence is consistent with Domitilla being a Christian. In contrast, the only evidence for her being Jewish is Dio's statement that she and her husband had slipped into "Jewish ways," which could undoubtedly include Christianity. A probability calculation (given in the note) considering all these points concludes there is a 96% probability that Domitilla was Christian and just 4% that she was Jewish.[14] This probability is before we allow for the abundant evidence that Domitilla was the author of Luke and Acts.

The painting in the catacombs

Veneranda and Petronella

The sacred heart of the Domitilla catacombs is the church of Saint Nereus and Achilleus, which was later dedicated to Saint Petronella. The apse is centered on tombs below the floor level that once held the remains of the two male saints. These two were supposedly buried near the tomb of Saint Petronella, which has never been found. But if we go down underground into the catacombs and walk just a short distance, some seven meters, from the tombs of the martyrs, we come to a small cubiculum. And in this little room is a fresco that does bear the name of Petronella.[1] The fresco decorates the space above the tomb of a lady called Veneranda (see Fig. 1, 3 and 4). It is painted in the arcosolium, the arched recess hacked out from the rock above the tomb. The left third as we look at it is missing, but the remaining two-thirds are in fair condition. The fresco was discovered by De Rossi in 1875. The best image is Fig. 4 which is a nineteenth century hand-colored photograph.[2] Comparison with more recent photographs (Fig. 1 and 3) shows that the fresco has undergone further deterioration since the nineteenth century. To protect the image, the cubiculum is no longer accessible to visitors.

The inscription records that Veneranda died on January 7th. Recording the day of death served a practical purpose, as an annual feast was held in the deceased's honor. No year is given, but the fresco is typically dated to shortly after 356 AD from an inscription for a neighboring tomb that was engraved on a stone that sealed the arcosolium. The Veneranda painting was made over this stone.[3] The sanctuary which preceded the church would have been in existence at this time, although the church itself was probably not yet built. Veneranda had been granted a prime position close to the sanctuary and the martyrs' graves. Her name means "she who must be venerated," which perhaps indicates that she was a leader in the local church or otherwise especially esteemed. The quality of the fresco and the position of her tomb show that she came from a wealthy family.

Veneranda is painted in the center, standing with her arms raised in the

Figure 1: The Veneranda fresco, Catacombs of Domitilla.

Figure 2: Bust of Julia Titi showing the Flavian toupet hairstyle.

Figure 3: The Veneranda fresco, Catacombs of Domitilla, detail. Veneranda stands in front with arms held out in the orans pose while Petronella escorts her to heaven. Petronella points to the scrolls, directing Veneranda's gaze towards them.

Figure 4: The Veneranda fresco, nineteenth century hand-colored photograph by Carlo Tabanelli. A comparison with the previous image reveals the additional deterioration of the fresco since its discovery. Note the markings in the book; three vertical strokes on the left, four on the right.

"orans" pose, which is very common in early Christian art, particularly in relation to women. A little to the right, and behind her, is a second female figure drawn to the same scale. The writing above her head reads "Petronella Mart" and identifies her as a martyr, Saint Petronella. She is escorting Veneranda to paradise, symbolized by a rose bush, most of which is missing now—it would have twirled through much of the lost area on the left.

Both the women are dressed in the finery that was customary for such images. Veneranda's clothes and hairstyle are contemporary to the time of the fresco. Petronella's costume, however, is old-fashioned, in the style of the early centuries. And she is dressed as an empress. She wears a pallium, the scarf-like width of cloth that comes down her front to almost full length. In the church, the pallium (called the omophorion in the east) denoted a bishop from at least the fourth century. The pallium could only be conferred by the pope in the catholic church and bishops wear it to this day. It was derived from the custom of the later emperors and other high officials to wear a special scarf to mark their status.[4] But why should Petronella be shown wearing the pallium? It is true that another female Roman saint, Agnes, wears a golden pallium in a seventh century mosaic in the church of Saint Agnes fuori le mura: she is dressed as a Byzantine empress. But this is almost three centuries after the Petronella fresco which can be seen as the precedent for portraying female martyrs in this manner.

The Petronella of the fresco is usually described as a girl or young woman. Yet nothing about the image suggests that Petronella is particularly young. The rather formal costume gives the impression of a matron, although it is impossible to reach a definite conclusion about the age of either figure based on such stylized portraits.

Petronella's hair is worn up high in the manner of the early centuries. We can compare it to the extravagant toupet coiffure popular among high-status women between 70 AD and 120 AD.[5] This style is worn by the Flavian women, Julia Titi and Domitia, in their formal portraits (Fig. 2). Domitilla would have worn her hair similarly on official occasions, although such a high-maintenance hairstyle would not have been carried over to everyday life. There are some similarities with Petronella in the way the hair rises in a dome above the brow, a feature of the hairstyle that the poet Martial likened to a "globe or orb."[6] Juvenal was less flattering when he compared it to a multi-storied building.[7] The hairstyle on the fresco is certainly archaic and could be an attempt by the fourth-century painter to represent a late first-century style they had never seen in real life. The artist also gives her the pallium, a symbol of imperial authority in his own time. Was he trying to depict her as a member of the imperial family?

The greatest mystery in the painting concerns the other items in the fresco; a floating book to the right of Petronella and a capsa, a container used for carrying and storing scrolls, in the lower right. The analysis below owes much to Christine Schenk, who in turn has drawn upon Dorothy Irvin's ideas.[8] In "Crispina and her Sisters" Schenk explains that such a capsa is a very common feature on funerary monuments. For pagans, the capsa scrolls would symbolize an interest in philosophy which was all the rage in the second and third centuries. In a Christian context, they would indicate that the deceased could read and study scripture.

We would not normally attribute much importance to the presence of a capsa. It was a way of flattering the dead by showing their intellectual pursuits. This might mean no more than that the deceased would occasionally read philosophy. But there are features in this fresco that are not at all typical. The first mystery is why we have both a codex and the capsa of scrolls. By the fourth century, the codex book form had replaced scrolls for Christians. The floating book represents the Christian scriptures and the gospels in particular. Veneranda's raised hand reaches out towards the codex and associates her with the gospels. She was someone who read and studied the gospels and perhaps taught them to others.

But what about the capsa? Scrolls were old-fashioned and obsolete for Christians by this time. But they would have been very appropriate for the time of Petronella, who, judging by her clothes and hair, lived in the early centuries. And it is Petronella who gestures to the capsa with her hand. With her other hand on Veneranda's shoulder, she directs the dead woman's attention to the capsa. The capsa is not some mere decoration extolling the achievements of Veneranda but the focal point of the image. The outstretched hand of Petronella and the rapt gaze of Veneranda direct the viewer's eyes towards the capsa.

It is essential to read the language of gestures on such frescos as they convey much of the picture's meaning. Petronella's outstretched hand tells us that she is the one associated with the capsa and its scrolls. A saint would be depicted with the objects that symbolized what they were best known for. Often this would be something connected to their martyrdom. But Petronella is not shown with instruments of torture but with the capsa. Which means she was renowned for something to do with the scrolls.

So what do the scrolls stand for? One theory is that they represent the Old Testament Hebrew scriptures and complement the codex representing the gospels. But this makes no sense. Why should Petronella be associated with the Hebrew scriptures? It was the gospels that were the means of salvation for Christians. They should be the focal point as Petronella escorts Veneranda to paradise.

Schenk's explanation is that both women were preachers and teachers.

In her view, both the codex and the scrolls represented the scriptures in the broader sense and were symbols of Christian authority. Veneranda's ministry was represented by the codex. Petronella's earlier ministry was symbolized by the scrolls, the form in which the gospels circulated in the early centuries. Schenk concludes that Petronella was an early female minister who lived sometime between the late first to early third centuries.

Schenk's analysis is extremely valuable—the significance of this image could not have been identified without it. But her conclusion is influenced by the contemporary debate around women priests and bishops. The idea that the scrolls symbolize some kind of formal ministry and authority for Petronella does not make much sense in the context of an ancient martyr. Something is going on in this painting, something which this conclusion does not fully explain.

It might help to look at a parallel. Nearby the Veneranda tomb, there is a fresco in which the apostle Paul stands beside a capsa of scrolls. Paul was renowned for his letters which were viewed as scripture by the Christians. The letters were distributed on scrolls in the early centuries before being incorporated into the codices that constituted the early New Testament. The scrolls on the image must represent these letters, the thing that Paul was best known for.

Applying this example to Petronella would indicate that the scrolls are not something she studied but something she wrote. And it was important enough for Veneranda to give it her rapt attention as she walks the path to heaven.

Bitalia and Cerula

To help understand the Veneranda fresco in context, we will look at two frescos from the San Gennaro catacombs in Naples. Like the Veneranda fresco, they are both painted in the arcosolium above a tomb, they both show a woman in orans pose, and they both involve floating gospels.

The first decorates the tomb of Bitalia (Fig. 5), whose name is written in the fresco.[9] Unfortunately, the fresco's condition is poor. It shows the upper body and head of the deceased woman who stands with her arms raised. The symbol of Christ, the staurogram or tau-rho symbol, can be traced above her head. The most remarkable feature is the two codices on either side of her head which are open and floating, just like the Veneranda codex. Dangling below the codices are red ribbon-like streamers; they are not bookmarks but flames representing the Holy Spirit.

The first three half codices are marked with the name of a gospel in Latin in a non-standard order; Joannis, Markus, and Matteus. The last

Figure 5: Bitalia fresco in the San Gennaro catacombs.

Figure 6: Cerula fresco in the San Gennaro catacombs.

Lucanus, and Matteus. The ordering is non-standard and different from that of Bitalia. Above Cerula's head are the signs of Christ, the staurogram with a paired alpha and omega. The arch above the tomb is also decorated with Christian symbols, including two more staurograms and a large alpha and omega.

Cerula is adorned in rich garments. She wears a wide-sleeved purple dalmatic over a white tunic decorated with gold bands near the wrists. But the most extraordinary element of her costume is the veil, which flows over her head and drapes around her shoulders. It is exquisitely decorated by dancing figures and circular shield-like details.

Recently the theory has been put forward that Cerula and Bitalia were female bishops. The justification is the four gospels with their flames of the spirit shown in close association with the women. At a bishops' ordination, the gospels would be placed on his head so that the spirit could enter into him. Against this idea is Cerula's veil which is not at all what we would expect a bishop to wear. The veil's dark figures are typical of Coptic garments manufactured in Egypt in the 5th to 7th centuries. The imagery seems pagan, with bacchic dancers cavorting across the space. Even if this decoration had lost any religious significance by this time, there is the aspect of cost. A veil of such quality imported from Egypt would be extravagantly expensive. It was an ostentatious display of wealth to be depicted on your tomb wearing such costly apparel. We know of other richly dressed Christians buried in San Gennaro who made such a display. But this is hardly appropriate behavior for a bishop.

So was Cerula a hypocrite, expressing her piety with the gospels and Christ symbols while flaunting her wealth? Perhaps not. Appendix C sets out the case that Cerula is shown as the bride of Christ using imagery from the beautiful Wedding Hymn in the apocryphal Acts of Thomas. If so, the veil is not a real garment to flaunt wealth but a symbolic expression of the divine marriage.

A symbolic meaning would bring all the elements of the arcosolium and the wall painting into harmony. Cerula, as Christ's bride, is shown alongside Christ's symbols with the gospels burning with the flame of the Holy Spirit on either side, and the whole flanked by Paul and Peter. It is unlikely that she was formally a bishop. If the flaming gospels represented a bishop they should be associated with the burials of male bishops, but this is not the case. In fact, the floating gospels only seem to be found on the tombs of women. We only have these three surviving examples, although others may have been lost.

The prototype would seem to be the earlier Veneranda fresco. The community who produced the San Gennaro frescos in Naples may have been linked to those who cherished the Veneranda fresco in Rome. Bitalia, half codex, which should indicate Luke, is unmarked. Has the name been lost through damp and disintegration of the surface? Although this is possible, the absence of any trace of paint suggests that the fourth half codex was left blank.[10]

Why would one gospel be unnamed? Schenk mentions a feminist theory that the women who arranged for the painting of the fresco rejected the Gospel of Luke because it preferred Peter's leadership to that of Mary the Magdalene. She wisely adds that this is "a larger hypothesis than the evidence can support."[11] It is actually unbelievable. There is no evidence that women in the ancient world rejected the Gospel of Luke. Indeed, we would expect the opposite. Most women were mothers, and Luke elevates and celebrates motherhood. Both Luke and Acts promote the idea that women can be prophets equally with men. And in Acts, women play powerful roles as leaders and teachers.

It would also be incredible if the fresco painters rejected the Gospel of Luke as the concept of the four-fold gospel was long established. The number four had a mystical significance expressed in the fresco by the two symmetrical and equal codices, each split symmetrically into two equal sides. As early as the end of the second century, these four gospels were widely accepted as Matthew, Mark, Luke, and John. No Christian in the fifth or sixth century would substitute another gospel for Luke.

Nor is the unmarked gospel portrayed any differently from the other three. The flames of the spirit emanate from it just as they do from the others. Which leaves only one possibility. Those who painted the fresco were not rejecting the gospel but the name "Luke." They have inherited a tradition about the real author but cannot write this person's name on the codex: to do so would invite a charge of heresy. So they make a silent protest and leave the space blank.

The second fresco of interest at San Gennaro follows an almost identical design to that of Bitalia, although it is much more refined in execution.[12] Discovered in 1977 by a team led by Don Nicola Ciavolino, it is beautifully well preserved. It is the memorial fresco to a woman called Cerula (Fig. 6) and dates to c.500, over a century after Veneranda's memorial. The arcosolium containing Cerula's portrait is positioned centrally in a fully decorated wall. She is flanked on the left side by a full-length wall painting of the apostle Paul. Most of the decoration on the other side has been lost, but it probably showed a matching picture of Peter. This was a richly decorated tomb.

Like Bitalia, Cerula is shown from the waist up with hands raised in the orans pose between two floating codices. The codices are each split into two, with the flames of the spirit coming from them. The four books are all named and identified in Latin as the four gospels; Markus, Joannis,

Cerula, and Veneranda can be seen as continuing a threatened tradition of women as esteemed Christian teachers and prophets that went back to the origins of Christianity. Initially, there was no central control over individual congregations and no rules for who could preach. As the church became an increasingly centralized institution, those who taught under the old informal traditions were marginalized to the fringe and eventually eliminated in favor of an exclusively male priesthood.

One other feature of the Cerula fresco may be relevant. The picture has a strong dynamic produced by the dancers on the veil who proceed from left to right. If we extend the lines of the veil in the direction of this movement, we find that four lines converge at a focal point at the bottom left corner of the Gospel of Luke. This dynamic draws the viewer's eye to that gospel. The same gospel may be signaled in the other fresco by Bitalia's hand, which is positioned directly beneath it.

Does this indicate a special interest in the gospel of Luke by the women (and perhaps men) of this Christian community in Naples? Maybe these are nothing more than chance alignments, but it is significant that Luke is the gospel that the Bitalia fresco refuses to name.

The ribbon

The two open codices represent the four-fold gospel in the Naples' frescos. So the surviving open codex in the Veneranda painting must have been matched by a symmetrical codex on the other side. There are no names on the Veneranda gospels, but there are some vertical lines. The left side of the codex has three such lines and the right side four. The lines are clear on the nineteenth century image of Fig. 4 and are discernable with a little more difficulty on more modern photographs.

The lines are Roman numbering.[13] The two halves of the visible codex are numbered three and four, so the missing codex would have been numbered one and two. Fig. 7 shows what the full fresco must have looked like. Most of the space on the left would have been occupied with the rose bush symbolizing paradise with the codex floating above. Would there have been a ribbon coming from this left side codex to match the one on the right? Probably not, as there was nowhere for it to go. Most likely, there were only the bush and codices on the left as the focus of attention is on the right.

The choice of numbers rather than names for the four gospels is intriguing. There is sufficient space on the codices to indicate the gospel names. But those who commissioned the fresco preferred to use numbers instead. Was this to avoid naming the Gospel of Luke?

Figure 7: Reconstruction of Veneranda fresco. The two floating books represent the four gospels which are numbered. The ribbon connects the third gospel to the scrolls.

The numbering of the gospels implies a fixed order. The familiar order of Matthew, Mark, Luke, and John was already well established by the fourth century.[14] It was followed, for example, by Jerome in his Vulgate translation of the gospels produced in Rome in 383 AD. However, alternative orderings, such as occur in the Naples frescos, are also sometimes found. Assuming that the Roman fresco follows the standard order, then the codex on the right side shows the gospels of Luke (III) and John (IIII).

There is one remaining feature that has not been explained—the ribbon. It comes from the gospel numbered three and snakes down in sinuous waves approaching the capsa. Although Fig. 4 seems to show the ribbon not quite touching the capsa, other photographs make it clear that the ribbon does just touch the container. It seems to serve no purpose and is far too long to be a bookmark. Is it purely decorative? That would be odd when everything else in the picture has a meaning.

The two women are focused on the scrolls, but it is the gospels that should lead the way to heaven. The ribbon provides the solution to this mystery. It flows from the third gospel and terminates precisely at the capsa. Its serves to visually connect this gospel to the scrolls. The implication is that the scrolls and the third gospel are the same thing. We have seen that the capsa is associated with Petronella and contains something she wrote. So, the fresco is telling us that Petronella wrote the third gospel which we call Luke.

We can see why the venerated Christian teacher Veneranda should want to be associated with Petronella, who lived hundreds of years in the past. Veneranda studied the gospels, but Petronella wrote one. She points to it with her hand as she places the other hand around Veneranda, protectively guiding her to paradise.

20

Saint Petronella

Who is Petronella?

Petronella (or Petronilla as the name is sometime spelt[1]) is the most confusing of saints. The various traditions about her are contradictory and do not gel into a single picture. She has long been celebrated in the church as the daughter of Saint Peter. But a more modern scholarly interpretation sees her as a wealthy benefactress who lived in the early 300s AD. Her sarcophagus was taken to the Vatican and its inscription recorded.[2]

One theme that does emerge is that she was associated with the two male saints, Nereus and Achilleus, who shared the same cultic center, the church in the Domitilla catacombs. The earliest evidence for Saint Petronella is negative; she was not included in the first calendar of the saints, the Depositio Martyrum of the fourth century.[3] This is usually taken as meaning that she must have lived after the cut-off date for that calendar which does not include any martyrs after 336 AD. However, 336 AD is perilously close to the standard dating of the Veneranda fresco at c.356 AD. Those who painted the Veneranda fresco believed that Petronella had lived in the distant past. Whether or not their belief is correct, she must certainly have lived long before their own lifetimes.

The other possibility is that Petronella was too early for inclusion in the calendar. The Depositio Martyrum does not include any martyrs before 203 AD except for Peter and Paul.[4] The only conclusion that makes sense of both the calendar and the fresco is that Petronella lived and died in the first two centuries.

Nereus and Achilleus are also omitted from the Depositio Martyrum. Yet the archaeological evidence tells us that their cult was well established by the early fourth century. They are usually thought to have been martyred in the persecution of Diocletian (284-305). But this is not consistent with the evidence of the early sanctuary and their omission from the Depositio Martyrum.[5] The inscription of Pope Damascus is vague and cannot be assumed to be reliable.

The obvious conclusion is that Nereus and Achilleus, like Petronella, lived in the first two centuries. This would pre-date the catacombs in which their remains were interred, but bones were often moved around.

The two could have been buried in the cemetery before their precious relics were moved into specially constructed tombs when the catacombs were dug. Later the sanctuary was excavated above the tombs and the church built on the site of the sanctuary.

We can conclude that the three saints, Nereus, Achilleus, and Petronella, belonged to the first two centuries and were probably connected somehow. When Pope Damascus came along, he froze out Petronella and dedicated the church to Nereus and Achilleus. However, Petronella would get her revenge on Damascus when she found fame as the supposed daughter of Peter.

Peter's daughter?

The earliest version of the story of Peter's daughter would originally have come from the Acts of Peter, which dates prior to 200 AD.[6] Peter has a beautiful daughter who is paralyzed on one side and lives stretched out in the corner of the room. The people who come to Peter for healing are surprised why he has not cured his own daughter. To demonstrate that this is not through a lack of power, he tells the girl to rise, and she gets up and walks. The people rejoice until Peter tells her to return to her place and resume her infirmity. Peter explains that he had a vision in which he was told that the girl would do harm to many if her body remained healthy. When she was just ten, a man called Ptolemaeus saw her bathing with her mother. He sent messengers offering marriage, but her mother would not agree. At this point, two pages of the manuscript are missing, but Ptolemaeus must have abducted her. God preserved her virginity and saved her from rape by paralyzing her on one side. The servants returned the girl leaving her outside Peter's house. Ptolemaeus himself was consumed with guilt and eventually converted to Christianity. He bequeathed the girl some land when he died, but Peter sold it to give the money to the poor.

There is no connection in this story to the Petronella of the fresco. She was an adult martyr who is shown standing and obviously not paralyzed. The only link is the unusual name Petronella, the feminine of Peter. The first time that Peter's daughter is called Petronella is in the retelling of the story in the Acts of Nereus and Achilleus. Petronilla (most manuscripts spell the name with an "i" rather than an "e") lies paralyzed. Peter is asked why he does not cure her, and to prove he has the power, he tells her to get up "and wait upon us." The girl rises up and is cured. Unfortunately, she is seen by an evil seducer called Count Flaccus, who becomes obsessed with her. He offers her marriage and for some unexplained reason, she cannot just say "no." To gain a respite from his attentions, she tells him to send "noble matrons and venerable virgins" to come for her in three days. Instead of preparing for marriage, she prays to God that she might be spared this terrible fate, and at the end of the three days, she expires in her bed. The women who have come to take her to her wedding instead bury her.

In the genre of martyrdom stories, the victim would be accused, tortured, condemned, and then put to death in some unpleasant way. None of these elements are present for Petronilla who just falls asleep and dies. The author of the Acts of Nereus and Achilleus has combined two separate traditions; one relates to Peter's daughter, and the other to the martyr, Petronella. To make Peter's daughter into Petronella, she has to become a martyr. The story is contrived and clumsy, yet it was to be highly influential. Petronella would soon become the patron saint of a new Europe.

Saint Petronella of the Franks

In October 753 AD, Pope Stephen II made an audacious journey from Rome, across the Alps, and into Gaul. He was responding to a political crisis that threatened the survival of Rome and the Papal States as an independent entity. For centuries the Roman Empire had been divided into the Western empire, controlled first from Rome and then Ravenna, and the eastern Byzantine empire ruled from Constantinople. The fate of the two halves was very different. The western empire collapsed to a mere shadow of its former self under successive waves of barbarian invasions. The eastern empire, however, was stable and continued to prosper.

In 533 AD, the emperor Justinian sent the Byzantine general Belisarius on an expedition to reconquer lost territory from the Vandals in North Africa. In a remarkable campaign, Belisarius succeeded in taking Carthage and the productive lands of North Africa. He went on to capture Sicily and then moved into Italy to fight the Goths, who controlled much of the peninsular. The population welcomed the Byzantine forces into Rome, but the Goths besieged the city. Belisarius only succeeded in holding it after a long and brutal war. But by 540 AD, he had taken much of Italy and was in command of Ravenna, which would serve as the Byzantine capital of Italy for two centuries.[7]

Italy and much of North Africa were now part of the Byzantine Empire. It must have looked as if the Roman Empire was being revived into something like its former glory. But it was not to be. Belisarius' victories marked the high tide in the fortunes of Constantinople. The relationship between the two chief Christian cities of Rome and Constantinople was always uneasy. They were separated by bitter theological differences which appear obtuse to the modern mind. But the real power lay in the east while Rome was falling into ruins.

It was the rise of Islam that caused an abrupt decline in the Byzantine Empire. Arab forces, fighting with religious fervor, rapidly conquered the rich lands of Egypt and the Levant, depriving the eastern empire of much of its resources. The Arabs went on to surge across North Africa, eventually reaching Spain. It was a disastrous loss of territory for Constantinople.

By 753 AD, Constantinople could no longer exercise military influence over Italy. Its diminished and hard-pressed armies were needed to defend the capital in the east. The power vacuum was filled by new invaders. The Lombards ("long-beards") crossed the Alps into northern Italy and gradually moved southwards, threatening Rome and the Papal States. Pope Stephen II knew that he could not call upon Constantinople for assistance, so he made an audacious move to secure a new alliance. He traveled to Gaul (France) to meet with Pippin, the king of the Franks. He actually had to pass through Lombard territory on his journey, but they, being good catholic Christians, granted him passage.[8]

The Franks welcomed Stephen, and the two parties forged a new alliance. The pope would give legitimacy to Pippin as the protector of Christendom. The Franks would, in return, support the pope's rule of the Papal States, a swath of territory across Italy from Rome in the west to Ravenna in the northeast. After a campaign against the Lombards, Pippin was able to return all the territory of the Papal States to Rome.[9] It was a historic agreement that would give rise to a new Europe with the center of power in the west rather than the east. The culmination came on Christmas day in 800 when Pope Leo III crowned Pippin's son Charlemagne, "Charles the great," as Holy Roman Emperor in St. Peter's in Rome.

In the early stages, the relationship needed nurturing, which is where Saint Petronella came in. The Franks adopted her as their patron saint. Whether this was the idea of Pope Stephen II or because there was an existing connection is unknown, although there is little evidence for a cult of Saint Petronella outside Rome. But it is certain that Stephen promised Pippin to make a chapel for her at St. Peter's. When Stephen died in 757 and was succeeded by his brother Paul, the new pope held a ceremony to remove the remains of Petronella from the Domitilla catacombs:

> From there he removed her venerable and holy body along with the marble sarcophagus in which it lay and on which were carved letters reading "To golden (Aurea) Petronilla, sweetest daughter." This made it certain that the carving of the letters could be identified as engraved by Saint Peter's own hand out of love for his sweetest child. (Life of Paul, Liber Pontificalis)[10]

The sarcophagus was placed into a specially converted side-chapel dedicated to Petronella. The cult of Petronella was now split from that of Nereus and Achilleus. The relics of the two male saints would have already been moved to their new church near the Baths of Caracalla, where they were joined by the supposed remains of Saint Domitilla. The three saints did not thrive in their new home as the area became depopulated and the church fell into dereliction. The old basilica in the Domitilla catacombs was abandoned and collapsed.

Petronella, however, was installed in splendor in the greatest church in the west. Paul would extravagantly decorate her chapel with "gold, silver and brocades" and "wondrously beautiful pictures." Subsequent popes would give it six arches of silver, six silver columns, and cornices. The altar was gilded with a jeweled diadem and a silver crown. Petronella symbolized the alliance between the Franks and the Catholic Church that was remaking Europe. When Pope Paul received the baptismal shawl of Pippin's baby daughter Gisela he placed it in the new chapel so that the girl might come under Petronella's powerful protective influence.[11]

The saint was the daughter of the supreme apostle, Saint Peter. The proof was that sarcophagus, carved by Peter's own hands for his beautiful, "golden" daughter. So what happened to this most precious relic of Peter and Petronella? In the early sixteenth century, a workman took a hammer and smashed it to pieces for hardcore filling for the rebuilding of St. Peter's. Nothing lasts forever.

The sarcophagus

Everyone feared the warrior pope Julius II (1503-1513) and his irascible temper. He was always spoiling for a fight and had even led the papal troops into battle. But he was also the renaissance pope whose vision operated on the grandest scale. He commissioned work from some of the greatest artists of the renaissance, including Michelangelo, who painted the ceiling of the Sistine Chapel, and Raphael, who frescoed walls in the papal apartments.

Julius had planned a most incredible tomb for himself in St. Peter's, a spectacular monument to be decorated by no less than forty life-sized marble sculptures by the greatest sculptor of the age, Michelangelo. But the pope decided that the old St. Peter's built by Constantine the Great was not good enough for his tomb. So he held a competition to rebuild the church. The winner was the architect Bramante. No one could ever accuse Julius of timidity. He immediately ordered work to begin on the demolition of the old St. Peter's and construction of the new church. In the event, the rebuilding would take a century.

During this work, the Petronella side-chapel was demolished. In an act of officially sanctioned vandalism, the sarcophagus was broken up for material to be used as filling beneath the floor. Fortunately, we have a description of the sarcophagus; it was strigillated and carved with four dolphins.[12] Although the dedication was supposedly to "Aurea Petronilla," meaning "Golden Petronilla," it did not actually say this. The inscription read:

AVR PETRONILLAE FILIAE DVLCISSIMAE

The letters AVR (Aur.) did not mean "golden" but were an abbreviation for the Aurelia gens. The woman buried in the sarcophagus was called Aurelia Petronilla. Her father's nomen would be Aurelius, so this Petronilla was certainly not Saint Peter's daughter.

The sarcophagus would have been an embarrassment to the church. Not only would a knowledgeable person realize that Aurelia Petronilla was a Roman, but there is not the slightest indication beyond the name Petronilla that she was even Christian. The dedication reads:

"Aurelia Petronilla, sweetest daughter."

It is an entirely standard Roman-style epitaph with no hint of martyrdom. Nor did the sarcophagus, with its pagan dolphins, exhibit any Christian symbols.

The first we hear of the sarcophagus is its relocation to St. Peter's in 757. If Petronella had written the Gospel of Luke, she would have lived 650 years before. That is a long time for her sarcophagus to survive and be identifiable as hers. She would have died a century before the catacombs of Domitilla were built, raising the question of where the sarcophagus was located over this period.

The only thing to connect the sarcophagus to the martyr Petronella is the name, and even that is not a perfect match. The nomen is included on the sarcophagus but not on the fresco. And the cognomen is spelled with an "e" on the fresco and an "i" on the sarcophagus. These might be considered minor points, but the sarcophagus should have been located within ten paces of the fresco when it was painted. So why did the artist not copy the name as it appears on the sarcophagus?

The Petronella of the sarcophagus does not seem to fit the Petronella of the fresco. The sarcophagus Petronella was probably a teenage girl because the dedication was by the parents. A married woman's tomb would be dedicated by her husband, if alive, or otherwise by her adult children.

A young widow could return to her parents, but she would quickly be married again. The brief nature of the inscription, "sweetest daughter," suggests a young girl below marriageable age. Such early deaths were tragically common in Rome, where mortality was high at all ages.

Compare this to the Petronella of the fresco, dressed as an empress with her hair in an archaic fashion. This Petronella is associated with a capsa of scrolls, meaning that she was renowned for her intellectual pursuits. This is difficult to square with the idea that she was a teenage girl; it takes maturity to acquire a reputation for learning.

Nor is there anything to connect the girl in the sarcophagus with martyrdom. The inscription is not what we would expect for someone who had died in the arena or suffered in some other way for their faith. There are no Christian symbols present as we would expect to find on a martyr's grave. Why has no Christian added as much as a tau-rho or chi-rho in several hundred years of supposed veneration before the sarcophagus was moved?

This brings us to the question of when Aurelia Petronilla lived. The sarcophagus was of the restrained style typical of the early centuries, but sarcophagi were often reused. After a hundred years, everyone would have forgotten the dead person. The bones could then be respectfully removed and added to those on a shelf, and the sarcophagus rededicated for a new occupant. This saved the considerable cost of a new sarcophagus.

The Aurelia were a respectable old plebeian gens. Many commentators have viewed Aurelia Petronilla as belonging to a noble Roman family of this gens related to the Flavians. However, in 211 AD the Emperor Marcus Aurelius Antoninus, better known as Caracalla, granted Roman citizenship to all the free men and women in the empire. The vast number of new citizens, perhaps 50% of the population, took the Aurelia nomen of the emperor. Also, many emperors from the second century came from the Aurelia gens, and droves of their imperial freedmen inherited the name. So many people were called Aurelius/Aurelia that it served no purpose to distinguish individuals and was only employed on formal occasions. This development would lead to the eventual abandonment of the Roman nomen. The abbreviated name, such as AVR, would come to mean nothing more than that a person was free rather than a slave.[13]

While it is possible that the sarcophagus belonged to a noble member of the ancient Aurelia clan, the probabilities are firmly against this. More likely, Aurelia Petronilla came from one of the many new families entitled to use the nomen after 211 AD. And a noble from the first two centuries was very unlikely to end up in a sarcophagus. Burial only began to make inroads on the traditional Roman practice of cremation in the late first century. The custom started with freedmen and was not adopted by the nobility until hundreds of years later.

Confirmation that Aurelia Petronella lived sometime after 211 AD comes from the use of the abbreviation. We would expect the nomen to be spelt out in full in the early centuries. The shortening tells us that the inscription comes from a time when the name was so common that it was customary to use the abbreviation.

Evaluation of the evidence

We can eliminate the idea that Petronella was Peter's daughter, which only emerged around 500 AD. In the earliest version of the story, Peter's daughter was not called Petronella, nor was she a martyr. The strongest evidence, apart from the name, was the sarcophagus carved by Peter's own hands for "golden Petronilla," his "sweetest daughter." But this reading was only possible once people had forgotten that "AVR" was actually Aurelia.

So who was Petronella, if not Peter's daughter? There is an unreconcilable conflict between the evidence of the fresco and that of the sarcophagus which has been recognized by others who have struggled with the problem. The Vatican catacomb expert Phillipe Pergola puzzled over the identity of the real Petronella for years. He developed the theory that she was not actually a martyr, but a holy woman who had died sometime after 313 AD. Nicola Denzey accepts Pergola's basic argument and his suggestion that she was a rich patroness who paid for work on the church.[14] They are both grappling with why the Petronella of the sarcophagus should have received a privileged burial at the site. The problem with their theory is that if Petronella died after 313 AD then why does the fresco, which dates from c.356 AD, show her as an early martyr? Did Christians really forget everything about the esteemed Petronella within living memory? Pergola attempted to deal with this problem by assigning a very late date to the fresco of 430-450 AD.[15] In this way he allowed a century for her memory to be forgotten. But he seems to have changed his mind later when he dated it to the second half of the fourth century.[16] Denzey accepts the conventional dating of c.356 AD, but does not seem to realize the resulting difficulty. She assumes that Christians would have forgotten all about the real Petronella in just twenty-five years and made the rich patroness, who some of them must have known, into an early martyr! If we reject this idea, then we must reject the theory of a late Petronella.

We will reconsider the three main lines of evidence:

1. The Veneranda fresco in which Petronella martyr is shown in the dress of the early centuries, wears the pallium of an empress and is associated with scrolls. The fresco is dated c.356 AD, but with some uncertainty.

2. The omission from the Depositio Martyrum which indicates that Petronella either lived before 203 AD or after 336 AD.

3. The sarcophagus of Aurelia Petronilla that was removed from the site 757 AD. The sarcophagus has a conventional dedication by Petronilla's parents, implying that she was a teenage girl, and there are no explicit indications of Christianity. It almost certainly dates from after 211 AD, perhaps centuries later.

We must give primacy to the best early evidence, that of the fresco, and accept that Petronella was a martyr who lived in the early centuries. The omission from the Deposito Martyrum implies that she died before 203 AD which means that the sarcophagus cannot belong to her. This is unsurprising. From the time of Constantine onwards, there was a huge demand for the relics of the saints and martyrs. We can expect there to have been many girls called Petronella in honor of the early saint. When the sarcophagus of one of these girls turned up, it was wrongly believed to belong to the martyr herself. The sarcophagus is a red-herring.

In the sixth century, the church of Nereus and Achilleus was rededicated to Petronella. This tells us two things. First, there had been a massive increase in the importance of Petronella because she was now believed to be Peter's daughter. Second, her bones were thought to be physically at the church. The discovery of the sarcophagus would explain both points.

The movable sarcophagus could have been brought to the site from elsewhere. More likely, it had always been there although everyone knew that its occupant, Aurelia Petronilla, was not the saint. Grieving Christians wanted their loved ones to be interred close to the martyrs. Who better than Saint Petronella to intercede for a young girl, her namesake, at the last judgment?

In support of this conclusion is evidence that Christians in the fifth century were not aware of the saint's supposed sarcophagus which should have been the center of her cult. Instead, Christians were using the flat stone top of the tomb in front of the Veneranda fresco as an altar for offerings to the martyr.[17] This indicates that Petronella's bones were believed to be somewhere in the cubiculum. If De Rossi was right about the niche in which the sarcophagus had lain, then all these Christians had to do was leave the cubiculum, turn right, take a handful of steps and they would come to the prominently located sarcophagus. They should have made their offerings at that place—it would be unprecedented for a saint to have two cultic locations at the same site. When the Acts of Nereus and Achilleus says that the two martyrs were buried near to the monument of Petronella, it must mean the fresco. But if Petronella was not buried at the site, then why is she connected with the catacombs of Domitilla?

The Acts of Nereus and Achilleus

The one consistent theme that emerges with Saint Petronella is that she is associated with Nereus and Achilleus. Apart from the inscription of Pope Damascus, our primary source of information about these two male martyrs is the Acts of Nereus and Achilleus (we will call it "the Acts" here—not to be confused with the Acts of the Apostles).[18] As a historical source, this is far from ideal; it is quite late, dating from the fifth or sixth centuries, and has more than its fair share of fantastic and unbelievable stories.

The Acts celebrates virginity and martyrdom, attitudes that have rather declined in popularity in the modern world. It is set in Christian Rome in the late first century and brings in an amazing cast of martyrs; Petronilla, Felicula, Nicomedes, Nereus and Achilleus, Eutyches, Victorinus, Maro, Sulpicius, Servilianus, Theodora, Euphrosyne, and the star of the show, Domitilla. It could more justly be called the Acts of Domitilla.

In the Acts, Nereus and Achilleus are the "eunuch chamberlains" of Domitilla who is a cousin of Domitian. The two brothers are slaves who belonged to Domitilla's mother, Plautilla, the sister of the consul Clement. This reflects Eusebius' account of Domitilla as Clemens' sister's daughter, which, as we have seen, is likely to have arisen from a grammatical misunderstanding. Plautilla was supposedly converted by the apostle Peter who baptized her whole household, including Domitilla, Nereus, and Achilleus. It is tempting to see all this as pure fiction. Undoubtedly Plautilla and the involvement of Peter are fiction, but the idea of Domitilla's household as converted Christians is consistent with other evidence.

When the Acts opens, both Plautilla and Peter are dead, and Domitilla is looking forward to her approaching marriage to a consul's son called Aurelian. Like any bride-to-be, she spends time on her dress and takes care over her appearance. This conduct shocks Nereus and Achilleus, who reprove their mistress before giving her a long and remarkable homily on the disadvantages of marriage. They tell her she will be powerless to her husband's will when she is married. He will probably abuse her, take female slaves to his bed, and physically beat her. Even if she is one of the lucky few who avoid having such a husband, she will still suffer all the discomforts, pain, and indignity of pregnancy and childbirth. These are described in graphic detail. With a high probability, her baby will be born seriously deformed. And in any case, her husband will almost certainly keep her shut up in the house and not let her out.

There is no romance, no love between man and woman, or joy in having children. To be a wife is to face endless misery with no prospect of a happy family life. The terrible fate of the married woman is contrasted with the delightful life of a virgin who will share the angel's table—"virginity outranks all the virtues" and is second only to martyrdom. Virginity is personified as a young girl who enters into the bridal chamber with Christ.

Domitilla accepts the arguments of her eunuch chamberlains and laments that she ever intended to marry. She goes to the early church father Clement to take a vow of virginity, and he gives her a monk's habit. If it reads like a recruiting brochure for a convent, that is because it was probably written by a nun. In fact, there were no "vows of virginity" or monasteries in the first century.

Domitilla rejects Aurelian, and he responds by appealing to Domitian, who exiles her along with Nereus and Achilleus to the island of Pontiana. Exile would have been enjoyable, with Nereus and Achilleus looking forward to enduring hard labor for Christ, except for the presence of two magicians, Furius and Priscus. They are the disciples of the notorious heretic Simon Magus who makes a brief appearance in Acts of the Apostles. To nullify their growing influence on the island, Nereus and Achilleus write a letter to Marcellus, "prefect of Rome," a fictional character from the Acts of Peter. He writes back with the story of how Peter bested Simon Magus in a competition of miracles and magic that ended with Simon having his clothes torn off by a dog and fleeing naked before taking up with Nero.

A digression brings in Petronilla and the story of her "martyrdom" to escape from the clutches of Count Flaccus. The Count then switches his attention to Petronilla's companion Felicula who also rejects him and suffers torture and martyrdom at the hands of the Vestal Virgins. Felicula's body is dumped in a sewer but is rescued and buried by Nicomedes. He, in turn, is then tortured and martyred. We learn from a letter that Nereus and Achilleus have also become martyrs. The three men who wrote the letter are also tortured and suffer martyrdom...but you get the picture.

Meanwhile, Aurelian has devised a cunning plan to get Domitilla to give up her vows. She is brought to Tarracina on the mainland with Theodora and Euphrosyne, the fiancées of two of his noble acquaintances. He hopes that these girls will persuade her to see the benefits of marriage. But the opposite happens: Domitilla performs healing miracles and converts her companions to Christianity.

Aurelian is moved to desperate measures. He comes to Tarracina with the would-be husbands of Theodora and Euphrosyne. Aurelian intends to rape Domitilla but unwisely celebrates the deed in advance by holding a party. He is unable to stop dancing and dies of exhaustion after three days. At this miracle, everyone else is converted. The role of persecutor is now taken by Aurelian's brother, Luxurius. He persuades Trajan to order the death of all the Christians, and Domitilla and the other virgins are locked in a room that is set on fire. They all die, but their bodies are preserved and buried.

We might be tempted to dismiss the Acts as ridiculous nonsense, but there are specific elements of historical truth. One example is that Nereus and Achilleus are said to be buried at the country villa of Domitilla one and a half miles outside the walls of Rome close to the monument to Petronilla. Archaeology has confirmed the location, found the Petronella fresco and found evidence that the land belonged to Domitilla. More generally, the Acts is very specific about the locations of the martyrs' graves:

Felicula - 7 miles from Rome on the Via Ardeatina
Nicomedes - Near the walls of Rome on the Via Noumentana
Eutyches - 16 miles from Rome along the Via Noumentana
Victorinus - At Amiternum, 60 miles from Rome along the Via Salaria
Maro - 130 miles from Rome along the Via Salaria
Sulpicius and Servilianus - 2 miles from Rome on the Via Latina
Domitilla, Euphrosyne, and Theodora - Tarracina
(Note: Roman miles are approximately 1.5 km)

We can deduce that the author of the Acts was familiar with the sites and tombs of Rome. One way of approaching the work is to compare it to the stories told by an imaginative tour guide. Much of what the guide says is unbelievable, but there are some genuine traditions and historical facts among the fiction. And the guide certainly knew the sanctuaries of the martyrs as they existed in their day.

Some commentators believe that the author of the Acts came from the Tarracina region because Nereus, Achilleus, and Domitilla are all martyred there. The locations of the martyrs' tombs do not support this idea. The sites with definite positions are either in the vicinity of Rome or along the Via Salaria, which ran east from Rome to the Adriatic. The location of Domitilla's tomb within Tarracina is unspecified, and the description of her burial is vague. We can conclude that the author was well acquainted with Rome and the Via Salaria but may never have visited Tarracina.

The title "eunuch chamberlain" given to Nereus and Achilleus is Byzantine. This could mean that the Acts date from the Byzantine conquest of Italy in 540. However, there was a substantial Byzantine influence even before this date. This can be seen, for example, in the Ravenna mosaics, many of which predate the conquest. And the Acts has some linguistic features which suggest an earlier date.[19] So the Acts could have been written anytime from the late fifth century to the mid-sixth century.

The most puzzling aspect of the Acts is the inconsistency with Pope Damascus' inscription where the two saints are Roman soldiers who laid down their arms. Most commentators assume that the Acts must be wrong and that the author invented the association of the saints with Domitilla because they were buried in her catacombs. But the puzzle lies deeper than this.

The author of the Acts has excellent knowledge of the sites of the martyrs in Rome and must have been aware of the church of Nereus and Achilleus. The two martyrs are decapitated in the Acts even though this was a punishment reserved for citizens and not slaves. In this respect, the Acts seem to have been influenced by the pillars inside the church showing the death of the martyrs by decapitation. Why, then, did the author completely ignore the church inscription that they were soldiers and make them into eunuchs? There must have been a strong pre-existing tradition that conflicted with the inscription, a tradition that Damascus had set out to suppress.

The names support the idea that the two were, in fact, slaves and not soldiers. Roman soldiers were recruited from Roman citizens and would be expected to have a Roman-style name. But both Nereus and Achilleus are Greek names as would be given to slaves.

Nereus is named after a Greek sea god. Paul includes a Nereus in his long list of greetings to the Christians at Rome in the 50s AD.[20] This would be some forty years before Domitilla's exile, so if our Nereus were associated with Domitilla, it is not the same man. Although Nereus could be a cognomen taken in honor of the earlier Christian, it may just be a coincidence.

The name Achilleus is more revealing. It comes from the Greek hero Achilles, the supreme example of a fighting man. A cook or a chamberlain would not be called Achilles. It is the name for a particular type of slave—a gladiator. If Nereus and Achilleus were gladiators, this would explain Pope Damascus' inscription; they were fighting men who gave up their arms upon converting to Christianity. The Pope thought they were soldiers. But they were actually gladiators who had fought and killed many men in the arena.

Why would Domitilla own gladiators? For the same reason that today's billionaires might hire ex-members of the special forces—as bodyguards. No one was going to mess with you if you had gladiators in your entourage. The Acts, however, was written hundreds of years later and sees Domitilla as a young virgin nun. She can hardly go around with two beefy gladiators as her intimate attendants! To preserve her purity, Nereus and Achilleus are made into eunuchs modeled on the chamberlains who would wait upon the imperial ladies of Constantinople in the author's day.

We can now put together a picture that is consistent with the evidence. Nereus and Achilleus were former gladiators who belonged to Domitilla's household and who had converted to Christianity under her influence. The two new Christians set aside their role as fighting men and were likely freed by Domitilla at this time. When Domitilla was accused of atheism, they were accused with her.

In the Acts, Domitilla, Nereus, and Achilleus are all killed in Tarracina; Domitilla is buried there, while the bodies of the other two are taken to Rome by boat, which is obviously unrealistic. The author of Acts knows:

(i) that all three were victims of the same persecution;
(ii) that the two men were killed before Domitilla and buried in Rome;
(iii) that Domitilla was killed and buried in Tarracina.

In reality, Nereus and Achilleus must have been among those who Cassius Dio says were executed in Rome rather than exiled. As freedmen they were dispensable, and as former gladiators, too dangerous to leave alive.

If this picture is correct, Pope Damascus got many of the details right. The two were fighting men who put down their arms, and they were killed by "the tyrant"—meaning Domitian rather than Diocletian. As Domitilla's freedmen, they would have been buried on the land she had granted for burials of her freedmen. When the catacombs were built, their remains would have been translated into more secure tombs underground. The cult of the two loyal martyrs then developed centered on these tombs.

Petronella and Domitilla

Where does this get us with Petronella? We can summarize the evidence:

- Petronella is portrayed as an empress wearing the dress and hair-style of the early centuries.

- Saint Petronella is associated with the catacombs of Domitilla, where she is shown on the fresco of Veneranda, although her tomb has not been found. Strangely, Saint Domitilla is not associated with the Domitilla catacombs in the early centuries.

- The church that was first dedicated to Nereus and Achilleus and then to Petronella is the cultic center of the Domitilla catacombs. An earlier sanctuary to the martyrs preceded the church, but there was never a cult of Domitilla at the site as far as we know.

- Petronella is closely linked to the two martyrs, Nereus and Achilleus. Most likely, the two were former gladiators and freedmen of Domitilla who were executed when she was exiled and buried in the cemetery she had established for her freedmen.

The obvious solution that reconciles all these points is that Petronella is another name for Domitilla. In the late first century, it was the fashion for Romans to have multiple cognomina, including additional names taken as adults. Given the intense hostility among Romans towards Christianity, it is unsurprising that Domitilla would have used an alternative cognomen for her Christian activities. To the Roman elite, she was Domitilla, and to the Christians, Petronella. Why, though, should she choose that particular name?

Petro

Early Christians and many later commentators did not doubt that the name Petronella was anything other than the female form of Peter. The name Peter comes from the Greek for "rock." It is unusual, almost unique. So Petronella was thought to have been connected to the apostle Peter. Hence the idea that she was his daughter.

Skeptical scholars did not accept that Petronella was Peter's daughter and began looking for other explanations. The closest common name among the Romans was Petronius, the nomen of the Petronia gens. The feminine nomen is Petronia, but it is possible that Petronella was a diminutive form used as a cognomen. So the name was explained away as honoring a Petronius ancestor without having any connection to Peter.

This is to ignore the obvious. If an early Christian martyr is called Petronella, then there is a high prior probability that the name has been derived from "Peter." The sarcophagus dedicated to Aurelia Petronilla by her parents has misdirected most investigators. If we rule it out as a later burial, the most obvious explanation of Petronella is a name adopted on conversion to Christianity as an adult.

But why should Domitilla take Peter's name? A cognomen was usually taken after an ancestor or family member or was descriptive of the person. Taking a Christian name would become almost universal, but it was not an established custom in Domitilla's day. And if the author of Acts were to take a Christian cognomen, then why not Paulina in honor of her hero Paul?

There is an excellent reason why Domitilla should be called Petronella. The closest Latin equivalent to Peter (Petros) was Petro and we know of only two Romans called by this name.[21] One was Granius Petro, a quaestor of Caesar. The other was Titus Flavius Petro, the Flavian patriarch and Domitilla's great-great-grandfather. Domitilla would have been very familiar with her ancestor Petro. When Vespasian became emperor, his relatively lowly family was the subject of malicious gossip focused on his grandfather. Petro is the first of the Flavians to whom we can attach a name. He had been a centurion in Pompey's army, the earliest known military connection in the family.[22]

The story went around that Petro's father had been a contract laborer who had come to Reate from the Gaulish side of the Po to work on the fields and stayed to marry a local girl. As a teenager, Domitilla would have been all too aware of this scurrilous story that ridiculed her family's background by suggesting that they were common workers and not even true Italians. When Suetonius wrote his life of Vespasian, he investigated this rumor but did not find any truth in it.[23]

After Domitilla converted to Christianity, it would have seemed an amazing coincidence that the family patriarch had the same unusual name as Jesus' chief disciple. The ancients, of course, did not believe in coincidence—it was God's way of showing Domitilla that she was destined to become a Christian. By adopting the cognomen Petronella, she honored the patriarch of the Flavians and the patriarch of the Jesus movement at the same time. It had the practical advantage of being explainable to pagans while full of meaning for Christians.

Many other things snap into place with the realization that the author of Luke felt a special connection to Peter. It explains why Acts is mainly concerned with just two apostles, Peter and Paul. The obvious hero-worship of Paul is understandable in a gentile Christian. But the author portrays Peter as the premier apostle virtually to the exclusion of the remainder of the Twelve. Then there is the apparent neglect of the Magdalene in favor of Peter at the resurrection appearances. It is not misogyny as some feminists have proposed, but a personal devotion towards Peter.

21

Flavian testimony

Josephus

The fresco in the catacombs is a strong and unexpected piece of evidence supporting the hypothesis that Domitilla wrote Luke and Acts. But it cannot prove the case. At most, it shows that a group of Christians living in Rome in the mid-fourth century thought that Petronella had written Luke. We have seen the evidence linking Petronella to Domitilla, but even if we accept these are two names for one person, we cannot be sure that those fourth-century Christians were correct in their belief. We need an eyewitness, someone who knew Domitilla and who would have known the truth. Given how little we know about the first century, it would be extraordinary to find such an eyewitness. By a fluke of history, we have just the right person.

Our eyewitness is Josephus, who would have known Domitilla from when she was a girl. Whether Domitilla was Christian or a Jewish sympathizer, we would expect her to have discussed her new faith with the Flavian client and premier Jewish expert in Rome. We know that Josephus exercised a strong influence on the author of Luke. So if Domitilla were that person, then Josephus would have known.

Josephus does not explicitly mention either Domitilla or Clemens in his surviving works. In the Life, he acknowledges the patronage of the Flavians but only names the emperors Vespasian, Titus, and Domitian and Domitian's wife, Domitia. This might be disappointing, but is further evidence that Domitilla was neither Jewish nor a God-fearer at this stage. Josephus is fulsome in his praise of high-status gentiles who converted, and he would surely have found some way to acknowledge Domitilla if that were the case.

Although we may regard Josephus as a complete hypocrite given his betrayal of his people, he kept up with Jewish observances and saw himself as a good Jew. As a Pharisee, he would have strongly disapproved of Christianity. Luke and Acts, with their anti-Jewish tone, would have shocked him. He would have regarded such works as a Roman attempt to appropriate Judaism. But Josephus was a dependant of the Flavians. After the death of Titus, he badly needed the support of the Flavian women, both Domitia and Domitilla. And he certainly could not afford to make an enemy of the woman who was likely to be the mother of the next emperor. Josephus would have had to thread the needle in dealing with Domitilla's religious views.

So we come to the most controversial passage in Josephus, the Testimonium Flavianum, so-called because it is the presumed testimony to Christ by Flavius Josephus. It comes from the Antiquities when Josephus is dealing with the governorship of Pontius Pilate:

> About this time there lived Jesus, a wise man, if indeed one ought to call him a man; for he was a doer of surprising deeds, a teacher of such people who receive the truth gladly. He drew to himself many of the Jews and many of the Greeks. He was Christ. And when Pilate, hearing him accused by the principal men amongst us, had condemned him to the cross, those that loved him at the first did not forsake him. On the third day he appeared to them alive again, for the prophets of God had fore-told these and many other marvelous things concerning him. And the tribe of Christians, so named from him, has not disap-peared to this day. (Josephus, Antiquities 18:63-64)

As a passage from Josephus, it is astonishing. It describes Jesus as per-forming miracles and hints that he was more than a man. Even more surprising, it says that Jesus was the Messiah, the Christ; that he was resurrected on the third day; and that he fulfilled the Jewish prophecies. The Testimonium appears in all Greek copies of the Antiquities and is quoted in its entirety by the early Church historian Eusebius writing c.324 AD. To Christians, it seemed remarkable that even a Jew like Josephus acknowledged Christ's miracles.

In a more skeptical age, scholars began to have doubts about the passage. As early as the sixteenth century, Scaliger suspected its authenticity.[1] It seemed extraordinary that a Pharisee would have written anything so positive about Jesus. Was Josephus a secret Christian? There was no hint in his later works, such as his Life and Against Apion, that he was anything other than a pious Jew.

It is suspicious that Josephus calls Jesus the Christ when he went out of his way to avoid using the word. It never appears in the Jewish War, even though Jewish expectations of the coming Messiah were a major cause of the war. Josephus had to keep very quiet on this subject because of his own revelation that the Messianic predictions were really about Vespasian.

He did not want the Romans probing too deeply into these prophecies. Even the word Christ, "the anointed one," was dangerous. The prophesied ruler was supposed to be the anointed king of Israel from the line of King David. How could this possibly fit Vespasian, the Roman emperor from Renate in Italy?

When Josephus was writing the Antiquities, Vespasian and Titus were dead, but he still had to be careful. His interpretation of the prophecies had become part of the mythology of the dynasty, and Domitian would not have had patience with anything that cast doubts upon Flavian legitimacy.

So it is incredible that Josephus would include a statement that Jesus was Christ in the Testimonium. However, he does not discuss the meaning of the word so Roman readers would not understand its connection to the Jewish prophecies. This is not the only time that "Christ" appears in the Antiquities. Later, Josephus describes James as "the brother of Jesus called Christ".[2]

Origen, writing c.250, seems to allude to both this passage about James and another passage in Antiquities about John the Baptist. However, he makes no mention of the Testimonium and says that Josephus did not believe that Jesus was Christ. The Testimonium appears in Antiquities close to the John passage, so many scholars have thought that the Testimonium in its complete form was not in Origen's copy.

One idea was that the claim that Jesus was the Christ was a gloss added by Christian scribes. However, the remainder of the passage was still more positive about Jesus than we would expect from Josephus. So a consensus developed that Josephus must have written something negative or neutral, which was revised by overzealous scribes. As Eusebius knew the Testimonium as found in manuscripts of the Antiquities, it was assumed that this rewriting took place sometime between Origen (250) and Eusebius (324).

Others maintained that the whole passage was a forgery. However, most scholars accepted the later reference to "James, the brother of Jesus called Christ" as genuine. And Josephus would not have introduced James in this way without already having explained to his readers who Jesus was. So, it was argued, there must have been a previous passage about "Jesus called Christ."

The question of the Testimonium Flavianum took on new importance with the growing popularity of the mythical Jesus theory that Jesus had not existed as a man. The Testimonium became exhibit A in the defense mounted by those who believed in a historical Jesus. Indeed, the debate often seems to revolve around this one passage. But this is to grant it more importance than it merits. Even if the Testimonium were proved genuine, this would not establish that Jesus existed. Josephus is not the ideal witness that some make him out to be. He was not even born at the supposed time of Jesus' crucifixion. He was writing the Antiquities some sixty years later, having spent twenty years living in Rome, a city with a significant Christian population. And there is nothing in the Testimonium that could not have come from the Christian gospels that had been circulating in Rome. On the other hand, even if Josephus had written nothing about Jesus, that would not be evidence that he had not existed. Realistically, the early Jesus movement would have been too insignificant and peaceable to interest a military historian like Josephus.

The Testimonium Flavianum as found in the Antiquities is not good evidence for Jesus' existence because it too obviously depends on the gospel accounts. The chief evidence for the existence of Jesus became the reconstruction of what Josephus was supposed to have written, evidence which, ironically, does not itself exist. The reconstructions are based on the assumption that a skeptical Josephus knew the historical Jesus, and it is circular logic to use them as evidence for that assumption.

The mythicists have typically taken the opposite tack of attempting to prove that both the Testimonium and the James reference are fakes dating from long after Josephus. A popular theory points the finger of accusation at Eusebius. It seems suspicious that the passage first appeared in his Ecclesiastical History and was not known by Origen seventy years earlier. Eusebius could have forged it for the Ecclesiastical History and then arranged for its insertion into the Antiquities. But there is no evidence to support such a far-fetched idea. Forgers are typically anonymous. They are not authors publishing under their own name and with a reputation to defend. The forgery would involve adding a new passage to a book that had already been in circulation for over two hundred years. This would surely be detected and condemned by both pagans and Christians. And how exactly would Eusebius have been able to get his forgery incorporated into all the copies of the Antiquities in existence? And if he had gone to all this trouble and taken all these risks, why does he attach so little importance to the passage in the Ecclesiastic History? He barely comments on it and is more interested in proving the historical existence of John the Baptist.

Such was the state of the controversy in 1995 when Gary Goldberg published a paper that would turn the debate upside down. He made a computer search to identify any similar passages to the Testimonium and found a most unexpected match in the Gospel of Luke.

The Road to Emmaus

The relevant passage comes from Luke's resurrection account. After Jesus' crucifixion, two of his followers are going along the road to Emmaus when Jesus, in the form of a stranger, comes up and walks beside them. The stranger asks them what they are talking about, and they are amazed that he does not know. They then describe Jesus of Nazareth and the events that had taken place. The stranger enlightens them about the meaning of the scriptures, and when they reach their destination, they invite him in for a meal. They sit down together, and he blesses the bread and hands it to them. At that moment, he appears in his true form and then vanishes.

Goldberg's analysis showed a close similarity between the conversation on the road and Josephus' Testimonium.[3] My comparison below is largely based on Goldberg and shows how the two narratives have an identical structure (J=Josephus; L=Luke 24:19-26):

J: About this time there lived Jesus…
L: Concerning Jesus of Nazareth…

J: …a wise man, if indeed one ought to call him a man…
L: …who was a man, a prophet..

J: …for he was a doer of surprising deeds…
L: …mighty in deed…

J: …a teacher of such people who receive the truth gladly. He drew to himself many of the Jews and many of the Greeks.
L: …and words before God and all the people.

[J: He was the Christ.]

J: And when Pilate, upon hearing him accused…
L: He was delivered up…

J: …by the principal men amongst us…
L: …by the chief priests and rulers of us…

J: …had condemned him to the cross…
L: …to the judgment of death and they crucified him.

J: …those that loved him at the first did not forsake him.

L: We, however, were hoping he was the one to redeem Israel.

J: Having the third day...
L: We are now having the third day from when these things came to pass...

J: ...he appeared to them alive again...
L: At this point Luke has a flashback to the women going to the tomb, finding it empty, and seeing the angels who told them Jesus was alive. This is followed by the words: Then he (Jesus) said to them...

J: ...for the prophets of God had foretold these (things)...
L: O foolish and slow of heart to believe in all that the prophets had spoken. Did not the Christ have to suffer these things and enter into his glory?

J: ...and many other marvelous things concerning him.
L: And beginning with Moses and the prophets, he interpreted to them all the things in the scriptures concerning himself.

Goldberg excluded Luke's flashback to the women at the tomb in his analysis, but as we can see that this fits nicely at the point where Josephus says, "he appears to them alive again." Note that the Testimonium statement "He was the Christ" has no match in Luke.

In total, nineteen points of similarity were identified between the two passages, all occurring in the correct order in the Greek. As a control Goldberg compared other similar passages to the Testimonium. A brief description of Jesus by Justin Martyr had at most four points of agreement and many disagreements. Some Acts passages were closer, as would be expected from the author of Luke, but still had only eight points of agreement. The probability of nineteen points arising in the same order between two passages by chance is close to zero. This structural similarity shows that the two passages must be related.[4]

If we turn from the structure to vocabulary, the degree of agreement is less impressive. The two texts typically describe the same thing using different words. However, there are some important exceptions to this general rule.

The most significant is the phrase translated above into literal but clumsy English as "having the third day." It is an unusual and ambiguous construction, although not unnatural in Greek. In the New Testament, the usual phrase is "on the third day," and "having the third day" only appears here. It is also a very unexpected and unique construction for

Josephus to use.[5] To find this unusual form of the phrase at the same point in both passages is a clear indicator that they are linked.

Another unusual phase for Josephus is "by the principal men amongst us." Josephus takes great care to distance himself from the action of the narrative: in the Jewish War, he even refers to "Josephus" using the third person. If Josephus had written the Testimonium, we would expect "the principal men among the Jews." But like Luke, it has "us."

Theories

Let us look at the possible theories to account for the Testimonium in the light of this close correspondence between the Testimonium and the Gospel of Luke's Emmaus passage.

1. Josephus originally wrote a negative/neutral passage about Jesus, which was revised into something more positive by Christian scribes.

This cozy consensus is blown out of the water by the similarity of the Testimonium to the Luke passage. The explanation envisages a two-step process; (i) Josephus writes something, and (ii) a later Christian scribe makes changes to Josephus' words. But such a two-step process will never result in a passage with a structure that closely resembles the Emmaus narrative. If Josephus was negative or neutral, he was not influenced by the Gospel of Luke and the probability that his original passage would be so similar to the Emmaus conversation is close to zero. The scribe revising Josephus could have used language taken from Luke. But a revision here and there will not give rise to a nineteen-point agreement in structure.

The consensus which has lasted for so many years must be wrong. The Testimonium cannot have arisen from a multi-step process but has been written in a way that generates a close link to Luke.

2. Josephus did not write any part of the Testimonium. The whole passage was added as a later interpolation by Christians.

This is the most obvious solution, but not without its difficulties. In this scenario, a scribe or Christian scholar such as Eusebius, living hundreds of years after Josephus, decided to add a passage about Jesus. The problem is why they should base their interpolation on an obscure section of the Emmaus story. The most memorable parts of the story are that Jesus appears to two disciples in a form different from his normal appearance, that he walks with them along the road, that they share a meal, and that the disciples recognize him as Jesus before he disappears. Yet all of these elements are absent from the Testimonium. The similarity is with the unmemorable discussion on the road.

We would have to assume that the author of the interpolation was unconsciously influenced by the Gospel of Luke and fell into the pattern of the Emmaus narrative. But it is difficult to see how this could produce the nineteen-point agreement in structure.

3. Josephus and the author of Luke both used a third source.

This is Goldberg's preferred explanation. The Emmaus story only appears in Luke, so Goldberg's idea is that both the author of Luke and Josephus used the same source, which was a short account of Jesus' life and resurrection. For the traditionally minded, it has the merit of providing independent evidence for Jesus' existence. The Testimonium would be based on a source for the resurrection story independent of the gospels.

However, this scenario has numerous problems. For a start, it requires the existence of a third document for which there is no evidence other than the mutual resemblance of the two texts. More seriously, it does not address the issue of why Josephus should include such a positive view of Jesus in the Antiquities. Once again, we would have to assume that a later Christian decided to extensively revise Josephus' words. This introduces an additional layer of complexity into the explanation. And would not these revisions disrupt the correspondence that we find between the texts?

It is also mystifying why the author of Luke should use the hypothetical third source for the conversation on the road. We can gain an idea of the contents of the source from the overlap between the Testimonium and the Emmaus story: it would have been no more than a brief summary, and contained nothing new to the author of Luke, who had just written a whole gospel about Jesus. Why then copy this source rather than write the short passage themself? Also, the conversation on the road reads as an integral part of the story rather than an insertion from elsewhere.

There is further evidence that rules out the third source idea. The Testimonium shows links to Luke/Acts beyond the Emmaus story, similarities that could not have arisen from a hypothetical third source. Take the line from the Testimonium:

"He drew to himself many of the Jews and many of the Greeks."

This is one of the author of Luke's favorite phrases:

Acts 14:1: "...a great multitude both of the Jews and also of the Greeks believed."

Acts 18:4: "...persuaded both Jews and Greeks."

Acts 19:10; "... all those who dwelt in Asia heard the word of the Lord Jesus, both Jews and Greeks."

Acts 19:17: "... and this became known to all, both Jews and Greeks..."

Acts 20:21: "... testifying fully both to Jews and Greeks ... "

The phrase does not appear anywhere in the Luke resurrection narrative, nor is it the type of thing a Christian scribe would interpolate into Josephus. So we have an agreement between Josephus and the author of Luke that the hypothetical third source cannot explain.

It is not the only such agreement. When are the members of the Jesus movement first called Christians? Paul never calls the followers of Jesus by that name, nor do any of the gospels. The first use of the title is either; (i) the Testimonium; or (ii) the Acts of the Apostles, whichever was written first. The name appears twice in Acts:

Acts 11:26: "And the disciples were called Christians first in Antioch"
Acts 26:28: "You almost persuade me to be a Christian"

It is essentially a Latin word and the author of Luke may have invented it. Whether or not this is the case, the use of "Christians" for members of the Jesus movement is a further link between the Testimonium and Luke/ Acts. Acts certainly shows knowledge of the Antiquities, so the two works seem to show mutual influence, a strong indication that the two authors are interacting. So we come to the final theory.

4. The Testimonium was written by the author of Luke and passed to Josephus to incorporate within the Antiquities.

This theory is not generally considered because it seems absurd. Yet it is where the evidence is pointing. The similarity with the Emmaus conversation occurs because they are two pieces written by the same person at around the same time. An author's mind tends to run in grooves when repeating similar content. The author of Luke either wrote the Emmaus conversation a short while before they supplied Josephus with the Testimonium, or it was the other way around, and the author of Luke had worked with Josephus on the addition just before writing the Luke resurrection narrative. Such repetition is very typical of the author of Luke. For example, the story of Paul's conversion on the road to Damascus is given three times with variations in Acts.[6]

The Testimonium is just the kind of short summary that the author of Luke loved to write. Its brevity is unlike Josephus, who tends to explain the reasons for events and give more circumstantial detail. The author of Luke often provides potted summaries of what has transpired, something we do not find in the other gospels. And they loved miracles while being uninterested in theology: the Testimonium stresses Jesus' "surprising deeds" and his resurrection after three days.

Readings

How was a book published in the ancient world? Making a copy of a book was expensive and time-consuming as it had to be laboriously written out by hand. To produce one copy of an extensive work such as Josephus' Antiquities might take a scribe a year or more. You would not make many copies in advance unless you were very sure of your market. The best approach is to only produce copies to order. To drum up interest, the author would hold readings to expose the work to the target audience and fish for these orders.

Readings were not just a marketing tool; they also helped the author fine-tune the work. Ancient authors did not have access to word processors or typewriters. If they were wealthy, they would dictate to a scribe, and if not, they would have to learn to write themselves. But it was as difficult for an author to dictate the final work straight off as it would be today. So a book would typically go through a few iterations, starting with a collection of notes, then a good draft, and finally a corrected polished version. Readings were an integral part of the process. Pliny the Younger gives us an account of his authorial methods:

> First of all, I go through my work myself; next, I read it to two or three friends and send it to others for comment. If I have any doubts about their criticism, I go over them again with one or two people, and finally I read the work to a larger audience; and that is the moment, believe me, when I make the severest corrections... (Pliny the Younger, Letters 7:17)

Pliny is describing his method for refining the speeches he had already given for publication. Although some questioned if it was appropriate to revise past speeches in this way, his defense makes it clear that this was the standard approach for works such as history. Pliny's audience would be select: "I do not invite the general public, but a select and limited audience of persons whom I admire and trust...". Such readings would not only help perfect the work but were also valuable in building support. A person who had contributed was more likely to order a copy and recommend it to their connections.

Josephus would not have waited for the Antiquities to be complete but would have given readings as he progressed. There was a very long interval between the Jewish War and the Antiquities, and such events would have been essential to maintaining his reputation as a historian. Who would Josephus have invited to his readings? His patron, Epaphroditus, would be there by right; it was part of the payback for a patron to host such gatherings. Both Josephus and Epaphroditus would have wanted the most distinguished audience to attend. The Emperor Domitian was a lost cause because of his anti-Jewish bias and because Josephus had been a favorite of Titus. Perhaps they could attract the emperor's wife Domitia, who Josephus said: "conferred many favors on me."[7] But the two members of the imperial family we would expect to be present are the two interested in Jewish matters, Clemens and Domitilla. We have seen how Josephus in the Life seems to draw on incidents in Luke and Acts and recast them as stories about himself. This is understandable if Josephus expected Domitilla to be present at his readings.

Imagine Domitilla reclining on a couch attending a reading of book eighteen of the Antiquities. It would have been a leisurely occasion with food, drink, and much discussion. Usually, an author would read the work himself, but Josephus admits his diction in Greek was poor, so perhaps one of his scribes, a slave or freedman, was the reader. The section on Pontius Pilate would have been of particular interest to Domitilla. It would have started with the story of Pilate bringing the ensigns into Jerusalem and the disturbance that caused. Then would come the story of Pilate taking money out of the temple to pay for an aqueduct causing more unrest. After this, there may have been a brief notice of Jewish unrest in Rome and then the story of a Samaritan who led his supporters to the top of Mount Gerizim and Pilate's brutal response. This last event caused Pilate's removal; the Samaritans accused him of an unjustified massacre, and Vitellius, the governor of Syria, sent him to Rome for judgment.

Domitilla would have been astonished that there was no mention of Jesus. She was just finishing the Gospel of Luke and knew that Jesus' ministry and crucifixion was the most important thing to have happened under Pilate. Naturally, she would point this out to Josephus, who would admit that he knew nothing of Jesus in Judea at this time. It was customary for the audience to make contributions to the work and even draft passages for inclusion. So Domitilla would offer to send him a section on Jesus, for which kind offer Josephus would have thanked her profusely.

When Domitilla's contribution came, Josephus may have been tempted to tone it down, but he had to be very careful. Some editing to suit his style could be justified, but he could not upset an imperial lady by significantly changing her production. So Josephus was forced to include a brazenly pro-Christian text in his Antiquities. He could not refuse Domitilla but would not have been happy. Josephus prided himself as a consummate trickster who would always win in the end. The man who had arranged for a whole cave of people to commit suicide would not allow the Testimonium to stand in his Antiquities without a riposte. He will get his revenge on the person who made him include the Testimonium, a person he regarded as a foolish and gullible young woman. It is Josephus' revenge that provides our final evidence.

Dates

Let us go back a stage. The evidence points to the Testimonium being written by the author of Luke. Josephus would have hated including it, so it must have come from someone he could not refuse. This gives a very small list of suspects; apart from Domitilla and Clemens, only Epaphroditus, his patron, and Domitia would have sufficient power over Josephus. Of these four, only Domitilla and Clemens have any potential connection to Christianity. If Domitilla had supplied the Testimonium, it would not necessarily prove that she wrote it, as the author could have been a member of her household or house church. However, taken as a whole, the evidence points strongly to Domitilla herself.

She must have written the Testimonium around the same time as the Emmaus narrative. This enables us to date both Luke and Acts approximately. The fixed point is that Josephus published the Antiquities in the 13th year of Domitian's reign while he was in his 56th year of age. This dates the publication between mid-September 93 and mid-March 94. He would have worked on the Life immediately afterward as it was intended as an appendix to the Antiquities. We have suggested that the Life shows knowledge of Acts and Luke. So Acts must have been finished around the same time as the Antiquities.

Working backward, Acts 5-12 shows pre-publication knowledge of Antiquities 20:97-104. The author of Luke must have attended a reading of this section while working on Acts. Allowing one year for Antiquities to be finished and made ready for publication gives a date for this reading of c.92 AD.

The Emmaus narrative comes at the end of Luke, so Domitilla would have been finishing the gospel when she attended a reading of the Pilate section of Antiquities, which is near the beginning of book 18. Allowing a year for Josephus to write books 18 and 19 places this reading in c.91 AD. To summarize:

91 AD - Luke completed; Testimonium written.
92 AD - Acts 5-12 written
93 AD - Acts completed

The timescale agrees with the generally accepted dating range for Luke/ Acts. It allows time for both Luke and Acts to be copied and distributed widely before Domitilla's downfall in 95 AD. Domitilla would have been around thirty when she wrote Luke. (Interestingly, Jesus is said to be around thirty in Luke.) If this scenario is correct, then "Testimonium Flavianum" is an apt title, not because Flavius Josephus wrote it, but because it was written by Flavia Domitilla.

22

James and Jesus

Tacitus

The argument that only the author of Luke can have written the Testimonium rests on the belief that it is an original part of the Antiquities. In this chapter, we will consider two lines of evidence that support this: the first is a passage from Tacitus, and the second is a later Josephus reference to "James, brother of Christ."

Like the Testimonium, the Tacitus passage is widely and wrongly used to prove that Jesus existed. It is a short passage from the Annals about Nero's persecutions of "a people hated for their shameful offenses whom the common people call Christians [or Chrestians]." Tacitus explains how this strange eastern sect originated:

> Christus, from whom the name had its origin, suffered the extreme penalty during the reign of Tiberius at the hands of one of our procurators, Pontius Pilatus, and a most mischievous superstition, thus checked for the moment, again broke out not only in Judaea, the first source of the evil, but even in Rome, where all things hideous and shameful from every part of the world find their center and become popular. (Tacitus, Annals 15:44)

The surviving manuscript originally had Chrestians (chrestiani) before a scribe changed the "e" to an "i" to give the more familiar Christians (christiani). The spelling with an "e" may be a mistake by a previous copyist, or it may go back to Tacitus; "Chrestians" was an alternative for the similar-sounding "Christians" in the early centuries.[1] The misspelling may even be deliberate, with Tacitus implying that the common people call them Chrestians out of ignorance.

Tacitus had no direct knowledge of Judea and was not writing until c.120.[2] There is nothing in the passage that could not have come from the gospels, which had been in circulation for over forty years. Some apologists have argued that Tacitus would have consulted imperial archives for the official record of Jesus' crucifixion. But the information about Jesus is nothing more than a minor aside in a story about Nero and a Roman historian is not going to waste days of effort on a parenthesis.

It is even doubtful whether the supposed records existed. The Romans kept archives for practical administrative purposes, and there was no useful purpose in keeping provincial records for as long as eighty years. And if there were such dated archives, Tacitus would have had a hard time finding the correct scroll. We do not know how many people were crucified in Judea during Pilate's ten-year term of office, but it was probably several hundred, if not thousands. We can expect tens or even hundreds of these victims to be called "Jesus," as it was a common name. But then Tacitus only calls him "Christus." And what was the point of Tacitus trying to find the correct record? He would have to know that Christ was crucified under Pilate before he could even begin looking in the right place. Yet he adds nothing to this very basic information. The gospels do not tell us what Jesus was accused of, and Tacitus does not seem to know either—he only says that he suffered the extreme penalty under Pilate, implying crucifixion. So why would he go through the effort of trawling through hundreds of old records and not tell us anything he found? He adds nothing that he could not have gotten from any Christian in Rome.

We can be sure that Tacitus did not consult imperial records because he gets Pilate's title wrong. Tacitus calls him a procurator, but the governors of minor territories, like Judea, only became procurators after Claudius. Under Tiberius, they were prefects, which is Pilate's title on the "Pilate Stone" inscription. For the Romans, such titles were a serious matter, and the official records will call Pilate by his correct title. So Tacitus must have used another source that confused him into thinking Pilate was a procurator.

If Tacitus did not use Roman records, what was his source for this passage? He would typically consult senate decrees and imperial records, which would be readily available to him, but his principal sources were the works of other historians. It was not the standard practice among Roman historians to acknowledge their sources, and Tacitus' use of other historians has been hidden because most other Roman historical works are lost. If Tacitus were looking for information about events in Judea in the recent past, then the only historian interested in that area was Flavius Josephus. So rather than spending days searching through old archive records, Tacitus would have consulted the scrolls of Josephus' Antiquities on the shelves of his own library.

That he did just that is demonstrated by the close correspondence between what he says about Jesus and the Testimonium. (I am indebted to a blog post by Steven Carlson for suggesting that Tacitus used the Testimonium and for the similarities below.)

Tacitus:
...whom the common people called Christians [or Chrestians]. Christus, from whom the name had its origin...
Josephus:
He was Christ.
And the tribe of Christians, so named from him, has not disappeared to this day.

Tacitus:
....suffered the extreme penalty during the reign of Tiberius at the hands of one of our procurators, Pontius Pilate...
Josephus:
And when Pilate...had condemned him to the cross
(Although Tiberius is not mentioned in the Testimonium itself, he is in the context of the Pilate passages in the Antiquities. For example, 18:89 makes it clear that Tiberius was emperor while Pilate was procurator.)

Tacitus:
...and a most mischievous superstition, thus checked for the moment, again broke out...
Josephus:
...those that loved him at the first did not forsake him. On the third day he appeared to them alive again, for the prophets of God had foretold these and many other marvelous things concerning him.

Tacitus:
...not only in Judaea, the first source of the evil, but even in Rome, where all things hideous and shameful from every part of the world find their center and become popular.
Josephus:
He drew to himself many of the Jews and many of the Greeks. (Note - Greeks/Hellenists would have included the Romans.)
And the tribe of Christians...has not disappeared to this day.

Everything in Tacitus corresponds to something in Josephus. They are not in the same order, and the agreements are not as impressive as between Josephus and Luke. But then Tacitus is writing a very brief passage from a Roman perspective. He despises both Christians and Jews and is going to recast the pro-Christian Testimonium into something more cynical and critical. Later we will see evidence that this is not the only passage from the Pilate section of the Antiquities that Tacitus has used.

Tacitus' use of the Antiquities would explain his uncharacteristic mistake in calling Pilate a procurator. Josephus, writing in Greek, does not use the Latin titles procurator or prefect. The words he uses are *epitropos* (governor/administrator) and *hegemon* (leader), and he employs them interchangeably for both procurators and prefects. In the Jewish War, he calls Pilate an *epitropos*, but in the Antiquities, he calls him a *hegemon*.[3] Tacitus could not have known Pilate's correct title from Josephus and so calls him by the familiar post-Claudian title "procurator."

If Tacitus had used Josephus, then it would destroy the significance of his passage as independent evidence for the existence of Christ. But it also proves that the Testimonium must have been original to the Antiquities, for it would have been impossible for any Christian to have modified Tacitus' copy.

James, son of Damnaeus?

The second line of evidence is a passage from book twenty of the Antiquities about James, "the brother of the Lord." It all started with the death of the procurator Festus who had sent Paul to Rome for trial. There was an interregnum of several months before the new procurator Albinus could reach Judea. During this period, Agrippa II replaced the high priest Joseph with Ananus, son of Ananus. It was a distinguished family: the elder Ananus had a long reign as high priest, and each of his five sons would also become the high priest. Josephus describes the younger Ananus as "rash and daring" and explains what happened in his brief term of office:

> He followed the school of the Sadducees, who are indeed more heartless than any of the other Jews, as I have already explained, when they sit in judgement. Possessed of such a character, Ananus thought that he had a favorable opportunity because Festus was dead and Albinus was still on the way. And so he convened the judges of the Sanhedrin and brought before them a man named James, the brother of Jesus who was called the Christ, and certain others. He accused them of having transgressed the law and delivered them up to be stoned. Those of the inhabitants of the city who were considered the most fair-minded and who were strict in observance of the law were offended at this. They therefore secretly sent to King Agrippa urging him, for Ananus

had not even been correct in his first step, to order him to desist from any further such actions. Certain of them even went to meet Albinus, who was on his way from Alexandria, and informed him that Ananus had no authority to convene the Sanhedrin without his consent. Convinced by these words, Albinus angrily wrote to Ananus, threatening to take vengeance upon him. King Agrippa, because of Ananus' action, deposed him from the high priesthood which he had held for three months and replaced him with Jesus, the son of Damnaeus. (Antiquities 20:199-203)[4]

To summarize: the strict Sadducee Ananus took cynical advantage of the gap between two procurators to get rid of individuals he considered lawbreakers. The prominent Jews appealed to the new procurator Albinus who was on his way and who was furious that Ananus had summoned the Sanhedrin without his consent. So Agrippa removed Ananus from the priesthood after just three months.

Only one of the supposed lawbreakers is named: "James, the brother of Jesus who was called the Christ." The passage as a whole reads very much like Josephus, and most scholars accept the James reference as genuine. But it would be odd for Josephus to call someone "Christ" without some explanation. So, it is argued, Josephus must have already explained who Jesus was in the Testimonium, two books earlier. The logic is circular; the James passage is used to argue for the existence of the Testimonium, and the Testimonium is then used to justify the phrase "who was called the Christ" in the James passage. Both could be genuine, but both could also be fake.

There is one thing about the passage which does not ring true; the prominent Jews go out of their way to intervene over the execution of James, the leader of the Christians. The academic consensus sees this as evidence supporting the idea that Christianity started as a subset of Judaism and was not a separate religion at this time. This strange belief is contradicted by virtually every early piece of Christian literature. The Christians did not see themselves as Jews, and they speak of an ever-growing discord between the two groups: Paul received the third-nine lashes from the Jewish religious authorities at least five times.[5] The Jews were particularly enraged by Christian recruitment of uncircumcised gentiles, and this was also the chief bone of contention between Paul, the self-styled apostle to the gentiles, and James. He had been appointed as the movement's leader in Jerusalem but had little success in exercising his authority outside Judea. Paul did not want his hard-won gentile converts to have to become circumcised because he knew few adult men would agree to this. James, however, wanted all males who joined the movement to be circumcised.

Most commentators have seen Paul as the innovator who had abandoned the law as it applied to gentiles. But the radical Jesus movement was all about freedom from the Jewish law, which had been replaced by the new spiritual law of Christ. It made no sense for Christians to be under the old law of Moses. Paul makes this point time and again in his letters. It is not Paul who is the innovator, but James who is the backslider. Paul expresses the real reason for James' insistence to the Galatians:

> Those who want to make a good impression in the flesh compel you to be circumcised so as to avoid persecution for the cross of Christ. (Galatians 6:12)

Paul's point is valid but also unfair. James, living in the jurisdiction of the Jewish priests, was under tremendous pressure for his movement to conform to the Jewish law. The sight of uncircumcised gentiles being accepted into the Jesus movement confirmed the worst fears of the Jewish establishment; the movement led by James was heretical to the core. For James, it was a matter of life and death. But his attempt to get the movement to conform to the law outwardly was doomed to failure. Paul says that the circumcised Christians "do not keep the law themselves." This is one of many clues that early Jewish Christians did not adhere to the law. Unlike the uncircumcised, their own non-compliance was less visible.

Because of Jewish persecution, James' followers found it necessary to abandon Jerusalem. Eusebius reports that the Jerusalem church relocated to Pella in Perea before the Jewish war began.[6] This town was actually in the extreme north of Perea and was administratively part of the Decapolis, falling under the Roman province of Syria. Eusebius says that the reason for the move was a revelation about the coming destruction. It makes more sense that the Christians were fleeing persecution. Suppose you traveled north from Jerusalem, avoiding the hostile area of Samaria. Then Pella would be the first town you would come to that fell outside Judea and the religious jurisdiction of the Jewish priests. The Sanhedrin had no authority in Pella. But it would not have been a safe place for Jewish Christians to sit out the war because of the murderous hostility between the Jewish and Syrian populations.

The idea that prominent Jews in Jerusalem would have intervened on behalf of James is ludicrous. They would have regarded the Christians as law-breaking, vagrant scum. So one idea is that James, the brother of Jesus, has been written into an existing passage as an interpolation. The best form of this theory only requires the addition of three Greek words. The original could have read "James, the brother of Jesus," meaning not the Christian Jesus, but Jesus, son of Damnaeus, who became high priest

after Ananus. This other Jesus could have been awarded the high priesthood in compensation for the death of his brother James. Later, a Christian
scribe would have mistaken James for the brother of Christ and added the
interpolation "called the Christ." This hypothesis has been put forward by
Richard Carrier, among others.

It is a neat theory, but is it true? It requires the coincidence that there
were two brothers, James and Jesus, the sons of Damnaeus with the same
names as the Christian James and Jesus. Since the names are common, this
is not an insuperable difficulty. A more significant issue is that it would
require Josephus to have written "James, the brother of Jesus" without
telling us who this Jesus was until several lines later. Josephus' regular
practice would have been to introduce the first brother as "James, the son
of Damnaeus" and then, at the end of the passage, say that "Jesus, the
brother of James" or "Jesus, the son of Damnaeus" became high priest. In
reality, there are always variations, and it is not impossible for Josephus to
have written "James, the brother of Jesus" before telling us who this Jesus
was. But it is unlikely. In fact, the theory involves a string of improbable
coincidences:

1. There happens to be a pair of Jewish brothers called James and Jesus,
with one of them, James, put to death by the Jewish authorities.
2. Josephus just happens to identify the first brother, James, in an
unusual way.
3. Much later, a Christian scribe misunderstands Josephus and makes
an interpolation at just this point.

We will give the theory the benefit of the doubt on the first point. But if
we take the probability of the second point as 1 in 100 and the third point
as 1 in 10, there is only a 1 in 1000 chance of the conditions for the theory
being met. Another problem is whether Agrippa would have given the
priesthood to Jesus, son of Damnaeus, as compensation for his brother
being stoned to death. James was condemned by the Sanhedrin as a law-
breaker and must have done something wrong in Jewish eyes. The high
priest was a most important position, and Agrippa would not have chosen
a candidate lightly.

James, brother of Christ

If we reject an interpolation as unlikely, how do we account for the contradiction between the idea that the senior Jewish citizens of Jerusalem
intervened on James' behalf and the reality of Christian and Jewish

relations? The understanding that Josephus has placed the Testimonium into book eighteen of the Antiquities at the behest of Domitilla provides the explanation. Josephus has drafted the James passage with Domitilla in mind. She is aware that James was put to death in Judea and is naturally interested in the circumstances. Josephus, bruised by his experience with the Testimonium, knows that he cannot keep silent about James, so he puts the best possible spin on events. His account is intended to shift the blame for the death of James away from the Jewish people in general and from Josephus in particular.

In the Testimonium, Christ is "accused by the principal men amongst us," implicating the Jews as a whole. The wording of the James passage is quite different: "...the inhabitants of the city who were considered the most fair-minded and who were strict in observance of the law were offended at this." Josephus excuses the Jews as a people and associates himself with the objectors by calling them "the most fair-minded." His assignment of guilt and innocence is multi-leveled:

1. The death of James is mainly due to the actions of one man, Ananus.

2. More widely, the death is attributed to the severe school of the Sadducees. The implication is that Josephus' own group, the Pharisees, are innocent.

3. Josephus, the author, associates himself with the fair-minded, who are shocked by the killing and demand the removal of Ananus.

This is not to say there was no historical truth behind the passage. The complaint of the leading citizens is that the death penalty had been applied without the proper authority as capital punishment was a reserved power of the procurator. They did not want the high priest to be able to wield this power and use it to settle internal disputes. Josephus has spun the episode as being all about James, which it was not. The real focus of the leading citizen's protests would have been the unnamed others put to death at the same time.

In later Christian accounts, there is a consensus that James, "brother of the Lord," was stoned to death. However, these later accounts could all be dependent, ultimately, on the Josephus passage. Our other early source, Acts, does not even hint at James' death by stoning, but it does give another account of the execution of a James:

> About that time, King Herod reached out his hands to harm
> some of those of the church. He put to death James, the brother
> of John, with the sword. (Acts 12:1-2)

Conventionally, James, the son of Zebedee and brother of John, is seen as a different person from James, the brother of the Lord. In the Rock and the Tower, I set out the evidence that the two individuals named James were actually one and the same person.[7] But even if there were two early Christians both called James, one could have been confused with the other. The description of the execution that James was condemned by "Herod" and beheaded with the sword is vague. Only the context identifies this Herod with Agrippa I. But if the episode really related to James, brother of the Lord, then the guilty party would be Agrippa I's son, Agrippa II.

That Agrippa II was a persecutor of the Jesus movement is indicated by his involvement in the trial of Paul, which should have been entirely outside his jurisdiction. In Acts, Agrippa and Berenice just happened to be around when Festus heard Paul's case. In reality, they would not be present at a trial like this by chance. Their attendance is a sign that they had been acting behind the scenes to get Paul condemned. The conservative Agrippa would have had strong religious objections to the Jesus movement and would have wanted to strike off its head with the removal of James and Paul. He faced the difficulty that such religious matters were of no concern for the Roman procurator Festus. Paul, though, had a habit of stirring up trouble, and Romans had little patience with trouble-makers. Agrippa and Berenice must have persuaded Festus to send Paul to Rome for trial. This was probably not because he was a Roman citizen but because his supposed offenses had been committed outside Judea.

James was a more complicated case for Agrippa; he was peaceful, avoided conflict, and had not caused trouble outside Judea. James may have been a deviant Jew, but in the eyes of Festus, he had done nothing wrong and presented no danger. The procurator's unexpected death presented Agrippa with the ideal opportunity to deal with James alongside his other political and religious enemies. It is informative to look at the sequence of events according to Josephus:

1. Festus dies.
2. Agrippa appoints Ananus as high priest.
3. Ananus convenes the Sanhedrin. Takes action against James and others.
4. "Fair-minded" Jews appeal to Agrippa.
5. "Fair-minded" Jews appeal to Albinus.
6. Albinus writes an angry letter.
7. Agrippa removes Ananus as high priest.

Ananus must have secured the agreement of most of the Sanhedrin, so the killings were not the actions of a single man. The establishment was behind him, and the Jews who objected would have been a small minority, probably the relations of the victims. Agrippa must have approved of the high priest's actions, for he had the power to remove him. Note how Agrippa ignored the appeals of the "fair-minded" until the new procurator wrote in anger. Agrippa only takes action when he has to appease his Roman overlord.

The series of events were instigated by Agrippa's appointment of Ananus, who is never going to act without the prior agreement of the king and other leading Jews. Agrippa disguises his action by hiding behind Ananus. Ironically, James was probably not even killed by the high priest but executed on the direct orders of Agrippa.

This is the inevitable conclusion assuming the James killed by Herod in Acts is the brother of the Lord. Agrippa would have possessed capital authority over his own citizens in his own territory, but James is unlikely to have been one of those citizens. So his execution would have been legally dubious. Most likely, it happened exactly when Josephus says it did, in the interregnum between Festus and Albinus, when Agrippa was not under the watchful gaze of a procurator. Agrippa's territories were far to the north with one exception: Nero added the city of Livias (called Julias by Josephus) to his kingdom along with fourteen surrounding villages.[8]

Livias was twelve Roman miles east of Jericho and the largest city in Perea. This is significant because we know that the Jerusalem Christians had relocated to Pella in the north of Perea sometime before the Jewish war started in 66 AD. Josephus places the death of James in 62 AD, and the relocation could have been underway by then. With such a complicated move involving many individuals and families, there would have been much toing-and-froing between Jerusalem and Pella. If you needed to travel the route avoiding Samaria, which was dangerous for a Jew, you would cross the Jordan near Jericho and pass close to Livias. You might even have to go through Agrippa's territory; we do not know its exact extent, but some of those fourteen villages lay several miles to the north of the town. Livias itself would have been an attractive stopping point and could even have served as a base for the movement before they fixed on Pella. As a gentile city out of sight of the Jewish priests but quite close to Jerusalem, it may have seemed like a safe haven for Christians. So one plausible scenario is that James was arrested and executed while traveling through the area or staying in the town.

If James were really executed by Agrippa, why does Josephus say he was killed by Ananus? Josephus was in Rome when all this was happening, and his most likely source is Agrippa. Domitilla would have looked on Agrippa as almost an uncle, given the close relationship between Berenice and Titus. After Titus's death, Agrippa, like Josephus, would have been dependent on the Flavian women for influence. When Domitilla became a Christian, his past as a persecutor of the movement came back to haunt him. If one of her sons became emperor, she would be in a position of considerable power. It was vital that Agrippa disguise his role in the deaths of both Paul and James. So he uses Ananus as a scapegoat.

Agrippa is also the most obvious source for the Acts account of the trial of Paul with its absurd conclusion that he and Berenice would have freed Paul had they been able. Perhaps it was Agrippa who suggested that Paul was a Roman citizen who had appealed to the emperor. His purpose would have been to shift the blame for Paul being sent to Rome for trial from himself and Berenice. Domitilla would have been easily fooled. It would have been almost impossible for her to accept that two people she had looked up to since she was a girl were responsible for the deaths of James and her hero Paul. So when she came across a Christian source telling her that James was killed by Herod with a sword, she assumed this must have been Agrippa I who ruled all of Perea. So completely did she absolve Agrippa II that she used a chiastic structure in Luke/Acts built around the king. His territories were listed at the start, and Acts was brought to its first climax with Paul being found not guilty by Agrippa and Berenice.

Ananus and Origen

Josephus' account of the death of James supports the idea that the Testimonium is original to the Antiquities. The two passages show clear signs of a Christian influence acting upon Josephus, and the only potential source of such influence is Clemens and Domitilla.

But there is a contrary piece of evidence. The church father Origen wrote that Josephus "was not believing in Jesus as Christ" in connection with a passage about John the Baptist, which occurs only fifty lines after the Testimonium.[9] Origen even gives the correct book number—eighteen. As the Testimonium explicitly states that Jesus was the Christ, some have seen this as proof that it could not have been in Origen's copy of the Antiquities. Origen lived in Caesarea, the same location from which Eusebius would later write his Ecclesiastical History. So, the argument goes, the Testimonium must have been interpolated into the Caesarean copy of Antiquities sometime between Origen and Eusebius, with the finger of blame often directed at Eusebius himself.

It seems like a strong case—until we look at Origen's actual words. Origen's statement that Josephus did not believe that Jesus was the Christ is made in conjunction with another claim; that Josephus said that the destruction of Jerusalem and the temple was divine punishment for James' death. Origen makes this claim three times; twice in Against Celsus and once in his commentary on Matthew.[10] But Josephus said no such thing.

Origen certainly could not have consulted book twenty of the Antiquities. He makes a blatantly false statement about what Josephus said about James and does not repeat anything that he actually did say. If Origen did not have access to book twenty, he probably did not have book eighteen either. Otherwise, he would have realized that Josephus did say something very similar about John the Baptist—Herod's defeat by king Aretas was divine revenge for his execution of John.

In fact, there is no evidence that Origen had access to a copy of the Antiquities when he was writing in Caesarea. He never quotes anything from Josephus word for word. His knowledge of the Antiquities could have come from his visit to Rome decades earlier, and memory can be fickle. Eusebius did have a copy of the Antiquities in Caesarea, but that was eighty years later. And as Eusebius' copy included the Testimonium, it cannot be Origen's supposed copy without the Testimonium.

There is another remarkable coincidence. Although Josephus does not say that the destruction of Jerusalem occurred because of the death of James, he does say this in respect of someone else. He describes this individual in the Jewish War:

> A man on every ground revered and of the highest integrity, with all the distinction of his birth, rank and reputation, yet he loved to treat even the humblest as equals. Utterly devoted to liberty and with a passion for democracy, he always put the public welfare above his own interests. To maintain peace was the aim of his life, for he knew that Rome was invincible. (The Jewish War, 4:319-20)

It continues that had this man lived, "hostilities would have ended; for he was an effective speaker who words molded public opinion and had already silenced his opponents."[11] Unfortunately, this man suffered an appalling death at the hands of the Jewish rebels. He was even denied a burial—his naked body was flung down from a tower to be eaten by dogs. Because of this murder, Jerusalem fell:

> I should not be far wrong in saying that the fall of the city began with Ananus' death, and that the overthrow of the walls and the downfall of the Jewish state dated from the day when they saw the high priest [Ananus], the champion of their cause, butchered in the heart of the city. (Jewish War 4:318)

Yes, this is the same Ananus, son of Ananus, who supposedly executed James! The man who is a paragon of virtue in the Jewish War becomes "rash in his temper," "daring," and "heartless" in Antiquities. Even for Josephus, this is quite a turnaround. It can be explained by his differing audiences for the two works. Josephus was writing for Vespasian and Titus in the Jewish War and cared nothing about anything that Ananus may have done to James. But he writes book twenty of the Antiquities with a very different audience in mind, Domitilla and Clemens, who care very much about James.

Now any Christian would regard Ananus' death as divine judgment for James' execution, particularly as it resembles the fate of the evil Jezebel. But Josephus also says that Ananus' death resulted in the fall of Jerusalem. So we have a chain of argument that leads to Origen's statement about James:

1. Josephus says in book eighteen of the Antiquities that Herod's execution of John the Baptist resulted in his army losing the war against Aretas (Antiquities).

2. Ananus had James unfairly executed through a cynical ploy (Antiquities).

3. Ananus met a horrible death, and his naked body was thrown down for the dogs (The Jewish War).

4. Ananus' fate was God's punishment for the death of James. (A natural Christian conclusion. In the Old Testament, Jezebel also had God's prophets executed; she was thrown down from a tower, with her body also left to be eaten by dogs.)

5. Josephus believed that Jerusalem and its temple were destroyed as a result of the death of Ananus (The Jewish War).

To Christians, James, brother of Jesus was greater than the Jewish John; his unjust death requires an even greater punishment than John's death. So Jerusalem was destroyed in an act of divine justice against the Jews for the death of James. Origen must be basing his statements on a secondary Christian source which comes to this conclusion by analyzing Josephus' comments on John the Baptist, James, and Ananus. Origen has misunderstood the secondary source as meaning that Josephus directly said that the destruction of Jerusalem was due to the death of James. He is amazed at this because he knows that Josephus did not think that Jesus was the Christ, something that would be obvious to anyone who knew that Josephus had hailed Vespasian as the Messiah.

We should not give too much credibility to Origen's specific mention of book eighteen for John the Baptist as this information could have come from his secondary source. In the Commentary on Matthew, Origen talks about Antiquities' twenty books, although it is clear he has not consulted these volumes since he makes a false statement.[12]

If Origen is using a secondary source, then none of this is pertinent to the existence or non-existence of the Testimonium. Origen does not consult the Antiquities as he writes and his source would not mention the Testimonium because it is irrelevant to the argument.

23

Josephus' revenge

Paulina

The Testimonium is a strange passage in Josephus' writings, but what comes after it is even odder. Josephus is a military historian and a historian of the Jews. He writes about Jewish wars, Jewish beliefs, and Jewish characters while showing no interest in matters that do not have some Jewish connection. But an exception to this rule comes immediately after the Testimonium:

> About the same time another outrage threw the Jews into an uproar; and simultaneously certain actions of a scandalous nature occurred in connection with the temple of Isis at Rome. I shall first give an account of the daring deed of the followers of Isis and shall come back to the fate of the Jews. (Antiquities 18:65)[1]

With these words, Josephus establishes an entirely spurious connection between his next story and the Jews. While covering events under the governorship of the procurator Pontius Pilate in Judea, he suddenly makes a diversion to the temple of Isis in Rome. Scholars have felt a sense of disquiet at the positioning of this story, coming as it does immediately after Josephus' account of Jesus. Are the two in some way connected? The story is scandalous and differs from anything else in Josephus.[2]

It starts with a woman living in Rome called Paulina, who was of noble birth and highly esteemed. She was happily married to a man named Saturninus, who was her match in reputation. Paulina was attractive, in the full bloom of womanhood, but also virtuous, with the marital fidelity that the Romans valued so highly in a wife. However, she had attracted the notice of a knight called Decius Mundus, who had fallen hopelessly in love with her. He sent her gifts, but she scorned his attentions. Becoming desperate, he offered her an enormous sum, 200,000 drachmas, if she would sleep with him just once. She refused.

Mundus decided that he could not live without her and resolved to die. But he had a freedwoman called Ida who, seeing his intention, devised a plan to help him get his way. She told him she would secure him a night of passion with Paulina for just 50,000 drachmas. He agreed and gave her the money. She did not go to Paulina who was too virtuous to consent to such a proposal. Instead, she approached the priests of the temple of Isis, knowing that Paulina was an avid devotee of the goddess. Ida offered the priests the 50,000 drachmas to carry out the plan she had devised.

The priests agreed, and the eldest went to see Paulina at her house. He told her that the god Anubis had fallen in love with her. The god desired her to dine in his temple and share his bed for the night. Paulina was delighted, telling both her lady friends and her husband about the god's summons. Saturninus agreed that she should go, trusting in her faithfulness. This idea of sleeping in a temple may seem odd to us, but not for the Romans. After Paulina reclined to eat at the god's table and made her bed in his temple, it would be expected that he would visit her in a dream. But her experience was to be much more carnal than that.

Paulina went to the temple and had her meal. The priests then turned out the lights and locked up the temple, leaving her to settle down in her bed. When all was quiet, Mundus, who the priests had hidden, came out and approached her. Thinking he was Anubis, Paulina gave him everything he desired, and they made love all night long. Mundus slipped away in the early morning before the priests began to stir.

The next day Paulina proudly told her friends and her husband about her experiences. They were incredulous, but because of her reputation did not know what to believe. On the third day, Mundus, his passion quenched, approached her:

> Well Paulina, you have indeed saved me 200,000 drachmas which you could have added to your fortune, yet you have rendered perfectly the services I urged you to perform. As for your attempt to flout Mundus, I was not bothered about names but about the pleasure of the act, so I took the name of Anubis as my own. (Antiquities 18:17)

Paulina was horrified and rent her garments in grief. She went to Saturninus and begged him to seek justice. Saturninus appealed to the emperor Tiberius. After ascertaining the facts of the case, Tiberius ordered Ida and the priests to be crucified. The temple of Isis was razed to the ground, and the goddess' statue was dumped in the river. Decius Mundus escaped with a sentence of exile since he had the excuse of passion.

Fulvia

After these "insolent acts" of the priests of Isis, Josephus introduces his second story, what happened "at the same time to the Jews in Rome."[3] There is another Roman noblewoman who was called Fulvia. Like Paulina, she was also married to a man named Saturninus, a coincidence that has caused further consternation among commentators. Whereas Paulina worshiped Isis, Fulvia worshiped the Jewish God—she was a God-fearer. However, she had fallen under the spell of a gang of Jewish rogues led by someone who had broken laws in his homeland. This man had put himself out as an interpreter of the Mosaic Law and was joined by three crooked confederates. Fulvia was duped by this group and met regularly with them. They persuaded her to send gifts of "gold and purple" to the temple in Jerusalem. But it was all a fraud from the start—they sold the gifts and spent the money. When Fulvia found out, she urged Saturninus to report the matter to Tiberius, "whose friend he was." But instead of punishing the guilty parties, the emperor ordered all Jews to be expelled from Rome. Josephus says that four thousand were sent to the island of Sardinia for military service. They endured many hardships because of their reluctance to break the Jewish law.

This second story does concern the Jews and is potentially more realistic as the type of thing that Josephus would write. But the offense is too trivial to merit the punishment of an entire people, and there are strange similarities with the Paulina story. We can compare Josephus' account of the expulsion of the Jews to that of Tacitus:

> There was also a discussion of driving out Egyptian and Jewish rites, and a senatorial decree was passed ordering 4,000 persons of the freedman class who had been infected with such superstition and who were also of appropriate age, to be transported to the island of Sardinia. There they were to be employed in putting down bandits, and if they perished because of the oppressive climate the loss would be slight. The others were under orders to leave Italy unless they cast aside their profane religious observances before a specific date. (Tacitus, Annals 2:85)

There are enough points in common to see that the two accounts are closely related. Tacitus says that the action was against both Egyptian and Jewish religion. Josephus has the incident at the temple of the Egyptian goddess Isis and the Jewish expulsion occurring at the same time. Most impressively, both agree that 4,000 were sent to Sardinia for military service, although Tacitus implies that devotees of Egyptian religion, as well as Jews, were involved.

Tacitus is writing after Josephus, and the similarities are best explained if he has used Josephus as one of his sources. Another coincidence supports this—in each case, the expulsion comes after an account of prostitution concerning a Roman noblewoman. Josephus has the story of Paulina, who is offered a large amount of money for sex, but who declines until she is tricked. Tacitus tells the story of a woman of praetorian rank called Vistilia who was brazen enough to declare before the aediles that she was willing to engage in sex for money. This caused the senate to enact a measure that "a woman was barred from prostitution if she had a grandfather, father or husband who was a Roman knight."[4] Tacitus would have read the Paulina story in Josephus, and it would have triggered his memory of the real case of Vistilia. So he places the senatorial decree about prostitution immediately before the Egyptian and Jewish expulsions in his Annals.

Suetonius also mentions the Jewish expulsion but with less detail. He says that Tiberius took action against both the Egyptian and Jewish cults and religions, "obliging those who practiced such rituals to burn their religious garments and all their paraphernalia."[5] Young Jewish men were sent to regions where the climate was severe "ostensibly on military service." The remainder of the Jews and "others of similar beliefs" were banished from the city. Suetonius' account is probably dependent on Tacitus.[6]

Finally, Cassius Dio also mentions the expulsion:

> As the Jews had flocked to Rome in great numbers and were converting many of the natives to their ways, he banished most of them. (Dio Histories 57:18:5a)

Dio is writing much later than Tacitus or Suetonius but can draw upon independent earlier sources. His account makes the most sense: it was the Jews' growing numbers and their success at attracting Romans to their religion that aroused Tiberius' ire. Significantly, Dio does not mention any action against the followers of Egyptian religion.

We can see how each of the three episodes in Antiquities 18:63-84 is reflected by something in Tacitus' Annals:

The Testimonium (Antiquities 18:63-64) - Nero's persecution of Christians.

The Paulina story (Antiquities 18:65-80) - Prostitution among Roman noblewomen, expulsion of Egyptian religion from Rome.

The Fulvia story (Antiquities 18:81-84) - Expulsion of Jews from Rome, 4000 sent on military service.

So Tacitus seems aware of the Testimonium and the two stories that came after, implying they were all in his copy of the Antiquities. The differences between Tacitus and Josephus are revealing:

The Paulina story is omitted entirely.

There is no mention of the destruction of the temple of Isis and the cultic statue of the goddess.

There is no mention of Fulvia or Saturninus as the reason for the Jewish expulsion.

The expulsion is dated to 19 AD rather than c.30 AD in Josephus.

As Tacitus had access to the senate decrees, we can be confident that his dating is correct, and Dio also places the event at the same time. So Josephus has moved the expulsion back eleven years to bring it within his Pilate section and position it immediately after the Testimonium. Tacitus is well informed about Roman matters, so it is significant that he says nothing about Paulina, Decius Mundus, Saturninus, or Fulvia. The Paulina story, in particular, is just the type of scandalous episode we would expect him to include. Its omission from the Annals implies that Tacitus regarded it as fiction.

The temple of Isis and Serapis

To the ancient mind, the most incredible part of Josephus' two stories would be the claim that Tiberius ordered the temple of Isis to be destroyed and the goddess' cultic statue dumped in the river. The Romans were very superstitious. If Tiberius had taken such an outrageous action, we would surely have heard about it from Roman writers. But none of the Roman accounts mentions this destruction of the temple or the mortal insult to the goddess. There is, it is true, a similar incident in Rome's past. Dio tells us that in 53 BC, the Roman senate decreed that those temples in Rome built by private individuals for the Egyptian gods Serapis and Isis should be torn down. This was because "they did not believe in those gods." Dio adds that this action against the gods caused great calamities.[7] The Romans came to regret this action against the temples and within ten years the senate voted for a new public temple for Serapis and Isis to appease the gods' anger.[8] It was this temple in the Campus Martius that Josephus says was destroyed by Tiberius.

There was further action against the Egyptian rites under Augustus. In 28 BC, the emperor banned the Egyptian rites within the city boundaries, and a similar action, this time including the suburbs, was taken by his governor Agrippa in 21 BC. Although the rites were banned, Augustus made strict provisions to maintain the temples.[9] This would be consistent with Suetonius' statement that the vestments and paraphernalia were burnt. The rites are banned, but the gods' temples, which are sacred spaces, must not be desecrated.

Certainly, the temple of Isis was standing in Vespasian's reign because it is depicted on one of his coins.[10] It had either been rebuilt or, more likely, never been destroyed. But why would Josephus lie about such a thing? Although he calls it the temple of Isis, it was actually the temple of Isis and Serapis. And Serapis was Vespasian's favorite god. Vespasian had performed his healing miracles in Alexandria by Serapis' power. And the miracle of the branches and cakes in Serapis' Alexandrian temple marked the news that Vespasian was now undisputed emperor. There is also a link between the temple of Isis in Rome and Domitian. In the civil war, he escaped from the burning temple of Jupiter Optimus dressed as a follower of Isis.

In Josephus' story, Paulina and Decius Mundus spend the night in the temple of Isis. Vespasian and Titus spent the night before their triumph for the Jewish War in the very same temple.[11] Vespasian would have chosen this place to honor and give thanks to Serapis. Josephus was an eyewitness to the triumph and may have been obliged to participate as the defeated general of Jotapata. Whether or not he did participate, the occasion would have been humiliating and distressing. The former temple priest would have to watch as the sacred temple treasures were paraded before the jeering crowds of Rome.

So we come to the idea that the two stories following the Testimonium are a secret satire by Josephus. He is careful to avoid directly mentioning Vespasian's patron god Serapis, but the god's temple is razed to the ground. And the cultic statue of Isis, Domitian's protective goddess, is dumped in the river. Is this literary revenge for the destruction of the Jerusalem temple?

A satire – part one

Josephus may be satirizing the Flavians, but his main target was Christianity. Certain aspects of this have been known for a long time but have been generally ignored because they do not fit established theories about the Testimonium.[12] Let us take the story of Paulina first.

The name Paulina happens to be the female form of Paul, another sign that something is going on below the surface with this story. Paulina was a common Roman name, so this has been dismissed as yet another coincidence.

What about the name of the love-struck villain, Decius Mundus? The cognomen Mundus is suspicious. It means the world/the earth/the sky/ the heavens; what we would call the universe. It was also used euphemistically for the underworld. But Mundus could also mean "perfumed," so it can be argued that Decius Mundus is presented as a perfumed ladies' man. We should bear in mind that Josephus needs to keep his satire hidden and so would choose a name that does have some such explanation.

The nomen Decius was carried by two famous patriots, father and son, who sacrificed their lives for Rome. It appears to be a respectable Roman name, but there is a hidden meaning. If we omit the two central letters, then Decius becomes Deus—"god." So:

De(ci)us Mundus = God of the World/God of the Universe

It would be incredible if this were just a coincidence. Decius Mundus represents Jesus Christ in a satire that mocks the Christian idea of Jesus as the god of the world. According to Josephus, this god is nothing more than a perfumed deceiver and villain.

In the story, Decius Mundus assumes the identity of the Egyptian god Anubis. The dog-headed Anubis was a god of the dead and the underworld. When Mundus tells Paulina that it does not matter if he is called Mundus or Anubis, his words have a hidden meaning—Mundus could also mean Hades. Mundus' transformation into Anubis represents Jesus' descent into the underworld after his crucifixion until his resurrection on the third day. The Testimonium says that Jesus appeared on the third day to those who loved him. Josephus would have secretly regarded all this as nonsense. His Jesus, Anubis, is also resurrected and appears to Paulina "on the third day" when he reveals the fraud and that he is really Mundus. So Mundus is not only called the god of the world but corresponds to Christ in both death (becoming Anubis) and resurrection on the third day.

Equating Jesus with Anubis is a further mockery. Roman statues show Anubis looking absurd with a human body and the head of a dog. So Jesus is represented as having a dog's head, an unclean animal to the Jews. The satire evokes the image of the foolish Paulina in bed kissing this supposedly dog-headed god without noticing that he was a perfectly normal man.

A further link to Christianity is that Ida and the priests are crucified. Mundus escapes the death penalty. But then, as a supposed Roman citizen, he could not be crucified, and perhaps no other death would be appropriate.

The satire is a secret, derisive commentary on the preceding Testimonium. But there is more to it than that. Commentators have long recognized that the story also appears to mock the virgin birth of Jesus, which the Testimonium does not even mention.

The virgin birth occurs in only two gospels, Matthew and Luke. Matthew's description of the divine conception is very brief: "His mother Mary was pledged in marriage to Joseph, but before their coming together, she was found to be with child of the Holy Spirit."[13] This Matthew nativity cannot have been the source for the Paulina story, and instead, we must turn to the Gospel of Luke. Several similarities show that the Paulina satire (P) is based on the Luke nativity (L):

L: The angel Gabriel appears to Mary in her house and gives her a message: "Greetings, you who are highly favored! ... Behold, you will conceive and give birth to a son."[14]

P: The oldest priest of Anubis comes to Paulina and gives her a message: "he said he had been sent to her by the god Anubis; the god had fallen in love with her and bade her come with him."

L: Mary answers the angel: "May it happen to me according to your word."[15]

P: Paulina's reaction to the priest is similar: "The message was what she would have wished."

L: The act of conception is described by the angel: "The Holy Spirit will come upon you, and the power of the Most High will overshadow you."[16]

P: Paulina goes into the temple, and the god comes to her bed.

L: The pregnant Mary visits Elizabeth, who recognizes her special state. The two women rejoice together, and Mary sings the Magnificat about how she is blessed.

P: After Paulina's night-time experience, she tells her husband and then her friends: "before the ladies, her friends, she put on great airs in talking about him."

The point here is not exact literary correspondences but that Josephus is satirizing the form of the virgin birth story that did not exist before the Gospel of Luke. Early Christians also recognized that the story was a satire on the virgin birth. Albert Bell has pointed out that the fourth century Christian writer going by the name Hegesippus included the story in his account of the Jewish War which was based on Josephus.[17] Hegesippus' version was much shorter than that of Josephus, and made the connection with the virgin birth story in Luke more obvious. For example, Paulina becomes pregnant after her encounter with the "god" and the language is closer to the Luke account. Hegesippus clearly knew that Josephus had intended the story as an anti-Christian satire.

We have seen that Acts shows familiarity with book twenty of the Antiquities. Assuming Luke was written a year or two before Acts, it could not have been completed much earlier than the Paulina story. How could Josephus know the Luke version of the virgin birth so early?

He has got it, of course, from Domitilla, the author of Luke. The Paulina story postdates the Testimonium, which was approximately simultaneous to the Emmaus story, which in turn postdates the virgin birth. So we can be confident that the Luke nativity was in existence before Josephus wrote about Paulina. Domitilla must have read her nativity account to an astonished Josephus. Ironically, he would have been among the first to hear the story, which would exert such an influence on Western culture. He would also be its first critic.

A satire – part two

The second story is the second part of the satire. There are links between the two stories; most obviously, the husband in each is called Saturninus. There are also close structural similarities. Fulvia, a God-fearer, is conned by some bad Jews. This is how their leader is described:

> There was a certain Jew, a complete scoundrel who had fled his own country because he was accused of transgressing certain laws and feared punishment on this account. Just at this time he was resident in Rome and played the part of an interpreter of the mosaic law and its wisdom. (Antiquities 18:81-2)[18]

Which sounds suspiciously like a description of Paul. A Jew such as Josephus would certainly have looked upon the apostle to the gentiles as a lawbreaker. Paul tells us that he was given the thirty-nine lashes five times by the Jewish religious authorities.[19] And he was an interpreter of the "mosaic law and its wisdom" in his letters. He argued that Christians were free from the old law because it had been superseded by a new law of the spirit. Josephus would have hated this idea. And according to Acts, Paul resided in Rome while under house arrest and taught both Jews and Gentiles.

In the satire, Paul is joined by three confederates "no better in character than himself." They must represent three other apostles, most likely Peter, James, and John Mark, the three leaders who Paul says he met in Jerusalem.[20] The four persuade Fulvia to send "purple (cloth) and gold" to the Jerusalem temple. This also matches something that Paul did. He mentions a collection for the Jerusalem church in several of his letters. In the story, the four use the gifts "for their personal expenses," which is exactly what happened. Paul was collecting to meet the living expenses of the brothers and sisters in Jerusalem, including James and the others. The Jews did send wealth and gifts for the Jerusalem temple, but that was not the stated purpose of Paul's collection. Josephus either misunderstood the collection or deliberately misrepresented it to make his satirical point that the Jesus movement is led by fraudsters and thieves.

In the story, the actions of the "bad" Jews (the Christians) result in the exile of the "good' Jews from Rome. There were certainly no Christians around in 19 AD, but Josephus could be conflating two different episodes. As well as an expulsion under Tiberius there may have been one under Claudius, who reigned until 54 AD. The evidence that Christians caused this Claudian expulsion comes from Suetonius:

> The Jews he expelled from Rome since they were constantly in rebellion at the instigation of Chrestus. (Suetonius, Claudius 25)

Chrestus was a common slave's name—it meant "useful"—but there was confusion in Rome between Chrestus and Christ, and most likely, Christ is meant here. It seems that Christian activity in Rome before 54 AD caused trouble with the Jews, which resulted in their expulsion from the city. Acts also refers to a recent expulsion of the Jews from Rome, which would fit this period. So Josephus could be combining the two expulsions for his satirical purpose and placing them during the governorship of Pilate, after the Testimonium.

To satirize Paul, Josephus must have had some knowledge of his letters. Acts alone is insufficient; the collection for the saints in Jerusalem is not even mentioned in Acts. We have seen that the Life also shows some knowledge of Paul's letters. Josephus is unlikely to have a copy of texts that would only have circulated among Christians. So his source would have to be Domitilla. We can expect her to have talked to Josephus about Paul and read extracts from his letters in an attempt to convert him to Christianity. What better way to persuade the pharisee Josephus than to quote the arguments of the former pharisee Paul? Mixed into all this would be her notions about Paul, which were coalescing into the form of Acts. So Josephus would have had access to a rich seam of information about the Jesus movement.

Why so subtle?

Josephus' satire is subtle, with multiple levels of meaning. He takes aim at the Flavians by indirectly mocking Vespasian's patron god Serapis. But his chief venom is reserved for the Christians. Jesus is a fraud who seduces women by presenting himself as the dog-headed god of the underworld resurrected after three days. The virgin birth is a big con, and Paul and the other apostles are law-breakers and thieves. We have not even uncovered all of the satire's secrets yet. The names Paulina and Decius Mundus have a hidden meaning, so what about Saturninus, Ida, and Fulvia?

Before exploring the satire further, we need to ask why so subtle? It might have been possible for an ancient reader to connect the Paulina story to the account of Jesus' death and resurrection in the Testimonium. But it is far from obvious. The virgin birth is not even included in the Testimonium, and most readers in the 90s would be unaware that Christians had such a belief. Similarly, appreciation of the satire on Paul would require knowledge of that apostle that the original audience did not possess.

The purpose of satire is to mock, but mocking requires the reader to be in on the trick. Why then write a satire which is impenetrable to the audience? In the ancient world, as in dictatorships today, this was necessary when you were mocking your rulers. Writing an obvious satire on the king or emperor would likely get you executed. So you wrote your satire to be understood by a small group of insiders. It was a subtle demanding craft, and the cost of getting it wrong could be death. Perhaps that was the source of its fascination. We can expect Josephus to have disclosed his satire to a small group of trusted Jewish confidants. Or perhaps it was enough for him to hide the satires in his work without sharing the meaning with a living soul.

We can understand why Josephus would have to keep his criticisms of the Flavians hidden, but why his anti-Christian satire? The emperor and the Roman ruling class despised Christianity. We would expect Josephus to make his anti-Christian feelings public to distinguish Jews from the Christians and win approval from his Roman patrons. The fact that Josephus needed to hide his satire shows the existence of a pro-Christian influence sufficiently powerful to counterbalance the anti-Christian attitude of Domitian and the nobles. The only realistic possibility is Domitilla and Clemens, the parents of the future emperor.

The existence of the satire proves that a pro-Christian Testimonium was placed in the Antiquities by Josephus. If Josephus had written an anti-Christianity or skeptical Testimonium, he would not have needed to follow it with a secret anti-Christian satire. We can also rule out the idea that the satire was a later interpolation. Such an interpolation would have to be written by a pagan or Jew who lived under circumstances in which Christians wielded political power. But Christianity had no such power in the first three centuries. Only after Constantine the Great's conversion in 312 AD did Christians gradually gain authority over pagans and Jews. The satire would have to date no earlier than the mid-fourth century, which is after the date when Eusebius quotes the Testimonium in full. This raises two questions:

1. Why would a pagan bother with putting an almost impenetrable satire in a Jewish history more than 200 years old and little read?
2. How did a pagan or Jew get their interpolation into all surviving Christian copies?

The Antiquities has survived to the modern age because it was preserved and copied in Christian monasteries and churches. The work was popular among Christians but not among Jews or pagans. It was translated into Latin quite early, and Christians would have rejected the addition of new stories. These considerations would apply with even greater force if the Testimonium were a later interpolation. We would then have to imagine a bizarre series of events:

1. Josephus wrote the Antiquities without the Testimonium or the two stories that come after it.
2. Eusebius, or some other Christian living around the time of Constantine, interpolated the Testimonium into the Antiquities.
3. A pagan or Jew somehow had access to Eusebius' scriptorium. They took Eusebius' copy, or a very early copy made from it, and added a further interpolation immediately after the Testimonium. This highly subtle anti-Christian satire was written skillfully as a piece from first-century Rome.
4. No one noticed that the copy had been doctored. It was used as the exemplar for producing many other Christian copies and was distributed widely around the Roman Empire.

Clearly, this never happened. If we accept that the two stories are anti-Christian satires, we can rule out the idea that the Testimonium is a later Christian interpolation. The Testimonium and the two satirical stories must all go back to Josephus.

24

Fulvia Paulina

The subject of the satire

The satire is Josephus' revenge for having to include the Testimonium in Antiquities. To find out who obliged Josephus to include it, we only need to ask: at whom is the satire aimed? Strangely, no one seems to ask this question, although the answer is straightforward. In both stories, the subject is the woman who is tricked and fooled owing to her incredulity and whose husband is too weak to intervene. The main target then is the woman called Paulina and Fulvia, with the secondary target being her husband, Saturninus. This raises the question: are Paulina and Fulvia intended to represent the same woman?

Most scholars have not realized that Paulina and Fulvia are satirical characters but regard them as real women. Some have argued that as they are both married to a man called Saturninus, they must be the same person. Others point out that Paulina is a devotee of Isis and Fulvia a Jewish God-fearer, so they have incompatible religious beliefs. Now, it would be incompetent for an author to have two stories, one after the other, involving a husband called Saturninus without making it clear to the reader whether or not they are two different men. And Saturninus is not the only link between the stories; there is a close structural similarity:

Both involve a Roman noblewoman, Paulina/Fulvia, described in similar terms.

Both stories center around a temple (Isis/Jerusalem temple).

In both cases, the woman is strongly religious but is duped by deceivers who take advantage of her religious beliefs.

In both stories, when she discovers the deception, she urges her husband Saturninus to seek redress.

In both cases, Saturninus appeals to the emperor, who inflicts a strong punishment.

It would be astonishing if two independent stories happened to be so

similar. The common factor of Saturninus is a clue that we are supposed
to link the stories together. A real woman cannot both be a follower of Isis
and a Jewish proselyte, but this consideration does not apply to satire! The
stories are satirical, and satire has its own rules. The subject of the satire
is represented as first Paulina and then Fulvia, which is why the two have
the same husband.

The satire mocks the Flavians and the Christians. This woman, then,
is a Christian who is a Flavian or associated with the Flavians. Josephus
satirizes her Christianity by first representing it as a pagan Egyptian
mystery religion and then attacking its supposed Jewish provenance. The
woman has compelled Josephus to include the Testimonium. Her husband,
Saturninus, supports her, and behind them lies the power of the emperor.
In the satire, the emperor is Tiberius, who must stand for the current
emperor, Domitian. Saturninus is a "friend" of the emperor; the Latin
equivalent is *"amici."* Every emperor had his *amici*, a group of office holders,
equestrians, and senators through whom he carried out his administration
alongside his freedmen.[1] So Saturninus is a senior Roman who was close
to Domitian and part of the imperial administration. Naturally, Clemens
would have been one of Domitian's *amici*.

These considerations enable us to eliminate Domitia as the subject
of the satire—her husband is the emperor himself and not Saturninus.
Epaphroditus is also eliminated because we hear nothing about his wife,
who could hardly be powerful enough to be the woman of the satire. Only
Domitilla and Clemens fit the profile, and they fit it perfectly. So:

Paulina/Fulvia = Domitilla
Saturninus = Clemens

The satire within Antiquities

If this picture is correct, neither the Testimonium nor the two satirical
stories were present in the initial draft of the Antiquities. When Josephus
was obliged to add the Testimonium to the original text, he included the
two stories mocking Domitilla as a foolish and gullible young woman.
Josephus had to be very careful to ensure that Domitilla would not pene-
trate his meaning. But dangling the satire right in front of her eyes would
have been all part of the fun.

If we look at the Pontius Pilate section of the Antiquities, we can see the
evidence that the Testimonium and the two stories have been added-in.
We start with the parallel section in the Jewish War, which has just two
episodes about Pilate:

Under cover of night, Pilate conveys the Roman ensigns (idols) into the city, leading to a riot by the Jews. Pilate has to give way and withdraw the ensigns. (2:169-174)

Pilate takes treasure from the temple for an aqueduct which causes another disturbance that he puts down ruthlessly. (2:175-177)

In the Jewish War, nothing more is said about Pilate's rule in Judea. We do not hear how or why he was replaced as governor. Turning to the Antiquities, the Pilate section has been greatly expanded:

Pilate brings the ensigns into the city as above. (18:55-59)

Pilate takes the money for the aqueduct from the temple resulting in a disturbance, as above. (18:60-62)

[The Testimonium. (18:63-64)]

[The Paulina story. (18:65-80)]

[The Fulvia story. (18:81-84)]

Expulsion of the Jews from Rome at the instigation of the Samaritans. [Later edited to remove reference to the Samaritans.]

A Samaritan attempts to lead an armed multitude to the top of Mount Gerizim, where the vessels of Moses were supposedly hidden. Pilate attacks the Samaritan crowd with his cavalry, and many die, both in the assault and afterward by execution. (18:85-87)

The Samaritans accuse Pilate of an unjustified massacre, and the Syrian governor Vitellius sends him back to Rome for judgment by Tiberius. But Tiberius is dead by the time Pilate reaches Rome. (18:88-89)

The items in square brackets are those that Josephus has added later. If we omit the Testimonium and the Paulina and Fulvia stories, the Pilate section makes good logical sense. Josephus includes the Samaritan disturbance to explain why Pilate was sent back to Rome. This account of this episode begins with the words: "The Samaritan nation too was not exempt from disturbance..." which follows on well from the two stories about rioting in Judea. This might suggest that the expulsion was not included in the original draft: it is in the wrong place under Pilate. But the reality is more complex. There is a strong indication that it was included at this position, although in a very different form from the Fulvia story.

The evidence lies in an ancient table of contents for the Antiquities that may go back to Josephus and which omits both the Testimonium and the Paulina story. The omissions have been taken as evidence for the Testimonium being a later interpolation, but this is to misunderstand the table. Unlike a modern table of contents, it does not list everything but provides a small series of signposts to certain episodes to help the reader navigate the text. There are three entries relating to Pilate, an unusually large number for a short section. One relates to the bringing of ensigns into Jerusalem, another to Pilate's recall to Rome, and in the middle is the expulsion of the Jews from Rome:

What happened to the Jews in Rome at this time at the instigation of the Samaritans. (Josephus, Jewish Antiquities, ToC 18 ix)

The table of contents shows the expulsion as being caused by the Samaritans and not the Christians! This makes sense because the expulsion would set the scene for the next two episodes about how the Samaritans got Pilate sent back to Rome. Josephus must have changed the text of the Antiquities by editing the story to bring in Fulvia and shift the blame from the Samaritans to the Christians. But he forgot to update the table of contents. At the same time, he would have added the Paulina story before the expulsion and the Testimonium before that.

Domitilla as Paulina and Fulvia

In Paulina, we have our first glimpse of Domitilla from someone who knew her in real life. It is ironic that the portrait is satirical, although not without its positive elements. Paulina is descended from noble Romans. She is universally acknowledged as virtuous, wealthy, and of "comely appearance." She is "at the age at which women are most exuberant yet devoted her life to good conduct."[2] We can conclude that Paulina was not a young girl in the first flush of youth, but neither was she middle-aged. Domitilla would have been around thirty when Josephus wrote the satire, an age that fits the description well.

Her husband Saturninus is "fully a match for her in reputation." This is a good description of Clemens, who, as her cousin, was Domitilla's equal in background. In fact, Paulina and Saturninus sound like the perfect Christian couple. The emphasis on Paulina's virtue and good deeds is particularly impressive coming from a strict Jew who would have regarded most Romans as thoroughly immoral. Yet she is no quiet introvert; Josephus calls her "exuberant." We can picture Domitilla as a lively risk-taker, a true daughter of Cerialis. This fits with our deductions about the author of Luke and Acts: she is self-confident to the point of arrogance, imaginative and inventive, but also undisciplined and careless with the facts.

Although Paulina is virtuous, she ends up playing the whore by being tricked by a fake god. Josephus takes great fun mocking her gullibility.

Paulina cannot resist letting everyone know that the god has specially chosen her. After her night of passion with Anubis, she gives herself airs while telling her husband and friends everything. We have the comic portrait of the virtuous young matron proudly recounting the pornographic details of her nighttime encounter while her audience exchanges incredulous looks.

Josephus mocks both Domitilla's religion and Domitilla herself. Paulina stands both for the virgin Mary and the young woman he knows. He sees Domitilla as a good person but easily deceived. At this time, Christianity was intensely spiritual, and Domitilla would have seen herself as the bride of Christ. For Josephus, Christianity is a semi-pagan falling away from the purity of Judaism. He sees Jesus not as her spiritual husband but as a trickster who has lured her into adultery. Josephus represents the Christian mysteries of the bridal chamber in crude physical terms, turning Domitilla into a temple prostitute.

When Paulina finds out the truth, Josephus says that she "rent her garment," a curiously Jewish expression of grief. Perhaps Josephus has fallen into this turn of phrase by habit. Or maybe it is intended as a further bridge to the second story.

Domitilla now becomes Fulvia, described simply as "a woman of high rank who had become a Jewish proselyte." Her rank is high indeed, for her husband Saturninus is an *amicus* of the emperor. Domitilla was almost certainly a Jewish God-fearer before she became a Christian; the author of Luke shows excellent knowledge of the Septuagint Greek scriptures. Fulvia is just such a God-fearer, but she falls under the spell of false teachers, led by the apostle Paul. He sets himself up as an expert on the Jewish law but is a hypocrite and a law-breaker. (We should note that in the first story, Domitilla is called Paulina. It would be too obvious to call her by this name in this second story about the corrupting influence of Paul.) The Christians are really only interested in Fulvia's money. They take advantage of her inherent generosity and persuade her to make expensive gifts to the Jerusalem temple, which they keep.

We should remember that Josephus had a reputation as a conman during his time in Galilee and was accused of enriching himself in the war. We have also seen how he would project his own dishonesty on those around him. Because Josephus has no sincerity, he cannot believe that others are sincere. So Josephus, the thief, represents the Christians as a gang of thieves.

Saturninus

If Domitilla is a well-meaning but gullible young woman in the satire, what about her husband, Clemens? As Saturninus, he does not share in his wife's enthusiasms or beliefs but is entirely under her influence. When Paulina tells him she will sleep with the god in his temple, he meekly agrees. Even afterward, when he has grave doubts about the incident, he does nothing. When Paulina finds out the truth, she is the one who urges him to take action, and he does what she tells him to do. If Domitilla is a bride of Christ, then Clemens is a cuckold.

Saturninus plays no part in the second story until Fulvia appeals to him to seek redress with the emperor. Once again, he meekly complies. By the masculine standards of Rome, Saturninus is a weak man who fails to control his headstrong wife. The portrayal is consistent with what we know about Domitilla and Clemens. Domitilla was the Christian, whereas Clemens was little more than a sympathizer. Yet he went along with her religious activities, which would cost him his life. The two are happily married, but there is no doubt who is in charge. It fits in with Suetonius's comment that Clemens was a man of "contemptible idleness."

This leaves the question of the name "Saturninus." Another name we have not explained is that of the freedwoman Ida, who arranges the whole deception on behalf of Decius Mundus. Saturninus is named in honor of the god Saturn, and Ida is a sacred mountain in Crete connected to stories of the origins of the gods. But why these names in particular?

If Domitilla wrote Luke/Acts, Clemens is Theophilus, "God-lover." Josephus is aware of this name and mocks it by turning it into Saturninus. To understand how this works, we must appreciate Roman speculations about the origins of the Jews. One popular Roman theory was that the Jewish God Yahweh was the same as Saturn. In Roman myth, Saturn ruled the world before being forcibly replaced by his son Jupiter. The Jews were seen as followers of Saturn who refused to accept Jupiter and the other gods. They originated on Mount Ida, the mountain where Saturn resided. The Jews' name, Judaei, was derived from the Idaei, the people who inhabited Ida during the early reign of Saturn. Supposedly these proto-Jews were cast out into the Libyan desert at the fall of Saturn before ending up in Judea. The entomology is entirely spurious but would have been convincing to a Roman. This theory is one that Tacitus reports:

> It is said that the Jews are refugees from Crete who settled in the furthest part of Libya at the time when Saturn was forcibly deposed by Jupiter. Evidence for this is sought in the name: Ida

is a famous mountain in Crete inhabited by the Idaei, whose name became lengthened into the foreign name Judaei. (Tacitus, Histories 5:2)

The importance the Jews placed on the sabbath was seen as evidence that their God was Saturn:

Others maintain that they do this in honor of Saturn, either because their religious principles are derived from the Idaei, who are supposed to have been driven out with Saturn and become the ancestors of the Jewish people; or else because, of the seven stars which govern the lives of men, Saturn moves in the topmost orbit and exercises the mightiest influence... (Tacitus, Histories 5:4)

Cassius Dio also connects the Jewish sabbath with Saturn: "Thus was Jerusalem destroyed on the very day of Saturn, the day which even now the Jews reverence most."[3] Josephus, living in Rome, would have been all too aware of these Roman speculations. He would have been enraged by these attempts to assimilate Judaism into Roman religion. To the Jews, Saturn and the other Roman gods did not even exist. Josephus would have seen Domitilla's Christianity as another Roman attempt to appropriate the Jewish God. So Josephus mocks Theophilus, the supposed "lover of God" (Yahweh), by making him into Saturninus, a follower of Saturn, the false non-god who was the Roman idea of Yahweh.

The name Ida comes from the mountain of Saturn, which was the place of origin for the Jews according to these false Roman ideas. In the Paulina story, Ida comes up with the whole scheme of establishing Decius Mundus as the fake god. So Josephus seems to be equating Christians to the Idaei, the Romans' fake Jews who came from Ida. What is fascinating is that Josephus is satirizing the Jesus movement as being founded by a woman. He represents her as a former slave and cynical schemer who ends up being crucified in Rome. In the Rock and the Tower, I argue that Christianity was founded by the woman we know under the characters of both the virgin Mary and Mary the Magdalene. As a person of mature age, she moved to Rome in the 50s AD and was martyred by some form of crucifixion following the fire of Rome in 64 AD. Josephus visited Rome in 61 and returned permanently in the early 70s AD. It seems that he knew something of Mary.

Fulvia Paulina

We come back to the names, Paulina and Fulvia. Why would Josephus use these particular names in a satire whose target is Domitilla? One is a nomen and the other a cognomen, so we can combine them to give the full name Fulvia Paulina. The Fulvia were a well-established Roman gens. The most famous, not to say infamous, Fulvia was the wife of Mark Antony, who became a notable politician in her own right.

However, it is suspicious that "Fulvia" is so similar to "Flavia." Suppose Josephus wanted to choose a gens name that resembled Flavia without being too obvious. Looking at the gens that start with an F, there are a few possibilities:

Fabia
Fadia
Flavinia
Fulvia

Of these, the closest to Flavia is perhaps Fulvia. It has the same number of letters, it starts and ends the same way, and five out of six letters are identical and appear in the same order. There are several hundred different gens to choose from, so this close similarity would be a remarkable coincidence. We can deduce that Josephus has chosen Fulvia as a disguised representation of Flavia.

The name Paulina is the feminine of Paul, which is surely also no coincidence in a satire about Christianity. We have seen that Domitilla had the alternative cognomen Petronella. The author of Luke has two heroes, Peter and Paul: the Acts of the Apostles could more accurately be called the Acts of Peter and Paul. Josephus obviously cannot use the name Petronella, so he switches from Petronella (fem. Peter) to Paulina (fem. Paul). He uses Paulina in the first story because it would be too obvious in the second story about Paul. Putting it all together, we get:

Fulvia Paulina = Flavia Petronella

Or, to give her more familiar name, Flavia Domitilla

25

The end of the Flavians

Assassination

On 18 September 96, Domitian was assassinated, and the Flavian dynasty came to an end. Our best source for the assassination is Suetonius' Lives of the Caesars, and it leaves us with many questions.[1] The regime that succeeded the Flavians, the succession of adoptive emperors, lasted for a hundred years. Anything that challenged the legitimacy of the first of the line, Nerva, would also challenge the legitimacy of his successors. This applies particularly to Suetonius, who writes c.120 AD under the reign of Hadrian, the adoptive son of Trajan and adoptive grandson of Nerva. We get the sense that he is only telling us half the story.

Suetonius says that the plot against Domitian involved "his friends (amici), his most trusted freedmen, and his wife."[2] So he blames the emperor's own household for the assassination. He then gives an extraordinary catalog of portents and ill-omens before the assassination, showing that Domitian was doomed by fate and the gods. In his final days, the emperor had become paranoid and even had the walls of his porticos lined with a shiny reflective stone so he could see if anyone was creeping up on him.

As a result of his paranoia, Domitian executed Epaphroditus, his secretary in charge of petitions, because he had helped Nero commit suicide.[3] This is extraordinary on several levels. It was almost thirty years since Nero's suicide, and it would be very odd for Domitian to employ the same Epaphroditus as his secretary. He had been a freedman of Nero, and an emperor would have been expected to use their own family's freedmen. Epaphroditus would have been old, perhaps around seventy. The name is the same as Josephus' patron, although he is not necessarily the same man.

Suetonius says about Clemens' execution: "It was this deed in particular that precipitated his (Domitian's) assassination."[4] So he represents the assassination as connected to Domitian's action against Clemens and (as we will see) Domitilla. He gives a long series of omens that indicated to Domitian the exact date and time of his death. This is followed by a factual and more believable account of the deed itself.[5] Domitilla's steward

Stephanus approached the conspirators with a plan and was the chief assassin. Stephanus wrapped a bandage on his arm and put it into a sling for several days, pretending it was hurt. The bandages had enough room to hide a dagger. He then requested an audience with Domitian, saying that he had uncovered details of a conspiracy.

Suetonius presents this as being on the day predicted for the emperor's death. Domitian feared the fifth hour, between 10 am and 11 am, but was told it was already the sixth hour. However, he had been tricked by the conspirators—it was still the fated hour. Pleased that he had averted the predicted assassination, Domitian was going off to his bath when Parthenius, in charge of the bed-chamber (a senior official), told him that a man wished to see him about something urgent. So Domitian went into the bed-chamber where he found Stephanus waiting. The doors were closed behind them to give them privacy to talk.

Stephanus produced the evidence for the conspiracy in the form of a document. While the emperor was reading this document, Stephanus took the dagger from his bandages and knifed him in the stomach. Domitian was a strong man of forty-four, and he grappled with his assailant, dragging him to the floor. A boy attendant was also in the room, and Domitian called to him to get a knife hidden under his pillow and summon help. But the conspirators had removed the knife's blade, and the doors were all locked. Domitian struggled with Stephanus on the floor, attempting to wrestle the dagger from his grasp. Ignoring the cuts to his hands from the blade, he tried to gouge out Stephanus' eyes.

The other conspirators, waiting outside, heard the sounds of struggle and rushed in to finish the job. Suetonius says they were Clodianus, a centurion's adjunct, Maximus, freedman of Parthenius, Satur, a senior member of the bed-chamber staff, and an unnamed gladiator. Domitian was overwhelmed by these new arrivals and butchered by seven blows.

His corpse was taken out in secret, as if for a paupers' funeral, and was cremated at the suburban villa of his old nurse Phyllis. The intention would have been to leave him no monument. But Phyllis smuggled the ashes into the Flavian temple and mixed them with Julia's. This is perhaps the best evidence for a relationship between Julia and Domitian. But Phyllis had her own reasons as she had nursed both Domitian and Julia and wanted the two buried together.

All the conspirators named by Suetonius are fairly low-ranking imperial freedmen. Cassius Dio is our next best source, and he implicates more senior individuals.[6] He says that Parthenius was fully involved in the plot and was the one who removed the blade from the dagger. Dio is not certain whether it was Parthenius or his freedman Maximus who actually participated in the killing. Dio's list of conspirators differs in some other respects from that of Suetonius; he includes Sigerus, one of the chamber-lains, and Entellus, in charge of petitions. More significantly, he implicates the emperor's wife Domitia and the two praetorian prefects, Norbanus and Petronius Secundus, as all knowing about the plot. Dio also says that the conspirators had lined up the future emperor beforehand. They had approached two others who had refused because they thought their loyalty was being tested. The third man they approached was Nerva who agreed. Dio includes a rather ridiculous story about Domitian writing down a list of his future victims on a two-leaved wooden tablet that one of Domitian's naked boy attendants stole and brought to Domitia. We need not give credence to this particular story, but Dio's overall picture makes sense of events after the assassination.

Dio adds one other thing about what happened after Parthenius or Maximus rushed in as Domitian struggled with Stephanus on the floor:

> Thus not only was Domitian murdered, but Stephanus, too, per-ished when those who had not shared in the conspiracy made a concerted rush upon him. (Dio 67:17:2)

Here we encounter a significant silence from Suetonius, who does not tell us that Stephanus was killed. He says that several men rushed in to help finish Domitian, but not what happened to them in the immediate aftermath. Another puzzle is why only Stephanus was killed when at least four other people attacked Domitian. Why did the supposed bystanders not kill them as well?

There are other questions about Stephanus's role. It was a well-planned and coordinated attack with involvement at the highest levels. The plot-ters even managed to smuggle an armed gladiator next to the emperor's bed-chamber. So why was Stephanus sent in alone to do the deed? Why did the gladiator not lead the attack? If four assailants were ready next door, why did they not all join the initial attack? It is suspicious that only Stephanus died, and it suggests that he was not killed by bystanders but by the gladiator and the others who finished off the emperor.

The conspirators have the problem of explaining the assassination to the pretorian guard. The senate, the Roman nobles, and the emperor's household all hated Domitian. They wanted him dead. But the army loved the Flavians and even Domitian himself. The conspirators could not be seen to be Domitian's murderers. They needed a fall guy. Someone to take the blame while they seized power. They needed someone like Stephanus.

Nerva

What happened after the assassination was extraordinary. Nerva was acclaimed as the new emperor on the same day, the 18 September 96, with his election confirmed by the senate no later than the following day.[7] The speed by which Nerva assumed the purple speaks volumes about the conspiracy. Dio tells us that Nerva was in on the plot, which makes sense; it was all planned before the assassination. The conspirators could not leave the choice of emperor to chance. He had to be someone on their side and under their control. And he had to be prepared to move quickly, for everything depended upon speed and surprise: act before others had a chance to think.

Nerva was by no means a natural choice, being elderly and in poor health, but the senate would have been amenable to any reasonable candidate. This is clear from their reaction to the assassination:

> The senators ... were so delighted that they eagerly filled the senate house and did not refrain from attacking the dead man in the most abusive and ferocious outbursts, giving orders that ladders should be brought and his shields and images be torn down and dashed to the ground while they looked on, and finally they decreed that his names were to be everywhere erased and that all reminders of him were to be destroyed. (Suetonius, Domitian 23)

The fear of the Roman ruling classes during Domitian's reign and their relief when his rule ended comes through from Tacitus and Pliny the Younger. As for the common people, Suetonius says that they were indifferent. Unlike the elite, they were not in the firing line from Domitian's paranoia and had no reason to hate him. But the most striking divergence was between the views of the army and the nobles:

> His assassination was ... a source of gravest dismay to the soldiers who immediately called out for him to be deified and would have attempted to avenge him, if they had leaders. Indeed, this objective was achieved not long afterward following repeated demands that those responsible for the murder be punished. (Suetonius, Domitian 23)

Somehow the conspirators had managed to get the praetorian guard to acclaim Nerva as emperor. This could only have been achieved through deception, by presenting the assassination as the work of a single man,

Stephanus, who was killed in the attack. The praetorian guard would have been bribed by a monetary reward, a generous donative from the new emperor, but by itself, this would not have been enough. The key to getting Nerva accepted by the soldiers was the influence of the two praetorian prefects, Norbanus and Petronius Secundus. Dio says that both were in on the plot, although this is questionable for Norbanus.[8] Petronius Secundus played the vital role and emerges as one of the two masterminds of the conspiracy.

It should be remembered that the Flavians were a military family and had strong appeal to the army. Both Vespasian and Titus were distinguished generals. Even Domitian had taken to the field. More significantly, he had increased the soldiers' pay by a third.[9]

In contrast, Nerva was a poet whose chief claim to fame was exchanging homoerotic verse with Nero. As an *amicus* of Nero, he had even been an informer during Nero's reign. A rumor circulated that Nerva had been a lover of the youthful Domitian. Whether true or not, it suggests that the two were close during the period when Vespasian and Titus were in Judea. It is likely that Nerva was a relative of Otho and would have been able to protect the young Flavian while Otho was emperor.[10] He must have given some such service to Vespasian because he received the surprising reward of an ordinary consulship alongside the emperor in 71 AD—only the second, after Titus, of Vespasian's reign. And in 90 AD, he was granted the considerable honor of a second ordinary consulship with Domitian. He was now a respected elder statesman, which is why he was chosen by the group of Domitian's "friends" who organized the assassination. But there was little about Nerva that would have impressed the army.

If the plan was to blame Stephanus alone, it soon fell apart. In the chaos of the immediate aftermath the conspirators controlled the news flow. But it was inevitable that the truth would leak out. It would have quickly become known that several others had taken part in the killing. While the senate attempted to obliterate every last trace of Domitian, the army asked for him to be deified. And they were growing increasingly angry. They had been deceived, and they knew it. They wanted the heads of those who were responsible. According to Suetonius, there were repeated demands for the punishment of the killers. The army lacked leaders but finally succeeded.

If we only had Suetonius, we might think the minor freedmen who carried out the assassination were the target of the army's quest for revenge. However, Suetonius himself hints that he is only repeating the official version of events.[11] It seems that the senior conspirators sacrificed the actual assassins, but it was not enough. Dio gives us the full story. In 97 AD, there was a major rebellion of the pretorians led by the pretorian prefect

Casperius Aelianus, who had also held the post under Domitian. The
rebels were out for the blood of the leaders of the conspiracy:

> Nerva resisted them stoutly, even to the point of baring his col-
> larbone and presenting to them his throat; but he accomplished
> nothing, and those whom Aelianus wished were put out of the
> way. (Dio 68:3:3-4)[12]

The epitome by John of Antioch explicitly names the men: "Nerva was
forced to surrender Petronius and Parthenius, who were very dear to
him..."[13] So the army's targets were Parthenius, the senior freedman in
charge of the bed-chamber, and Petronius Secundus, the former pretorian
prefect. The epitome of Caesaribus adds the gruesome detail that while
Secundus was killed by a single blow, Parthenius was castrated and his
genitals stuffed into his mouth. The army was really not happy.[14]

Nerva's vigorous defense of the two men is one of the surest signs that
he had foreknowledge of the conspiracy. His failure to shield them was
a catastrophic collapse in his authority. Suetonius does not feel at liberty
to name the men, probably because this would implicate Nerva. But the
involvement of Parthenius is strongly implied in his account—it is he
who intercepted Domitian as he was going to the baths, directing him
instead to the bed-chamber where he met his death. Suetonius does not
even mention Petronius Secundus who was very close to Nerva. It is significant that although Suetonius avoids naming those punished by the
army, he accepts their guilt.

Ironically, Nerva is popularly regarded as one of the five so-called "good
emperors." But after the rebellion, his rule was a busted flush: Rome tee-
tered on the brink of a new civil war. Nerva was forced to adopt a military
man, Trajan, as his son and successor to appease the army. Nerva was
now emperor in little more than name and died shortly afterward on 27
January 98 from natural causes. Trajan was acclaimed as the new emperor.

Stephanus

We must return to the fall guy, Stephanus, and ask: why him? Dio says that
Stephanus led the attack because he was stronger than the others, which
makes no sense. Stephanus was not a fighting man but a steward who
would have been responsible for managing Domitilla's estate. Domitian was
strong and had received military training. Even though Stephanus got in the
first blow by surprise, Domitian still managed to wrestle him to the ground
and seemed likely to have killed him had the other assassins not burst in.

Suetonius gives a different reason; the conspirators did not know how to go about the killing until Stephanus came forward with his plan. This makes no more sense than Dio's explanation. The plot was very well organized and supported by a group of the emperor's *amici* and his own wife, Domitia. The plotters controlled access to the emperor and were able to get four assailants, including military men and a gladiator, into the room next to Domitian's bed-chamber. Such clever planners would not need to be approached by a steward to tell them what to do. There is one thing in Suetonius's account that is a significant clue; Stephanus was not one of the instigators but was brought in late to commit the deed.

As for Stephanus' motive, Suetonius says he was under investigation for embezzlement. It is the obvious charge, real or fabricated, that could be made against any steward. Even if Stephanus were in some trouble, it would be absurd to attempt to get out of it by killing the emperor. His best option would have been to keep a low profile and wait for the plotters to strike. Alternatively, he could have informed upon the conspirators to Domitian, who was known to be very generous to freedmen who betrayed others. Volunteering to strike Domitian, with the considerable risk that he would not survive, would have been insane. So Stephanus must have had a deeper motive than saving his own skin.

Suetonius is, once again, not telling us the whole truth. He does say that Domitian's action against Clemens led to his death. Stephanus must have been motivated out of loyalty toward Domitilla, his mistress. Their relationship is so strong that he is ready to die for her. This raises the fascinating possibility that Stephanus was a Christian.

Domitilla and her sons would have been alive at the time of the attack, for Domitian is never blamed for their deaths. Stephanus would have expected that Domitilla would return from exile after the assassination, and one or other of her sons would be declared emperor. As the boys were probably still adolescents, she would have been the effective regent while they matured. The other conspirators had no intention of letting this happen. No one could know how the young Vespasian and Domitian would turn out, and past experience was not good. The conspirators did not want another Caligula, Nero, or Domitian. Their aim was not to restore Domitilla but to end the Flavian dynasty for good. They would give power back to the nobles by selecting a mild, elderly, and ineffectual senator as the new emperor. Stephanus would have been told none of this.

This brings us to the real reason why the conspirators would have chosen Stephanus; he was Domitilla's steward. By making Stephanus the sole assassin, they were implicating Domitilla by association. She might be in exile, but everyone would believe that her freedman acted under her orders.

The plan would have been for Stephanus to attack Domitian while the other four waited in the next room. When Domitian was dead, the four would rush in and kill Stephanus in a display of grief and outrage. If Stephanus failed to do the deed, they would finish off Domitian while pretending to come to his aid and kill the steward at the same time. The tearful conspirators would then go to the Pretorian guard and tell them that Domitilla's steward had assassinated Domitian so that one of her sons could become emperor. The enraged pretorians would demand the punishment of the plotters and agree to the ascension of Nerva. The senate would be back in control.

However, no plan of engagement survives contact with the enemy. Domitian fought back far harder than expected: it required five men and repeated stabbing to kill him. There were too many witnesses, and it soon got out that Stephanus was only one of several assailants. The army realized they had been tricked into accepting Nerva by the masterminds of the conspiracy.

Domitilla

This brings us to the elephant in the room about which all our ancient sources are silent. Domitian had two adoptive sons when he was killed. Not a single source tells us what happened to the young Domitian and Vespasian. The pair were Domitian's acknowledged successors, and we would expect one or both of them to become emperor on his death. If they were too young, why does no source tell us that? And what was their ultimate fate? Adoption was taken very seriously by the Romans. The two boys would have been Domitian's legal children and heirs. And yet we hear nothing more about them. Our lack of knowledge about Domitian's sons is unprecedented.

The boys' problem was that they were friendless. Their father had been executed, and their mother was in exile. They had no close surviving relatives in any position of influence or power. The army loved the Flavians, but the boys had no one to present them to the Pretorian cohorts. We do not know their whereabouts at the time of the assassination. Were they in Rome, or was Domitian keeping them somewhere secure out of fear of rebel factions? We would hear from his army of detractors if he had them killed.

The silence speaks volumes about the boys' ultimate fate. The Flavians had been in power long enough to become a dynasty. The last survivors of that dynasty were Domitilla and her sons. They posed the gravest threat to the new regime of Nerva and Trajan. The history of the Julian-Claudian dynasty demonstrates that family members would almost certainly be killed sooner or later unless they became emperor. All three of Claudius' children were put to death by Nero: Britannicus was poisoned, and Octavia and Claudia Antonia were executed. Claudius himself only survived the murderous reign of his nephew, Caligula, because he had some kind of disability: Caligula had too much fun at his expense to kill him. The other family members were not so lucky, and Claudius was the sole survivor. Domitian also executed adult male family members, both Sabinus and Clemens. And he was very careful to keep close control over Titus' daughter Julia.

Dio says that Nerva brought back the exiles:

> Nerva also released all who were on trial for treason and restored the exiles …. and no persons were permitted to accuse anybody of treason or of adopting the Jewish mode of life. (Dio 58:1:2)

We would expect Domitilla and the boys to be explicitly mentioned if they were included in the amnesty. But it would have been foolish for Nerva to allow them to return to Rome while the army was on the brink of rebellion. The conspirators and their supporters had achieved power and would not give it away lightly. Domitian's wife Domitia was allowed to live out her life in Rome in peace, but she was involved in the assassination plot. Besides, as a childless widow in her forties and not even a Flavian, Domitia posed no risk.

Domitilla's sons were far more dangerous. They were closely related to three former emperors through both mother and father. And Domitilla herself was a Flavian and still of child-bearing age. Anyone who married her would have a good claim to be emperor.

Trajan, of course, was one of the "good emperors." In the correspondence with Pliny, he comes over as sensible, pragmatic, and reasonable. But we should not forget that he was a military commander who expanded the empire to its greatest extent. This expansion would have involved many thousands of deaths. Trajan, the soldier, would not have blinked to take what action was required to secure his rule. Better to kill a few individuals than risk a new civil war like the terrible year of the four emperors in which thousands of Romans died.

Dio reports that Trajan promised not to take action against any Roman without recourse to the law:

> When he became emperor, he sent a letter to the senate, written with his own hand, in which he declared, among other things, that he would not slay nor disfranchise any good man; and he

confirmed this by oaths not only at the time but also later. (Dio 68:5:2)

We only have this part of Dio's works in an epitome, an abridgment, so we cannot tell whether the placing of the following lines was deliberately ironic:

He sent for Aelianus and the Praetorians who had mutinied against Nerva, pretending that he was going to employ them for some purpose, and then put them out of the way. (Dio 68:5:4)

Trajan owed his adoption to the rebellion against Nerva. So Aelianus and the other rebel leaders must have been expecting some reward. Trajan, however, "put them out of the way"—implying that he had them quietly killed. The alternative interpretation that he made them retire does not explain why he would trick them into coming to him. Trajan's treatment of the pro-Flavian rebels is an ominous indication of the action he would have to take with the surviving Flavians.

Our only hint of Domitilla's fate comes from the Acts of Nereus and Achilleus, which has her killed at Tarracina on the orders of Trajan. The Acts is a fanciful text written four hundred years after events, but it has accurately remembered some traditions; for example, that Nereus and Achilleus were attendants of Domitilla. In the Acts, Trajan takes action against Domitilla and the other Christians for religious reasons, but the real motive would have been political. Tarracina was the Roman coastal town closest to the island of Pontia and also close to Pandateria. If Domitilla had been taken from exile to the mainland, Tarracina would be the logical place to hold her while Nerva dithered over her fate. At Tarracina, she could have been quietly "put out of the way" by the more decisive Trajan. Her sons would have either shared her fate at Tarracina or were dealt with elsewhere.

Is this too gloomy an assessment? The evidence is scant. An inscription may turn up one-day recording that Domitilla lived to an old age under Trajan or Hadrian. But from our knowledge of Roman dynastic succession, a happy ending seems unlikely.

It might be objected that if Trajan had ordered Domitilla or her sons killed, we would have heard something from our Roman sources. They are certainly not reticent about the dynastic murders committed by earlier emperors. But these accounts were written after the emperor's dynasty had come to an end. The so-called adoptive emperors ruled for a hundred years, with the reigns of Trajan, Hadrian, Antonius Pius, and Marcus Aurelius widely recognized as the pinnacle of the Roman Empire. Trajan was not involved in Domitian's assassination, and his rule was a great success. Before long, neither the army nor anyone else wanted the Flavians back.

So there was an excellent reason to keep quiet about any regrettable deeds that Trajan had to commit to secure the peace of the empire. The aim of historians under Trajan and Hadrian was to blacken Domitian. It was convenient that Domitilla had been exiled by him, for he could be held responsible for whatever happened to her. Held under guard in some remote place away from Rome, she was vulnerable. And no one would have wanted to know about her fate—except, that is, for the Christians who gave testament to her memory.

26

Stephen and Joanna

Stephen

Today the name Stephanus, meaning crown or crowned, is very common in Christian cultures. The popularity of the name goes back to the author of Luke. In Acts, Stephanus, "Stephen" in English, is the first Christian martyr and given more prominence than anyone other than Peter and Paul. (To avoid confusion, I will use "Stephen" for the character in Acts and "Stephanus" for Domitilla's steward, although the names are identical.) But did Stephen even exist? He is not mentioned in any early source outside Acts, and aspects of his story suggest that his martyrdom was invented to illustrate the early persecution of the church.

Stephen is a Jewish-Christian preacher in Jerusalem accused of blasphemy by Jews unable to refute his arguments. He is tried before the Sanhedrin, where he gives a long, defiant speech. Shocked by his supposed blasphemy, the Jews immediately drag him out and stone him. Although Paul (called Saul at this time) does not participate in the actual killing, he looks on with approval—the executioners lay their cloaks at his feet. After Stephen's death, a great persecution of the church breaks out led by Saul/Paul.[1]

The purpose of the story in Acts is to introduce Paul and provide the background to the persecution he confesses in his letters. Paul twice says that he persecuted the church in Judea, although he does not mention Stephen or give any details.[2] The Acts account of Stephen's trial is based on the trial of Jesus before the Sanhedrin in the gospels. Stephen's speech at the trial is also odd, with no explicit Christian elements until the end. He describes the covenant with Abraham, the story of Moses and the escape from Egypt, the building of the tabernacle, and then the construction of the temple by David and Solomon. We might wonder why he covers such basic Jewish beliefs before the learned Sanhedrin. He continues that even from the time of Moses, the Jews neglected the true worship of God and turned to the "host of heaven." He adds that God does not reside in temples of stone, so rejecting the Jerusalem temple. He then claims that his listeners, and their forebears, killed the prophets and "the righteous one" (Jesus), as well as disobeying the law, which he says was "sent by angels."

The author of Luke has access to a very early source for the first part of this speech, as it gives hints to the Israelite background of Christianity. (The interested reader is referred to my book, The Judas War.) The climactic ending comes straight from the Gospel of Mark:

> "Behold, I see the heavens opened, and the Son of Man standing on the right hand of God" (Acts 7:56)

Compare this to Jesus' words in front of the Sanhedrin: "...you will see the Son of Man sitting at the right hand of power and coming with the clouds of heaven."[3] As a result of this assertion, Jesus is condemned to death for blasphemy. Similarly, the Sanhedrin condemns Stephen for blasphemy in Acts and he is dragged out and stoned to death.

It all points to Stephen being a fictional character. Is it just a coincidence that he shares the name of Domitilla's steward? Domitilla was certainly ready to use people she knew in her narrative. She gives prominence to Agrippa's family, and the story of Felix has been crafted as a warning for Clemens/Theophilus. Agrippa, his sisters, and Felix were all historical persons involved in Roman-ruled Judea. But they do show how Domitilla would introduce people close to her into the narrative.

Stephanus must have been very close to Domitilla, for he was ready to sacrifice his life for her. Suetonius describes him specifically as Domitilla's steward rather than Clemens' steward. This suggests that Stephanus started as a family slave who served her before her marriage, and his Greek name indicates a slave or freedman. The two may even have grown up together. He would have been freed sometime after age thirty and given the very responsible job of steward. We may wonder if there was a sexual attraction between Stephanus and Domitilla. Acts' description of Stephen is suggestive: "his face was like the face of an angel."[4]

Stephen is introduced in Acts as the head of a group called the Seven. There has been a dispute between two factions of Christians in Jerusalem called the Hellenists (Greeks) and the Hebrews. The disagreement concerns the daily distribution of food for the "widows" of each group. To resolve the issue, the Twelve apostles make an announcement:

> So the Twelve summoned the multitude of the disciples and said, "It is not acceptable for us to neglect the word of God to minister [diakonein} on tables. Select, therefore, brothers, seven men from among you full of the Spirit and wisdom whom we will appoint over this task. [...] They chose Stephen, a man full

of faith and of the Holy Spirit, and Philip, and Prochorus, and Nicanor, and Timon, and Parmenas, and Nicolaus, a proselyte of Antioch. (Acts 6:1–3;5)

The task of the Seven is to administer the daily rations and serve at tables. Effectively, they are stewards. Which makes Stephen, who comes first, the head steward. The list of names in the passage above is probably purely imaginary. The real Seven seem to have been a group appointed to replace the Twelve when the movement was reorganized under the leadership of James. The gentile author of Luke turns the Seven into Hellenistic Christians, but in reality, most or all of them would have been Jewish Christians. Both the Twelve and the Seven "ministered" to the movement—the word used is *diakoneo* which usually means to supply with food and drink. But in the Jesus movement, the word had a symbolic meaning for the spiritual food and drink, the bread and the wine. The English word "deacon" comes from the related word *diakonos*, "one who ministers." The author of Luke makes the mistake of taking *diakoneo* in a literal sense.

Not only is Stephen a steward, he is also a freedman:

> Now Stephen, who was full of grace and power, performed great wonders and signs among the people. But opposition arose from what was called the Synagogue of the Freedmen, including Cyrenians, Alexandrians, and those from Cilicia and Asia. They disputed with Stephen, but could not withstand his wisdom or the Spirit by whom he spoke. (Acts 6:8-10)

We have no evidence for the existence of this Synagogue of the Freedmen outside of Acts. There were many synagogues in Jerusalem, including at least one for Hellenistic Jews.[5] However, the idea of a synagogue for freedmen in Jerusalem is odd because the freedman class was a Roman concept. A freed Jewish slave was just a Jew to his fellow Jews, and there would be no reason for such freed slaves to form a separate synagogue. In fact, all the members of this supposed synagogue seem to have come from outside Judea. A diaspora Jew might want to visit Jerusalem to attend feasts and visit the temple, but why would they join a synagogue?

The Romans, however, were very conscious of class distinctions, and a freedman would be most comfortable associating with other freedmen. Former gentiles might have felt out of place in an ethnically Jewish synagogue. We know from Tacitus that most Jewish converts in Rome came from the freedman class.[6] So, a synagogue of converted freedmen would make perfect sense in Rome but not in Jerusalem. It seems that Domitilla has based the supposed Jerusalem synagogue on a Roman example with which she was familiar. Which suggests that Stephen in Acts is modeled on Stephanus and that he was a Jewish convert before becoming a Christian. The dispute between Stephen and the other freedmen at the synagogue would represent the arguments arising after Stephanus converted to Christianity in Rome.

The crafty steward

If Domitilla has rewarded Stephanus by putting him in Acts, then he must have been a Christian. Did he assist her in writing Luke and Acts? This would explain a very odd parable, that of the crafty steward in Luke 16:1-9. A rich man has a steward whom he accused of squandering and wasting his possessions. He calls in the steward to give him notice of dismissal. If the steward loses his position, he will be in trouble—he cannot dig and is too proud to beg. So he comes up with a devious plan to get himself looked after:

> And he called in each one of his master's debtors and said to the first, "How much do you owe my master?"

> "A hundred measures of olive oil," he answered. 'Take your bill", said the steward. "Sit down quickly and write fifty."

> Then he asked another, "And how much do you owe?" A hundred measures of wheat,' he replied. He told him, "Take your bill and write eighty."

The amounts owed are substantial, equal to the annual production of a sizeable vineyard and wheat production from a farm some twenty times larger than an average family holding.[7] This is no Judean peasant landlord, but the owner of a great estate with many tenants running sizeable productive farms. It is the scale of operations of a rich landowner such as Domitilla.

The steward's idea is that by falsifying the bills payable by his master's tenants, they will look after him when he loses his job. The master's reaction to the fraud is surprising:

> The master commended the unrighteous steward because he had acted shrewdly. (Luke 16:8)

In reality, a Roman master would have been furious with a freedman who had cheated him like this. The gospel adds that the people of this world are shrewder in dealing with their own kind than the people of light, before coming to its conclusion:

> And I say to you, make friends for yourselves by the wealth of unrighteousness, that when it fails, they might receive you into the eternal dwellings. (Luke 16:9)

This train-wreck of a parable is trying to illustrate the principle that you should forgive others so that God might forgive you.[8] But by using the example of a corrupt manager who dishonestly forgives his master's debtors, it goes horribly wrong. The steward intends to gain a future benefit from these same individuals—a kickback. But the Christian principle of charity is that you forgive your debtors without any expectation or hope of reward in this world.

Perhaps it is a matter of perspective. A Roman steward would know that if he wanted to be forgiven for some of the things he had to do as part of his job, he would exercise forgiveness on those who came under his considerable power. It suggests a steward was involved in coming up with the parable. We should remember that Stephanus was supposedly under suspicion of embezzlement. Like the steward in the story, his accounts may not have been in good order. We could even imagine the germ of the parable arising from banter:

> D: "Your accounts are a mess! You are squandering my wealth. What would you do if I dismissed you?"

> S: "I would forgive your tenants half of their debts so that they would treat me well later."

> D: Laughing - "You are a clever scoundrel!"

Imagination aside, the crafty-steward parable points to Stephanus' involvement in Luke. A wealthy Roman would look for help from their trusted slaves and freedmen. A female Christian author would be working under a considerable disadvantage compared to a male pagan who could write openly and draw upon a circle of connections and acquaintances. She would have to be cautious about who she consulted, and her first choice would have been Christian members of her own household. A steward would be better educated than most slaves or freedmen and would be close to his master/mistress by the nature of his job. If Stephanus helped Domitilla, he might not have been the only one—the steward may have had a wife.

Joanna

Joanna appears twice in the Gospel of Luke. We first come across her as one of the women who accompany Jesus and support him financially:

> The Twelve were with him, and certain women who had been cured of evil spirits and infirmities: Mary called Magdalene, from whom seven demons had gone out, Joanna the wife of Herod's steward [*epitropos*] Chuza, Susanna, and many others. They were ministering to them out of their own means. (Luke 8:1-3)

She appears again at the resurrection:

> It was Mary Magdalene, Joanna, Mary the mother of James, and the other women with them who told these things to the apostles. (Luke 24:10)

Both times she is given a prominent place among the women followers of Jesus, second only to Mary the Magdalene. And yet none of the other gospels mention Joanna. The author of Luke seems to have introduced her into the resurrection narrative from nowhere.

We have already seen that the idea that Joanna, the wife of Chuza, could accompany Jesus is completely unrealistic. To be Herod's steward was a most senior role, and Chuza's wife would never be allowed to follow a vagabond preacher. Chuza, like Joanna, is not mentioned in any of the other gospels, nor do we have any historical information about him. In fact, we can be sure he did not exist. In the analysis below I am indebted to Richard Bauckham's summary of the evidence for the name, although I come to a very different conclusion.[9]

Chuza/Kuza means "jug" in Aramaic, but occasionally appears as a name. Bauckham's theory is that Chuza was a Nabatean and he cites the evidence for the name appearing in Nabatean contexts. An unfinished Nabatean tomb was built for "Hayyan son of Kuza." A roughly carved Nabatean inscription on a rock by a trade route could be a boast that one Muhaiyal had defeated a man called Kuza—or it might be a message left for a fellow trader that Muhaiyal had acquired a jug. There are two inscriptions in Old Syriac that mention a Kuza, and one of these may show Nabatean influence. So out of some 1,500 Nabatean inscriptions that are extant, we have evidence of at least one and possibly as many as three Nabatean individuals called Kuza. Bauckham confidently argues that the

Chuza of Luke was a Nabatean based on these examples. That does not follow: Aramaic was spoken over a wide area, and the name could have cropped up in many different contexts and groups. There is, in fact, an Assyrian record of the name that is not mentioned by Bauckham. Dating over seven hundred years before the first century, it records that a belt-maker called Kuza went mysteriously missing on a journey in Assyria.

But there is a more relevant piece of evidence than these inscriptions. Bauckham considers, and then disregards, a Jewish source that says that Chuza was the son of Pontius Pilate! This source is a genealogy of Haman in a targum on the Book of Esther, a Jewish romance from the Persian period. Haman, the villain of the Book of Esther, was the viceroy of the Persian king. He devised a plan to kill all the Jews within the Persian Empire but was foiled by the king's beautiful young Jewish wife, Esther. She intervened with the king who was outraged by the plot and ordered Haman to be hung. For the Jews, Haman became archetypal of the cruel overlord seeking their destruction.

The fictional genealogy traces Haman's origins all the way back to the Amalekites, hereditary enemies of the Jews from the book of Samuel. It starts with Haman and his father (from the book of Esther) and ends with the names of the two sons of Haman (also from Esther), followed by figures from Genesis, back to Esau. There is a list of thirteen ancestors between these two blocks of biblical names that do not come from any known source.[10] Kuza, the great-grandfather of Haman, is second in this block of names. The first name, that of Kuza's son, has been corrupted, and differs in various versions of the genealogy. The name after Kuza is Apolitus which has long been recognized as a barely disguised reference to Pilatus—Pontius Pilate. The genealogy is saying that Kuza was the son of Pilate!

Following this clue, scholars discovered other names in the list related to first-century Roman figures. A plausible case has been made for Fadus and Flaccus, procurators of Judea, for L. Vitellius, governor of Syria, and for the client kings Antipater and Herod. They all lived in the first century, in the period leading up to the Jewish war. There are differing suggestions for some names, and not all the identifications are certain. One problem is that many of the names have been corrupted in transmission, which shows that the Jews who used and copied the targum had lost the understanding of what they meant. It all supports the idea that the list of names comes from the first century when it was necessary to refer to the hated Roman overlords in a disguised code.

Bauckham thinks that the Roman names only started with Apolitus and that the two names before, including Kuza, did not represent Roman rulers. He sees a link between the name before Kuza and the names at the end of the genealogy which come from Genesis.[11] But this would not explain the name Kuza which does not relate to anything in Genesis. The natural conclusion would be that Kuza is the first of the Roman names, but Bauckham never considers this idea. Instead, he suggests that the authors of the Esther genealogy wanted to include a Nabatean name in Haman's ancestry and fixed on Kuza because "it seemed appropriate." To call this argument weak is an understatement! Bauckham's problem is that the Kuza of the genealogy is obviously not a Nabatean, which undermines his theory that the name is only found in Nabatean contexts.

Kuza does not end with the "os" that indicates a Latin name, but then nor do several other names in the Roman section of the genealogy. They all mean something, but not all are straightforward transliterations from Latin. The others are probably derogatory nicknames whose significance has long been forgotten. There is some evidence that the names closer to Haman were regarded as more wicked by the Jews. Pilate, the great-great-grandfather of Haman, is near the beginning. He was notorious for bringing the ensigns into the holy city and his vicious putting down of the aqueduct riot. In contrast, Vitellius, the governor of Syria, acted favorably towards the Jews and sent Pilate back to Rome for trial. He is much further away from Haman, second to last in the Roman section. If this is correct, then Kuza is someone even worse than Pilate. And if Bauckham is right about the name before Kuza, then Kuza is the first Roman name and the evilest Roman of them all.

The obvious candidate is Gessius Florus, whose massacre in the Upper Market Place set off the Jewish war—this suggestion was first put forward by H.L. Strack.[12] If so, then "jug" must have been an offensive term for Florus. Josephus tells us that the procurator suffered mockery from the Jews and that his sensitivity to their shouted insults triggered the Jewish war. Florus' corruption was at the center of these insults; the Jews collected bronze coins in a basket for him, as if for a beggar.[13] Most likely, then, the name Kuza refers to his avarice—the Jews' wealth was disappearing into the commodious Florus-jug. In the ancient world gold and silver coins were stored in ceramic vessels; Paul talks of holding treasure in "clay vessels."[14] And many thousands of buried ancient coin hordes have been found, invariably stored in clay jars or jugs.[15]

The two names that come after Pilate, Jos, and Josos, are also interesting. It has been proposed that Jos (Deus) stands for Zeus and Josos for Dionysus. But why would Jews incorporate gentile gods into a list of Roman rulers of Judea? Perhaps a double level of disguise was required for these two figures, with Zeus being Vespasian and Dionysus being Titus. Both Vespasian and Titus were deified, so the Jews would be mocking the idea of men becoming gods. Dionysus was Zeus' son and the god of wine, an appropriate fit for the playboy Titus. If this is correct, then the list must have been compiled after Titus' death and deification in 81 AD. Which means that Florus, the worst procurator of them all, would certainly have to be included somewhere. And if Chuza represented Florus, then the four individuals who start the Roman portion of Haman's genealogy would be the four Roman rulers who, above all others, had sought the Jews' destruction—Florus, Pilate, Vespasian and Titus. They were all fitting ancestors of Haman.

But if Chuza is Florus, then why does the Gospel of Luke call him Herod's steward? The word the gospel uses for "steward" is *epitropos*. Josephus and other Jewish writers use this exact same word to mean "procurator". In fact, Josephus actually calls Florus an *epitropos*. If Domitilla had come across a reference to an *epitropos* called Chuza, she would not have realized that this was the disguised name of a Roman procurator. She would have thought that the odd sounding name Chuza belonged to the steward of a local king.

So Chuza, Herod's steward, did not exist; he arose through a misunderstanding of a Jewish satirical source. This means that his wife, Joanna, is a fictional character. Why would the author of Luke introduce such a character? The example of Stephen suggests that Domitilla wanted to reward Joanna with a cameo role. The idea that the author would include people she knew in her gospel will horrify the biblical literalist, but that is where the evidence is pointing. Medieval patrons of religious art would have themselves painted within a scene giving homage to Jesus or the Virgin alongside apostles and saints. So perhaps the idea only seems odd to the modern mind.

What can we deduce about the real Joanna? The name is Jewish. In Luke, she is one of the women who bankroll Jesus, so the real Joanna must have been relatively wealthy. Joanna must have been very close to Domitilla to be written into Luke. And she was married to a steward. The most obvious possibility is that Joanna was Stephanus' wife. She may have been a Jewish aristocrat who came to Rome with Agrippa and Berenice. If so, then Stephanus, a freedman, would be marrying well above himself. But he had imperial patronage and we should recall the example of Felix, the freedman favorite of Claudius, who married three queens. Stephanus may have had to go the whole way and become circumcised before he could marry Joanna—we know that gentile men would consider circumcision to secure a worthy, and wealthy, Jewish bride. The couple would have converted to Christianity under Domitilla's influence.

Whether or not Joanna and Stephanus were really married to each other, they would have been Christians and close associates of Domitilla. They were written into Luke/Acts, suggesting that they assisted Domitilla in producing the two works. We are getting a picture of Luke and Acts as a collaborative production, led by Domitilla but drawing on the help of her most trusted clients.

27

Conclusion

It is sometimes said that the gospels were left anonymous because it did not matter who wrote them. This sentiment can only remain valid as long as the author is unknown. An anonymous author belongs in the realm of the general and hypothetical. Identifying an actual person brings us crashing down to earth into the particular. Any flesh-and-blood man or woman brings baggage, not least a member of the Roman imperial family.

Our only real hope for determining the author of one of the four gospels lies with the Gospel of Luke. We have seen the considerable evidence pointing to Flavia Domitilla, aka Flavia Petronella, as the author of Luke and Acts. If she were the author, it would explain many odd features, including the dedication to Theophilus, the indications of female authorship, the pro-Roman attitude, and the strange emphasis on Agrippa II and his circle. In particular, it is difficult to see any other way of explaining the Testimonium than that it was passed to Josephus by Domitilla.

On a personal note, it was the Testimonium that triggered my obsession with the author of Luke. It all started when I came across the paper by Goldberg setting out the structural links between the Testimonium and the Emmaus narrative. This became a hot topic online among those who discussed whether or not Jesus had been a historical person. The paper effectively eliminated the scholarly consensus that had ruled for so long; that Josephus had written something about Jesus that was then modified by Christian scribes. Most scholars ignored the paper, while most mythicists seized upon it as proof that the whole passage was a later interpolation. I was not so sure. Goldberg himself had rejected this conclusion and had made some good points. Was it really likely that a later scribe would follow the obscure conversation on the road to Emmaus so closely when interpolating into Josephus?

I was also influenced by a blog post that suggested that the source for Tacitus' account of Christ was the Testimonium. The evidence of links between Tacitus' passage and the Antiquities was convincing but led to a seeming absurdity. No Christian could have interpolated into Tacitus' copy, so Josephus' Antiquities must have contained a pro-Christian passage closely linked to a passage in Luke. Was Josephus a secret Christian?

It was intriguing that Luke/Acts was influenced by Josephus, and Josephus' Testimonium was influenced by Luke. I pondered ways of explaining this coincidence while still thinking that the Testimonium was likely a later interpolation. But nothing fitted. The evidence was dragging me to a more radical hypothesis that the author of Luke and Josephus must have known each other and belonged to the same circle. The author of Luke had given the Testimonium to Josephus.

In the meantime, I was forming a picture of this person who had written Luke/Acts. The evidence that the author was a woman was strong. There was the prominence given to female characters, the authorial lapses into a woman's perspective on events, and the rewriting of Matthew's nativity to make Mary the central character. I could not imagine any man inventing John's leap of joy in the womb as he recognizes Jesus. And the only explanation of the dedication that made sense was that the author was either married to the most excellent Theophilus or his mother or sister.

The author of Luke must have been living in Rome in the early 90s AD to have known Josephus while he was writing book eighteen of the Antiquities. This narrowed things down. However, we know absolutely nothing about most people who lived at that time, and it was unlikely that a particular candidate would ever be identified. Most positively, the author must have been someone important, of at least equestrian rank, so it was possible that some scrap of information had survived. It was worth searching for an individual, so I began looking and immediately came across Domitilla and Clemens. They fitted the profile perfectly. Yet it seemed absurd to suggest that the emperor's niece had written Luke and Acts, although that was where the evidence was pointing.

This was as far as I had got when I published The Rock and the Tower, which contains a strong hint pointing to Domitilla as the author of Luke.[1] The subject was originally going to form two chapters of that book, but I removed them because the volume was becoming unmanageably long, and it deserved more space. That was fortunate.

The great physicist Richard Feynman said that the acid test of a theory was whether it explained evidence that was not known when the hypothesis was framed. The Domitilla theory meets this test because some of the best evidence was unknown before I began working on this book several years later. The first piece was the fresco which I came across while researching the catacombs of Domitilla. Reading Schenk's analysis, the realization came that the fresco showed Petronella as the author of Luke. It was almost shocking to see the hypothesis I had been nursing in private for years appear pictorially before my eyes. But why Petronella? There were so many connections between her and Domitilla that it did not take long to work out that the name must be an additional cognomen. Everything now clicked neatly into place, including the relationship between the Petronella name and Domitilla's ancestor Petro. The sarcophagus was discordant but could be discounted as its existence was first recorded in 750 AD, and it could have belonged to any girl named after the early saint.

The second major piece of evidence was the satire that followed the Testimonium. I had not previously given these stories much attention, which is unsurprising because they were virtually never mentioned in discussions around the Testimonium. One exception was the writer Joseph Atwill who had drawn attention to the Paulina story in relation to his theory that the Flavians invented Christianity to pacify the Jews. It was an absurd conspiracy theory projected onto Roman history that relied on the type of far-fetched parallels that it is always possible to find between two large bodies of unrelated information. The more knowledgeable mythicists rejected Atwill's theories out of hand. Yet perhaps with the Paulina story, he was on to something.[2]

He was not the only one. Other more conventional scholars had also noticed that the stories seemed to be satirizing Christianity. Yet because it was difficult, even impossible, to explain how such a satire should follow the Testimonium, the idea was shrugged off. It was a phenomenon that I have come across time and again. The anomaly that does not fit the theory is the key to a greater understanding, yet it is precisely such unexplained anomalies that will be sidelined by the established experts. The anomaly puts the consensus at risk and must be ignored.

The Domitilla hypothesis, though, explained the satire beautifully. Josephus would have hated including the Testimonium in his Antiquities, and the satire was his revenge. It was not just aimed at Christianity, but at one individual and her husband in particular. The Domitilla theory was necessary to understand the satire, and the satire was the final evidence for the theory. Josephus had even craftily pointed to the target's name.

What then is the significance of Domitilla as the author of Luke? It impacts the controversy as to whether Jesus existed by removing two key pieces of evidence. Ironically, the Testimonium would be proved to be original to Josephus' Antiquities but could not be classed as independent evidence for Jesus' existence. And Tacitus' passage on Christ would be based on Josephus, so it could also be eliminated. This would leave no independent evidence for Jesus having existed as a flesh and blood man. (We can exclude Pliny the Younger's letter to Trajan, as it is evidence for Christians in the early second century but not evidence for Jesus' existence.)

The implications are less clear-cut than we might expect. Josephus and Tacitus were never the independent early witnesses that some made them out to be. Josephus was writing at least sixty years after events, and there is nothing in his or Tacitus' account that could not have come from the Christians of Rome. On the other hand, even if Josephus did not have first-hand knowledge of Jesus, that does not mean that Jesus did not exist. There were many religious sects and Messiah aspirants in Judea, and Josephus only mentions a few of them.

The idea that a woman wrote almost a third of the New Testament would have implications for the role of women in the church, but only if the established churches accepted the Domitilla hypothesis, which seems unlikely. The problem is that identifying the real author would destroy the idea that the gospels are authoritative. It would become embarrassingly clear that much of Luke and Acts are fiction. However, a book can be inspired literature without being literally true. The Gospel of Luke remains a beautiful work regardless of who wrote it.

Then there is the issue of Domitilla's family who were guilty of killing hundreds of thousands. Although both Vespasian and Titus adhered to the rules of ancient warfare, those rules were brutal. It was accepted that the massacre or enslavement of a whole city was a just price to be paid for a refusal to surrender. As emperors, they were both remarkably tolerant in their civil rule. Yet Roman society was inherently cruel even in peacetime, with crucifixion used to keep the slave population under control and thousands of gladiators dying in the arenas for the amusement of the populace. There is some evidence that Vespasian abhorred the killing: yet he was responsible for many deaths in war.

However, Domitilla did not command armies, nor was she guilty of atrocities. She was a mother of seven who was perhaps a God-fearer before becoming a Christian. Josephus may have satirized her as a foolish young woman, but he also regarded her as living a virtuous life even by Jewish standards. Christianity offered a stark alternative to the callousness of Roman society. In God's eyes, the life of a slave was as valuable as that of an emperor. The riches of the world were illusionary, with spiritual wealth being the only reality. The world was ruled by demons and evil angels who operated through the possession of human avatars. It was tempting for the Christian to fight these powers physically and politically, but if you did, you would become like them and fall under the angels' spell. The Christian must reject the rulers and their world but not offer any physical opposition or disobedience. It was a surprising philosophy for a member of the imperial family to embrace. Nothing could be further from the Roman respect for strength and contempt for weakness. And yet Christianity would conquer the Roman Empire.

Much of the success of Christianity was due to the heroism of the martyrs whose unflinching acceptance of death for Christ persuaded some Romans that there was something in this strange new religion. As Christianity gained more converts, the martyrs were increasingly revered for following in the path of Jesus even to death. The remains of these martyrs were hallowed and believed to have healing powers and other miraculous properties.

Domitilla was one of those martyrs. Under the name of Saint Petronella, the Christians of Rome kept her cult alive through the centuries alongside that of her faithful attendants, Saints Nereus and Achilleus. It seems she had a particular appeal among women. It is true that if she was killed on the orders of Trajan, this would have been for political rather than religious reasons. Yet it is certain that Domitilla suffered greatly for Christ. Her downfall was total, and she lost everything, including her husband and probably her family. Yet she also left an enduring legacy. Domitilla deserves to be remembered and acknowledged as the author of Acts and Luke.

Appendix A: The twin pattern in the Luke nativity

It has long been recognized that the Luke nativity stories draw heavily upon the Septuagint ancient Greek translation of the Hebrew Bible. We do not have to envisage a separate writer as this dependence can be explained by the subject matter. In this section, the author has the opportunity to innovate and draw upon their knowledge of the Septuagint.

The account of the childless couple, Zechariah and Elizabeth, who have a baby in old age, retells the story of Abraham and Sarah. Sarah is barren until God promises Abraham that his wife will conceive. Abraham and Sarah both laugh at this idea, but Sarah becomes pregnant and bears Abraham a son, Isaac, whose descendants will become the Jews (Genesis 17:1-22; 18:9-15). Zechariah also disbelieves the angel's message and is struck dumb. The major theme of the Abraham story is the covenant that Yahweh makes with Abraham and his descendants (Genesis 12:1-8; 13:14-17; 15:1-7; 18:9-15). Paul says that the Abrahamic covenant comes spiritually true through Christ and applies to the Christians, who will inherit the new earth (Romans 4:16-25; 9:6-9, Galatians 3:6-18; 4:22-28). The author of Luke has picked up on this idea and retold a version of the Abraham story. Paul talks about the two "seeds of Abraham." In Luke, the physical seed, the Jews, are represented by John and the spiritual seed, the Christians, by Jesus.

The Gospel of Luke alludes to more than the story of Abraham and Sarah. Mary's song of praise echoes the prayer of Hannah in the temple at Shiloh. Hannah was barren until Yahweh answered her prayers, and she conceived a son, the great prophet Samuel. When the boy was still young, she dedicated him to the service of God at the temple, as she had promised. The thanksgiving song seems more appropriate to Elizabeth than to Mary, but such swapping around is part of the style of the author of Luke. The nativity borrows themes and even phrases extensively from the Hebrew Bible, but everything is mixed up as jazz rather than logical exposition. The author of Luke is a poet and a novelist, not a commentator or historian.

The nativity is beautifully structured, with themes like threads woven

through the fabric on a Roman matron's loom. Twinship is the basic principle; everything is twinned with something else. Sometimes this is obvious,
sometimes subtle. The following shows the structure following the dedication up to the genealogy:

Family qualifications
Family of John's parents, Zechariah and Elizabeth. (Luke 1:5)
Genealogy of Jesus' supposed father, Joseph. (Luke 3:23-38)

An angel announces a coming pregnancy
The angel appears to Zechariah in the temple and announces that his
wife, Elizabeth, will give birth to a prophet to be called John. Elizabeth
becomes pregnant. (Luke 1:8-17;24-25)
The angel appears to Mary, telling her that she will conceive the Son of
God by the spirit. He is to be called Jesus. Mary becomes pregnant. (Luke
1:26-45)

Doubt (male) and faith (female)
John's father, Zechariah, doubts the angel and is struck dumb. (Luke
1:18-22)
Jesus' mother, Mary expresses her faith in the angel's message. (Luke 1:38)

The Holy Spirit
John will be filled with the spirit from the womb. (Luke 1:15)
The spirit descends upon Jesus at his baptism. (Luke 3:21-2)

Jesus to be born from the spirit
The angel tells Mary how she will conceive; "The Holy Spirit will come
upon you and the power of the most high will over-shadow you." (Luke 1:35)
The Holy Spirit comes over Jesus in the shape of a Dove, and God calls
him his Son. Some texts add; "today I have begotten you." (Luke 3:21-2)

John recognizes Jesus
John acknowledges Jesus in the womb. (Luke 1:41)
The adult John predicts Jesus' coming to the crowd. (Luke 3:15-17)

Hymns of praise
Mary gives a hymn of praise (the Magnificat) for her pregnancy with
Jesus. (Luke 1:46-55)
Zechariah gives a hymn of praise after John is born. (Luke 1:67-79)

Births
John is born. (Luke 1:57-8)
Jesus is born. (Luke 2:3-7)

Holy birth announced.
Angels tell the shepherds. (Luke 2:8-14)
The shepherds tell everyone. (Luke 2:15-20)

Circumcision and miraculous signs
John is circumcised on the eighth day. This is marked by the miraculous return of Zechariah's speech. (Luke 1:59-66)
Jesus is circumcised on the eighth day. This is followed by the presentation of Jesus at the temple, where Simon and Anna make miraculous prophecies about him. (Luke 2:21-38)

Time markers
There is a Roman-style time marker for the birth of Jesus; the census in the time of Augustus Caesar when Quirinius was governor of Syria. (Luke 2:1-2)
There is a Roman-style time marker for the commencement of John's mission, the fifteenth year of the reign of Tiberius Caesar. (Luke 3:1-2)

Teaching
The boy Jesus questions the Jewish teachers in the temple and then gives them the answers. (Luke 2:41-51)
John teaches the Jews in the wilderness. (Luke 3:3-14)

Typically, one item of the pair relates to John and one to Jesus, although this is not always the case. The second part normally follows shortly after the first, except for the beginning and end, which have a symmetrical, chiastic structure:

Ancestors of John's parents, Zechariah and Elizabeth
{Angel appears to Zechariah; John will be filled with the spirit.
{Angel appears to Mary; she will conceive the Son of God by the spirit.
John acknowledges Jesus in the womb.
Other twin pairs—not chiastic.
John acknowledges Jesus to the crowd.
The spirit descends upon Jesus, who is acknowledged by God as his Son.
Genealogy of Jesus' supposed father, Joseph.

The two angelic visits are paired with each other, but when taken together, they form a pair with the spiritual baptism of Jesus:

The angel tells Zechariah that John will be filled with the spirit in the womb. He tells Mary that she will conceive by the spirit which will over-shadow her.

At his baptism, the spirit descends upon Jesus (overshadows him) and God acknowledges Jesus as his Son.

The baptism ties up the loose ends; Jesus now has the spirit as well as John, and the spiritual birth of Jesus at the baptism completes the spiritual conception experienced by his mother, Mary. It is all very clever.

This chiastic structure resolves the problem of the apparently odd place-ment of the genealogy, which actually makes perfect sense. The author of Luke completes the nativity with Jesus' baptism, so the genealogy ends the section dealing with the birth of John and Jesus. The genealogy also bal-ances the family background of John in Luke 1:5 which starts the nativity account. It is the "same but different" pattern all over again; the author of Matthew precedes his nativity account with Jesus' genealogy, so the author of Luke follows her nativity account with Jesus' genealogy.

Appendix B: The long ending of Mark

The so-called long ending of Mark 16:9-20 records Jesus' resurrection. Although this is widely believed to be a much later addition to the gospel, we will show that it must actually be very early; it was attached to the gospel no later than c.80 AD and was available to both the authors of Matthew and Luke.

This appendix borrows heavily on The Rock and the Tower, Chapter 10. When I wrote that book, I was not aware of James Snapp Jr.'s excellent defense of the long ending from a traditional perspective. The sections here relating to the textual evidence and the church fathers owe a particular debt to Snapp's publication "Authentic: The Case for Mark 16:9-20." But all the opinions expressed are my own.

The case against the long ending seems at first sight to be overwhelming:

The language of the start of the long ending is more appropriate for the start of a new text rather than the continuation of the previous account. Also, the long ending seems to re-introduce Mary the Magdalene.

The language of the long ending is not typical of the remainder of Mark.

Matthew and Luke follow Mark closely until the long ending when they diverge from each other and from Mark.

There is a suspicious silence about the ending of Mark from most of the early church fathers.

Eusebius of Caesarea, writing c.320 AD, casts doubt on the genuineness of the long ending, saying that it is missing in most Greek copies of the gospel.

The best early Greek manuscripts omit the long ending.

There is an alternative "short ending" in some Greek manuscripts.

The cumulative case against the long ending seems insurmountable, and almost all scholars believe that the long ending was a much later addition. But almost all scholars can be wrong! If we take a more complete look at the evidence, we will find that it points to the long ending being part of Mark from a very early stage.

The supposed ending is not feasible.

This is the most obvious objection to the idea that the long ending was added later. It would mean that Mark would have originally ended immediately after the visit of the women to Jesus' tomb where they have seen an angel:

> And, having come forth quickly, they fled from the sepulcher, and trembling and amazement had seized them, and said nothing to anyone, for they were afraid. (Mark 16:6)

It is difficult to conceive a more unlikely end to an ancient text, particularly a gospel which was intended to persuade potentially skeptical readers of the truth of Christianity. We would expect Mark to end on a positive note with a strong affirmation of the truth of the resurrection. This is how the other three gospels end. There are two approaches to this problem among those who dismiss the long ending. As the above ambiguous and doubtful ending appeals to some modern tastes, the first approach is to regard the author of Mark as an ancient post-modernist. I think we can dismiss this idea as an unhistorical fudge!

The second approach is to assume that the original ending was lost and was replaced by the long ending. Although this is a more realistic solution, it greatly complicates matters. We now have to account not just for an added ending, but also for an ending which has somehow disappeared. And it rases the obvious objection: why has no copy of this original ending survived?

The evidence of the Greek manuscripts

What about the evidence of the Greek manuscripts of Mark? Surely the omission from the "best copies" proves that the ending is a later addition? The evidence here is normally presented in a very misleading way. It is common to find statements along the lines of—"all good early Greek copies omit the long ending." Or even—"the long ending only appears in a few, poor later copies of Mark." There are some 1,600 known early Greek manuscripts of Mark. So how many of these omit the long ending entirely? One thousand? Five hundred? One hundred? Actually, it is three.

Now it is true that a few copies have the so-called short ending. This "short ending" consists of a few lines summarizing the long ending and it is found in six copies. However, in these copies it is almost always followed by some or all of the long ending, so it is inaccurate to call it an ending.

There are also fourteen copies which include notes saying that some other copies omit the long ending. None of these notes suggest that most copies or the best copies omit the ending, and the majority positively support the view that the long ending is genuine. The idea that other manuscripts indicate the doubtful nature of the long ending by asterixis in the margin has been shown by James Snapp to be myth based on a misreading of lectionary marks in a tiny number of copies.

So why do the skeptics assert that all the best copies omit the long ending? The three copies missing the long ending include both Codex Sinaiticus and Codex Vaticanus, the two texts most esteemed by textual analysts. However, to say that these are the best surviving manuscripts is very different from saying that they are perfect. Both manuscripts are of the Alexandrian type which originated in Egypt. The dry environment of Egypt and the Levant has yielded the earliest manuscripts, so it is no surprise that the two best surviving examples come from this area. Although they are the two earliest complete copies, they only date from c.350 AD, at least 250 years after the gospels were written. That is plenty of time for them to have accumulated many errors and idiosyncrasies.

Textual scholars may give a high weighting to Sinaiticus and Vaticanus, but they take into account all surviving manuscripts in their reconstructions of the original text. Comparing the two Alexandrian manuscripts to their reconstructions demonstrates that there are indeed many errors in the pair. Their value for determining whether the long ending was initially attached to Mark is therefore limited. The third manuscript that completely omits the long ending is called 304 and is a relatively late medieval copy dating c.1300 AD. It would not attract much attention were it not for Sinaiticus and Vaticanus.

What about the short ending? Skeptics make a great deal about this supposed alternative ending, but it is easy to see what has happened. A scribe in Egypt has copied a text of Mark without the long ending, and has improvised by adding a few words summarizing the ending from memory. This text has in turn been copied by other scribes, but the long ending has then been added in part or full to these copies from intact exemplars.

While two of the three manuscripts lacking the long ending come from the same locality, the manuscripts including the long ending, accounting for over 99% of the total, derive from all over Europe and the full extent of the Roman Empire. Such an extraordinary wide distribution can only be explained if the long ending were attached to the gospel very early, before the gospel was copied throughout the Empire. Otherwise, we would have to imagine some way in which all those copies without the long ending could somehow acquire the ending. Perhaps a little imp with a pen flew thousands of miles adding the long ending to the copies which lacked it.

Was Eusebius of Caesarea the culprit?

What about Eusebius' statements that the text ended after the frightened women "in almost all copies of the gospel"? He wrote this in a letter to a Christian called Marinus and published it in a collection of letters known as "Gospel Problems and Solutions." Reading his words in context gives a more nuanced view. Eusebius is addressing an inconsistency between the Mark and Matthew accounts and offers two answers; one by a person who believes that "the accurate copies" omit the long ending, and then the view of a person who accepts the long ending. I believe that Eusebius prefers the first solution and is greatly exaggerating the number of copies missing the ending for rhetorical effect. But he prevaricates by saying that this is something that a person who doubts the long ending might claim, rather than saying it is actually true.

It is likely that Eusebius was also directly or indirectly responsible for the omission of the long ending from Sinaiticus and Vaticanus. Some have proposed that Sinaiticus was one of fifty copies of the gospels that the Emperor Constantine ordered Eusebius to produce (Eusebius, Life of Constantine, 4:36). Whether or not this is the case, it is certain that Sinaiticus was influenced by Eusebius because it includes one of his inventions; canon tables to help the reader correlate passages across the four gospels. These canon tables were very new when employed in Sinaiticus, indicating that the manuscript had some connection to Eusebius.

Vaticanus, which is slightly older, does not include a cannon table, but that does not mean that it was not also influenced by Eusebius. It dates from the later part of his life, or just after his death, when his reputation was at its peak. Eusebius was the premier scholar in the church and enjoyed the patronage of the emperor, so his views were authoritative. It has even been proposed that Vaticanus was manufactured at Caesarea where it would have been made under Eusebius' supervision or by one of his pupils.

It is thus a reasonable hypothesis that both Sinaiticus (certainly) and Vaticanus (probably) were influenced by Eusebius' theories as to the genuineness of the long ending. And there is evidence that this is the case because both codices show knowledge of the long ending. James Snapp has shown that the Vaticanus scribe left a space, including a blank column, exactly large enough to fit in the long ending. This is the only blank column in the entire codex other than a few required for production purposes such as the change from one scribe to another, or a change in number of columns on a page. It seems that the scribe was instructed not to include the long ending in Vaticanus, but disagreed and left enough space for it to be added later.

The situation with Sinaiticus is the opposite, in that the scribe went out of his way to ensure nothing could be added after 16:8. The final version of the end of Mark was copied by scribe D, a supervisor who was responsible for correcting the work of others. Not only did he drastically space out the preceding column to avoid leaving a blank column, he even executed an elaborate arabesque on the final line of Mark, the only such arabesque design in the entire codex. It was his way of saying "It ends here—add nothing more!"

So both Vaticanus and Sinaiticus show signs that the long ending was omitted as a deliberate editorial decision reflecting Eusebius' belief that it was not genuine. He must have had some reason for this conclusion and was doubtless aware of some copies that omitted the long ending. But it seems that he was the one who propagated the idea more widely and greatly exaggerated the evidence.

Eusebius' influence continued after his death and was responsible for many later commentators expressing doubt over the long ending. For example, in Jerome's published letter "To Herbia" he says that "almost all Greek codices are lacking it." This statement by Jerome has been highly influential. So how many Greek manuscripts did Jerome examine to come to this sweeping conclusion? The answer is none. Herbia's question and Jerome's answer are clearly taken from Eusebius' "To Marinus" which they closely follow. Jerome is a plagiarist who is just copying what Eusebius wrote on the subject

The testimony of Irenaeus

What about the supposed silence from the church fathers such as Clement and Origen? Absence of evidence is not evidence of absence. Just because someone does not comment on a particular passage does not mean that passage is not in their copy of the gospel. And the long ending was quoted or alluded to by many authors in the third century including Tertullion (195-220), Hippolytus (235), Vincentius (256), and the author of De Rebaptismate (c.258) (all these examples are taken from Snapp's book—he gives many more). And one of the earliest church fathers of them all was far from silent on the topic.

Irenaeus gives us the best possible proof that the long ending is early. In Against Heresies 3:10:15 he quotes word for word from the long ending as part of the gospel of Mark. Irenaeus writing c.180 AD trumps Sinaiticus, Vaticanus and the writings of Eusebius, which all date from 150 to 200 years later. He was the most informed scholar of his time in the proto-orthodox church. Aged about fifty when he wrote Against Heresies, he had been in the church since his youth. Irenaeus is not going to quote from an addition to Mark penned in his own lifetime. His evidence shows that the long ending was attached to Mark and widely accepted before c.150 AD.

The evidence of Irenaeus is so damaging to the skeptics' cause that they are forced to discredit it—unless they ignore it completely. It has been alleged that the long ending quote is an interpolation as our earliest copy of Against Heresies is quite late. However, the quote makes perfect sense in its context. And there are two pieces of further evidence which strongly point to it as being from Irenaeus. The first is that there seems to be another allusion to the long ending, although not word for word, in Against Heresies 2:20:3. The allusion cannot be accounted for as an interpolation and implies that the full quote is also genuine.

The second piece of evidence concerns a scribe called Ephraim who copied notes in the margin of the long ending in a tenth century manuscript designated 1582. His notes were copied from an exemplar which would have been produced centuries earlier. Indeed, the notes may go back as far as the fourth century. Ephraim's note states that Irenaeus quoted from the long ending in Against Heresies. It provides independent evidence that the text we find in our later copies is correct and that Irenaeus did regard the long ending as an integral part of Mark.

The evidence of Matthew and Luke

We can conclude that the long ending was attached to Mark before 150 AD when it was accepted without question by the church's premier scholar. But we need to go further and establish that it was present in the author of Luke's copy of the gospel c.90 AD.

I have gone through the evidence in detail in The Rock and the Tower (Chapter 10) and will summarize the arguments here. One method is to look at the resurrection accounts of the two gospels, Matthew and Luke, which use Mark as a source. All three accounts diverge and the skeptics think that this proves that the long ending cannot have been attached to Mark. But they are wrong! All the gospel writers are grappling with two contradictory traditions about the resurrection; (i) that Mary the Magdalene first saw the risen Christ and (ii) that it was Cephas who first saw him. They take different approaches to resolving the problem which explains the divergence.

To prove that the authors of Matthew and Luke did know the long ending we first assume the opposite; that it was not attached to Mark. Both authors would then have had at least two sources available to them— Mark ending with the frightened women, and Paul's statement about the resurrection in 1 Corinthians. We can reconstruct how the authors should have ended their gospels using these two sources: there should have been a resurrection appearance to Peter and the disciples in Galilee. This ending is certainty visible in Matthew, but that gospel also inexplicably introduces an earlier appearance to Mary the Magdalene and a companion. The Luke account diverges even more radically from what we would expect; it moves the resurrection to Jerusalem and has an appearance to two people on a road. By correlating the alterations both writers make to what they should have written we can conclude that they both used a third source which we can call LE (to take two letters at random). It turns out that LE is remarkably similar to the long ending of Mark. If the long ending did not exist it would be necessary to invent it. We would have to hypothesize something like the long ending to explain the Matthew and Luke resurrection accounts.

The frightened women

One other piece of evidence is that odd line in Mark 16:6 which is supposed to have ended the gospel; the women are frightened and tell no one. What most commentators miss is that this line cancels out the previous line in which the angel gives the women a task: he instructs them to tell Peter and the disciples that Jesus will appear in Galilee. But the women say nothing to anyone—meaning that they have disobeyed the angel's instruction.

Such a line only makes sense if it is followed by something else: its purpose is to explain why Jesus does not appear next to Peter. Instead, Jesus has to come first to Mary the Magdalene because she has failed to pass on the message to the disciples. The line provides a transition to the long ending but occurs even in the copies which lack the long ending. As these manuscripts copy the transitional line, they must be derived ultimately from manuscripts which did possess that ending. The same is true for those manuscripts containing the so-called short ending. So every copy of Mark that has come down to us is derived ultimately from a copy that had the long ending.

In the Rock and the Tower, I proposed that the long ending was originally a stand-alone text in existence before the Gospel of Mark. The author of Mark used this text as a source but ended the original draft of his gospel with the positive message of the angel. However, the long ending was then appended in full, together with the transitional line about the frightened women. This happened very early and was in all the copies that were distributed around the Roman Empire, including those used by the authors of Matthew and Luke. This explains why the language of the long ending is rather different form the rest of Mark and why the start is more appropriate for an independent text.

Acts and the long ending

Finally, we have the evidence of Acts. As I pointed out in The Rock and the Tower, the whole of Acts can be seen as one great elaboration of the words in Mark 16:14-20. Peter's speech near the beginning of Acts and Paul's teaching at the end are chiastic, and give effect to Jesus' command to preach the gospel to every creature, along with his warning that those who believe will be saved and those who do not will be condemned.

Then we have the specific miracles in Acts which match those in the long ending. In the Rock and the Tower, I saw this as part of the chiastic structure of Acts. In this book we go further and see how it is the "we" passages that copy the long ending miracles in the same order and using similar language. The person who wrote those "we" passages was certainly familiar with the long ending which must have been in existence before Acts was written.

Appendix C: Cerula and the Wedding Hymn

This appendix sets out the case for believing that the veil of Cerula in the Naples fresco (Fig. 6) is intended to be symbolic: the deceased woman is depicted as the bride of Christ using imagery from the Wedding Hymn in the apocryphal Acts of Thomas.

The Wedding Hymn is a beautiful piece that is undoubtedly older than the third-century Acts of Thomas within which it has been preserved. It celebrates the divine union between "the father of truth and the mother of wisdom." For an individual like Cerula, it would celebrate her mystical marriage with Christ. The Wedding Hymn describes the bride of the marriage, and several aspects correlate with the Cerula fresco. We will go through them one by one.

> In the crown of her head the king is established
> With his ambrosia feeding those who are founded upon him
> Truth is set upon her head.

The king, Christ, is established above the head of the bride. So on the fresco, the symbols indicating Christ, the staurogram, and the alpha and omega are set directly above Cerula's head. We find the same placement with Bitalia. This is very unusual for ancient images which do not normally have a symbol of Christ situated directly above a person's head. It continues:

> Her two hands signify signs and secret patterns, proclaiming
> the dance of the blessed ages.

Likewise, Cerula's hands are raised in the orans pose.

> Surrounding her, her groomsmen keep her, their number is seven
> Whom she herself has chosen
> And her bridesmaids are seven,
> And they dance before her.

This ties in with the top two rows of dancers on the veil. The top row does surround her because the dancers go all the way from one side to another. Seven dancers are in this row; the seventh is small and close to her left shoulder, but it is definitely there with a head and arm visible. In the row below, there are also seven dancing figures. These must be the bridesmaids. We cannot tell if the dancers are male or female because they are too small and simplified. However, there are two groups of seven, and the hymn explains why the figures are dancing. They are not celebrating a bacchic feast but the mystic Christian wedding. The hymn continues:

> And twelve are they in number that serve before her
> And are subject to her
> Their aim and gaze is on the bridegroom

There are another four dancers in the lowest row of Cerula's veil. Dancers also go up the veil on either side of her face. There are four on the right side, and there should be a matching number on the left, although these are indistinct. In total, we have twelve dancers in addition to the two groups of seven, corresponding to the twelve and two groups of seven in the hymn. We cannot say whether the twelve gaze towards the bridegroom, but those on each side of the veil progress towards the staurogram above Cerula's head.

More generally, the wedding is for the "eternal ones" who put on "royal robes" and are "arrayed in splendid raiment." Cerula is displayed in just this fashion. We should not be put off from this interpretation because her veil is similar to actual luxury items at the time. The artist will model symbolic clothing on the type of rich garment familiar to him.

Bibliography

Acton, Karen, *Vespasian and the Social World of the Roman Court* (The American Journal of Philology, Vol. 132 No. 1, 2011) pp. 103-124.

Alexander, Loveday, *Luke's Preface in the Context of Greek Preface-Writing* (Novum Testamentum, Jan., 1986, Vol. 28, Fasc. 1), pp. 48-74.

Allison, Penelope, *"Soldiers' Families in the Early Roman Empire"* in *A Companion to Families in the Greek and Roman Worlds* (Blackwell Publishing, 2011) Chapter 10.

Atwill, Joseph, *Caesar's Messiah: The Roman Conspiracy to Invent Jesus* (CreateSpace, 2011).

Barrett, C. K., *The First New Testament?* (Novum Testamentum, Vol. 38, Fasc. 2, 1996), pp. 94-104.

Bartman, Elizabeth, *Hair and the Artifice of Roman Female Adornment* (American Journal of Archaeology, Vol. 105, No. 1, 2001) pp. 1-25.

Bauckham, Richard, *Gospel Women: Studies of the Named Women in the Gospels* (T&T Clark, 2002).

Bell, Albert A. Jr., *Josephus the Satirist? A Clue to the Original Form of the "Testimonium Flavianum"* (The Jewish Quarterly Review, New Series Vol. 67, No. 1, July 1976), pp. 16-22.

Bisconti, Fabrizo, *"The Art of the Catacombs"* in *The Oxford Handbook of Early Christian Archaeology* (Oxford University Press, 2019).

Bosworth, A. B., *Firmus of Arretium* (Zeitschrift für Papyrologie und Epigraphik , 1980, Bd. 39) pp. 267-277.

Braconi, Matteo *"Figurative Imagery of the Deceased in the Catacombs of Domitilla in Rome"* in *Catacombs of Domitilla: Conservation in its Making* (Vatican City, Pontificia Commissione Di Archeologia Sacra).

— *"L'Arcosolio Di Cerula nelle catacomb di San Gennaro a Napoli: Prime inuizioni e recenti scoperte"* in *Campania Sacra, Rivista di Storia Sociale e Religiosa del Mezzogiorno Vol. 46-7* (Naples: Verbum Ferens, 2016), pp. 129-146.

Bruce, F.F., *The Book of Acts* (Grand Rapids: Eerdmans, 1988).

Butler, H.E., *The Institutio Oratoria of Quintilian* Vols I-IV (Loeb Classical Library, 1920-22).

Caragounis, Chrys C., *Peter and the Rock* (Berlin & New York: Walter de Gruyter, 1990).

Cary, Earnest (trans.), *Dio's Roman History Vols 1-9* (Loeb Classical Library, 1914-27).

Catholic Encyclopedia (New York: The Encyclopedia Press,1907-14).

Collins, Andrew W., *The Palace Revolution: The Assassination of Domitian and the Accession of Nerva* (Phoenix, Vol 63 No 1/2, 2009) pp. 73-106.

Crook, John A., *Titus and Berenice* (The American Journal of Philology, 1951, Vol. 72, No. 2, 1951), pp. 162-175.

D'Ambra, Eve, *Mode and Model in the Flavian Female Portrait* (American Journal of Archaeology Vol. 117 No. 4, 2013), pp. 511-525.

Denzey, Nicola, *The Bone Gatherers: The Lost Worlds of Early Christian Women* (Boston: Beacon Press, 2007).

Du Plessis, I. I., *Once More: The Purpose of Luke's Prologue (Lk I 1-4)* (Novum Testamentum, Vol. 16, Fasc. 4, 1974), pp. 259-271.

Ehrman, Bart D., *Lost Christianities: The Battles for Scripture and Faiths we Never Knew* (New York: Oxford University Press, 2003).

Louis H. Feldman, *Loeb Classical Library: Josephus Jewish Antiquities* (Cambridge, Massachusetts: Harvard University Press, 1965).

Frere, S. S. et al., *The Roman Fortress at Longthorpe* (Britannia, 1974, Vol. 5) pp. 1-129.

Fyfe, W.H. (trans.) and Levene, D.S., *Tacitus: The Histories* (Oxford: Oxford University Press).

Gallivan, Paul, *The Fasti for A.D. 70-96* (The Classical Quarterly, Vol. 31, No. 1, 1981) pp. 186-220.

Gambash, Gil, *To Rule a Ferocious Province: Roman Policy and the Aftermath of the Boudican Revolt* (Britannia Vol. 43, 2012) pp. 1-15.

Goldberg, Gary J., *The Coincidences of the Emmaus Narrative of Luke and the Testimonium of Josephus* (The Journal for the Study of the Pseudepigrapha 13, 1995) pp. 59-77.

Goodson, Caroline, *"To be the daughter of Saint Peter: S. Petronella and forging the Franco-Papal Alliance"* in *Three Empires, Three Cities: Identity, Material Culture and Legitimacy in Venice, Ravenna and Rome 750-1000* (Turnhout, Belgium: Brepols, 2015), pp. 159-184.

Green, Joel B., *The Gospel of Luke* (Grand Rapids: Eerdmans, 1997).

Gummere, Richard M., *Seneca Ad Lucilium Epistulae Morales* (Loeb Classical Library, 1925).

Herrin, Judith, *Ravenna: Capital of Empire, Crucible of Europe* (London: Allen Lane, 2020).

Hughes, Margaret, *Boudica's Last Battle: The Mancetter Candidacy* (academia.edu).

—*The site of Boudica's Last Battle* (academia.edu, 2013).

Jones, Brian W., *The Emperor Domitian* (London & New York: Routledge, 1993)

Keresztes, Paul, *The Jews, the Christians, and Emperor Domitian* (Vigiliae Christianae, Vol. 27, No. 1, 1973) pp. 1-28.

de Kleijn, Gerda, C. *Licinius Mucianus, Vespasian's Co-ruler in Rome* (Mnemosyne, Fourth Series, Vol. 66, Fasc. 3, 2013) pp. 433-459.

Knudsen, Johannes, *The Lady and the Emperor: A Study of the Domitian Persecution* (Church History, Vol. 14, No. 1, 1945) pp. 17-32.

Lampe, Peter, *From Paul to Valentinus: Christians in Rome in the First Two Centuries* (Minneapolis: Fortress Press, 2003).

Laurie, S.P., *The Rock and the Tower* (London: Hypostasis, 2016).

— *The Thomas Code: Solving the Mystery of the Gospel of Thomas* (London: Hypostasis, 2018).

— *The Judas War: How an Ancient Betrayal Gave Rise to the Christ Myth* (London: Hypostasis, 2020).

Lightfoot, J.B., *"Clement the Doctor", Introduction to S. Clement of Rome, Apostolic Fathers Part I Vol. I.* (London and New York; Macmillan and Co., 1890).

Mancinelli, Fabrizio, *The Catacombs of Rome and the Origins of Christianity* (Firenze: Scala, 1998) pp. 25-7.

Mason, Steve, *Josephus and the New Testament*, 2nd Ed. (Peabody, Massachusetts, 2003).

McWhirr, Alan, *The Early Military History of the Roman East Midlands* (Reprinted from Transactions of the Leicestershire Archaeological and Historical Society, 1969, Volume XLV).

Morgan, M. Gwyn, *Vespasian and the Omens in Tacitus "Histories" 2.78* (Phoenix , Vol. 50 No. 1, 1996) pp. 41-55.

Myers, E.A., *The Ituraeans and the Roman Near East: Reassessing the Sources* (Cambridge: Cambridge University Press, 2010)

Nicolai, Vincenzo Fiocchi *"The Catacombs" in The Oxford Handbook of Early Christian Archaeology* Ed. Caraher, Davis, and Pettegrew (Oxford University Press, 2019).

Noble, Joshua, *Common Property and the Golden Age Myth in the Book of Acts* (Online article in The Bible and Interpretation, 2020)

— *Common Property, the Golden Age, and Empire in Acts 2:42-47 and 4:32-45* (London: T&T Clark, 2021).

Northcote, J. Spencer and Brownlow, W.R., *Roma Sotterranea, Some Account of the Roman Catacombs* (London: Longmans, Green, Reader and Dyer, 1869).

Pearse, Roger (Ed.), *Eusebius of Caesarea: Gospel Problems and Solutions* (Ipswich: Chieftain Publishing, 2010).

Pergola, Philippe, *Christian Rome: Early Christian Rome Catacombs and Basilicas* (Rome, Vision S.R.L., 2000).

Pervo, Richard I., *"The Acts of Nereus and Achilleus, A New Translation and Introduction" in New Testament Apocrypha: More Noncanonical Scriptures Vol. 2*, Tony Burke Ed. (Grand Rapids: Eerdmans, 2020) pp. 241-63.

Power, Tristan, *Suetonius' Tacitus* (The Journal of Roman Studies, Vol. 104, 2014) pp. 205-225.

Ramsay, G.G. (trans.), *Juvenal and Persius* (Loeb Classical Library, 1918).

Rolfe, J.C. (trans.), *Suetonius*, Vols. 1-2 (Loeb Classical Library, 1914-20).

De Rossi, Cav. Giovanni Battista, *Bullettino Di Archeologia Christiana* (Rome, 1865; 1874; 1875; 1878; 1879).

Saghy, Marianne, *Pope Damascus and the Beginnings of Roman Hagiography* (academia.edu).

Salway, Benet, *What's in a Name? A Survey of Roman Onomastic Practice from c. 700 B.C. to A.D. 700* (The Journal of Roman Studies, Vol. 84, 1994), pp. 124-145.

Salway, Peter, *Roman Britain* (Oxford: Oxford University Press, 1981).

Saydon, P.P., *The Order of the Gospels* (Scripture 4 No 7, July 1950), pp. 190-6.

Scheidel, Walter, *Emperors, Aristocrats, and the Grim Reaper: Towards a Demographic Profile of the Roman Elite* (The Classical Quarterly , 1999, Vol. 49, No. 1) pp. 254-281.

Schellenberg, Ryan S., *The First Pauline Chronologist? Paul's Itinerary in the Letters and in Acts* (Journal of Biblical Literature, Vol. 134, No. 1, 2015) pp. 193-213.

Schneemelcher, Wilhelm, *"The Acts of Peter" in New Testament Apocrypha Vol. 2* (Westminster: John Knox press, 1989, English trans. 1992) pp. 271-321.

Schenk, Christine, *Crispina and her Sisters: Women and Authority in Early Christianity* (Minneapolis, Fortress Press, 2017) pp.147-157.

Smallwood, E. Mary, *Domitian's Attitude toward the Jews and Judaism* (Classical Philology, Vol. 51, No. 1, 1956) pp. 1-13.

Smith, Robinson, *Fresh Light on the Synoptic Problem; Josephus a Lukan Source* (The American Journal of Theology, Vol. 17, No. 4, 1913) pp. 614-621.

Snapp, James Jr., *Authentic: The Case for Mark 16:9-20* (Kindle, 2016)

Strack, Hermann L., *Jesus die Haretiker und die Christen* (Leipzig: J.C. Hinrich'sche Buchhandlung, 1910)

Townend, Gavin, *Some Flavian Connections* (The Journal of Roman Studies, 1961, Vol. 51, Parts 1 and 2) pp. 54-62.

Vinson, Martha P., *Domitia Longina, Julia Titi, and the Literary Tradition* (Historia: Zeitschrift für Alte Geschichte , Bd. 38, H. 4, 1989), pp. 431-450.

Weaver, P. R. C., *Epaphroditus, Josephus, and Epictetus* (The Classical Quarterly, Vol. 44, No. 2, 1994) pp. 468-479.

Webster, Graham, *Boudica: The British Revolt Against Rome AD. 60* (Routledge, 1978).

Williams, Margaret H., *Domitian, the Jews and the 'Judaizers': A Simple Matter of Cupiditas and Maiestas?* (Historia: Zeitschrift für Alte Geschichte, Bd. 39, H. 2, 1990) pp. 196-211.

Wood, Susan, *Who Was Diva Domitilla? Some Thoughts on the Public Images of the Flavian Women* (American Journal of Archaeology Vol. 114, No. 1, Jan 2010) pp. 45-5.

Yardley, J.C. (trans.), Barrett, Anthony A. (intro. and notes), *Tacitus: The Annals* (Oxford World Classics, 2008).

Notes

Chapter 1

1   The best account of the rebellion is Tacitus Annals 14:29-37 which is the source for most of the details in this section.
2   Cassius Dio 62:2:1-3.
3   Tacitus, Annals 14: 29-30.
4   Tacitus, Annals 31.
5   Cassius Dio 62:2:1.
6   S. S. Frere et al, The Roman Fortress at Longthorpe (Britannia , 1974, Vol. 5) pp. 38-9.
7   The Ninth would be made up to full strength again from among two thousand legionaries sent to Britain from Germany after the rebellion.
8   Tacitus, Annals, 14:32.
9   Tacitus, Annals, 14:33.
10 Tacitus Annals 14:33.
11 Gavin Townend, Some Flavian Connections (The Journal of Roman Studies, 1961, Vol. 51, Parts 1 and 2) pp. 58-59.
12 That Vespasian and his elder brother Sabinus were the only surviving siblings is clear from Suetonius, Vespasian 1. The story in Vespasian 5 records that Vespasian's mother had three children including a girl who died in infancy. Vespasian's own three children are named in Vespasian 3.
13 See Walter Scheidel, Emperors, Aristocrats, and the Grim Reaper: Towards a Demographic Profile of the Roman Elite (The Classical Quarterly , 1999, Vol. 49, No. 1) pp. 273-9 for the fertility of Roman marriages and the extraordinary variation between couples. Because of this variation, an estimate of Domitilla's age based on the number of her children is subject to wide uncertainty. One later empress, Faustina the Younger, had seven children before she was twenty-five although these included at least two sets of twins. She is, however, the most fertile example in 600 years. An average of a child every two years is more typical of imperial couples with large families. If Domitilla gave birth at this rate she could have been as young as thirty at the time of the death of her husband assuming that the first child was born when she was around seventeen. Most aristocratic Roman marriages had a much lower birth rate. The average for senator's wives was only around five births over twenty-five years of child-bearing age.
14 This theory was put forward by Gavin Townend, Some Flavian Connections (The Journal of Roman Studies, 1961, Vol. 51, Parts 1 and 2) p. 58 n.16.
15 Suetonius, Titus 4.

16   Cassius Dio 61:30:1.
17   A. B. Bosworth, Firmus of Arretium (Zeitschrift für Papyrologie und
      Epigraphik , 1980, Bd. 39) pp. 267-277.
18   Bosworth, p.276 n.35.
19   See chapter 15 for a discussion of this issue. If Rufus did not exist then
      Firmus would have to be Cerialis' oldest surviving son which makes it all
      the odder that he did not share one or more of his father's names.
20   The date of the founding of the Lincoln fortress is uncertain, but it seems to
      have been occupied in the late 50s and certainly no later than c.60 AD. See
      Alan McWhirr, The Early Military History of the Roman East Midlands
      (Reprinted from Transactions of the Leicestershire Archaeological and
      Historical Society, 1969, Volume XLV) pp. 8-10.
21   See Penelope Allison, "Soldiers' Families in the Early Roman Empire" in
      A Companion to Families in the Greek and Roman Worlds (Blackwell
      Publishing, 2011, Chapter 10) pp.161-82.
22   Penelope Allison, "Soldiers' Families in the Early Roman Empire" pp. 169-72.
23   Tacitus, Annals 14:34.
24   Peter Salway, Roman Britain (Oxford: Oxford University Press, 1981) pp.119-20.
25   Tacitus, Annals 14:37; Cassius Dio 62:12:6.
26   The Mancetter theory was first put forward by Graham Webster in
      Boudica: The British Revolt Against Rome AD60 (Routledge, 1978) p.97;
      111 f. Margaret Hughes gives a summary of the Mancetter and alternative
      theories in The site of Boudica's Last Battle (academia.edu, 2013) and
      Boudica's Last Battle: the Mancetter candidacy (academia.edu).

Chapter 2

1   Irenaeus, Against Heresies 3:9.
2   Revelation's four creatures are a development of Ezekiel 1:10.
3   S.P. Laurie, The Thomas Code: Solving the Mystery of the Gospel of
      Thomas (London: Hypostasis, 2018).
4   Augustine of Hippo, The Harmony of the Gospels (1:2:3-4).
5   The two-source hypothesis was first formulated in 1838 by the German
      scholar Christian Weisse. The symbol "Q" was given to the sayings source
      by a later scholar, Johannes Weisse.
6   S. P. Laurie, The Rock and the Tower, (London: Hypostasis, 2016) pp. 87-90.
7   Juvenal 6:185-8.
8   Joel B. Green, The Gospel of Luke (Grand Rapids: Eerdmans, 1997) p.8.

Chapter 3

1   Suetonius, Vespasian 1.
2   Suetonius, Vespasian 2.
3   Suetonius, Vespasian 2.
4   Brian W. Jones, The Emperor Domitian (London & New York: Routledge,
      1993), p. 3.

5   Suetonius, Vespasian 3.
6   Suetonius, Claudius 29; 38; 41-2 3.
7   Suetonius, Claudius 28; Vespasian 4.
8   Peter Salway, Roman Britain pp.70-94. Our main ancient sources for the invasion are Suetonius Claudius 17; Vespasian 4, and Cassius Dio 60:19:1-60:22:2.
9   Suetonius, Vespasian 4.
10 The main source for Messalina's "marriage" to Silius is Tacitus, Annals 11:26-38. See also Suetonius, Claudius 26, and Dio 61:31:1-5.
11 Tacitus, Annals 12:1-9.
12 Tacitus, Annals 12:25-26; 58.
13 Tacitus, Annals 12:66-69.
14 Suetonius, Vespasian 4; Tacitus Annals 13:2.
15 Tacitus Annals 13:45-46.
16 Tacitus Annals 14:1-8.
17 Tacitus Histories 2:97; Suetonius Vespasian 4.
18 Tacitus, Annals 16:4-5; Suetonius, Nero 23-24; Vespasian 4.
19 Suetonius, Vespasian 4.
20 Suetonius, Vespasian 14.
21 Benet Salway, What's in a Name? A Survey of Roman Onomastic Practice from c. 700 B.C. to A.D. 700 (The Journal of Roman Studies, Vol. 84, 1994), pp. 130-3.
22 As suggested by Gavin Townend. Some Flavian Connections (The Journal of Roman Studies, 1961, Vol. 51, Parts 1 and 2) p. 58 n.15.

Chapter 4

1   Loveday Alexander, Luke's Preface in the Context of Greek Preface-Writing (Novum Testamentum, Jan., 1986, Vol. 28, Fasc. 1), pp. 48-74.
2   For a discussion of Alexander's hypothesis, see Joel B. Green, The Gospel of Luke (Grand Rapids: Eerdmans, 1997) pp. 4-5.
3   Antiquities 17:78; 18:123; 19:297; 20:223. Against Apion I:216.
4   Acts 23:26; 24:3; 26:25.
5   Applied to Mettius Modestus in Pliny the Younger, Letters 1.5.
6   Tacitus, Annals 15:44.
7   Pliny the Younger, Letters 10.96-7.
8   Tacitus, Annals 13:32.

Chapter 5

1   The account of Nero's end is given in Suetonius, Nero 40-49.
2   Suetonius, Galba 11.
3   Titus Vinius and Cornelius Laco, along with a freedman Icelus. Tacitus, Histories 1:6; 13; Suetonius, Galba 14.
4   Suetonius Galba 11; Tacitus Histories 1:6.
5   Suetonius, Galba 16.
6   Suetonius, Galba 16; Tacitus, Histories 1:12.

7   Suetonius, Galba 17; Tacitus, Histories 1:14-16.
8   Tacitus, Histories 1:27; Suetonius, Galba 19.
9   Tacitus, Histories 1:34-35.
10   Tacitus, Histories 1:40-44;48; Suetonius, Galba 19-20.
11   Tacitus, Histories 1:50-57; Suetonius, Otho 8; Vitellius 7-8.
12   Tacitus, Histories 1:61.
13   Tacitus, Histories 1:76.
14   Tacitus, Histories 2:11-26.
15   Tacitus, Histories 2:27-31.
16   Tacitus, Histories 2:32-33; 39-45.
17   Tacitus, Histories 2:46-49, Suetonius, Otho 10-11.
18   Suetonius, Vitellius 10;14.
19   Tacitus, Histories 2:1-7; 74-78.
20   Tacitus, Histories 2:74; 85; 96.
21   Tacitus, Histories 2:79-86.
22   Tacitus, Histories 2:97-98.
23   Tacitus, Histories 2:82.
24   Tacitus, Histories 2:86.
25   Tacitus, Histories 3:2.
26   Tacitus, Histories 2:99-101.
27   Tacitus, Histories 3:12-15.
28   Tacitus, Histories 3:15-18.
29   Tacitus, Histories 3:23-25.
30   Tacitus, Histories 3:26-34.
31   Tacitus, Histories 3:40-44;62.
32   Tacitus, Histories 3:59.
33   Tacitus, Histories 3:63-65.
34   Tacitus, Histories 3:59.
35   Tacitus, Histories 3:59.
36   Tacitus, Histories 3:67-69.
37   Tacitus, Histories 3:78-79.
38   Tacitus, Histories 3:71-74, Suetonius, Domitian 1.
39   Tacitus, Histories 3:82.
40   Tacitus, Histories 3:83-85.
41   Tacitus, Histories 4:2-4, Suetonius, Domitian 1.

Chapter 6

1   Luke 1:42.
2   Steve Mason, Josephus and the New Testament, 2nd Ed. (Peabody,
       Massachusetts, 2003) pp.273-77, Louis H. Feldman, Loeb Classical Library:
       Josephus Jewish Antiquities Books 18-19 (Cambridge, Massachusetts:
       Harvard University Press, 1965) p.2 n. a.
3   Luke 2:16.
4   Luke 2:19.
5   Luke 2:35.
6   Luke 2:15.

7   Tertullian, Against Marcion 1:30;3:6;4:4.
8   For an overview of Marcion see Ehrman, Bart D., Lost Christianities:
    The Battles for Scripture and Faiths we Never Knew (New York: Oxford
    University Press, 2003) p.p.103-9.
9   Tertullian, Against Marcion, 4:7.
10 Tertullian, Against Marcion, 4:4-6.
11 Tertullian, Against Marcion, 4:4.
12 Tertullian, Against Marcion, 4:2.
13 Tertullian, Against Marcion 4:2.

Chapter 7

1   Josephus, The Life 14-16. I have added a little color to Josephus' brief
    account.
2   Josephus, The Life 13; 16.
3   Tacitus, Annals 14:60-4; Suetonius, Nero 35.
4   Tacitus, Annals 13:45-6, Suetonius, Otho 3.
5   2 Corinthians 11:24-25.
6   Josephus, The Life 5.
7   Josephus, The Life 414-5.
8   Josephus, The Life 416; 426-7.
9   Josephus, The Life, 1-5. There are gaps between generations of 65 years
    (Matthias Curtus and Joseph) and 76 years (Joseph and Josephus' father
    Matthias). This indicates that at least two generations have been omitted.
    Josephus has either suppressed or is unaware of the names of some of his
    ancestors, including his grandfather.
10 Josephus, The Life 6.
11 Josephus, The Life 9-12.
12 Antiquities 20:97-98.
13 Jewish War 2:261-263, Antiquities 20:167-172.
14 Jewish War 1:408-416.
15 Antiquities 19:356-9.
16 Jewish War 2:266-70; 284.
17 Jewish War 2:284-92.
18 Jewish War 2:293-96.
19 Jewish War 2:297-305.
20 Jewish War 2:306-8.
21 Jewish War 2:309-14.
22 Jewish War 2:315-30.
23 Jewish War 2:331-2.
24 Jewish War 2:333-5.
25 Jewish War 2:333-41.
26 Jewish War 2:402-7. Josephus has Agrippa give the people a long speech
    about the need to submit to the Romans (Jewish War 2:345-401). Such
    set-piece speeches were a convention of history writing and not accurate
    reportage.
27 Jewish War 2:408-10.

28   Jewish War 2:418-19.
29   Jewish War 2:433-40.
30   Jewish War 2:441-56.
31   Josephus, The Life 17-23.
32   Jewish War 2:457-68.
33   Jewish War 2:487-98.
34   Jewish War 2:559-61.
35   Jewish War 2:499-516.
36   Jewish War 2:517-522.
37   Jewish War 2:523-537.
38   Jewish War 2:531; 538-40.
39   Jewish War 2:541-50.
40   Jewish War 2:551-54.
41   Jewish War 2:555.
42   Josephus, The Life 24.

Chapter 8

1   Acts 22:4; see also Acts 9:2.
2   Acts 5:1-11.
3   Acts 12:12-17.
4   Acts 6:1.
5   Acts 9:36-41.
6   Mark 5:41.
7   Acts 25:13-26:32.
8   Acts 26:30-31.
9   Acts 17:34.
10   S.P. Laurie, The Rock and the Tower, pp.155-6.
11   Luke 24:1-11.
12   1 Corinthians 15:3-7.

Chapter 9

1   Jewish War 2:562-8.
2   Jewish War 2:569-84. Josephus gives the number of his army at over 100,000
     in 2:576, but only enumerates around 65,000 in 2:583.
3   Jewish War 2:585-94.
4   Josephus, The Life 79.
5   Josephus, The Life 95;105.
6   Josephus, The Life 115-9.
7   Josephus, The Life 28-9; 62-3; 77.
8   Josephus, The Life 77-8.
9   Josephus, The Life 43-45.
10   Josephus, The Life 189-93.
11   Josephus, The Life 193-203.
12   Jewish War 2:590-2.

13 Josephus, Jewish War 2:590-2; The Life 29;73.
14 Josephus, The Life, 75.
15 Jewish War, 590.
16 Josephus, Jewish War 2:599; The Life 134.
17 Josephus, The Life 62-67.
18 Josephus, The Life 68.
19 Josephus, The Life 69.
20 Josephus, Jewish War 2:595; The Life 126-7.
21 The name is similar to Annaeus.
22 Josephus, Jewish War 2:596-7; The Life 128-131.
23 Exodus 23:4.
24 Josephus, The Life 118-120.
25 Josephus, Jewish War 2:598-99; The Life 132-5. Exodus 20:15.
26 Josephus, Jewish War 2:600-4; The Life 136-138.
27 Josephus, Jewish War 2:605-9; The Life 138-144.
28 Josephus, Jewish War 2:610-2; The Life 145-8.
29 Josephus, The Life 189-96; Jewish War 4:319-20.
30 Josephus, The Life 197-212.
31 Josephus, The Life 277; 284.
32 Josephus, The Life 294-304.
33 Josephus, The Life 309-32.
34 Josephus, Jewish War 2:632-641; The Life 157-169.
35 Josephus, Jewish War 2:642-4; The Life 170-3.
36 Jewish War 3:6-8; 29.
37 Jewish War 3:9-28.
38 Jewish War 3:30-4; 59-63.
39 Jewish War 3:64-9; 129-30.
40 Jewish War 3:130-1; 135-40.
41 Jewish War 3:132-4.
42 Jewish War 3:158-60.
43 Jewish War 3:141-57.
44 Jewish War 3:161-70.
45 Jewish War 3:171-7.
46 Jewish War 3:178-85.
47 Jewish War 3:193-204.
48 Jewish War 3:213-25.
49 Jewish War 3:226-35.
50 Jewish War 3:240-50.
51 Jewish War 3:251-7.
52 Jewish War 3:258-70.
53 Jewish War 3:271-75.
54 Jewish War 3:276-82.
55 Jewish War 3:283-88; 316-22.
56 Jewish War 3:323-335.
57 Jewish War 3:336-339.
58 Jewish War 3:341-3.
59 Jewish War 3:343-50.
60 Jewish War 3:351-6.
61 Jewish War 3:357-60.

62   Jewish War 3:361-86.
63   Jewish War 3:387-89.
64   Jewish War 3:390-1.
65   Titus was born in December 39 AD, Josephus in 37 AD.
66   Jewish War 3:392-8.
67   Jewish War 3:399-408.

Chapter 10

1   Acts 20:3.
2   Acts 21:1-8.
3   Acts 21:14.
4   Acts 27:2; Philemon 1:24.
5   Acts 27:1-6.
6   Acts 27:7-15.
7   Acts 27:21-26.
8   Acts 27:27-44.
9   Colossians 4:14.
10   Philemon 1:23-24.
11   2 Timothy 4:11.
12   1 Corinthians 14:23.
13   Galatians 1:15-17.
14   Acts 9:1-30.
15   S.P. Laurie, The Rock and the Tower, Ch. 10. I show how Acts uses the long
      ending of Mark in a chiastic structure reflected in the first and last speeches
      in Acts which are made by Peter and Paul, respectively. This is matched by
      the first and last miracles in Acts which also come from the long ending. The
      last two miracles are the snake and the cure of Publius' father, whereas the
      first is the speaking in tongues which takes place at Pentecost in Jerusalem.
16   F.F. Bruce, The Book of Acts (Grand Rapids: Eerdmans, 1988) p.310.
17   For Acts use of Paul's letters for its account of his travels see Schellenberg,
      Ryan S., The First Pauline Chronologist? Paul's Itinerary in the Letters and
      in Acts (Journal of Biblical Literature, Vol. 134, No. 1, 2015) pp. 193-213.

Chapter 11

1   Jewish War 3:438-442.
2   Jewish War 3:409-431; 438-442.
3   Jewish War 3:422-502.
4   Jewish War 3:503-5;522-31.
5   Jewish War 3:532-42.
6   Jewish War 4:4-35.
7   Jewish War 4:62-80.
8   Jewish War 4:84-120.
9   Jewish War 4:441-5.
10   Jewish War 4:451;476-7.

11   Jewish War 4:497-502; Tacitus Histories 1:10.
12   Jewish War 4:588-621; Suetonius Vespasian 6; Tacitus Histories 2:74-80.
13   Jewish War 4:629.
14   Suetonius, Vespasian 4.
15   Jewish War, 3:118.
16   Isaiah 40:4.
17   Tacitus Histories 4:81; Suetonius Vespasian 7.
18   Mark 7:35; John 9:6.
19   Such is the version of the story in Suetonius Lives of the Caesars: Vespasian
     7. Tacitus repeats the same story (Histories 4:81) but places it while
     Vespasian is waiting for a fair wind for Rome. He makes Basilides a noble
     and sees the augury as lying in his name which means "son of a king."
20   Jewish War 4:658-63.
21   Jewish War, 4:660-61. Translation by H St. J. Thackeray.
22   Jewish War 4:132.
23   Jewish War 4:147-54.
24   Jewish War 4:155-7.
25   Jewish War 4:225.
26   Jewish War 4:196-207.
27   Jewish War 4:208-236.
28   Jewish War 4:289-314.
29   Jewish War 4:315-344.
30   Jewish War 4:345-53;389-97.
31   Jewish War 4:503-14.
32   Jewish War 4:515-37.
33   Jewish War 4:560-3.
34   Jewish War 4:566-76; 5:527-31.
35   Jewish War 4:577-84; 5:11-26.
36   Jewish War 5:39-46.
37   Jewish War 5:52-65.
38   Jewish War 5:69-97.
39   Jewish War 5:98-105.
40   Jewish War 5:261; 541-7.
41   Jewish War 5:275-83; 299-302.
42   Jewish War 5:317-47.
43   Jewish War 5:424-36; 499-518; 6:193-219.
44   Jewish War 5:421-2; 446-91; 550-2.
45   Jewish War 6:26-8.
46   Jewish War 6:29-95; 129-56; 164-8; 177-92; 220-35.
47   Jewish War 6:236-59.
48   Jewish War 6:260-6; 281-4.
49   Jewish War 6:316.
50   Jewish War 6:268-270. Josephus puts this final destruction 1130 years after
     the building of the temple by Solomon and 639 years after the rebuilding
     under Cyrus. Both numbers are too high, although the story of the
     building under Solomon is mythical and the precise date is unknown. The
     time from Cyrus should be 589 years.
51   Jewish War 6:323-7; 358-420.
52   Jewish War 6:317.

53   Jewish War 6:433-4; 7:26-37.
54   Josephus, The Life 417-21.
55   Josephus, The Life 422.

Chapter 12

1   Luke 3:14.
2   Mark 15:39.
3   Luke 23:47.
4   Acts 10.
5   Acts 27.
6   Acts 21:32.
7   Acts 22:23-29.
8   Acts 23:17.
9   Acts 23:23.
10   Acts 24:23.
11   Acts 23:16.
12   Galatians 1:13-24.
13   2 Corinthians 11:24-25.
14   Acts 16:22-24; 35-40.
15   Josephus, The Life 13.
16   Tacitus, Histories 15:44.
17   Acts 28:14
18   Acts 17:1-9.
19   Acts 18:6-8.
20   Acts 18:12-17; Bruce, The Book of Acts, pp. 351-4.
21   Acts 19:37.
22   Acts 19:23-41.
23   Matthew 25:14-20.
24   Matthew 25:24.
25   Matthew 25:30.
26   Luke 19:11-27.
27   Josephus, The Life 341-3, 410.
28   Luke 23:6-11.
29   Luke 23:16.
30   The Jewish War 5:19.
31   Mark 13:14; Matthew 24:15.
32   Luke 21:24.

Chapter 13

1   Jewish War 7:100-11.
2   Jewish War 7:218.
3   Jewish War 7:112-131.
4   Jewish War 7:132-57.
5   Jewish War 7:158-62.
6   Jewish War 1:3;6.

7   Against Apion 1:50.
8   Antiquities 20:264-6.
9   The work was published while Vespasian was alive and refers to the
     temple of Peace, which was dedicated in 75 AD.
10   Josephus The Life 361-367; Against Apion 47-52.
11   Suetonius says that Titus divorced Marcia Furnilla after acknowledging
     her daughter as his (Titus 4) and that Jerusalem was captured on his
     daughter's birthday (Titus 5). If Titus only had one daughter, Julia, then
     this implies that she was born in August 64 AD. But Suetonius may be
     referring to two separate daughters; Julia's unexpected name is more
     explicable if she were the child of Titus' first wife, Arrecina Tertulla, who
     was related to the Julia gens. If there was a second daughter then she must
     have died young, for we hear no more about her.
12   Paul Gallivan, The Fasti for A.D. 70-96, The Classical Quarterly , 1981, Vol.
     31, No. 1, pp. 213-5. The Sabinus who married Julia was a consul suffectus
     in 82 AD. Most likely he is the son of the Sabinus who was consul in 69 and
     72 AD, but it is just possible that the elder Sabinus was consul three times.
     If so then Julia's husband would have been quite old.
13   Suetonius, Domitian 15.
14   Antiquities 20:145-6.
15   Translation by G.G. Ramsay, Juvenal and Persius (Loeb Classical Library, 1918).
16   Josephus Antiquities 19:276-7; 354, 20:145-6.
17   Suetonius, Titus 7.
18   John A. Crook, Titus and Berenice (The American Journal of Philology,
     1951, Vol. 72, No. 2, 1951), pp. 166-8.
19   Antiquities 19:354-5, 20:139.
20   Antiquities 20:141-2.
21   Suetonius, Claudius 28.
22   Suetonius, Claudius 28; Tacitus, Histories 5:9.
23   Tacitus, The Histories, Translated by W.H. Fyfe, revised and edited by D.S.
     Levene (Oxford: Oxford University Press) p.291 note p.239.
24   Jewish War 2:252-70, Antiquities 20:141-3; 162-66; 182.
25   However, Suetonius (Titus 7) implies that Berenice was sent away to
     placate public opinion after Titus became emperor.

Chapter 14

1   Chalcis, in the Biqa valley, has been variously identified as modern Anjar,
     Majdal Anjar or Baalbek.
2   For a comprehensive summary of the evidence relating to the Ituraeans
     see E.A. Myers, The Ituraeans and the Roman Near East: Reassessing the
     Sources (Cambridge: Cambridge University Press, 2010).
3   Jewish War 2:247.
4   The evidence concerns a possible southward Ituraean expansion onto the
     slopes of Mount Hermon at the southern extreme of the anti-Lebanon
     range and further beyond to the Golan Heights in north Gaulanitis. A
     pottery type called Golan Ware dating from the second century BC has

been found in both the Golan Heights and Mount Hermon. It has been proposed that the Golan Ware was made by the Ituraeans and it has even been called Ituraean Ware although there is nothing to definitely link it to Ituraeans. See Myers pp. 42-64 for a lengthy discussion of the Golan Ware.

5   Although much of the land ruled by Philip had previously been under the control of Zenodorus and hence in the Ituraean kingdom of Lysanias. This territory included Trachonitis, which Luke lists separately from Ituraea, and Batanaea. Myers pp. 166-7.

6   Jewish War 2:178-181 and at much greater length in Antiquities 18:168 ff.. The tetrarchy of Lysanias is only mentioned at Antiquities 18:237.

7   Jewish War 2:215; Antiquities 19:274-5.

8   Jewish War 2:220; 223; Antiquities 19:360-3; 20:104.

9   Also Jewish War 2:247.

10   Translation Louis H. Feldman, Loeb Classical Library.

11   Jewish War 2:247.

12   In Antiquities 19:275, Josephus says that Claudius gave Agrippa I lands including Abila and "all the land in the mountainous region of Lebanon as a gift out of his own territory." However, this mountainous area would have previously been part of the tetrarchy of Soaemus who ruled Ituraea. Upon Soaemus' death Claudius took the tetrarchy back into direct Roman rule (Josephus, The Life 52; Tacitus, Annals 12:23). Soaemus, however, did not die until several years after Agrippa I, so Josephus seems to have confused Agrippa I and Agrippa II here. We can deduce that Varus must have been awarded his tetrarchy sometime after the death of Soaemus and that it returned to Roman administration when he in turn died, allowing Claudius to award it later to Agrippa II. This hypothesis is supported by the fact that Agrippa II's regent was also called Varus. He was a descendant of Soaemus and probably the son of the older Varus. Josephus says that this younger Varus hated the Jews and attempted to get Agrippa II executed to inherit his kingdom. He was qualified for the kingdom by his royal birth (Josephus' Life 48-61; Jewish War 2:481-3).

13   Jewish War 2:252; Antiquities 20:159. In the Jewish War, Abila was included in the towns granted by Nero and Trachonitis was included as part of Philip's former territory (2:247).

14   Acts 22:22-23:24.

15   Acts 24:5.

16   Acts 24:22.

17   Acts 25:1-12.

18   Acts 25:13-27.

19   Acts 26:1-28.

20   Acts 26:30-2.

21   Josephus, The Life, 360.

Chapter 15

1   Tacitus, Histories 5:22.

2   Tacitus, Histories 4:12.

3   Tacitus, Histories 4:13;54-62.
4   Tacitus, Histories 4:68.
5   Tacitus, Histories 4:75.
6   Tacitus, Histories 4:86.
7   Tacitus, Histories 4:71-2.
8   Tacitus, Histories 4:75-7.
9   Tacitus, Histories 4:77-8.
10 Tacitus, Histories 5:23.
11 Tacitus, Histories 5:24-6. At this point the surviving text of the Histories stops as the ending is lost. We do not know the fate of Civilis although it seems likely that he was allowed to live.
12 Tacitus, Histories 4:72.
13 Tacitus, Agricola 8,17. Also Jewish War 7:82 where Josephus misspells his name Petilius Cerealius.
14 Suetonius, Vespasian 8, 12.
15 Suetonius, Vespasian 21.
16 Cassius Dio 65:13:2.
17 Suetonius, Vespasian 17,23.
18 Suetonius, Vespasian 23-4.
19 Suetonius, Titus 6-7.
20 Suetonius, Titus 6, Cassius Dio 66:16:3-4.
21 John A. Crook, Titus and Berenice, (The American Journal of Philology, 1951, Vol. 72, No. 2, 1951), pp. 168-171.
22 Suetonius, Titus 7.
23 Tacitus, Annals 15:21.
24 Suetonius, Nero 20; Tacitus, Annals 15:33-34.
25 Pliny the Younger, Letters 6:16; 20.
26 Antiquities 20:144.
27 Suetonius, Titus 8; Cassius Dio 66:24.
28 Suetonius, Titus 10.
29 Suetonius, Titus 11; Cassius Dio 66:26:2-3.
30 Cassius Dio 67:2:5-7.
31 Suetonius, Domitian 2,13.
32 Suetonius, Domitian 10.
33 Suetonius, Domitian 22; Cassius Dio 67:3:2; Pliny the Younger, Letters 4:11.
34 Suetonius, Domitian 8.
35 Suetonius, Domitian 8, Pliny the Younger, Letters 4:11.
36 Susan Wood, Who Was Diva Domitilla? Some Thoughts on the Public Images of the Flavian Women (American Journal of Archaeology Vol. 114, No. 1, Jan 2010) p. 56. Wood interprets this as a sign of Domitia's popularity and influence as Corbulo's daughter rather than being due to the emperor's wishes. But it is naive to suppose that regional governors would not be primarily trying to please the emperor. And a fatal problem with Wood's argument is that Titus' daughter, Julia, should have been even more popular than Corbulo's daughter.
37 See Wood, Who Was Diva Domitilla?
38 BRMCRE 2:312, No 68. See Wood, Who Was Diva Domitilla?, page 49 for an image and discussion. She concludes that the engraver portrayed

Vespasian's wife as resembling her husband! But it makes more sense that the woman is Vespasian's daughter.

39   See, for example, Brian W. Jones, The Emperor Domitian p.207 n.113.

40   Paul Gallivan, The Fasti for A.D. 70-96, p. 212.

41   Bosworth, Firmus of Arretium, pp. 275-6, argues that if Cerialis was the son of the disgraced senator Q. Petillius Rufus then his career may have been held up by the disrepute of his father, so that he was only appointed legionary legate in 60/61 AD in his late thirties. But would the ambitious and politically savvy Vespasian have married his only daughter to such a son-in-law?

Chapter 16

1   Josephus, The Life 364.

2   Louis H. Feldman, Josephus: Jewish Antiquities, Book 20 (Loeb Classical Library, 1965) p.53 n.d..

3   Antiquities 20:171.

4   Robinson Smith, Fresh Light on the Synoptic Problem; Josephus a Lukan Source (The American Journal of Theology, Vol. 17, No. 4, 1913) pp. 614-621.

5   Steve Mason, Josephus and the New Testament, 2nd Ed. (Peabody, Massachusetts, 2003) pp.277-82.

6   Antiquities 19:343-50.

7   Acts 12:20-23.

8   Antiquities 19:338-42. Marsus, the Roman governor of Syria, thought that the other local kings were far too friendly with Agrippa.

9   Vespasian had to rebuke them for insulting Agrippa II. Josephus Against Apion 70; The Life, 407-8.

10   The Jewish War 2:119-166; Antiquities 18:11-25.

11   Luke 1:52.

12   Luke 6:24.

13   Translation Richard M. Gummere, Seneca Ad Lucilium Epistulae Morales Vol 3, (Loeb Classical Library, 1925). See also Mason, Josephus and the New Testament, p. 285.

14   This hypothesis is summarized by Joshua Noble, Common Property and the Golden Age Myth in the Book of Acts (Online article in The Bible and Interpretation, 2020). Also, set out at greater length by the same author in Common Property, the Golden Age, and Empire in Acts 2:42-47 and 4:32-45 (London: T&T Clark, 2021).

15   Acts 5:17; 15:5; 26:5.

16   See Mason, Josephus and the New Testament p.288-9.

17   Acts 27:27; Josephus, The Life 15.

18   2 Corinthians 11:24-25.

19   Luke 3:1-18.

20   Mark 1:6; Matthew 3:4.

21   Luke 3:9.

22   Jewish War 3:351-54.

23   Steve Mason, Josephus and the New Testament p. 128.

24   Jewish Antiquities 20:189-196.

Chapter 17

1   Suetonius, Domitian 15.
2   Translation by H.E. Butler, The Institutio Oratoria of Quintilian, Vol. II (Loeb Classical Library, 1921).
3   Suetonius, Domitian 15.
4   Translation by Earnest Cary, Dio's Roman History, Vol. 8 (Loeb Classical Library, 1925).
5   Translation by J.C. Rolfe, Suetonius, Vol. 2 (Loeb Classical Library, 1920).
6   Exodus 20:4-6; Duet 5:8-10.
7   Cassius Dio 67:14:3.
8   Philostratus, Life of Apollonius 8:25.
9   An alternative reading of Philostratus is that Domitian required Domitilla to marry another husband. See J.B. Lightfoot, Clement the Doctor, Introduction to S. Clement of Rome, Apostolic Fathers Part I Vol. I. (London and New York; Macmillan and Co., 1890), p. 113.
10 Peter Lampe, From Paul to Valentinus: Christians in Rome in the First Two Centuries (Minneapolis: Fortress Press, 2003) p.199.
11 The same point is made by J.B. Lightfoot, Clement the Doctor, Introduction to S. Clement of Rome, Apostolic Fathers Part I Vol. I. (London and New York; Macmillan and Co., 1890), p. 49. Lightfoot offers a few different suggestions for how a confusion between Clemens' sister's daughter and Domitian's sister's daughter could have arisen, including grammatical ambiguity.

Chapter 18

1   Catholic encyclopedia entry for "Bosio." Also J. Spencer Northcote and W.R. Brownlow, Roma Sotterranea, Some Account of the Roman Catacombs, (London: Longmans, Green, Reader and Dyer, 1869) pp. 5-8.
2   Northcote and Brownlow, p.5.
3   For a description and the text of the inscriptions see J.B. Lightfoot, Clement the Doctor, Introduction to S. Clement of Rome, Apostolic Fathers Part I Vol. I. (London and New York; Macmillan and Co., 1890), pp. 36-7; pp. 114-5.
4   CIL 6:16246.
5   CIL 6:948.
6   CIL 6:8942.
7   See for example Peter Lampe, From Paul to Valentinus: Christians in Rome in the First Two Centuries, p.33 including n. 44. His dismissive argument scarcely considers two of the stone inscriptions and he omits to even mention the evidence of Acts of Nereus and Achilleus. His conclusion also relies on faulty logic—not establishing to 100% certainty that a hypothesis is true does not mean that hypothesis is false and can be disregarded.
8   Marianne Saghy, Pope Damascus and the Beginnings of Roman Hagiography, p.1.
9   Nicola Denzey, The Bone Gatherers: The Lost Worlds of Early Christian

Women (Boston: Beacon Press, 2007) pp.193-200; Christine Schenk, Crispina and her Sisters, Women and Authority in Early Christianity (Minneapolis, Fortress Press, 2017) pp.336-8.

10   Marianne Saghy, Pope Damascus and the Beginnings of Roman Hagiography, p.2-6.

11   Cav. Giovanni Battista De Rossi, Bullettino Di Archeologia Christiana (Rome) 1875 p.12; 1878 pp. 133-5.

12   Translation by Richard I. Pervo.

13   Fabrizo Bisconti, "The Art of the Catacombs" in The Oxford Handbook of Early Christian Archaeology Ed. Caraher, Davis, and Pettegrew (Oxford University Press, 2019).

14   The calculation assumes that points 1 to 3 are mutually independent. Point 4, that Domitilla was a Christian saint, could be dependent upon Eusebius' evidence and so it not taken into account. We evaluate the evidence assuming (i) that Domitilla's religion was Christianity and (ii) that it was Judaism. The prior probability for each of these is taken as 50%. The probabilities that we would see the evidence we observe under (i) or (ii) is taken as follows: Point 1 (Dio); Christianity—100%, Judaism—100%. Point 2 (Eusebius); Christianity—100%, Judaism—20%. Point 3 (Catacombs); Christianity—100%, Judaism—20%. The combined probability that Domitilla was Jewish is (1*0.20*0.20)/(1*1*1) which equals 4%.

Chapter 19

1   The Catacombs of Rome and the origins of Christianity, Fabrizio Mancinelli (Firenze: Scala, 1998) pp. 25-7. Also, Caroline Goodson, "To be the Daughter of Saint Peter: S. Petronella and forging the Franco-Papal Alliance" in Three empires, three cities: identity, material culture and legitimacy in Venice, Ravenna and Rome, 750-1000 Ed. Veronica West-Harling (Turnhout, Belgium: Brepols, 2015), pp. 165-7.

2   Photo by Carlo Tabanelli, from J. Wilpert, Die Malereien der Katakomben Roms, Freiburg, 1903, vol. 2, fig. 213. This image is reproduced in Caroline Goodson, To be the Daughter of Saint Peter, p.167.

3   De Rossi, Bullettino Di Archeologia Christiana (Rome). 1875 pp.15-17. Nicola Denzey, The Bone Gatherers, The Lost worlds of early Christian Women (Boston: Beacon Press, 2007) p.126; p.247 n.8.

4   Encyclopedia Britannica entry for "pallium". See also Catholic Encyclopedia "pallium".

5   Elizabeth Bartman, Hair and the Artifice of Roman Female Adornment (American Journal of Archaeology, Vol. 105, No. 1, 2001) pp. 8-12. Eve D'Ambra, Mode and Model in the Flavian Female Portrait (American Journal of Archaeology Vol. 117 No. 4, 2013), pp. 523.

6   Martial, Epigram 2.66.

7   Juvenal 6.502.

8   Christine Schenk, Crispina and her Sisters, pp.147-157.

9   Christine Schenk, Crispina and her Sisters, pp. 149-41.

10   Christine Schenk, Crispina and her Sisters, pp. 141.

11 Christine Schenk, Crispina and her Sisters, pp. 141.
12 Matteo Braconi, "L'Arcosolio Di Cerula nelle catacomb di San Gennaro a Napoli: Prime inuizioni e recenti scoperte" in Campania Sacra, Rivista di Storia Sociale e Religiosa del Mezzogiorno Vol. 46-7 (Naples: Verbum Ferens, 2016), pp. 129-146.
13 Although the number 4 is more familiar as IV it was often represented as IIII.
14 P.P. Saydon, The Order of the Gospels (Scripture 4 No 7, July 1950), p. 191.

Chapter 20

1 The name is variously spelt in ancient sources. I have followed the fresco in using "Petronella" for the early martyr but also use "Petronilla" when the context makes it appropriate.
2 De Rossi gave the first full account of Petronilla's sarcophagus and its fate in Bullettino Di Archeologia Christiana (Rome); 1878 pp.125-46; 1879 pp.1-20; 139-160.
3 Christine Schenk, Crispina and her Sisters, p. 155; Caroline Goodson, To be the Daughter of Saint Peter, p.167.
4 Catholic encyclopedia, Petronilla.
5 See Christine Schenk, Crispina and her Sisters, p.156.
6 Wilhelm Schneemelcher, "The Acts of Peter" in New Testament Apocrypha Vol. 2 (Westminster: John Knox press, 1989, English trans. 1992) pp. 278-9; 283.
7 Judith Herrin, Ravenna; Capital of empire, crucible of Europe (London: Allen Lane, 2020) pp.156-9.
8 Herrin, Ravenna p. 343.
9 Herrin, Ravenna pp.343-46.
10 Translated by Davies, Eighth Century Popes p. 81 from Caroline Goodson, To be the Daughter of Saint Peter, pp. 160-1. I have substituted the English "golden" for "Aurea."
11 Caroline Goodson, To be the Daughter of Saint Peter, pp. 161-3.
12 Nicola Denzey, The Bone Gatherers, p.132; Christine Schenk, Crispina and her Sisters p.155.
13 Benet Salway, What's in a Name? A Survey of Roman Onomastic Practice from c. 700 B.C. to A.D. 700 (The Journal of Roman Studies, Vol. 84, 1994), pp. 133-40.
14 Nicola Denzey, The Bone Gatherers, p.131-3.
15 Nicola Denzey, The Bone Gatherers, p.247 n.8.
16 Pergola gives the fresco a date of "the second half of the 4C" in Philippe Pergola, Christian Rome: Early Christian Rome Catacombs and Basilicas (Rome, Vision S.R.L., 2000) p. 27.
17 Nicola Denzey, The Bone Gatherers p.140.
18 Richard I. Pervo, The Acts of Nereus and Achilleus, A new translation and introduction in New Testament Apocrypha Vol. 2, Tony Burke Ed. (Grand Rapids: Eerdmans, 2020) pp. 241-63.
19 Richard I. Pervo, The Acts of Nereus and Achilleus, pp. 243-4.
20 Romans 16:15.
21 Chrys C. Caragounis, Peter and the Rock (Berlin & New York: Walter de

Gruyter, 1990) p.19 including n.16.

22   Suetonius (Vespasian 1) reports claims in circulation that Petro's son
      Sabinus had been a centurion even though he actually had no military
      experience. It makes more sense for Petro to have been the centurion.

23   Suetonius, Vespasian 1

Chapter 21

1   Louis H. Feldman, Josephus: Jewish Antiquities, Books 18-19 (Loeb
      Classical Library, 1965) p.49 n. b.

2   Antiquities 20:200.

3   Gary J. Goldberg, The Coincidences of the Emmaus Narrative of Luke
      and the Testimonium of Josephus (The Journal for the Study of the
      Pseudepigrapha 13, 1995) pp. 59-77.

4   Goldberg pp. 6-8.

5   Goldberg pp. 9-10.

6   Acts 9:1-19; 22:4-16; 26:9-18.

7   Josephus, The Life 429.

Chapter 22

1   J.C. Yardley (trans.), Anthony A. Barrett (Introduction and notes), Tacitus:
      The Annals (Oxford World Classics, 2008) p.495 note to p.359.

2   The Annals are usually dated by an assumed reference in book 4 to Trajan's
      victory over the Parthians in 116 AD (Yardley & Barrett, Tacitus: The
      Annals xvii). The passage about the Christians comes much later in book
      15 and was probably written shortly before Tacitus' death which occurred
      sometime after 117. Tacitus took several years to write the shorter Histories,
      so allowing for writing time between books 4 and 15 gives an estimate for
      the Christian passage of c.120, although a later date is quite possible.

3   Jewish War 2:169; Antiquities 18:55. It may be that Josephus' knowledge of
      the titles of the governors before Nero had become more precise during
      his long residence in Rome because in Antiquities he only uses epitropos
      for Fadus onwards (Antiquities 20:97), perhaps indicating that it was
      equivalent to procurator. But it is more likely that he uses hegemon and
      epitropos interchangeably without making any distinction between a
      prefect and a procurator.

4   Translation by Louis H. Feldman, Loeb Classical Library.

5   2 Corinthians 11:24-25.

6   Eusebius, Ecclesiastical History 3:5.

7   S.P. Laurie, The Rock and the Tower, Ch.19.

8   Antiquities 20:159; War 2:252.

9   Origen, Against Celsus 1:47

10   Origen, Against Celsus 1:47; 2:13; Commentary on Matthew 10:17.

11   The Jewish War 4:321.

12   Origen, Commentary on Matthew 10:17.

Chapter 23

1   Translation by Louis H. Feldman, Loeb Classical Library.
2   Antiquities 18:65-80.
3   Antiquities 18:81-84.
4   Tacitus, Annals 2:85.
5   Suetonius, Tiberius 36.
6   Suetonius finished his Life of the Caesars between 119 and 122. Tacitus would have written Book 2 of his Annals sometime before 116 AD, the date usually assigned to Book 4. Both were friends of Pliny the Younger, and we would expect Suetonius to have attended readings by Tacitus even if he did not possess a copy of the Annals.
7   Cassius Dio 40:47:3-4.
8   Cassius Dio 47:15:4.
9   Cassius Dio 53:2:4-5; 54:6:6.
10   Copper alloy sestertius of Vespasian, 71AD. British Museum No. 1852,0609.1.
11   Jewish War 7:123.
12   See for example Albert A. Bell Jr., Josephus the Satirist? A Clue to the Original Form of the "Testimonium Flavianum" (The Jewish Quarterly Review, New Series Vol. 67, No. 1, July 1976), pp. 16-22. He correctly identifies both parts of the satire, although he fails to realize its full extent.
13   Matthew 1:18.
14   Luke 1:28;31.
15   Luke 1:38.
16   Luke 1:35.
17   Albert A. Bell Jr., Josephus the Satirist? pp. 16-22.
18   Translation by Louis H. Feldman, Loeb Classical Library.
19   2 Corinthians 11:24-25.
20   Galatians 2:9.

Chapter 24

1   The amici were an assorted and ill-defined group rather than a formally acknowledged office. See for example Brian W. Jones, The Emperor Domitian, pp. 50-71.
2   Antiquities 18:66.
3   Cassius Dio 66:6:2.

Chapter 25

1   Suetonius, Domitian 15-17.
2   Suetonius, Domitian 14.
3   Suetonius, Domitian 14.
4   Suetonius, Domitian 15.

5   Suetonius, Domitian 17.
6   Cassius Dio, 67:15-18.
7   Andrew W. Collins, The Palace Revolution: The Assassination of Domitian and the Accession of Nerva (Phoenix, Vol 63 No 1/2, 2009) pp. 98-100.
8   Cassius Dio 67:15:2.
9   Brian W. Jones, The Emperor Domitian, p.131.
10   Andrew W. Collins, The Palace Revolution, pp.92-96.
11   Andrew W. Collins, The Palace Revolution, p. 80.
12   Translation Earnest Cary, Dio's Roman History Vol. 8.
13   Earnest Cary, Dio's Roman History Vol. 8., p.365 n.1.
14   Andrew W. Collins, The Palace Revolution, p.88.

Chapter 26

1   Acts 7:1-8:3.
2   Corinthians 15:9; Galatians 1:23.
3   Mark 14:62.
4   Acts 6:15.
5   F.F. Bruce, The Book of Acts, pp.124-5.
6   Tacitus, Annals 2:85.
7   Joel B. Green, The Gospel of Luke, pp.591-2.
8   Mark 11:25-26.
9   Richard Bauckham, Gospel Women: Studies of the Named Women in the Gospels (T&T Clark, 2002) pp.150-58.
10   Hermann L. Strack, Jesus die Haretiker und die Christen (Leipzig: J.C. Hinrichs'sche Buchhandlung, 1910) pp. 45*-47*. The number of names differs slightly in different versions of the genealogy.
11   Richard Bauckham, Gospel Women p.157. Two of the several variations in the name of Kuza's son are Anah and Adah, who appear in Genesis 36:16 and 36:18.
12   Hermann L. Strack, p. 46*.
13   Jewish War 2:295.
14   2 Corinthians 4:7.
15   Mark Wilson, "Treasures in Clay Jars" (Bible History Daily, September 6, 2022) makes a connection between Paul's words and the coin hordes.

Chapter 27

1   S.P. Laurie, The Rock and the Tower, pp. 91-2.
2   Atwill, Joseph, Caesar's Messiah: The Roman Conspiracy to Invent Jesus (CreateSpace, 2011) pp. 279-301.